European Business and Marketing

Second Edition

Edited by

Phil Harris and Frank McDonald

SAGE Publications
London • Thousand Oaks • New Delhi

SAGE Publications Ltd
1 Oliver's Yard
55 City Road
London EC1Y 1SP

SAGE Publications Inc
2455 Teller Road
Thousand Oaks, California 91320

SAGE Publications India Pvt Ltd
B-42, Panchsheel Enclave
Post Box 4109
New Delhi 100 017

British Library Cataloguing in Publication data

A catalogue record for this book is available
from the British Library

ISBN 0 7619 6604 8
ISBN 0 7619 6605 6 (pbk)

Library of Congress Control Number 2003109266

Typeset by C&M Digitals (P) Ltd., Chennai, India
Printed in Great Britain by The Cornwell Press Ltd, Trowbridge, Wiltshire

To our parents:

Albert and Miriam

Burnet and Margaret

Thank you so much for your ability to teach the useful things in life.

Contents

List of Figures and Tables and Exhibits

FIGURES

TABLES

EXHIBITS

Case Study Contributors

IN THE BOOK

Paul Baines
Is a Principal Lecturer in Marketing and a Director of Business Development at Middlesex University Business School, London. He holds bachelors, masters and doctoral degrees from Manchester School of Management, UMIST. He is a Chartered Marketer and a full member of the Market Research Society. He is the author and co-author of numerous journal articles and book chapters on the use of marketing techniques in non-conventional services environments, particularly for political parties and candidates. With Bal Chansarkar he is co-editor of *Introduction to Marketing Research* and co-author of *Introducing Marketing Research*. He is also co-author, with Ross Brennan and Paul Garneau, of *Contemporary Strategic Marketing*. His latest book, co-written with John Egan and Frank Jefkins, is a text on 'Contemporary PR Practice' and is due out shortly. Paul's recent marketing consultancy projects include work for a number of organizations including a high-profile football club, a large aerospace maintenance company, a national charity, an advertising agency and an examination board.

Sukhbinder Barn
Is currently Senior Lecturer in Marketing at Middlesex University Business School and is Programme Leader of the MA in Marketing Management. He is also the Business School's co-ordinator for educational collaborations and exchanges in India. Sukhbinder has spent a number of years in industry where he worked for Coca-Cola & Schweppes Beverages Limited. During that time he was actively involved in the development and launching of new products and services within the newly established vending division. His current research and teaching interests are in the areas of branding and advertising and developing communication strategies for targeting hard to reach markets. Sukhbinder has published in academic journals, and has presented papers at international marketing conferences. He has led many professional workshops, particularly based upon the use of business simulation games, and has undertaken consulting activity for a variety of government organizations. Additionally, he has been

involved in developing branding and communication strategies with sporting organizations in London.

Maureen Benson-Rea
Is a Lecturer in the Department of International Business at the University of Auckland, where she teaches European business. Her research interests also include International Business Strategy, particularly Business Networks and she has had a number of journal articles and case studies published in these areas.

Kevin Boles
Is an Enterprise Manager and Senior Lecturer in Strategy and Entrepreneurship. Based at the Centre for Enterprise, Manchester Metropolitan University Business School, Kevin is actively engaged in researching strategic management in small firms. He is Course Leader and Regional Project Manager for the New Entrepreneur Scholarship programme and responsible for developing the MSEC project within Manchester Metropolitan University. He has published a number of papers on enterprise related issues and is a fellow of the Royal Society for the Arts.

David Carson
Is Professor of Marketing at the University of Ulster, Northern Ireland. His research interests lie in marketing for SME's and quality in marketing in service industries, particularly in travel and tourism. He has published widely in both of these areas. He has wide business experience both in consultancy and directorship roles. He is joint editor of the *European Journal of Marketing* and Vice President of the Academy of Marketing UK. He is a Fellow of the Chartered Institute of Marketing (CIM) and a member of the CIM Academic Senate.

Julia Clarke
Is a lecturer in Accounting at Leeds University Business School. Her research interests are in the areas of corporate social responsibility and reporting.

David Davies
After graduating in History and Politics from London University, he spent several years as a journalist and editor specializing in the food and manufacturing industries. He has extensive experience in the public relations industry including Rex Stewart Grayling PR where he was Northern Regional Director, and Stowe Bowden Wilson (now part of McCann Ericcson) and has run his own independent consultancy. He lectures on Manchester Metropolitan University Business School's MA in PR course and is a consultant specializing in the food sector and Business to Business sectors especially food manufacturing and retail industries.

Julia Djarova
Is a Unit Manager at the Netherlands Economic Institute (NEI) in Rotterdam and a part time Associate Professor at Erasmus University Rotterdam. NEI is the leading economic research and policy advisory bureau in the Netherlands. julia

teaches at the Faculty of Economics and Business Administration of Sofia University and she is Programme Director of the joint Sofia University Erasmus Master's Programme in Economics and Management. She is also a guest professor at the Higher School of Economics, Moscow and the Academy of Engineering and Economy in St Petersburg.

Matthew Dodd

Is Head of Strategic Planning at News International based in London. He graduated from Manchester Metropolitan University in 1991 with a Degree in Business Studies and then completed an M Phil in Management Studies at the newly created Judge Institute of Management Studies at the University of Cambridge. His thesis examined the symbiotic relationship between small high technology firms and large corporations.

Matthew has worked in a variety of research and planning roles with the Daily Mail General Trust Group. He is now Head of Strategic Planning at News International where he is responsible for planning and research across both the newspaper and online brands. In his time at NI he has been involved in a number of leading communication research projects. He regularly publishes articles and presents at conferences on understanding the consumer interaction with advertising.

John Fraser

Is a Marketing Intelligence Manager and an experienced marketing practitioner. He has worked in the e-business industry and has many publications around e-commerce and e-business areas.

Hanne Gardner

Was born and brought up in Denmark. After graduating from UMIST she worked as a marketing manager for major consumer and business to business companies covering both the UK and much of Europe. After 15 years of commercial experience she became a senior lecturer at Manchester Metropolitan University. Her research interests include different aspects of marketing such as political marketing and business to business marketing.

Monica Gibson-Sweet

Is Assistant Dean and Head of the School of Business Strategy at Leeds Metropolitan Business School. Prior to joining LMU in September 2002, Monica held posts at the University of the West of England, Bristol as Head of the Corporate Business and Regional Team and at the University of Wales College, Newport where she was Dean of the Business School. Her commercial experience was in the aircraft industry as a business analyst. Monica studied at Manchester Polytechnic and Manchester University and she has qualifications in business, marketing and education.

She has a range of research interests and has published in the areas of corporate social responsibility, business education and SMEs. Monica is a Chartered

Marketer and a member of the Institute of Learning and Teaching in Higher Education.

Audrey Gilmore

Is Professor of Services Marketing at the University of Ulster. Her teaching and research interests are in service marketing and management, SME marketing, competencies and networking. She has published in a variety of international journals on these themes. Much of her research has involved the development of qualitative methodologies for marketing studies. She is joint editor of the *European Journal of Marketing* and is currently the Academy of Marketing Regional Chair for Ireland.

Richard Hadley

Is a former Master's student in the Department of International Business at the University of Auckland. He has been working as a Research Analyst in the Electronic Banking Department of the ASB Bank, Auckland and is now in Europe.

Irene Harris

Is a member of the Human Resource Management and Organizational Behaviour Group of Manchester Metropolitan University Business School. She is a Senior Learning and Teaching Fellow at MMU Business School and her teaching and research interests include management development, management learning and government interventions in training and development. Before becoming an academic she was a senior civil servant with the Department of Employment and worked in many areas of national training provision.

She holds a Business Studies Degree from Hertfordshire University, obtained a Masters in Management Learning from Lancaster University and a Post Graduate Diploma in Education from Bolton Institute. She is an external examiner on national and internal programmes in Management and has a particular interest in Organizational Change.

Phil Harris

Is Co-Director of the Centre for Corporate and Public Affairs at Manchester Metropolitan University Business School. He is a past chairman of the UK based, Academy of Marketing, member of the Academic Senate and International Board of Trustees of the Chartered Institute of Marketing and Global Marketing Board of the American Marketing Association.

He is co-editor of the *Journal of Public Affairs* and a member of a number of international editorial and advisory boards. He has over 100 publications in the area of communications, lobbying, political marketing, relationship marketing and international trade in such journals as the *European Journal of Marketing, Journal of Communication Management, Management Decision, Journal of Marketing Management, Journal of Psychology and Marketing* and *Journal of General Management*. He is a consultant and advisor to various organizations, in the corporate, government and not for profit sectors. He coined the phrase

'Machiavellian Marketing' to describe modern campaigning and pressure group activity as an integral part of modern marketing management.

Hans Joachim Schmengler

Was marketing and distribution manager in some large German production and retailing companies. He is presently Professor for international marketing and retail management at FH Bochum – University of Applied Sciences, Germany. His research focus has been on strategic marketing of Mittelstand Firms and relationship marketing. He is also a Business consultant and management educator, as well as a member of the jury for the Award of Science of the German Marketing Association.

Dr Nuran Fraser

Is a senior lecturer in Manchester Metropolitan University Business School. She teaches international Business and supply chain management and does research around e-supply chain/e-procurement management and e-commerce/ e-business areas and its impact on business operations. She had many articles published around those areas.

Carla CJM Millar

Is currently Dean of TSM Business School, a Graduate School of the Universities of Groningen and Twente in the Netherlands, and a professor of International Marketing & Management. Her career has spanned marketing practice in major European and US multinationals, as well as academic research and teaching, consultancy and the development and management of executive education in the UK, Europe, Asia and Australia. Her work reflects her familiarity with continental European, Anglo American and several emergent business cultures. Her research can be found amongst others in the *Journal of Management Science*, *British Journal of Management*, *Journal of Business Ethics*, *Management International Review* and has co-published three books in International Business. She has been an officer of the Academy of International Business and the Marketing Education Group in the UK and is an enthusiast for International Business Research.

Danny Moss

Is co-Director of the Centre for Corporate and Public Affairs at the Manchester Metropolitan University and is Course Leader for the University's Master's Degrees in Public Relations. Previously, as Director of Public Relations Programmes at the University of Stirling, he was responsible for the introduction of the first dedicated Master's Degree in Public Relations in the UK in 1987. He is the co-founder and organizer of the annual International Public Relations Research Symposium which is held Lake Bled, Slovenia. He is also the co-editor of the *Journal of Public Affairs* and is the author of a number of books and articles including Public *relations cases: International perspectives, Public relations in practice: A casebook, Global Sources, Public relations research: An international perspective*, and *Perspectives on public relations research*.

Camille Schuster

Is founder of the specialist consultancy Global Collaborations and has been a Professor of Marketing at Xavier University. She is an adjunct faculty member at Arizona State University, a member of the Executive Committee of the Southern Ohio District Export Council, a member of the Board of Trustees of the Global Marketing Special Interest Group of the American Marketing Association and has served on the boards of various international organizations in Cincinnati.

She has published *Global Business: Planning for Sales and Negotiations*, with Michael Copeland, as well as *The Consumer Or Else! - A Consumer-Centered Business Paradigm*. She has also recently co-written with Don Dufek and their book will be published shortly. A third book, *Keep Your Focus on the Consumer and Integrate Your Marketing Communication*, will be published in Singapore next year.

Matthias Thieme

Studied business administration in Bochum, Germany. As a Post-graduate he did scientific works at the Entwicklungszentrum für Internationales Marketing. In 1993 he started working in several functions in the sales department of Mannesmann Mobilfunk. In 2000 he became Head of Sales Department for specialised Trade.

Claudio Vignali

Is the Arnold Ziff Professor of Retailing at Leeds Metropolitan University Business School. Prior to this role he was at the School of Consumer, Tourism and Hospitality Management at Manchester Metropolitan University, where he was the Consumer Section and Research Head for three years. Prior to this he was the postgraduate diploma course leader in the department of Retailing and Marketing.

He has written more than 50 articles and books in the field of Retailing and Marketing and is the editor of two academic journals: *The British Food Journal* and the *International Journal of Management*.

In the past, Professor Vignali has worked for Crown Berger Paints, part of Akzo Nobell, and Benetton, where he held positions from brand manager to export director and developed distribution and retail operations in Europe and the Middle East.

Gianpaolo Vignali

Holds a degree from UMIST and a past president of the students' association

Liz Walley

Joined the Department of Business Studies at MMU eleven years ago. Her teaching and research subject area is sustainable development/environmental management. Prior to MMU, she spent 15 years' working in consultancy, banking and industry. Liz has published in the areas of environmental management and transition in Eastern Europe. Her current research focus is organizational greening, specifically the role of environmental champions and green entrepreneurs.

ON THE WEBSITE

John Fraser
Is a Marketing Manager at General Systems Ltd, Cheshire.

Nuran Fraser
Is a Lecturer in the International Business Unit, Manchester Metropolitan University.

Olga Kuznetsova
Is a research fellow within the International Business subject group at Manchester Metropolitan University Business School. Her Research interests are: Economics of Transition, Enterprise Behaviour in Transition Economies, Modelling Enterprise Behaviour, Corporate Governance Development in Transitional Countries of Europe, Institutional Dimension of Transition and Corporate Social Responsibility. She is widely published and has taught and researched across Europe.

Andrei Kuznetsov
Is Reader in International Business at Manchester Metropolitan University Business School and is a member of the International Business Group. He has a PhD in Economics (Moscow) and a PhD Social Sciences (Florence). His research interests are Economics of Transition, Organizational Theory, Corporate Governance, International Economics and Foreign Investments. He is the author of *Russian Corporation: The strategies of survival and development* as well as numerous book chapters and journal articles on the subject of post-communist economic transition that have been published across Europe and North America.

Chris Lewis
Is a Principle Lecturer at Nottingham Business School in the Department of Strategic Management and Marketing. He has a BA in Spanish and French, and a doctorate from Cambridge University. In addition he has an MBA and Diploma in Marketing from the Chartered Institute of Marketing. He teaches International Business and International Marketing and has research interests in the international brewing industry and cross-cultural issues in relationship marketing.

Frank McDonald
Is Professor of International Business Strategy at the University of Plymouth. He has co-authored books in the area of European and International business.

Robert Tatham
Is at the Universitié de Savoie, Chambéry, France, with a particular interest in the broadcast media.

Giovanna Vertova

Is Assistant Professor of Political Economy, Department of Economics, University of Bergamo and was previously a researcher at MMUBS International Business Unit. She has a PhD in Economics and an MA in International Business and Economic Integration, from the University of Reading. Her first degree is in Economics and Social Sciences, from Bocconi University, Milan. She has substantial teaching and research experience in Italy and the UK. Her main research interests are Economics of Innovation, Technological Change Local and Regional Economics Italian Economic Development.

Preface

This second edition of *European Business and Marketing* has been produced in response to market need and kind requests from colleagues and students to update and extend the original text, which was published by Paul Chapman in 1994. We apologise to all those who have been waiting far too long for a new edition; it is entirely our fault for being caught-up in a number of more pressing projects until now. The European Union (EU) has moved on dramatically in those 10 years and we now think it is right to fundamentally review the original text and comprehensively extend and update it.

The book was originally produced in answer to a need for a straightforward text that addressed both business and marketing strategy from a European perspective. At the time, in 1994, there was only a limited range of written texts on European business and our desire was to plug that gap with a practical text for the advanced undergraduate and post graduate market.

We have now substantially re-written the original text and added three new chapters covering Europe and the world economy, business culture, and marketing and public affairs.

Naturally the text does not cover every issue, but we believe it addresses the core business questions and themes that academics and practitioners in Europe are seeking answers to. Rather than being a standard text, we have commissioned what we believe are a wide and thought-provoking range of modern case studies which emphasise the issues outlined throughout the book.

Our starting point in writing and pulling together the text has always been to consider how it can be used in undergraduate and graduate teaching. We believe we have achieved this by using a range of case studies that reflect many of the core issues and new phenomena impacting upon European business and its world trade. The 21 cases are all new with the exception of EVC1, which has been retained as a result of requests from tutors and has been complimented with the addition of the new case EVC2. The authorship of the cases reflect a cross-section of educators, managers, practitioners and writers who have taught on a international range of international business school and management programmes and have experienced the diversity and vitality of European business in practice. A number of authors have been leading managers in European businesses, others are researchers and academics who act as advisors and consultants to a range of organisations dealing on a day-to-day basis with European markets and business.

'Europe' in the text primarily refers to the enlarged EU of 2000, from the Atlantic coast to the boundaries of the *Lander* of a reunited Germany and the boundaries of Arctic-touching Finland. The relationships between the EU and the rest of Europe are specifically covered in Chapter 2. The text itself addresses the core features of the EU, the harmonisation of trade and the global marketing issues facing Europe. Our argument naturally leans towards a UK perspective as both the editors come from that tradition, although they reflect distinct regional perspectives in that one is Scottish and the other English. Consequently the book particularly reflects northern and western European views more so than other regions, although we have tried to compensate for this by deliberately including material from an Italian, a Dane, an American and two New Zealander amongst others to give balance and a world perspective to the work.

Naturally we concentrate on the EU and the way this market of 340 million people is evolving. Is it distinct? Does it have conditions which are unique to Europe? Or is it just a collection of states trying to arrest relative decline and reduced influence in the world?

Will the growth of the Pacific Rim and now particularly China naturally lead to Europe going into relative decline and becoming an area that had a high historic profile but is now retreating into its own fortress Europe of state regulation and subsidised internal trade? Using state protection and restrictive contracts to stave off decline in an ever more competitive global market, as Quelch, Buzzell and Salama argued in 1991? What of the knowledge economy, will we see perpetual decline as this moves away from continental Europe and relocates and focuses on the large and more opulent North American markets? Pharmaceutical companies are increasingly moving most of their operations to the US because of European restrictions, animal activism and the major funding from market demand for new drugs; will the same apply to advanced technology industries such as information systems management where restrictions on high-tech personnel working patterns are leading to a decline in this core industry in Europe?

What do we make of Europe and the EU as we face such major issues as civil war on its borders and the fracturing of a consensus on EU foreign policy post the 2003 Iraqi War? The EU seems to have been politically neutered by the events in Bosnia Herzegovina and the tribalism breaking out between ethnic groups within the boundaries of the old Yugoslavia. Has the linkage between Europe and America been much reduced by the Iraqi conflict and previous EU inactions? Is it easy for the US to reduce its military involvement in Western Europe and extend its involvement in the Middle East for better strategic reasons such as energy supplies?

Are Europe's close links with the US reducing? Does this mean that some of the solutions to European problems will be based less on North American perspectives? Much of the business, marketing and strategy debate in Europe has been driven by the intellectual power-houses of the US and Canadian business schools since the early 1950s, with modern marketing theory being popularised by Kotler (1993) and Levitt (1960) and developed into texts that have remained in the same basic structure for almost 30 years. The dominance of North American academic thinking in strategy has been based on the work of Porter (1980) and Mintzberg (1983), and in management through Drucker (1954) and Peters and Waterman (1982). North American authors tend to shape and develop the ways in which the study of business is undertaken. Consequently much of the literature on marketing and strategy is written from a North American point of view. The question therefore arises as to whether a more European perspective can provide new insights into the study of European business?

In this text we aim to give an overview of the EU, its market and how it works, and we have tried to show the variety and breadth of issues impacting upon Europe. We have deliberately commissioned a range of cases that reflect both small companies and multinationals. We have not shied away from the restructuring, regional and collaboration issues which have become more frequent and sometimes turbulent as the world gets smaller. We realise we have missed out some issues by not including cases that relate directly to consumer products. We feel, however, that by concentrating on organisational and inter-organizational business issues we give an overview of the core marketing phenomena emerging as a result of the impact of the changes in the European environment.

European Business and Marketing is presented in three parts.

PART I: STRUCTURE OF THE EU AND CORE ISSUES

This section outlines the structure of the EU and the core issues impacting upon it. Its four chapters introduce the subject, outline historic development, how it works economically, politically and socially and its pivotal role in world trade. Key issues and developments are covered throughout the chapters such as enlargement, the euro, trade relations and internal cohesion. This section comprises four chapters.

Chapter 1: The New Europe – Myths and Reality

This introductory chapter outlines the major global and regional changes impacting upon European business and marketing within the EU.

Chapter 2: The Policies of the Single Economic System of the European Union

This chapter considers the policies and programmes that are involved in the creation and development of the single economic system and the implications for business.

Chapter 3: The European Union and the Business Environment

This chapter assesses the historic origins and development of the EU and the evolution of core economic and social policies. It then explores the economic and social environment of the EU and compares and contrasts it with other major trading blocks and economies, notably the US.

Chapter 4: The European Union and the World Economy

This chapter outlines the trade policies of the EU and how with the US it is one of the two superpowers of world trade. It deals with trading relationships, enlargement and the role of the euro amongst other major European business issues.

PART II: TACTICS AND IMPLICATIONS FOR THE EU

In four chapters we look at core tactics and implications within the EU. This section includes developments and practice in modern European marketing, for instance the special needs of European marketing and the increasing importance of public affairs and political marketing within Europe. An assessment of the importance of joint ventures and strategic alliances as pivotal corporate organisational structures to gain competitive edge in the new Europe is made. And finally we look at the emerging and crucial area of business and international culture and its impact upon the emerging EU.

Chapter 5: European Marketing

This chapter looks at the special features impacting upon marketers in Europe such as Euroland, culture and various structural issues. It outlines emerging best practice and theoretical understanding of this complex market.

Chapter 6: Political Marketing and Public Affairs

This chapter explores the complexities of policy making in Europe and the increasingly important role of public affairs management and especially lobbying within the EU. It outlines the importance of relationship marketing to the policy process in the modern Europe and the development of political marketing and public affairs.

Chapter 7: Joint Ventures and Strategic Alliances – A European Perspective

This chapter considers the critical importance and role of joint venture equity companies and strategic alliances for organisational and commercial success both within the EU and to compete in highly-competitive global markets, for instance Airbus in the aircraft manufacturing industry. EU examples are given and the reasons for successful joint venture and strategic alliance formation are outlined:

Chapter 8: European Business and Culture

This chapter argues that it is crucial for businesses operating in Europe to have a comprehensive appreciation of national and corporate culture in order to be successful and benefit from the synergy of a multi-culturally diverse organisation. Cultural comparisons are made with organisations in the EU and North America to aid understanding.

These eight chapters introduce the advanced student in European business marketing and management to the core concepts and issues impacting upon the modern European manager and offer a text for staff from which to teach effectively these vital issues for success. We also hope that the text offered is a useful toolbox of history, practice and theory relating to operating in the modern EU and is a starting point for the modern manager or practitioner dealing with this ever complex and rapidly changing market on a day-to-day basis.

PART III: CASES STUDIES

The text is supported by 21 case studies, 16 in Part Three and 5 on a dedicated website at www.sagepub.co.uk/resources/harris.htm. They cover the European brewing, broadcasting, chemicals, consumer, dairy products, electronics, energy, engineering, food, financial services, furniture, retailing, sports, toys and wine industries amongst others. In addition the cases deal with environmental, regional development and transition economy issues. The cases include such types of corporate entity as state control, joint ventures, family businesses, multinationals and private companies led by entrepreneurs. The cases in Part Three are:

Case 1   Evaluating European Potential and Expansion Posibilities for a US Furniture Company
Case 2   What's Your Beef? The Role of the Meat and Livestock Commission after the UK BSE Crisis
Case 3   Blending Ethics and Modernity the Co-operative Way
Case 4   Boutinot Wines Limited
Case 5   EVC, 1986–1994. The European PVC Industry and the Creation of the European Vinyls Corporation (EVC): An Anglo-Italian Joint Venture Company, a Marriage made in the market place.

The five aditional case studies can be found on the website at: www.sagepub.co.uk/resources/harris.htm. They are:

The core business and marketing questions and themes covered by each case study are listed in the matrix on page xxxv. The support package for tutors using this book will be available to those who adopt the book for their courses and can be accessed on the SAGE website.

We hope you enjoy the book and gain some new insight in the continuing development of European business and management. We would very much welcome your comments on the text and suggestions for improvements.

Phil Harris
Manchester Metropolitan University Business School,

Frank McDonald
Plymouth Business School

REFERENCES

Drucker, P.F. (1954) *The Practice of Management*. New York: Harper and Row.

Kotler, P. (1993) *Marketing Management: Analysis, Planning and Control, 8th edn*. New Jersey: Prentice-Hall.

Levitt, T. (1960) 'Marketing myopia', *Harvard Business Review*, Vol. 38, July-August.

Mintzberg, H. (1983) *Structures in Fives: Designing Effective Organizations*. Englewood Cliffs, New Jersey: Prentice Hall.

Peters, T. and Waterman, R.J. Jr (1982) *In Search of Excellence*. New York and London: Harper and Row.

Porter, M.E. (1980) *Competitive Strategy*. New York: Free Press.

Quelch, J.A., Buzzell, R.D. and Salama, E.R. (1991) *The Marketing Challenge of Europe 1992*. Reading, Massachusetts: Addison Wesley.

Acknowledgements

It is always difficult when one pulls together a multi-faceted book over time to remember all those who have helped contribute to this revised edition. We started planning revising the book in the last millennium and finally completed our work this year. So we think that initially we should thank our readers, supporters and publishers for being patient with us as because of our eclectic mix of interests and pressures, deadlines have slipped once or twice. So first, we thank all those contributors of case studies in the revised edition for their considerable help, support and perseverance. We would also like to thank all those students and practitioners who have fed in comments to us in order to revise the edition: these have been greatly appreciated.

A number of institutions have offered support to us whilst we have carried out our research and writing for this revised edition. First, we would like to thank Manchester Metropolitan University Business School and Professors Nigel Healey and Andrew Lock for their considerable support during the planning and thinking for this book. We would also like to thank our colleagues from the Business School for constructive comments and helpful advice during the construction and development of the book. We would also like to thank Otago Business School, New Zealand for the facilities and support it gave Phil Harris over the last couple of years to complete the book.

For the hard work of putting all the words on disk, assistance in editing, graphics and general support in pulling together the final edition, we must thank some wonderful administrative staff and in particular Heather Standeven, Helen Winsor and Maddie Maher. We also thank the staff of Manchester Metropolitan University Library for their research support and colleagues for reading and commenting on draft chapters.

We would particularly like to thank those who have been involved in developing the text, including our publishers. First, Paul Chapman, who initiated the original text and stimulated us to get on with the second edition and as we signed our draft contract promptly sold his business to Sage. We always wondered whether it was significant! In recent times we have benefited from the great support of Kirin Shoman, who provoked us into getting on with the text and gave us a number of suggestions as to how we could improve and strengthen it for the modern user. We also thank Delia Alphonso-Martinez, who aided us as we completed the text over the last few months. Her support and patience is greatly appreciated.

Finally, and perhaps most importantly, we would like to thank those who have put up with us writing the book. We would like to thank Irene Harris, Mhorag, Sarah, Rachel and Duncan McDonald who had to endure us whilst putting this book together and who were an endless source of encouragement.

Phil Harris
Frank McDonald

List of Abbreviations and Acronyms

ABB	Asea Brown Boveri
ACP	African, Caribbean and Pacific (countries which are former colonies of member states of the EU)
AEBF	Asia–Europe Business Forum
APEC	Asia–Pacific Economic Cooperation
ASEM	Asia–Europe Meeting
BA	British Airways
BAe	British Aerospace
BBC	British Broadcasting Corporation
BHS or BhS	British Home Stores
BP	British Petroleum
BRITE	Basic Research in Industrial Technologies for Europe
BSE	bovine spongiform encephalopathy
BTO	build-to-order
CAP	Common Agricultural Policy
CBI	Confederation of British Industry
CCP	Common Commercial Policy
CCT	compulsory competitive tendering
CEE	Central and Eastern Europe
CEN	Comité European de Normalisation (European standards body)
CENELEC	Comité European de Normalisation Electronique (European standards body for electrical equipment)
CEO	Chief Executive Officer
CET	common external tariff
CJD	Creutzfeldt-Jakob Disease
CMEA	Council for Mutual Economic Assistance (also known as COMECON)
COR	Committee of the Regions
COREPER	Committee of Permanent Representatives (permanent Civil Servants in the Council of Ministers)
CSSR	Union of Soviet Socialist Republics
D1	German Telecom
D2	Mannesmann Mobilfunk
DCC	digital compact cassette

DCI	compact disk interactive
DFI	direct foreign investment
DML	Devonport Management Limited
DTH	direct to home
DTI	Department of Trade and Industry
DVD	digital video disc
EAGGF	European Agricultural Guidance and Guarantee Fund (the funding for the CAP and for the reconstruction of the agricultural sector)
EBRD	European Bank for Reconstruction and Development
EC	European Communities
ECB	European Central Bank
ECE	United Nations Economic Commission for Europe
ECJ	European Court of Justice
ECSC	European Coal and Steel Community
ECU	European Currency Unit
EEC	European Economic Community
EFA	European Food Agency
EFA	European Fighter Aircraft
EFSA	European Food Safety Authority
EFTA	European Free Trade Association
EMS	European Monetary System
EMU	Economic and Monetary Union
Eni	Ente Nazionale Idrocarburi
EP	European Parliament
EPA	Environmental Protection Act
ERDF	European Regional Development Fund
ERM	Exchange Rate Mechanism
ESC	Economic and Social Committee
ESCB	European System of Central Banks
ESF	European Social Fund
ESPRIT	European Strategic Programme for Research and Development Technology
EU	European Union
EURAM	European Research in Advanced Materials
EURATOM	European Atomic Energy Community
EVC	European Vinyls Corporation
FC	football club
FMCG	fast moving consumer goods
GATS	General Agreement on Trade in Services
GATT	General Agreement on Tariffs and Trade
GDP	gross domestic product
GDR	German Democratic Republic
GM	General Motors
GMO	Gentically Modified Organism

GMS	Global System for Mobile Communication
GSP	Generalised System of Preference
HDI	Human Development Index
ICC	International Chamber of Commerce
ICI	Imperial Chemical Industries
ICT	Information and communication technologies
IMF	International Monetary Fund
IMP	Industrial Marketing and Purchasing
ISTAT	Istituto Nazionale di Statistica
JIT	just-in-time
LDC	less developed country
MAAF	Ministry of Agriculture, Fisheries and Food
MBO	management buyout
MEP	Member of the European Parliament
MFA	Multi-Fibre Arrangement
MFN	most favoured nation
MHS	The Meat and Hygiene Service
MIS	management information systems
MITI	Japanese Ministry of International Trade
MLC	Meat and Livestock Commission
MNC	multinational corporation
MOD	Ministry of Defence
MP	Member of Parliament
NAFTA	North American Free Trade Area
NAFTA	North American Free Trade Association
NAP	North American Philips
NATO	North Atlantic Treaty Organisation
NFC	National Freight Corporation
NFP	Not for Profit
NGO	non-governmental organisation
NIC	newly industrialised countries
NPD	new product development
NTA	New Transatlantic Agenda
NTB	non-tariff barrier
NUTS	Nomenclature of Territorial Units for Statistics
NZDB	New Zealand Dairy Board
OECD	Organisation for Economic Co-operation and Development
OTMS	Over Thirty Months Scheme
PCC	Philips Consumer Communications
PEST	political, economic, social and technological factors
PHARE	Actions pour la Reconversion Economique Poland and Hungary
PR	public relations
PSB	public service broadcasters
PVC	polyvinyl chloride

R&D	research and development
REC	Regional Environmental Centre for Central and Eastern Europe
RLF	receiving licence fee
RNIB	Royal National Institute for the Blind
RSC	Rowland Sallingsbury Casey
SBO	specified bovine offal
SBU	strategic business unit
SEA	Single European Act
SEM	Single European Market
SEP	Single European Programme
SIF	Stitching Ingka Foundation
SME	small- and medium-sized enterprise
SWOT	strengths, weaknesses, opportunities and threats
TABC	Transatlantic Business Dialogue
TACD	Transatlantic Consumer Dialogue component
TQM	total quality Management
TUC	Trades Union Congress
UNCTC	United Nations Centre on Transnational Corporations
UNICE	Union of Industrial and Employers' Confederations of Europe
UPS	United Parcel Service
USMEF	United States Meat Export Federation
USSR	Union of Soviet Socialist Republics
VCM	vinyl chloride monomer
VCR	video cassette recorder
VHS	video home system
VW	Volkswagen
WTO	World Trade Organisation

Matrix: Core business and marketing questions and themes

Theme	C1	C2	C3	C4	C5	C6	C7	C8	C9	C10	C11	C12	C13	C14	C15	C16	C17	C18	C19	C20	C21	C22
Branding	*														*	*	*		*	*	*	*
Business strategy	*	*	*	*	*	*	*		*		*	*	*	*	*	*	*	*	*	*	*	*
Competition policy			*	*		*	*				*	*	*	*	*	*	*				*	
Cultural differences	*			*			*	*		*				*	*	*	*	*	*	*	*	*
Culture management	*		*	*	*		*	*	*					*			*			*		*
EU competition policy	*		*	*	*		*	*	*		*	*	*	*			*		*	*	*	*
EU law	*		*	*			*	*	*	*	*						*		*	*	*	
EU market entry	*	*	*	*	*		*	*							*					*	*	*
Entrepreneurialism		*				*			*									*				
Environmentalism				*	*	*	*	*					*				*		*	*		
FDI	*									*												
Global marketing	*		*	*	*		*	*			*			*	*	*	*	*	*			*
Globalism	*		*		*		*	*								*	*	*				
Joint ventures			*	*	*		*	*								*	*					
Lobbying							*	*		*						*	*		*		*	
Mergers and acquisitions	*		*																		*	
Pricing policy	*						*	*													*	
Product innovation			*	*	*		*	*	*	*	*		*	*		*	*	*		*	*	*
Rationalisation			*	*	*				*	*	*	*	*	*	*			*		*		
Regionalism		*	*	*	*				*	*		*	*						*	*	*	*
Regionalism/culture			*	*			*	*	*	*		*		*	*		*	*	*	*	*	
Regulation of markets			*	*	*		*	*			*	*		*	*	*	*	*	*	*	*	*
Restructuring		*	*	*	*		*	*	*		*	*		*			*			*		
Retailing	*	*			*				*			*		*	*	*	*	*	*	*		*
SEM	*		*	*	*		*	*	*				*	*	*	*		*	*	*	*	*
SME's		*		*	*	*			*	*	*								*			
Societal marketing																	*	*	*	*	*	*
State controlled business			*	*										*								
Strategic alliances	*		*	*			*	*	*								*		*	*		
Technology transfer							*	*	*					*			*		*			*
Urban regeneration												*										
Wholesaling	*	*	*	*	*		*	*												*		*

PART I: STRUCTURE OF THE ECONOMIC UNION AND CORE ISSUES

1   THE NEW EUROPE – MYTHS AND REALITY

'In the end each nation
is no more than a flock
of timid and hardworking animals
with each government as its shepherd'

Alexis de Tocqueville, 1835

Throughout the 1990s and the early years of this millennium, Europe, and particularly the European Union (EU) has become less glamorous to students, researchers and business people because of popular anti-EU mythology. The EU is frequently attacked as being over-bureaucratic, yet its civil service is smaller than that of the UK's Scottish Office. 'It just subsidises large farmers,' is one cry, yet its grant aid is steadily being increased to foster industrial competitiveness and regional restructuring rather than agriculture. 'It's too bureaucratic and is not accountable to anyone,' is commonly heard, yet the EU publicly asks for information and is open to lobbying and to calls for public information, in contrast to the secrecy of many state governments.

The above examples are just some of the myths of the new Europe in terms of popular political misconceptions, but perhaps these distortions reflect themes and issues within this most advanced and potentially culturally complex market in the world, with its immediate market of 380 million people and linkages directly to many more. The distortions, arguments and myths around the EU reflect the many sides fighting for power within the economic and political structure of the EU, whether they be nation states, political parties, media, business interests or non-EU trading blocks and nations attempting to exert pressure on its EU import, export or subsidy policies. More recently issues over enlargement, whether or not to join the euro, and the war in Iraq have exacerbated these perceptions and beliefs. Internally its citizens voice their views from the ballot box to the barricading farmers of France protesting at the reductions in the common agricultural policy (CAP), to the unemployed of the new Lander of Germany devastated at the ending of full employment or campaigning for peace in mass protests against military involvement.

THE IMPORTANCE OF SMALL AND MEDIUM-SIZED ENTERPRISES TO EUROPE

But what of European business markets, enterprises and their interests? Are there myths associated with these? Perhaps the most popular myth in this area is that most businesses are multinational corporations (MNCs). This is clearly wrong and distorts our view of business in Europe. For according to the EU (Eurostat, 2002), Europe's 20 million non-primary sector private enterprises employ 122 million workers. And over 99 per cent of these enterprises are small and medium-sized enterprises (SMEs). Distinct features of these European businesses include:

- Two-thirds of all enterprise sector jobs are in SMEs. Very small firms (under 10 employees) provide one-third of all jobs.
- The average size of a business in Europe is six workers (19 in the US, 10 in Japan).
- European SMEs provide a relatively large share of private sector employment (66 per cent, as against 46 per cent in the US and 33 per cent in Japan).
- SMEs are saying ever more often that their main growth constraint is lack of skilled labour.
- The share of SMEs in Europe with more international business contacts than five years ago is growing rapidly, rising from one-quarter in 1999 to one-third in 2001.

- Women own 22 per cent of European SMEs (ranging from 14 per cent in Greece to 30 per cent in France).

Local and national governments across the EU perceive the formation of more SMEs as the most effective way to counter recession, by creating employment opportunities as industrial manufacturing and multi-nationals contract. In the UK there was a major drive to expand the SME sector from 1982; this grew dramatically until late 1987 when recession hit it dramatically and earlier rapid growth was mirrored by a rapid increase in liquidations as credit became restricted.

The SME sector shows many reasons for growth, high incomes creating higher demand and many people looking for alternative employment opportunities. The squeeze on the SME sector has been made worse by over-bureaucratic demands of government requiring more detailed tax accounts, tax assessments, VAT returns and so on, all of which take time and increased expertise, often to the detriment of the enterprise. Late payments by MNCs to the SMEs has also become an EU issue, as the larger companies avoid prompt payment of their bills to smaller dependent companies and squeeze many of them into liquidation. There has been much criticism of this unfair practice and active lobbying to make it illegal and to protect small companies across Europe. This lobby has also started to counter the over-bureaucratic 'quality' movement world which is demanding BS 5750 and its European equivalent by all companies to show their commitment to just-in-time (JIT), total quality management (TQM) and the concepts of quality operations management currently in vogue. These may be justifiable processes to adopt and be acredited for by the MNCs and larger SMEs, but for the smaller organisation the amount of effort involved can be dangerous in taking away energy and funds from the core business. If resources have to be taken away from the business to achieve this qualification, is it worth it? Consultancy rates for the small SME invariably are too high and *de facto* preclude them. The question for many organisations is 'Is it worth it for the SME or is it another way of reducing entry and access to quality markets for the small producer/supplier?'

In Germany the SMEs have articulated their concern at the amount of bureaucracy brought by harmonisation of the market and how it is contributing unduly to costs. Banks in the UK are being criticised for their lack of support for small businesses and their bias towards larger SMEs. As recession bites, one can expect there to be more outcries against expensive bureaucracy SME entrepreneurs. There are parallels in the nineteenth century when arguments were propounded against government intervention in the economy and the over-bureaucratic tax systems which were seen as encumbrances on entrepreneurs.

Across the EU policies are being developed at regional, national and transnational government level that see SMEs as the only positive way of creating employment and generating increased local growth for the community. Enterprise initiatives, European Social Fund (ESF), European Regional Development Fund (ERDF) and other funds are being geared up to stimulate the development of SMEs. However, as a high proportion of SMEs are small retailers, does this mean there is a conflict of interest between the large retail chains – such as ASDA (Wal Mart), Sainsbury, Tesco, Aldi, Netto – and the small family business? Clearly the large out-of-town sites and sheds, whether they be supermarkets, hypermarkets or malls like the Trafford Centre in the north-west of England, are trying to attract and dominate a core sector of the European retail market. Could this type of behaviour, which is closing down many small retailers and reducing choice, be deemed anti-competitive behaviour? Or is it just a change in market pattern? The case study on e-shopping (see www.sagepub.co.uk/resources/harris.htm) explores these and other emerging retail issues in Europe.

It is only recently that SMEs and voluntary organisations have begun to confederate across the EU to lobby collectively on their own behalf and amend or reform discriminatory practices. As Saki, quoted in Grass (1983), commented, 'Every reformation must have its victims. You can't expect the fatted calf to share the enthusiasm of the angels over the prodigal's return.' Five case studies give particular insight into the SME area and its importance to the EU economy:

- The Boutinot Wines case is a good example of an entrepreneurial SME operating in the growing wine business in the north of England and outlines its everyday marketing problems.
- The Starobrno case gives insight into how a Czech brewery faces market change and repositioning post economic transition.
- Gruppo Massone outlines how an Italian food company plans to enter the UK Market.

- The Perkins case shows how public relations and reputation can be used to boost effectively an organisation's products in the market place.
- The Fulham FC case outlines how a brand in sport can be established and the struggle that football teams have to compete successfully in the top English football leagues.

CHALLENGING MARKETING ORTHODOXY

Many of the marketing texts argue that marketing is a logical process with a natural structure that can be viewed primarily as a method of: understanding the marketing environment; using the marketing mix (product, price, promotion and place); developing a marketing plan based upon the use of this mix; implementing the plan through a strategy; and, finally, using a control method to ensure that the strategy is adhered to. This marketing process is reviewed and evaluated regularly and modifications made to the use of the mix to take account of market changes impacting upon competitiveness. This is subsequently elaborated upon in texts with variants being developed for international (Czinkota and Ronkainen, 1993), industrial (Webster, 1984) and not-for-profit marketing (Kotler and Levy, 1969). More recently elements of debate in the services and retail marketing fields have emerged. This process has led to a new orthodoxy in marketing that seems to be rearticulating what can almost be deemed a reductionist view of markets and how they work.

This view of marketing seems to suggest that much of marketing theory, by its frequent use of consumer marketing case studies (chocolate, soap powder, shampoo and numerous chocolate bar examples) relates to multinational enterprises which are internationally based and have global ambitions. Invariably the marketing view is based on an orthodox corporation shape that uses standard methods to gain entry to markets and eventually dominates them, using branding and bought advertising. The basis of most of the quoted companies is either joint stock or private corporation and therefore much of this thinking ignores SMEs, family businesses and, more importantly, state holdings in strategic business sectors. This seems strange, as the new orthodoxy does not apply as rigidly in Europe where the socio-political scene has traditionally been much more interventionist. The family concern still dominates countries such as Spain, where

Anglo-Saxon based banks from the US and UK adopted their usual MNC orthodox approach, failed to gain any significant share of the Spanish market in the 1980s and were forced to withdraw. It is only in the last 10 years that some UK- and US-style banks have modified their style of operation to take account of the Spanish family business style and consequently have re-entered the market, and as a result have been more successful.

The recognition of the family business and its importance as an organisational business strategy has only recently begun to be explored. We include one example of this type of business amongst our case studies: LEGO, the Danish toymaker that has internationalised its product range but is still family based. LEGO shows how a highly regionally-based company that focuses on Europe and wider markets can develop. It is a specialist company yet it has managed to target the toy sector and become one of the world leaders in toy manufacture, despite being based in a remote region of Denmark away from the so called 'Golden Triangle' at the centre of the EU.

A NETWORK APPROACH TO EUROPE

Another core issue in marketing is the growth and importance of theories in networking and interaction. This has been much developed by the Industrial Marketing and Purchasing Group and is outlined in Hakansson (1982), Ford (1990) and in the Uppsala School research, especially Johanson and Mattson (1987). The area has been further augmented by views on developing the interface between service operations and marketing by the use of 'relationship marketing', through the work of Christopher, Payne and Ballantyne (1991). This area also has substantial work in the political domain and has a rich body of literature supporting political interaction around 'the public corporate affairs' area with Jordan (1991) and Harris and Moss (2001) supplying good qualitative research in the UK, whilst Mazey and Richardson (1993), Pedlar (2002) and Van Schendelen (2002) have outlined political interaction and corporate influence on an EU basis.

Much of this work looks at the way in which companies and organisations interact and consequently network with each other to gain commercial advantage in world markets. The network can be using similar subcontractors, components, sharing research and development costs or operating within the same governmental framework. Clearly being within the EU is beginning to foster its own network norms as companies and organisations collaborate on, for example, such diverse EU-funded initiatives as the European Strategic Programme for Research and Development in Information Technology (ESPRIT), Basic Research in Industrial Technologies for Europe (BRITE) and Pologne-Hongrie: Actions pour la Reconversion Economique (PHARE). Being within a trading block with no internal barriers creates its own networks. Collaborations in aerospace, vehicle manufacture and engineering have all sponsored the development of a European outlook based on its own internal market network.

This network and interaction approach to marketing shows the substance of being able to influence decisions by knowledge of how a human network works or how it interacts. The IMP group of researchers have concentrated on industrial interactions over the last 20 years by looking at the process of buying and selling interaction, by use of the Hakansson (1982) interaction model. This has been quantified and developed to lend understanding to complex industrial markets where organisations interact across a number of intricate markets. It shows how research and development decisions are made, what influences them, and what the procurement cycle is likely to be. If the seller or business is trying to influence the state, this can take time and energy over a significant period as it has to contend with the political processes. In military markets influencing buying decisions and project funders of projects can take place at many levels and take more than five years. The £40 billion (includes 25 years' procurement support costs) investment in the Aircraft Carrier Replacement programme in the UK is now looking well judged and will provide important work for a substantial section of the UK defence industry. Whether UK Prime Minister Blair overruled the original preferred bid from the prime French owned supplier because of government relations with France is one of those rumours one will have to wait 25 years under official secrecy agreements to clarify. The European Fighter Aircraft (EFA) project took five years to develop and has been redesigned to take account of the end of the Cold War and, more importantly, in the short term the recession in Europe combined with the public-sector borrowing requirement in the new united Germany, which has led to drastic cuts in what are now deemed non-standard needs. In addition, the UK sees it as crucial to

maintain its technology base by supporting British Aerospace (BAe) in the advanced armaments industry. The importance of weapons manufacture to the EU and especially to the former colonial powers France and the UK should not be forgotten. Worldwide Arms Agreement export sales in 2001 were:

USA	$9.7 billion (45.6 per cent of all sales)
UK	$4 billion
Russia	$3.6 billion
France	$2.9 billion

Collaborative projects in Europe have included Concorde, Airbus, Eurotunnel and the European Bank for Reconstruction and Development (EBRD), which all lend themselves more readily to a network approach to increase understanding rather than a more traditional approach. Thus a framework that looks at human interaction across organisations is particularly useful for understanding markets and opportunities.

The network approach and interaction models have also been applied to the public sector and to analysing how it works against the background of new liberal economics and divestment of public-sector activities to the private-sector. For example, understanding the interaction process in health purchasing and how decisions are made in health care is very important to the success of the pharmaceutical companies and providers of numerous health care services. Network analysis can also be applied successfully to other sectors such as local authorities or local and regional government. Finding out who makes the decisions, who influences them, how the tenders are constructed and who has prior knowledge is an important part of understanding the procurement process and can lead to commercial success or failure. An understanding of interaction models can significantly reduce the latter.

PRIVATISATION AND PUBLIC PROCUREMENT

In Europe compulsory competitive tendering (CCT) is impacting upon much of public provision, resulting in many protective barriers coming down and the opening up of the public sector to increased competition. It is well known that in certain regions and countries particular local businesses and interests have been favoured. This has its origins in the development of industrialisation in Europe. In Germany business has a complex web of interests woven into it. The banks, regional government, pension funds, assurance groups and trade unionists have traditionally put themselves behind supporting their own industrial investments and interests and precluded competition. Under CCT, though, these semi-closed markets should be open to competition. In Britain we already see French companies competing for refuse collection contracts, and under privatisation French water companies own UK water suppliers, and it is known that the German Bahnhof is interested in some UK rail franchise operator contracts.

With pressure on the public sector, from growing care demands, an aging population and the desire to reduce state involvement in public provision of services, an inevitable consequence has been the growth of the private providers and more interestingly the voluntary (not-for-profit) sectors. Europe has an aging population, with the only sizable exception being Eire. This and a general increase in people's expectations of the level of care has meant that there has been great pressure on the public provision of health and community support, which state systems are finding increasingly difficult to fund. New organisations have sprung up to address these issues, whilst the traditional charity and voluntary movement has modernised and new organisational structures have developed such as cooperatives and credit unions. Age Concern, the UK-based charity for the elderly, besides its charity shop interest has many other significant business interests. In its broad care provision it is also involved in the market by endorsing quality insurance with a leading independent brokerage, holidays (Saga) and across the UK the provision of community care in collaboration with local authorities.

Age and a rising life expectancy is a critical market factor across Europe and this sector of consumers is perhaps the fastest growing. This phenomenon is not restricted to Europe and is a truly transatlantic phenomenon as many Europeans observe when they see the maturing population of American tourists. The Japanese population is also in a similar situation. This has implications for markets and the types of goods that are growing in importance and the type of services needed and the provision of those services. The extent, wealth and limited regulation of the aging market in North America is seeing a steady drift of major pharmaceutical and health companies from Europe to the US.

A recent example of this is the former Swiss multinational Novartis, which is now headquartered in the US.

Clearly health insurance and pensions provided by the state will be under increasing pressure as demographics impact upon the national and wider European economies. This is leading to a growth in private provision. The increasing growth in the provision of state benefits to the elderly and the unemployed is becoming unsustainable as numbers rapidly increase and demands on a shrinking workforce become more and more of a burden as the aging population increases and gross domestic product (GDP) does not rise commensurably. All this, as well as ideology, is putting pressure on European economies to prune back public expenditure and think of ways of targeting social benefits more effectively. This has resulted in large-scale privatisation in the UK, with companies from British Petroleum (BP) to the National Freight Corporation (NFC) being taken out of state ownership and privatised. Privatisation has been replicated across Europe and has resulted in privatised telecom and utility companies across France, Germany and the rest of the EU.

In the new united Germany the funding of reunification has meant the privatisation of the Bundesposte (post office including telecommunications) and other assets, whilst in Italy corruption and a change of government has forced change, resulting in suggestions that even art galleries should be privatised. The movement towards privatisation is happening all over Europe, from the Atlantic to the Urals. In fact, some of the most dramatic privatisations have occurred in Central and Eastern Europe, where the newly-formed democratically elected states, such as the Czech Republic and Poland, have moved rapidly to a free enterprise economy by selling off state assets to private bidders in order to reduce state involvement. Thus Skoda is now owned by Volkswagen (VW), much of Poland's industrial base is in private hands, and the Estonian banking sector is Swedish owned.

Ways of reducing state control is one of the major issues within European markets, whether it be reducing trade barriers or moving from a state-controlled economy to one that is free to run its own affairs. The understanding of how state-controlled businesses ran in former planned economies is little understood and consequently there is little comprehension of how the old system of business operation can be reformed to sustain employment and generate profits. An awareness of how difficult it is to operate a business under a state-dominated system in a transition economy can be seen in the Russian Entrepreneurship, Shell, Starobrno and Unilever case studies. The differences between state-controlled planned economy and a free-market economy is dramatic. The case studies give an insight into the constraints of such a system, its weaknesses and social strengths. For the manager, academic or student wishing to appreciate how Eastern and Central Europe work, these are good starting points. Only by having this appreciation of the way business organisations in Eastern and Central Europe are run will we be able to build successful developments, based on learning from experience for a successful future. As is being found out, just transferring a Western capitalist answer to the East does not always bring the best solution.

The new Germany with its refurbishment of the Eastern Lander offers many opportunities for market development; the Treuhand (the government agency for privatising enterprises in the former East Germany) has been the main agency for transformation either via sales of former state assets, joint ventures or closure. This has brought about major change, shutting down pre-1945 chemical plants and complexes and closing coal mines that produced lignite brown coal. This has led to high unemployment, a concept not known before 1989 in the old German Democratic Republic (GDR). All this is having a major impact upon the local population. In Poland transition to a market-based economy has also been rapid, with everything from shipyards to tractors having been privatised.

This process of transference from the state to private control is inevitably going to be a major theme of European marketing and strategy over the next 20 years, and our knowledge of this process and the best methods for market success is only now being established. The issue of regional investment is explored in the Industrial Districts in Italy case study and the development of new markets in Germany in the Mannesmann Mobilfunk case study.

USE OF LOBBYING

The importance of being able to influence government has consequently become correspondingly more important to business as the state considers selling off assets. It has been argued that the British Airways' (BA) former chairman Lord King was able to lobby very effectively to the benefit of BA in the 1980s, and more recently this has been the case with his successor Lord Marshall. The significance of political influence as part of corporate strategy can be seen very clearly in the BSE case study where a whole industry faced a loss of market and access to world markets, and has diligently regained much access and sales through judicious lobbying. The New Zealand Dairy Board case study outlines the importance of the EU market to this far-distant country and particularly the UK market to its product Anchor Butter, and how custom rules can be used to block imports or make them very expensive. These case studies outline very effectively the benefit of lobbying and the use of law to block competitive imports into the EU and how this was countered. Philips, the Dutch electric group has always shown great interest in protecting its home market and has been accused of being too effective a lobbyist of the EU for its own long-term competitive good. It was able to negotiate price-protection for its newly invented compact disc system against Japanese industry, and by the end of the 1980s Philips had gained approval from DG XIII for a research and development (R&D) subsidy for a total of almost 150 projects, involving 10,000 man-years of work (Van Schendelen, 1993). The Philips case study shows the complexity of the business areas it operates in and how it is restructuring to meet new challenges.

The public affairs interface between government and business is crucial, for with intervention in business activities by government bodies such as the EU being common, there is a growing need for regular dialogue between state and businesses. Across Europe this is reflected in groups and companies organising to lobby the EU to amend community legislation and programmes. The EU and its organisations are geared up to be influenced by member states, companies and individuals. Therefore, there is a strong incentive for companies to lobby EU institutions directly; for instance, much of the legislation on the environment is derived from that source. McCormick (1991), commenting on UK environmental lobbying, argues that 'Membership of the community also fundamentally altered the position and the powers of the environmental lobby. Groups can now by-pass domestic governmental institutions and appeal to a higher level of authority, and a more diverse array of institutions and legislative processes.'

It has been argued that over 70 per cent of member state legislation is generated in Brussels.

This may not suit every member state and some may try to slow down legislation and regulation, but the growth of this is inevitable. These issues are further explored in Chapter 3 and lobbying in particular in Chapter 6. Environmental issues are explored and developed in the Shell case study and the ethical values of businesses outlined in the Cooperative Bank case study. Notable features of this growth in regulation have been the growing use of environmental audits by companies and the growth in emissions legislation and monitoring. Many types of environmental legislation need to be international to be effective, as major environmental disasters like Chenobyl's radiation fall-outs do not recognise state boundaries. This area of legislation consequently impacts upon major industries like vehicle production, farming, construction, oil and chemical industries to name but a few. This growing awareness of environmental issues amongst Europeans and Americans is having its impact on corporate strategy and marketing as it adjusts to a new environment that is theoretically greener and cleaner.

In the UK, lobbying has grown dramatically as a result of globalisation, deregulation policies and multi-layer government with quango, quasi-quango and agency institutional systems which are open to compete for business and influence who gets it. It is also argued that the UK's centralised government structure lends itself to lobbying in a more covert way than is the case with the EU. The ever-complex government system and international business demands has meant that it is essential for an effective dialogue to be maintained between government and business. Issues on harmonisation connected to the Single European Programme (SEP) and enlargement lend themselves very much to both the general and specialist lobbyist. As transnational business organisations have grown, their desire to influence their operating environment across boundaries has developed. Therefore to be able to amend, delay or even initiate legislation can give the company or organisation significant competitive advantage and cost savings.

Commercial lobbying as a business initially crossed the Atlantic and developed in Europe where it has continued to develop and has become significant in EU, national and regional government centres. Contracts can be won or lost depending upon the effectiveness of lobbying. This is not just about direct influence: politicians and officials must be briefed on issues surrounding a case to ensure that legislators have sufficient information to make an unbiased and informed judgement.

REGIONALISM

Another feature within Europe is regionalism and the distinct needs and culture of both separate states and constituent parts within the EU. This has led to dramatic differences in outlook. In Italy, northern Italians see themselves as distinctly different from their southern compatriots. Recently this has led to a growth in regional nationalism. The Lombard League has suggested that the country be broken into two, with the Lombard League state being based on Milan, Bologna, Florence and Turin – the 'Golden Belt' of northern Italy. Regional issues are seen very clearly in the Industrial Districts in Italy and Stena case studies.

In Spain, regional awareness was generated by the 1992 Barcelona Olympic Games, which opened many people's eyes to the distinct historical differences between Catalonia and the rest of Spain. Spain has a wide variety of unique regions, for instance, Galicia in the west has distinct Gaelic ancestry, much like Brittany in France or the highlands and islands of Scotland. Also within Spain is the Basque country, centred on the port and old steel and banking centres of Bilbao and Pamplona. Spain also has the Mediterranean regions of Valencia and further to the south Andalucia. The geography and cultural history of Spain therefore lends itself to a rich patchwork of distinct regions within the Iberian Peninsula. In the sixteenth century the capital Madrid was established in the centre of the country, to give central government a base from which to pull the different regions together. Within Spain, though, there are other influences. The Moorish influence has enlivened its culture by giving a distinct Islamic influence to its agriculture and architecture. The proximity of Catalonia to France has meant that it sometimes takes more of a lead from its French neighbour than Madrid. This is historically not surprising as the neighbouring region within France, centred on Perpignan, was originally part of a greater Catalonia. The North African influence can also be seen within Spain as its southern coast is close to Morocco, Tunisia, Algeria and so on. There is a significant colonial history that intertwines North Africa with France and Spain. This has had a major historic and cultural impact on this part of the EU.

Common interest in political and cultural issues can link economies in alliance; for instance, many of the regions and countries facing the Mediterranean have common agriculture and capital formation interests. Southern Italy, France, Spain and Greece have similarities that link them in common interest groups within the EU – the so-called Mediterranean group. They also seem to have similar problems in terms of the labour market, that is, in restricting immigration; in the case of France and Spain, particularly from the famine-stricken and economically disadvantaged African continent and in Greece from the unstable Balkans. Economic migration from Eastern Europe to the prosperous West is clearly an issue that EU enlargement will clearly have to address.

This federation of regional interests is not just restricted to Spain; across Europe most of the states are made up of distinct regions. In France the differences in the economic and business needs and cultural traditions of Bordeaux, Provence, Paris and Corsica can be immense, whilst in Germany the Hanseatic and Calvinist traditions are in marked contrast to the Roman Catholic and Hapsburg background of Bavaria. Belgium is one of the youngest states, composed of Wallonia and Flanders with distinct differences in ethnic groups and two state languages. The region of Wallonia is the former French-speaking heartland, based on heavy industries such as steel, coal and textiles, whilst Wallonia was until recently heavily dependent on agriculture. The dominance of the old French-speaking area has been reversed in recent years, with a transfer of economic power away from the industrial east to Flanders with its base of agriculture and light industry. These regional differences have parallels that apply across Europe and have their equivalents in other states such as The Netherlands, Austria, Portugal, Sweden, Finland and Denmark. The UK is made up of separate states and has recognised this with separate legal systems for Scotland, Wales and Northern Ireland. England, with its political centre in Whitehall, appears to be homogenous, but upon further inspection it can be seen to be made up of regions with their own cultural and economic identities. Clearly there is a dramatic difference between the economies of Cornwall and north-west England. Cumbria has its own unique needs, whilst the urban regions of Merseyside, Greater Manchester, the West Midlands, West Riding of Yorkshire and London may have a common link in their urban ecology and understanding of business networks.

Regions within Europe have also joined in common cause because of common interests such as language, finance and education systems. One grouping that has been particularly vocal has been Strathclyde in Scotland with Wallonia in Belgium and Catalonia in Spain, who linked up to influence the EU on their common industrial restructuring needs. The Atlantic-facing regions of Belgium, France and Spain also regularly link up to lobby on behalf of common infrastructure and agriculture issues within the EU. Northern Regions can be linked; for instance, the Orkneys and Shetland Islands of the UK with those of Denmark and its islands; The Netherlands Sweden and Finland with German Schleswig-Holstein on northern European issues within the Community.

There are also the first signs of Germany's new Lander having common interests with some of its pre-Iron Curtain trading partners, for instance, links between Halle, Leipzig and the north-west of England seem to be re-emerging after the collapse of the Soviet empire. A thriving regional trading area that appears to be re-emerging post the collapse of the Iron Curtain is that of 'Mittel Europe'. Northern Italy, Slovenia, Croatia, southern Switzerland, Hungary and Austria formed a major trading area within Europe, centred on Trieste, for a number of centuries, which was artificially cut off by the development of new nation states and the rise of Communism. This now appears to be re-establishing itself although, conflict in the former Yugoslavia slowed down this development.

These links that we have focused on within Europe are not limited to the borders of the EU. Germany has always held a pivotal role in Central and Eastern Europe, as can be seen in its substantial trade with these countries. It is very heavily involved in the Republics of Belarus, the Baltic States, Ukraine and Russia. Many of the new Lander were traditionally involved as trading and financial service centres for Eastern European prior to 1945. These are now being reactivated as free market centres, alongside the traditional western financial service centres for Central and Eastern Europe of Helsinki and Vienna alongside the new Berlin.

CULTURE AND LANGUAGE

Language plays an important part in the complexity of Europe. The linguist knows that using a native speaker's language effectively is like using a key to open a door. Knowledge of the vocabulary, grammar and cadence of knowing a native speaker's language gives insight into the person's thinking, outlook and prejudice. Within the EU there are nine official languages of which three predominate: English because it is the world commercial language, French which is adopted as the diplomatic language of the community, and German which is frequently seen as the lingua franca in Central and Eastern Europe. Spanish has wide use because, together with Portuguese, it is the language of Latin America.

It is well known that most people respond better if spoken to in their own language; this may appear obvious but seems to have been overlooked by many anglophiles who, having once belonged to a dominant culture, do not put much effort into developing a second European language. This is due partly to the internationalism of English, which has made the learning of a second language inessential but can also be attributed to the lack of access to language teaching within the English education system. It is interesting to note that this lack of language provision is less of a problem in Wales, Scotland or Northern Ireland, which all have their own independent language traditions. The Netherlands, Belgium and Denmark have developed extensive skills in other languages, which have allowed them to be very much at the heart of internationalism within modern Europe.

Proficiency in a foreign language and the ability to communicate with trading partners in their native tongue can lead to better understanding and increased business. A Frenchman seeking to trade with a British company is more likely to choose one with French-speaking members than one whose staff have no language skills. Also it is very apparent that those who speak no languages other than their own will have to use third parties to communicate and therefore place themselves at a disadvantage Clearly, to understand instantly what is being spoken of in a negotiation is essential, as slowness or misunderstanding could lose the business.

Europe has a number of major national languages at its heart: an inability to be able to interpret, evaluate, understand and assess can put the organisation at an immense advantage. Austrians, Germans, French, Fins, Spaniards, Swedes, Irish, Danes, Dutch, Portuguese, Greeks and Italians are all proud of their language and culture and will normally respond to those who respect it by having an understanding of its richness. Sometimes to understand is more important than to be able to speak fluently; therefore those who wish to

market in the new Europe need to be aware of the nuances and culture of the EU.

Another feature of Europe in any assessment of its business is its diversity of culture and heritage. We have briefly discussed the importance of language to the rich cultural underpinnings of Europe, but the many forms of art and the various religious influences, whether they be they be Calvinist, Roman Catholic, Jesuit, Moslem, Jewish or Orthodox Christian, have all had their impact upon the richness of the continent's diverse artistic and intellectual verve. Education also has it's impact: the Grande Ecole system of France perhaps produces a privileged intelligentsia of technocrats, who some would argue are chauvinist, whilst it has created a number of original technical individuals with a good engineering sense capable of being able to manage across a range of management disciplines; the German system with its long training and high degree of technical input, where some industries (chemicals, oil) are dominated by those with PhDs, thus showing a commitment to advanced education and especially science; the difference between academic education and scientific education and the divide between, say, Hogeschule and University which leads to a structuring of the workforce. Variations in the curriculum are also important. In the UK it is only in the last 10 years that there has been any effective recognition that the school system is failing to produce students with sufficient levels of foreign languages and a balance of numerate skills to form the basis for effective scientific enquiry.

Education and language contribute to the substance of the European market and are augmented by the richness of its cultural ancestry. The Italians and French have a traditional flair and verve for design, while in engineering the Germans can bring a certain order and logic to many of the finer and everyday things in life. The English, meanwhile, have a certain relaxed approach to structures, which can bring about successful diplomacy. Certainly Spain, Denmark, The Netherlands and the other members of the community are all contributing to the richness of what has become the largest fully-fledged free trading zone in the world.

GLOBALISATION AND RATIONALISATION IN EUROPE

Examples of failure litter company files of US companies that have not understood European national thinking: the lack of success of US brewers, with the exception of Budweiser Anhauser and perhaps Miller, in entering a complex European market is another example. It seems strange that two of the major beer products in the UK are Labatts and Mousehead lagers from Canada. The Canadians appear to be more successful in modifying their products and fitting them to European needs, which is very important. Häagen-Dazs ice-cream, based on a Canadian company's production, was originally intended for up-market New Yorkers and now dominates the French premium ice-cream market where the largest production operation is now based.

Japanese manufacturers and suppliers have had a different approach: direct entry followed by the establishment of local production. Japanese motor manufacturers Nissan, Toyota and Honda, in order to ensure access to the EU have opened up manufacturing in the UK, whilst Mazda has opened up its manufacturing plant in France. To ensure that Japanese cars manufactured in Europe are considered to be of European manufacture they have to adhere to component quota of at least 60 per cent and many are now at the level of 80 per cent. Consequently, European component suppliers are benefiting rather than being supplanted by cheaper imports. The entry of Japanese car manufacturers into production in Europe will mean that existing manufacturers will merge or be squeezed out of the market. In 1993, VW announced its first ever loss, whilst Fiat has experienced loss throughout the last decade and is fundamentally rethinking its strategy. Volvo and Renault embarked on a series of joint venture equity arrangements in truck manufacture to share costs and gain some competitive advantage in an over-supplied market with reducing demand. This initial collaboration collapsed and eventually Volvo was purchased by Ford, who also acquired Jaguar and Land Rover in the UK to add to its portfolio. Saab has also been acquired by General Motors (GM), whilst Mercedes-Benz has taken over Chrysler in the US. Japanese manufacturers have been hit by the Asian recession and many are now part-owned by European and US manufacturers.

German manufacturers continue to maintain market share in the declining truck market, perhaps because they have a long-term strategy. Increasingly, cheap trucks will enter the market from low-cost Eastern European production sites. This may lead to the use of more advanced, quality orientated equipment in plants based

within the EU. Rationalisation within Europe and the reorganisation of production has been very much in evidence in the last two decades. The oil crisis and recession of the late 1970s and early 1980s reduced output because of the high raw material costs and political and economic uncertainty of the period. In the late 1990s the Asian Rim recession, which dramatically impacted upon Japan and Korea, was brought about by financial overheating and a rapid fall in demand. Recent recessionary signs are likely in the short term to be strengthened by the impact of the Iraq War.

Besides the impetus of government-fostered restructuring, the marketplace has had its impact on industries through overcapacity, reduced demand and superseded technology. The petrochemical industry saw this in the early 1980s with many large suppliers reducing capacity by closing old plant or withdrawing from the production of certain products. In the UK some swapping of manufacturing interests and patents between producers took place. In the early 1980s, for instance, BP swapped its polyvinyl chloride (PVC) interests for ICI's polyethylene interests in a bid to rationalise these heavy loss-making bulk commodity polymer markets. The impact of restructuring and the use of joint venture companies to achieve this is illustrated in the EVC1 case study and further developments within the European plastics and chemical industries can be seen in the EVC2 and Shell case studies, which show how companies and organisations developed strategies to address fundamental shifts in demand. The petrochemicals market had excess capacity in its building block chemicals ethylene and polypropylene, as oil producers and related chemical industries attempted to add value to oil and gas refining businesses by moving downstream in the production process seeking higher margins. This led to over-capacity of manufacturing plant by the early 1980s, which resulted in downward pressure on prices for bulk chemical and plastic producers. Only reduced savings, rationalising supply arrangements and markets could allow surviving players to generate profits. Many of these bulk commodities gave substantial profits to producers in the 1970s and early 1980s as a part of an integrated business production process. However, as increased lower-production capacity from outside the EU has become available, so basic building block chemicals and polymers are becoming less viable to produce, which can only be reversed if there is a move towards a speciality product category or a competitive cost advantage can be created.

This process is still evolving in the European chemicals markets with suppliers such as ICI having broken-up into many businesses including Zeneca (pharmaceuticals, and renamed Asta-Zeneca following its merger with the Swedish Astra group) and ICI (paints and specialities). The German chemical industry triumvirate of BASF, BAYER and Hoechst continue to rationalise, slowly taking a long-term view that they may be the last players in the market because of advantages of controlled markets and scale. Nevertheless they face the pressure of recession, with all European chemical companies reporting regular losses. In this industry, the Italian industry, which is dominated by the state and Ente Nazionale Idrocarburi (ENI), is in the process of being privatised and consequently the hidden subsidies to ENI may come under closer scrutiny and further rationalisation may result. The state has played a major political role in this industry, with manufacturing plant being located in areas to gain employment to serve political interests.

The Anglo-Italian joint venture of ICI's and ENI's PVC interests into a European PVC sales and marketing operation was delayed formal recognition for six months until the Commission was satisfied it was not anti-competitive. The two case studies on EVC outline the complexities of rationalisation in a global industry and the management issues associated with this and establishing a joint venture company. The second case study deals with the company's share launch, coping with increasing operating losses and its eventual merger into a new chemical industry management company INEOS as part of the need to continually adapt to market circumstances.

Clearly, in a rationalising world competitive advantage can be gained in delaying competitors' strategic rationalisation, and an additional fear of the EU and national anti-competitive bodies is that consumers will lose out and unfair profits will be made, so the Commission watches this area closely. Interestingly, the Commission has been very active since its inception in monitoring prices and reporting and fining individual companies for price fixing and collusive behaviour in such markets as cement and polypropylene through to car pricing policy. The question for the researcher in the new Europe can sometimes be 'What is the difference between strategic rationalisation across borders and collusion?' The difference is sometimes hard to tell and perhaps can only be judged in the fullness of time. This is the approach being adopted by the EU. When it looks at the setting up of joint ventures and mergers, are they in the consumer's interest or against it?

Clearly the loss of an indigenous source of a strategic supply of a product is problematic to the community, but it may be against its short-term interest, which is set at being against competition policy. These contradictions are further explored when we consider joint ventures and competitive advantage in Chapter 7.

In technology-based industries such as computers and aircraft where it is necessary for European interests to be successful, alliances, joint ventures and other collaborative arrangements are deemed essential. CD Thomson's chairman stated in 1991 that Europe must hold on to its position as a micro-processor producer or face becoming a technological backward area dependent upon imports from Japan and the US. Already there are now no indigenous producers in the UK, since Inmos disappeared after being granted over £50 million of British state investment. This seems odd, as commentators have said in modern business that 'semiconductors will be the oil of tomorrow' (Dauvin, 1991). The only producers left in the semiconductor market are French (Thomson-SGS) and German (Siemens). Clearly, technology within the EU is vulnerable and perhaps EU financing, which gave $30 billion to agriculture against $2 billion to electronics in 1990, gives some clue to the problems of economic direction within the community. The increasing loss of the knowledge industry (science based) from mainland Europe appears to raise similar questions.

To be successful in the new Europe, companies need clear strategies of how they should respond to these global pressures. The world market is becoming more global with products rapidly being switched from one production source to another to gain competitive advantage, and already there is some evidence that governments are openly competing against one another in Europe to attract non-EU national companies to open production facilities in their territory.

Although the globalisation of markets is having its impact upon certain markets, some remain decidedly regional. For instance, quality clothing is still very much dominated by indigenous producers in Europe who also have distinct regional variations. The Barbour coat of the UK, which was very much a regional sport weatherproof product, has built on this base and has become a common world fashion accessory. Cars have their distinctive market orientations and adaptations in Europe. The famous small cars of Italy, the peasant farmer cars of France and the grand tourers of France and Germany to cater for the autoroutes and autobahns of those two countries, are variations on this theme.

Inward investment is championed by many city, regional and national based organisations. Clearly the lobbying within the EU for ERDF funding can be of major benefit to an economy. This process of bidding for major structural funds is explored more fully in the section on the cohesion fund in Chapter 2 and in the Gruppo Massone and the Industrial Districts in Italy case studies.

CONCLUSION

The EU is a rich, diverse market with a vibrant and varied cultural heritage; this means that although there has been a harmonisation process within the 15 states as a result of SEM, there are still distinct differences. Rather than business being simpler as a result of SEM, it should be recognised that because of regulation and the need to restructure in a globalising market it can be highly complex.

It should be remembered that the bulk of Europeans have high incomes and like their cultural differences to be recognised. Those who recognise this have a good chance of developing a successful marketing strategy to meet their needs.

REFERENCES

Christopher, M., Payne, A. and Ballantyne, D. (1991) *Relationship Marketing*. Oxford: Butterworth Heinemann.

Czinkota, M.R. and Ronkainen, I.A. (1993) *International Marketing*, (3rd edn.). Fort Worth, TX: Dryden.

Dauvin, J.-P. (1991) 'The future of the European Semicondictor Industry'. May, Corporate Communications Department of the Thomson Group, Paris France.

Eurostat (2002) *National Income Statistics*. Official publications of the EC, Luxembourg.

Ford, D. (ed.) (1990) *Understanding Business Markets – Interaction, Relationships, Networks*. London: Academic Press.

Grass, J. (1983) *The Oxford Book of Aphorisms*. Oxford University Press: Oxford.

Hakansson, H. (ed.) (1982) *International Marketing and Purchasing of Industrial Goods: An Interaction Approach*. Chichester: John Wiley.

Harris, P. and Moss, D. (2001) 'In search of public affairs', *Journal of Public Affairs*, 1 (2): 102–10.

Johanson, J. and Mattson, L-G. (1987) 'Interorganizational relations in industrial systems: a network approach compared with the transactions-cost approach', *International Studies of Management and Organization*, 17 (1): 34–48.

Jordan, G. (ed.) (1991) *The Commercial Lobbyists*. Aberdeen: Aberdeen University Press.

Kotler, P. and Levy, S.L. (1969) 'Broadening the concept of marketing', *Journal of Marketing*, 33 (1): 10–15.

Mazey, S. and Richardson, J. (eds) (1993) *Lobbying in the European Community*. Oxford: Oxford University Press.

McCormick, J. (1991) *British Politics and the Environment*. London: Earthscan.

Pedlar, R. (2002) *European Union Lobbying*. London: Palgrave.

Schendelen, van, M.P.C.M. (1993) *National, Public and Private EC Lobbying*. Dartmouth, Aldershot:

de Tocquevile, A. (1990) *Democracy in America*, (transcribed from the original text of 1836). London: Penguin.

Van Schendelen, R. (2002) *Machiavelli in Brussels*. Amsterdam: Amsterdam University Press.

Webster, F.E. (1984) *Industrial Marketing Strategy*. New York: John Wiley.

The EU arose in the aftermath of the Second World War among a group of Western European countries that had a strong commitment to stop the periodic outbreaks of war in Europe. In the post-Second World War period the six Western European countries (France, Germany, Italy, Belgium, Luxembourg and The Netherlands) were committed to the idea of European economic integration, but only in the limited area of coal and steel. The impact of the early integration process on business activities was minor and in most areas it had no noticeable effect on companies. However, this integration process developed in size and importance and by the end of the 1990s the EU had 15 member states, including the four largest economies in Europe, and was the largest economic bloc in the world. Its laws, policies and programmes influenced nearly every industrial and business activity in the member states. The EU has also developed strong economic links with most European countries and is likely to be enlarged to cover many of the countries of Central and Eastern Europe (see Chapter 4). Every company that conducts business with or in the EU is strongly affected by the activities of the EU. The laws of the EU influence the legal framework under which companies and organisations must operate. The policies of the EU shape the economic environment and EU programmes in the areas of R&D, environmental protection and towards small- and medium-sized enterprises (SMEs) and has a profound effect on companies and organisations. In a period of less than 50 years the integration process that led to the EU has resulted in one of the most important governmental organisations in the world and the bulk of its work directly affects companies, of every size.

THE ORIGINS AND DEVELOPMENT OF THE EU

In the aftermath of the Second World War the economies of the continent of Europe were severely damaged. The UK was unable and unwilling to lead the integration of Europe. This refusal to take the lead in the process of integrating Europe led to the emergence of a Franco-German alliance that led the integration project. The Cold War divided Europe into two opposing blocs, based on American leadership of Western Europe with Central and Eastern Europe controlled by the Soviet Union. Germany was divided into two parts and the need to integrate West Germany into the emerging western bloc raised problems as to how to create an appropriate political and economic structure for post-War Europe.

The defence and security of Europe became the centre of the Cold War conflict between the US and the Soviet Union, with European countries playing only a minor role in deciding the strategy and implementation of defence and security policy. The economic weakness of West European economies meant that the dollar became the currency used to finance the reconstruction of Western Europe. The dominance of the dollar was reinforced by the establishment of the Bretton Woods system that fixed most West European currencies against the dollar, thereby giving the US significant influence over macroeconomic policies in Western Europe. Consequently, by the beginning of the 1950s major political and economic developments in Western Europe were led by the US. Therefore, attempts to integrate the countries of Western Europe could not be based on defence and security policies or on major economic policies, for these were largely led and developed by the US.

Nevertheless, some of the countries of Western Europe, notably France and Germany, were eager to create new political structures to avoid the disturbing tendency for European countries to resort to war to settle their differences. The method that was selected to achieve this objective was to integrate the industries of the countries of Western Europe. The selection of the coal and steel industries as the starting point was very appropriate for such an outcome because these industries were at the heart of the war machine in the middle of the twentieth century. Therefore, European integration began with policies and programmes that directly affected companies. However, the main objective was not to make these companies more efficient or to promote the interests of business. The prime objective was political – to integrate the economies of European countries to prevent war. The integration of business activities was a means to this end. The legacy of these origins still has resonance today, for the EU is primarily concerned with the political objective of uniting the countries of Europe. For historical reasons most of the policies and programmes to achieve this objective affect companies, but the driving force for these developments continues to be political considerations (Pinder, 1995; Swann, 1998).

The UK chose not to join the European Coal and Steel Community (ECSC), founded by the original six countries in 1951. This lead to the emergence of two competing economic integration projects in Western Europe, one led by a Franco-German alliance that eventually developed into the EU and the other led by the UK. In 1957, the founding members of the ECSC developed the project to integrate their economies by founding the European Economic Community (EEC) and the European Atomic Energy Community (EURATOM). These three communities – the ECSC, the EEC and EURATOM – became the foundation of an integration project that developed into the EU. In response to the establishment of the EEC the UK formed, in 1960, the European Free Trade Association (EFTA). This agency was composed of Austria, Denmark, Norway, Portugal, Sweden and the UK. In Central and Eastern Europe the Council of Mutual Economic Assistance (CMEA, also know as COMECON) was founded to help to develop economic and trade relationships between the communist bloc countries. In defence and security matters Europe

was divided into two opposing alliances: the North Atlantic Treaty Organisation (NATO) linking most West European countries into an alliance with the US, and the Warsaw Pact Agreement binding the countries of Central and Eastern Europe with the Soviet Union. Therefore, by the beginning of the 1960s, Europe was split into two defence and security blocs and three economic blocs.

In the area of economic integration the EEC came to dominate and EFTA gradually melted into the EEC, or the European Communities (EC) – the merging of the ECSC, the EEC and EURATOM. Denmark, Ireland and the UK joined the EC in 1973, Greece in 1981 and Spain and Portugal in 1986. Austria, Finland and Sweden joined what had come to be known as the EU in 1995. Therefore, by 1995 nearly all of the countries of Western Europe were members of the EU. In the communist bloc dramatic events in the late 1980s and early 1990s saw the end of the Soviet Union and the fall of communism in the countries of Central and Eastern Europe. The response of most of these countries was to establish strong links with the EU and to seek full membership.

By the mid-1990s the EU had developed to include nearly every country in Western Europe and was developing strong links with Central and Eastern European countries. The EU has evolved from a project to integrate coal and steel industries to become a major influence on the legal and economic environment of all industries. An area of free movement of goods, services, labour and capital embracing all of Western Europe has been created. It has also established a strong influence in policies towards agriculture, competition, the physical environment and employment and working conditions. To accomplish this the EU created a large number of laws that influence nearly every aspect of business activities. Monetary integration has also been developed and 12 member states have joined a monetary union with a single currency. Increasingly the EU is developing a role in foreign policy and in security and defence issues. In addition it is involved in immigration and home affairs. The EU has developed from an agency primarily involved with the integration of the economies of the member states to embrace nearly every aspect of business, social and political life. This was the hope of the founders of the project that developed into the EU. However, the main focus of the EU remains the integration of the economies of the member states. Thus far, it is companies that are most influenced by the laws, policies and programmes of the EU.

THE INSTITUTIONAL STRUCTURE OF THE EU

The EU is based on a number of treaties that commit the member states to the objectives of integrating the countries of Europe (Nugent, 2002). The treaties also provide the basis for the institutional structure of the EU and for the creation and development of laws, policies and programmes to further the integration objective. An outline of the treaties is given in Exhibit 2.1. There are five main institutions in the current structure of the EU:

1 The Council of the European Union
2 The European Commission
3 The European Parliament (EP)
4 The European Court of Justice (ECJ)
5 The European Central Bank (ECB)

The Council of the European Union

The Council of the European Union (commonly called the Council of Ministers) is composed of the relevant government ministers of the member states, for example, proposals concerned with agricultural matters are considered by the ministers of agriculture from the member states. The Presidency of the Council of the European Union rotates around the member states every six months. Voting in the Council of Ministers can be by unanimity (including matters connected to industry, taxation, culture, R&D programmes and regional and social funds) or by qualified majority (including issues related to agriculture, fisheries, the internal market, the environment and transport). The Council of Ministers is assisted by a standing secretariat composed of representatives from national governments who are based in Brussels and who work on proposals that are brought before the Council for the decision of national ministers. This secretariat is called the Committee of Permanent Representatives (COREPER). The Council of the European Union holds regular summit meetings of the heads of government of the member states – the European Council. Matters connected to decisions to enlarge the EU and to engage in major changes to the institutional structure and to the policies and programmes of the EU are made by the European Council.

The European Commission

The European Commission is currently composed of 20 Commissioners, two each from Germany, France, Italy, Spain and the UK, and one from each of the other member states. The Commission is split into a number of departments (directorates-general) that have specific areas of responsibility (see the Commission's page on www.europa.eu.int for a list of the current directorates-generals and their responsibilities). All proposals for new EU legislation are initiated by the Commission on the basis of the treaties, or the decisions of the European Council. The Commission is the guardian of the treaties and is responsible for monitoring and policing EU law. The Commission has the power to investigate suspected breaches of EU law by governments, companies and individuals, and can impose fines if it considers that EU laws have been broken. The governments and national courts of the member states are obliged to ensure that the decisions of the Commission in these matters are implemented unless they dispute the ruling of the Commission. When this occurs the case is sent to the European Court of Justice (ECJ). The day-to-day operation of EU policies and programmes is also under the control of the Commission.

The European Parliament

Since 1979 the European Parliament (EP) has been directly elected by the citizens of the EU. Most proposals for new EU laws require the approval of the EP and it has power to submit amendments to the Council and the Commission on proposed legislation. The EP can dismiss the Commission and can refuse to approve the budget of the EU. It has influence on the appointment of the Commission and has the right to refuse to accept the nominations for the President of the Commission. The EP also investigates the activities of the Commission by use of a series of committees that examine the working of the various policies and programmes of the EU.

The European Court of Justice

The European Court of Justice (ECJ) should not be confused with the European Court of Human

---

EXHIBIT 2.1   THE TREATIES OF THE EU AND THE EUROPEAN CONVENTION

- *The Treaty of Paris 1951*: established the ECSC a free trade area with common policies for coal and steel. The ECSC provided the first Community institutions with limited powers to make law and policies.
- *The Treaty of Rome 1957*: established the EEC and EURATOM a customs union and common market with some common laws and policies and the basic institutional structure of the Council, Commission, EP and ECJ. The Treaty of Rome remains the bedrock of much of the institutional system and the legislation and policies to create free movement of goods, services, capital and labour.
- *The Single European Act (SEA) 1987*: Amendments to the Treaty of Rome, in particular to allow for the completion of the Single European Market (customs union and common market). The SEA also extended the Treaty to provide the basis for regional, environmental and R&D policies. The SEA also provided a framework for the political cooperation procedures of the EU.
- *The Treaty on European Union (Maastricht Treaty) 1992*: amendments to the Treaty of Rome. The major changes were a commitment to establish economic and monetary union (the EMU) with a single currency and a new European central bank (the ECB). The EP was given greater powers to amend proposed legislation in many areas by granting the use of co-decision making with the Council of Ministers. The Treaty also created intergovernmental procedures to develop common policies in foreign and security issues and in justice and home affairs.
- *The Treaty of Amsterdam 1997*: amendments to the Treaty on European Union that consolidated and expanded on the Maastricht Treaty. The use of the co-decision procedure was extended to cover most legislation and the Commission was made more accountable to the EP
- *The Treaty of Nice 2000*: amendments to the Treaty on European Union to permit enlargement. Reform of the Commission and EP to reduce the number of members of the EP and Commissioners such that the EU can grow to up to 27 members. Smaller member states would have to take turns at having a Commissioner as the Treaty envisages a Commission of less than 27 members. The use of qualified majority voting at the Council on Ministers is to be expanded, but unanimity is retained for important policy areas such as taxation, social policy and the external relations.
- *European Convention (2002)*: a convention of European politicians, industrialists and representatives of various interest groups. The Convention was set four main questions:

1 How should the division of competence between the institutions of the EU and the member states be organised?
2 How should the institutional structure of the EU be organised such that they are effective and able to incorporate an expanded membership?
3 How should the EU relate to the rest of the world?
4 How should the institutions of the EU be made more democratically accountable?

To achieve these objectives the European Convention is proposing a Constitutional Treaty that includes:

- the objectives of the EU;
- division of powers between EU institutions and the member states; and
- reform of the Common Foreign and Security, and Justice and Home Affairs policies to incorporate them into institutions of the EU rather than by intergovernmental arrangements within the EU.

This Constitution, if it were approved, would replace the above treaties as the basis for law and policy making of the EU. Such a development would be a major development because it could set the conditions for a type of federal Europe. However, the nature of this federation is not clear. The political arguments about the proposed Constitutional Treaty indicate that this proposal has little chance of being approved by major political powers (France, Spain and the UK). However, there is support for such a Constitutional Treaty in Germany and among the smaller member states. Whatever happens to the proposed Constitutional Treaty, it does demonstrate progress towards some type of a federal European state.

Details on the treaties can be found on the website of the EU at www.europa.eu.int and on the European Convention at www.europa.eu.int/futurum.

Rights. The latter court is part of the Council of Europe and its judgements are based on the European Convention on Human Rights. The ECJ is composed of 15 judges who are appointed by the member states and it sits in Luxembourg. It is responsible for interpreting EU law and making judgements when there are disputes on this law. The ECJ is the final court to which disputes on EU law can be brought and national courts must accept and implement the judgements of the Court. The ECJ normally takes about two years to reach a decision on a case. This factor plus the high legal costs associated with taking cases to the ECJ tends to discourage large-scale recourse to the Court. Often disputes are solved in negotiations between national governments and the Commission or organisations and the Commission.

The European Central Bank

The European Central Bank (ECB) is a type of a federal bank on similar lines to the Federal Reserve Bank of America. The bank is independent of national governments and the other institutions of the EU. The ECB is responsible for monetary policy for Euroland and for the management of the exchange rate of the single currency (the euro) against other currencies. The prime objective of the ECB is the pursuit of price stability. The Bank reports to the European Council and the EP, but they cannot interfere in the duty of the ECB to pursue price stability. The central banks of the members of Euroland compose the European System of Central Banks (ESCB). The ESCB is the operating arm of the ECB in the member states and helps in the construction and implementation of the common monetary policy.

There are two other significant institutions in the EU that influence law and policy making. These institutions are: the Economic and Social Committee (ESC) and the Committee of the Regions (COR). The ESC is a forum for interest groups and sectional interest (for example, farmers, trade unionists and representatives of employers) that expresses opinions on proposed legislation. It does not have any powers other than to express opinions on proposed legislation. The COR is composed of representatives from regional and local authorities. This Committee is appointed by the Council on the recommendation of the national governments of the member states. It must be consulted by the Commission and the Council on matters that affect the regions, but the COR need not be consulted on matters that do not directly affect the regions of the EU. In this respect the COR would appear to have less power than the ESC. It may, however, issue an opinion on its own initiative. There are a number of other EU institutions and agencies that work in technical and specialist areas (details of these can be found on the website of the EU at www.europa.eu.int).

The institutional frameworks of the EU are basically those that emerged when the institutions of the EEC were incorporated with those the ECSC and EURATOM in 1968 to form the European Community (EC). There have been various reforms to the institutional framework since 1968, especially with the direct elections to the EP in 1979 and the subsequent extension of its powers to amend proposed legislation. The extension of majority voting at the Council of Ministers also strengthened the powers of the institutions of the EU. The Maastricht, Amsterdam and Nice treaties developed and consolidated the institutional frameworks and also provided a basis for the extension of the powers of the Community in areas of political integration. These treaties still provide the basis for the institutional and decision-making systems of the EU (see Exhibit 2.1). However, the institutional structure is basically the same as the system that was developed for the original six member states in 1957. At that time the level of involvement of Community institutions in economic and social issues was minimal and in many areas, such as foreign affairs, defence and security and home affairs and immigration, the institutions had no real impact. As the EU expanded in terms of numbers of member states and the depth of its involvement to nearly all major economic, social and political affairs, the weaknesses of the institutional framework have become evident. The demands on the institutional frameworks will rise when the EU is enlarged to encompass many of the countries of Central and Eastern Europe. Against this background the EU has established a European Convention to propose a system that would be capable of effectively governing the increasing range of issues and areas of policy and law making that the EU has to cope with and that is also able to incorporate a membership of possibly 27 or 32 member states. The European Convention has developed a draft Constitutional Treaty that could, if it were approved, provided a constitutional basis for the EU that would help to overcome many of the problems associated with the lack of clarity over competencies of the EU institutions and national government agencies. Details on the progress of the Convention can be found on the website of the EU at www. european-convention.eu.int.

LAW MAKING IN THE EU

The legislative process of the EU is complex as it involves a variety of different institutions and ways of making law (Cairns, 1997). The EU has five main methods of making law and issuing rules:

1 *The treaties*: some of the articles of the treaties have direct effect in the member states and organisations, and individuals can base a court case in their national courts on articles in the treaties.
2 *Regulations*: these are issued by the Commission, normally to clarify or expand upon legal requirements derived from the treaties or directives, and they have direct effect in the member states.
3 *Directives*: these outline basic legal principles connected to a wide variety of economic and social interactions between individuals or organisations (including governmental organisations) or between individuals and organisations. They must be incorporated into the law of

the member states in accordance with their national legislative and administrative practices.
4 *Decisions*: these are binding rulings by the Commission on specific issues. They are directly applied to governments, companies and individuals.
5 *Recommendations and opinions*: these have no legal standing but they provide indications of the view of the Commission on legal and administrative practices.

In practice most EU law making is done by issuing directives. The use of regulations and decisions is mainly used for minor amendments, or to clarify policies that have already been agreed. The method of approving directives involves a series of protracted discussions and negotiations between the Commission, the EP and the Council of Ministers with opinions from the ESC and in some cases the COR. Since the Maastricht Treaty, the approval of directives is primarily done by the co-decision procedure. The Amsterdam Treaty extended the use of the co-decision procedure to cover most proposals that relate to economic matters. A schematic outline of the co-decision procedure is given in Figure 2.1.

The institutional structure of the EU is complex, with many different bodies responsible for decision making and for the implementation, monitoring and policing of Community laws and policies (Carins, 1997; Nugent, 2002). Furthermore, in the case of directives the governments of the member states must transpose the objectives specified in the directives into national law. They are also largely responsible for monitoring and enforcing EU law. The differences that exist in institutional and cultural characteristics among the member states can result in EU law having a differential impact on individuals and organisations according to the member state in which they are located. These differences arise from the ways that directives are transposed into national laws and by the manner in which EU law is monitored and enforced by national institutions.

Member states can 'gold plate' directives by adding to, or enhancing, the conditions that are specified in EU legislation (McDonald, 2000). It is not illegal to 'gold plate'. However, adding to the requirements of directives will impose costs that will not arise for those companies that are located in member states that do not 'gold plate'. The UK government has been accused of 'gold plating' many of the directives connected to food safety (particularly those

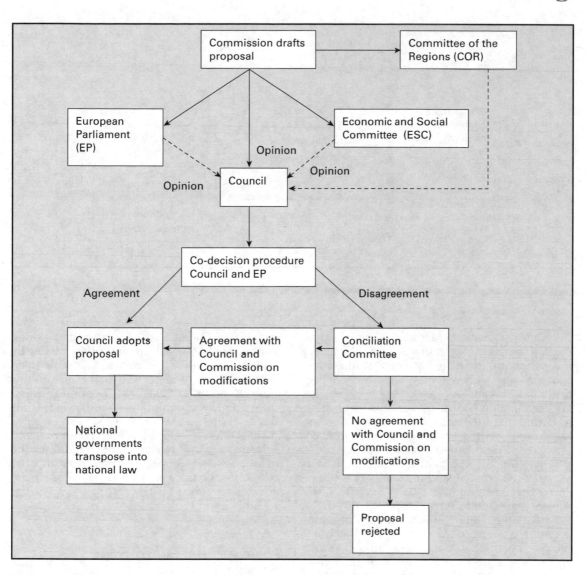

Figure 2.1 *The co-decision procedure*

relating to the processing and distribution of meat), leading to higher costs for some types of food processing in the UK compared to other EU member states. Problems can emerge with 'gold plating' if the enhancement of the conditions are not deliberate, that is, the national governmental agencies make mistakes in implementing directives by over-legislating. In these cases, costs are added to business operations not because the intention is to institute higher conditions but simply due to incompetent actions by national government agencies. It is possible that much of the 'gold plating' that has been

alleged in food safety directives in the UK was due to incompetence by the Ministry of Food, Fisheries and Agriculture. In some cases 'gold plating' may be a legitimate and correct action by governmental agencies. This will be the case when the directive is used as the basis to ensure conformity with EU law but where the national government decides that the directive does not go far enough to meet their objectives. EU law normally allows such higher conditions to prevail in those member states that decide that they want higher standards that those specified by EU directives.

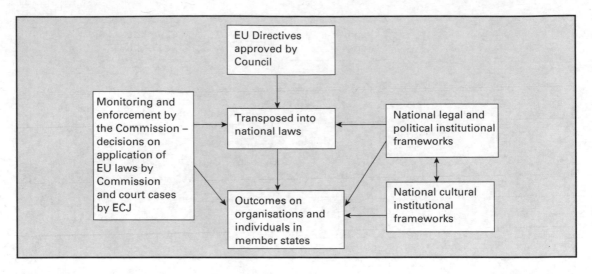

Figure 2.2 *Interrelationship between EU laws and national systems*

Member states can under implement directives leading to national laws that do not fully reflect the conditions that are specified in directives. National governments may also fail to effectively monitor and enforce EU law. Such actions are illegal, but it is difficult for the Commission to ensure that the requirements of directives are fully implemented, monitored and enforced. The Commission can only take steps to correct shortcomings by national government if it is aware of the problem and if a strong case can be made that member states have not effectively transposed, monitored or enforced directives. When national governments or organisations dispute the ruling of the Commission the case is brought before the ECJ for a decision. The case law that is generated by referral to the ECJ is important factor in the development of the legal environment in the member states. Cases brought before the ECJ take a long time before a decision is made and enforcement of the decisions of the ECJ rests with the governments of the member states. When the case is against the government of a member state it can be very difficult for the decisions of the ECJ to be enforced. The case of the French government refusing to obey the judgement of the ECJ on the importation of UK beef in the aftermath of the BSE crisis has highlighted this problem.

The culture and institutional characteristics of member states may also contribute to the under-, full, or over-implementation of EU laws and also contributes to the attitudes that prevail in the monitoring and enforcing of EU law. For

example, in member states that have a strong commitment to equal opportunities, backed by institutions set up to monitor and promote equal opportunities, it is more likely that EU law in this area will be fully implemented, monitored and enforced. The number and type of complaints and cases that go to the Commission and the ECJ about failings in implementing, monitoring and enforcing EU law can be found by visiting the website of the European Commission and the ECJ at www.europa.eu.int. The main interrelationships between EU law and national systems are outlined in Figure 2.2.

LOBBYING THE INSTITUTIONS OF THE EU

The institutions of the EU exercise a great influence on the legal and economic environment in which companies operate (Mazey and Richardson, 1993). Therefore, access to this system, to lobby and to seek advice, is important for those companies and organisations that are significantly affected by the laws and policies which emerge from the EU. Companies and organisations may wish to lobby the institutions of the EU for four main reasons:

1   To influence the content of proposals for new directives.
2   To seek redress when they believe that they have suffered from unfair practices by governments,

companies, organisations or individuals during the conduct of cross-frontier business activities.

3 To attempt to change laws, policies and programmes of the EU so that they are more beneficial or less harmful than the existing ones.

4 To obtain advice on whether the proposed activities of companies or organisations will breach EU laws or run contrary to the policies of the EU.

Lobbying the Commission before proposals are published is one of the most effective methods of affecting the content of proposals for new laws. The EP can also be lobbied because it has the power to modify proposals as part of the co-decision procedure. However, the Council of Ministers has the most significant power in the approval process for new legislation. The Council of Ministers is composed of government ministers from the national governments of the member states. Therefore, lobbying the relevant ministries in national governments and national politicians is the best way to influence the Council of Ministers. Directives have to be transposed into national law so it is possible to lobby national governments to seek to influence the way that directives are implemented in the member states. This can be a very effective way of influencing the impact of directives on companies and organisations because national governments often have considerable latitude to adopt a number of different methods of achieving the objectives outlined in directives. Indeed, it is possible to undermine the harmful aspects of directives by under-implementing them, or to add to them by 'gold plating' the directives.

The ECS and the COR can be lobbied. However, these committees have only an advisory role in the legislative process and consequently lobbying these bodies may have only limited value. Nevertheless, in areas connected to technical details the opinion of the ESC may have some influence in altering very complex technical details. In some cases these technical details can have very important effects on the implications of EU laws and policies on companies and organisations. Lobbying the COR is useful to influence the policies, programmes and funds of the EU that seek to promote regional development objectives.

It is possible for companies and organisations to approach the Commission directly to seek advice when they believe they have been victims of inequitable trading practices or have been placed in an unfair position by the laws and policies of the governments of the member states. Advice may also be sought to clarify the legal position of proposed courses of action. Campaigns to alter EU laws and policies can also be mounted by lobbying the Commission and the EP. Exerting influence on national governments is also important if companies wish to change EU laws and policies.

Large companies and organisations usually have their own offices in Brussels to lobby the institutions of the EU and to gather information on proposals for new laws and policies. Others make use of a large number of professional PR and lobbying firms that have offices in Brussels. Most SMEs normally cannot afford to retain offices or PR companies in Brussels. Therefore, they mostly rely on representation by trade associations and other types of associations that represent their interests.

In the area of employment and working conditions, employers and trade unions have a very direct influence on proposals for new laws and policies through the role of the Social Partners in the institutional structure of the EU (McDonald, 2000). In some cases the Social Partners can draft proposals for new directives in this area that the Commission pilots through the legislative process – this happened in the case of the parental leave directive. The Social Partners are also involved in providing advice to the Commission on matters connected to employment and general issues connected to the world of work. This provides a powerful means to influence proposals for new laws and for the development of policies in these areas. The Social Partners are composed of European associations representing private and public sectors employing organisations and trade unions (see Table 2.1). These European associations are based on national associations. Therefore, lobbying national associations such as the Confederation of British Industry (CBI) and the Trades Union Congress (TUC) in the UK can provide a direct and powerful method of influencing EU laws, policies and programmes in the area of employment and working conditions.

SINGLE ECONOMIC SPACE

The main economic objective of the EU is the creation and development of a single economic space that permits economic transactions across the frontiers of the member states without undue hindrance by laws and policies that

Table 2.1 Social partners

General cross-industry organisation

Union of Industrial and Employer's Confederation of Europe (UNICE)
Representing private sector organisations

European Centre of Enterprises with Public Participation (CEEP)
Representing public sector organisations

European Trade Union Confederation (ETUC)
Representing trade unions

Association of European Chambers of Commerce and Industry (EUROCHAMBRES)
Representing European chambers of commerce and industry

Specific cross-industry organisations

European Association of Crafts, Small and Medium Sized Enterprises (UEAPME)
Representing small- and medium-sized enterprises

Confédération europeenne des cadres (CEC)
Representing employees involved in management activities

Sectoral organisations

EUROCOMMERCE
Representing employers in the retail, wholesale and international trade organisations

COPA/COGECA
Representing employers in agricultural organisations

Plus 20 other employer's organisation involved in a wide variety of sectors and 15 organisations affiliated to the ETUC

Details can be found on the website of the EU at www.europa.eu.int.

---

restrict or prohibit such transactions (see Chapter 3). When these conditions exist there is free movement of goods, services, capital and labour (see El Agraa, 2001; McDonald and Dearden, 1999 for analysis of the implications of free movement). Where limitations to free movement exist they should be for good reason, for example, to provide for public safety, to promote legitimate economic and social priorities and to protect the physical environment. Furthermore, any laws or policies that limit economic transactions must be subject to the control to ensure that these limitations or restrictions are not for the purpose of confining supply to the domestic economies of the member states.

Single economic spaces require frameworks that permit the effective free movement of goods, services, capital and labour. They also can have macroeconomic policies to secure stable economic conditions. To achieve effective free movement and a stable economic environment five main frameworks must be created and maintained.

1 Legal frameworks that create, develop and maintain the legal conditions that permit free movement to exist.
2 Taxation frameworks that do not unduly distort free movement.
3 Economic and social policies that do not hamper the development of the effective free movement.
4 Macroeconomic policy frameworks that secure a stable economic environment.
5 Political frameworks that clearly identify the competencies of government bodies in matters connected to free movement and the creation and maintenance of stable economic conditions.

Comparison of the characteristics of these frameworks in the EU and the US illustrates the similarities and the differences between these two single economic spaces.

Legal frameworks

Legal barriers to free movement exist in some nation-states that would be regarded as single real economic spaces. For example, technical regulations that govern the production and sale of goods and services in the US vary in the different states. Therefore, companies that wish to trade across state frontiers have to conform to the different technical regulations that prevail in the different states of America. In practice, the technical regulations of large states such as California tend to be used as the norm for the production and sale of goods and services. This is because the economic size of the large states means that the demand from these states is a significant share of the total sales of goods and services. For example, the technical regulations of California on emission levels from motor vehicles determine the emission levels for all cars sold in the US. Nevertheless, in the US there are considerable differences across the states in technical regulations for the production, distribution and sale of many goods and services. There are also federal laws governing the safety of food and drugs and other regulations in matters connected to public safety.

Federal laws ensure that markets (for inter-state trade) are not distorted by anti-competitive practices. However, the governments of the states are free to limit their public procurement contracts to state-based companies. Federal procurement contracts are open to all US-based companies. Federal procurement, particularly in the defence sector, is very large. There are also no federal laws that restrict the use of government aid by states that wish to subsidise the operations of companies which are located within their area of jurisdiction. However, the states cannot hinder the free movement of labour or capital. Companies are also free to establish production, distribution and sales subsidiaries or branches in all the states of the US. They must, however, conform to the laws of the host state.

The EU has adopted a different approach from the US to removing legal barriers to free movement. To remove barriers associated with technical regulations the member states are required to accept the technical regulations that prevail in the member states with minimum harmonisation to ensure public safety and technical compatibility. The use of mutual recognition of national technical regulations with selective harmonisation means that companies must conform to any EU technical regulations, but they are not obliged to conform to the national regulations of countries that they supply.

The Commission has powers to investigate and stop anti-competitive practices that interfere with cross-frontier trade between the member states. The EU has laws that make most public procurement contracts open to Community-wide competition. However, most contracts linked to defence procurement are not open to EU-wide competition. Government aid to industry is monitored by the Commission and they can be prohibited or modified if they are considered to be for the purpose of limiting intra-EU trade. However, companies do not have the same freedom as in the US to establish production, distribution and sales subsidiaries or branches in all the member states. Moreover, member states have greater powers than the states in America to limit or prohibit the free movement of labour and capital.

Taxation frameworks

Taxation systems vary among the states of America. The goods and services that are subject to sales taxes and the level of these taxes differ from state to state. State income tax and taxes that relate to income from savings are also different. In the US inter-state trade takes place at the taxation rates that prevail in the exporting state. When a good or service is exported from South Dakota to North Dakota, the taxes levied in South Dakota are paid by the importer in North Dakota. In these circumstances it maybe cheaper to buy from another state that has lower taxes on the good or service to be imported. Differences in state taxation systems can therefore distort inter-state trade. However, there are no federal laws to prevent or limit such distortion. In America the states can decide to place their companies at a disadvantage by levying higher and more widespread taxes on goods and services than in other states. These differences in taxes can also provide incentives for consumers to engage in cross-frontier shopping for personal use to obtain goods and services that are subject to lower taxes than in the home state. The states also have the right to levy corporation taxes on companies located in their state and to grant tax breaks and concession to companies. Taxes on savings and investments are also subject to state tax systems. The effect of these state rights to have their own taxation systems is to generate a degree of tax regime competition between the states. This competition tends to promote a low business tax environment because companies can and do relocate from high tax states and consumers (who live near state borders) can cross borders to shop more cheaply.

In the EU differences in taxation treatment on the sale of goods and services and on income from savings are considered to be a serious distortion of free movement. Therefore, plans have been put forward to harmonise the taxation systems for goods, services, savings and profits. Thus far there has been little progress in harmonising taxation systems across the member states. However, when inter-EU trade takes place, goods and services that are exported are not subject to taxation. When a good or service is exported from the UK to France it is not subject to the VAT and excise duties of the UK. The good or service becomes subject to French taxation when it crosses the frontier. This system is called a destination principle tax system because tax is levied in the country of destination of goods and services that are exported. The costs of this system largely fall on companies because they have to keep records of their intra-EU exports and imports to enable national tax authorities to make adjustments to tax liabilities for products that cross frontiers. The EU plans to introduce a harmonised VAT and excise duties system based on the origin principle. This would mean that tax would be levied in the country of origin of goods and services that are exported. In this system tax induced distortions would be limited by the imposition of a tight band of permissible tax differences in the member states. This plan, if it is approved, will lead to significant changes to rates and coverage of VAT and excise duties in many member states.

Differences in taxation of goods in the member states do not distort inter-EU trade. However, consumers have an incentive to engage in cross-frontier shopping because personal purchases are only subject to the taxes of the country where the good is bought. The large-scale purchases by UK consumers of alcoholic beverages bought in France is a good example of the incentives that exist for cross-frontier shopping because of differences in taxation systems between the member states. These tax differences are also an incentive for illegal re-selling of goods bought by consumers in lower taxation countries. The high level of UK purchases in France of alcoholic beverages provides a clear example of this incentive to engage in illegal re-selling to profit from tax differences. The growth of cross-border shopping within the EU on the Internet may well increase this problem. In both the US and the EU there are incentives for consumers to engage in cross-frontier shopping to take advantage of tax differences. However, in the EU, unlike in the US, cross-frontier trade for the purpose of legally re-selling or for non-household consumption is not distorted by differences in the taxation systems in the member states.

The taxation of savings in the EU poses many difficult problems. Currently, in matters of taxation the member states have the right of veto in the Council of Ministers for proposals connected to taxation. The UK used the veto to prevent the imposition of a minimum withholding tax on investments. Luxembourg has also vetoed plans to improve the transparency of cross-frontier financial transfers that would help national tax authorities to track the movement of funds. In both of these cases the governments exercised their right to veto to protect their national interests. The UK used the veto to protect the eurocurrency market that is based in the City of London. Luxembourg was concerned to keep its large flow of savings from Germany because many German savers are keen to avoid the high taxes on savings if they save in domestic banks and financial institutions. Both governments claimed that the markets would relocate to a country that is not in the EU if these tax advantages are removed. In the case of the eurocurrency markets this would mean the loss of a very significant industry.

The Commission set up a High Level Working Group composed of leading civil servants, tax lawyers and business leaders to investigate the taxation of companies in the EU. The work of the Group led to Code of Conduct. The Code of Conduct seeks to develop mechanisms that would prevent harmful tax competition between the member states by coordinating tax policies that affect companies. This approach allows the member states to have different and in some senses competing tax regimes. Employer's organisations and some of the member states regard this as important to encourage a low business tax environment that is conducive to growth and therefore employment. However, there have also been attempts to promote tax harmonisation to create common tax systems on businesses (Aisbitt, 2002). There are also pressures to eliminate tax breaks and concessions that might induce companies to relocate to member states that grant preferential tax treatment to incoming companies.

These attempts at tax harmonisation have created considerable opposition from some member states (those with low taxes on businesses) and from employer's organisations such as Union of Industrial and Employers' Confederations of Europe (UNICE). There is, however, broad support for tax harmonisation to remove distortions and obstacles to cross-border collaboration between companies and in merger and acquisition activities. UNICE favours the development of single European Corporation Tax that would eliminate at one stroke the many tax distortions and obstacles to cross-border activities. Harmonization of taxes on bond and equities trading would also remove distortions caused by tax systems and would help to create a single economic space for these financial instruments. However, the likelihood of the member states agreeing to such a European corporation tax and in the taxation of financial instruments is small. Furthermore, UNICE and other employer's organisations and many banks and financial companies fear that if such a tax system was created it might lead to attempts to impose high taxes that could drive many types of business outside of the EU.

Economic and social policies

The differences between the US and the EU become more evident when policy frameworks that are concerned with the allocation of resources and in matters of equity are considered. The US adopts a more market-based approach, while the EU is more geared towards a social market approach. The market-based approach is based on limited interference by the government agencies in the working of the market process. This approach has a strong emphasis on anti-trust policies to limit the ability of companies to acquire monopoly power and to use anti-competitive practices. Efficiency considerations are regarded as a separate issue from equity or even considered to conflict with equity concerns. The social market approach regards the promotion of competitive markets as important, but also links equity issues to efficiency concerns. Thus, policies to promote social cohesion and to help disadvantaged groups are seen as an important function of governments to help the economy to deliver high living standards.

In terms of industrial policy, both the US and the EU promote particular industries and in some cases, for example, agriculture, there is large-scale subsidies. Government help for the development of R&D is more pronounced in the US because of the large-scale contracts to develop technologies in the areas of defence and space. The EU has only a small budget allocated to industrial policy issues compared to the US

but most of the help for companies to develop in the EU is provided by the member states. This could mean that the large-scale federal projects in the US are more effective than the multitude of member state projects backed by small-scale EU projects.

In matters connected to environmental policy, many areas in the US are decided by the states and in some cases (for example, recycling) by counties in the states. In the EU, most of these matters are determined, at least minimum standards, by the EU. However, in the US many of the decisions of large states such as California are adopted across all or most states because the state market is so large that it makes sense to adopt the standards of, say, California so that products can be sold in this state and many other states that have adopted Californian environmental standards. In both the US and EU differences in areas such as recycling and packaging vary across the states. The EU is progressively imposing minimum standards in these areas, while in the US there is little movement for federal direction of the states in this matters. Indeed, the constitution of the US makes it difficult for the federal government to interfere in the areas where the states have autonomy. In the EU, the treaties are less precise than the constitution of the US and this gives the EU the ability to interfere with the policies of the member states in those areas covered by the treaties.

The attempts to adopt policies to curb emissions of 'greenhouse gases' involve the federal government and the EU because these policies have to curb emissions of a global scale. However, neither the federal government nor the EU has made much progress in this area. Indeed, perhaps the most significant progress to curb emissions from cars has been made by California, where dramatic reductions have to be in place within 10 years. This Californian law is likely to lead to radical changes to car design, including the use of electric cars or fuel cell cars. These developments could spread to not only the rest of the US but to the whole world.

The differences between the US and the EU should not be overstated. The federal government of the US intervenes in employment and working conditions. Indeed, in areas such as the federal minimum wage and in equal opportunities policies, the federal government has a stronger influence on employment and working conditions than does the EU. However, there is no equivalent in US federal law to the EU laws on working time, worker participation and rights for part-time workers. In general, the federal government of the US is less interventionist than the EU and in many areas the states have autonomy to choose economic and social policies that influence the allocation of resources. Nevertheless, the member states also have autonomy to pursue different economic and social policies from those that come from the EU. In particular, the member states are often able to have higher levels of social protection than the minimum levels specified by EU policies. This is perhaps the biggest difference; in many areas the federal government does not specify any conditions that the states must apply, but leaves the states to decide these matters.

Macroeconomic policy frameworks

Macroeconomic policies affect the business environment because monetary, fiscal and exchange rate policies influence the inflation and growth environment in which companies operate. The US has a common monetary policy with a single currency that is managed by a federal central bank – the Federal Reserve Bank. Therefore, in the US monetary and exchange rate policies connected to maintaining a stable economic environment are clearly the responsibility of federal institutions. In most single economic spaces fiscal policies are normally harmonised so that the central or federal governments have a strong influence on taxation, expenditure and the borrowing policies of lower levels of government within the single economic system. However, the federal government of the US has no power over the taxation and expenditure decisions of the states. Nevertheless, the federal budget is large and exercises a strong influence on the level of economic activity. Consequently, if there are asymmetric shocks whereby some states suffer a more serious decline in economic activity than other states, federal tax revenues (linked to income) automatically fall and federal expenditures (linked to income) automatically rise. Hence there is an automatic transfer of income to states that suffer from asymmetric shocks. Therefore, in the US federal monetary, exchange rate and fiscal policies largely control the inflation and growth environment and federal tax and expenditure systems automatically help states suffering from asymmetric shocks.

Currently, 12 member states (Euroland) are members of European monetary union with a common monetary policy and a single currency that is managed by a type of a federal central bank – the ECB. Therefore, for Euroland monetary and exchange rate policies are the responsibility of institutional systems that are similar to those in the US. The EU is seeking to impose control over the fiscal policies (particularly government borrowing) of those members states that are members of the EMU. The budget of the EU is small in relation to the size of the economy of the Union. Therefore, unlike the federal budget in the US, the EU budget does not exert a significant influence on the level of economic activity. However, by controlling the level of borrowing by national governments it is possible to exercise influence on the impact of the fiscal policies of the member states on the inflation and growth environment in the members of Euroland. A significant difference between Euroland and the US is that there is no automatic transfer to member states suffering from asymmetric shocks because the EU does not have significant taxes and expenditures linked to income. Consequently, Euroland has a similar system of macroeconomic control as the US, based on a common currency with a strong degree of control over the impact of fiscal policy on inflation and growth levels. However, there is no automatic help via income transfers to member states suffering from asymmetric shocks. As the exchange rate is also fixed, because of the single currency this means that adjustment to asymmetric shocks has to be mainly accomplished by lowering costs of production to make products competitive.

Political frameworks

In the US the respective competencies of state and federal governments and the institutions responsible for governmental activities are constrained by a constitution and state and federal courts. A Supreme Federal Court makes the final decision when there is dispute about competencies. The President of the US has power and the means to enforce federal law in the states, including the right to use force. In most cases federal institutions monitor and enforce federal law. In addition, the US has a well-defined federal political system with political parties and institutions for making and modifying federal laws and policies.

The EU does not have a constitution but uses a series of treaties to determine the relationship between the member states and the institutions of the EU. Furthermore, the competencies of national governments relative to those of the institutions of the EU are often not clear. The ECJ has the right to clarify the meaning of EU laws and the treaties but it lacks the power and breadth of jurisdiction of the Supreme Federal Court. There is no agency in the EU that has the power or the means to enforce EU law in the member states. In most cases national institutions monitor and enforce EU law. Moreover, the EU does not have a well-defined political system with pan-European political parties to make and modify EU laws and policies.

The US has a governmental system with strong federal powers in matters connected to restrictions on inter-state trade and on the provision of a stable economic environment. The federal government has less power over microeconomic and social policies. In contrast, the EU is stronger on microeconomic and social policies but lacks strong institutional structures to ensure that its laws and policies are fully implemented and enforced. The important role of governments and institutional frameworks in the member states means that in principle companies and organisations should face the same or similar legal conditions governing free movement regardless of their location within the EU. However, this is often not the case. The ways in which member states implement, monitor and enforce EU law can lead to different legal conditions depending on the location of companies and organisations (see Law Making in the EU, p. 7). The establishment of European monetary union in 12 of the member states means that these countries are on a path towards strong EU control of the policies that affect economic stability. Furthermore, this is backed by strong institutional structures, in particular the European Central Bank (ECB). However, not all member states are part of the EMU and many of the expected new members from Central and Eastern Europe may not be able to join the monetary union for a number of years after they have joined the EU.

THE DEVELOPMENT OF THE SINGLE ECONOMIC SPACE

Much of the debate about the characteristics of the single economic space that the EU is seeking to create and develop is centred on whether it requires strong macroeconomic integration such as a monetary union. Increasingly the vexed issue of the taxation of businesses and savings is also creating heated debate in the EU. There is also controversy over the wisdom of taking a market-based or social market approach to the common or harmonised laws and policies of the EU. The origins of the EU have tended to favour a social market approach with a strong emphasis on using government laws and policies that encourage economic and social priorities which are sometimes contrary to the generation of high rates of return to capital. However, the enlargement of the EU (particularly the membership of the UK) and the growing pressure for companies to attain competitiveness because of the internationalisation of business activities has increased the focus on efficiency. Nevertheless, the EU appears to be reluctant to focus on free movement and a stable economic environment while leaving the member states to decide how far they wish to pursue economic and social polices to attempt to achieve equity objectives. In Europe, there has been a long tradition of regarding efficiency and equity questions as being interconnected. Therefore, interference in market allocation in social conditions and employment and working conditions has been seen as being important for encouraging the development of a productive economic system.

IMPLICATIONS FOR COMPANIES OF DIFFERENT TYPES OF SINGLE ECONOMIC SPACES

Clearly there are significant differences between the single economic space of the US and the emerging space in the EU. These differences mean that companies face significantly different conditions when they operate in the single economic space of the EU as compared with the space in the US. These differences are often thought to be mainly connected to the cultural and linguistic diversity of the EU. However, the matters discussed above are not directly connected to cultural differences but to differences in institutional frameworks. Moreover, the US also has a high level of cultural diversity and the growth of a large Spanish-speaking population in the US has led to a degree of linguistic difference. Nevertheless, the EU certainly has larger linguistic differences compared to the US.

The institutional differences make the EU a more complex single economic space than the US. Furthermore, although the US continues to evolve its single economic space it is not expanding geographically. The federal government is taking an increasing role in influencing the laws and policies that impact on business strategies and operations. The process by which this happens is clear, as it is defined by a Constitution with well established and effective legal and political systems to draft, approve, implement, monitor and enforce federal laws and policies. In contrast, the EU is rapidly expanding geographically and in the areas covered by EU laws and policies. Moreover, the EU lacks a Constitution and a clear and effective legal and political system to develop its laws and policies. The major institutional differences and the implications for companies are summarised in Table 2.2.

In the US companies have a number of advantages compared to EU-based companies. In particular, the free movement of goods, services, capital and labour is backed by a strong federal system to implement, monitor and enforce the laws and policies. This means that it is easier for US companies to locate anywhere they wish within their single economic space and to obtain access to the markets of the US from their selected locations. US companies also find it easier to obtain capital and labour from any part of their single economic space. The size of many federal procurement contracts means that US companies have access to very large public contracts that are normally considerable larger than those that EU companies face. In the US common monetary and exchange rate policies result in synchronised inflation and growth trends across the single economic space, whereas in the EU inflation and growth trends do not display the same level of synchronisation. However, European monetary union has already led to greater synchronisation among the members of Euroland. Nevertheless, for those member states that are not members of Euroland there can be considerable differences in inflation and growth trends. This means that trend developments in the economic environment that US companies face is more uniform than is the case in the EU. Moreover, the economic and social policies frameworks in the EU are more likely to lead to the development of employment and working conditions that result in higher non-wage costs than is the case in the US.

These advantages mean that the opportunities to develop economies of scale and scope are greater for US as compared to EU companies. Moreover, US companies find it easier to expand at given locations (because of the high level of mobility of capital and labour) or to relocate to other sites within the single economic space that confer better advantages. US companies also obtain advantages from their strong and large home base. This enables them to obtain advantages that give them a strong position in international markets. Moreover, the large federal defence and space contracts provide US companies with large high-technology markets that allow them to develop new technologies and products. EU companies normally do not benefit from these advantages because the single economic space in the EU is less conducive to free movement. SMEs in the US are also able to have lower-cost access than EU SMEs to a large and high-income domestic market because of the strong federal laws on free movement for inter-state trade. Moreover, state governments are more able to provide state aid to companies than is the case in the member states of the EU. It is also easier in the US for state governments to favour SMEs and other companies when allocating state procurement contracts.

Nevertheless, differences in tax systems and the diversity of technical regulations across the states means that US companies may face problems with conforming to technical regulations and distortions caused by tax differences. The emphasis on a market-based approach to economic and social policies in the US also leads to more income inequality than is the case in the EU.

CONCLUSIONS

The single economic space that is emerging in the EU has many similarities to that of the US. However, the companies that are located in the US have advantages in terms of reaping economies of scale and scope that are not yet available to EU companies. Furthermore, the well-developed federal system in the US ensures that federal laws and policies that affect free movement and the business environment are effectively implemented, monitored and enforced. The single economic space in the EU is based on complex interrelationships between EU and national government institutions. This system is probably less effective at securing low cost free movement. The EU also adopts a more social market approach that encourages higher non-wage costs than is the case in the US. The macroeconomic policies

TABLE 2.2   Comparison of the single economic space of the EU and the US

Legal frameworks			
The EU	**Implication for companies**	**The US**	**Implications for companies**
1 Free movement of goods and services with some limitations on the movement of capital and labour	1 Few limitations restricting supply of EU markets from any location within the Union. However, some markets not fully open and restrictions on movement of labour and some types of financial instruments.	1 Free movement of goods, services, capital and labour.	1 No limitation on ability to supply US market from any location in the US.
2 Mutual recognition of technical regulations with selective harmonisation of regulations.	2 Need to comply with EU regulations even if no intra-EU trade	2 Technical regulations of goods and services vary across the states.	2 Need to conform to the technical regulations that prevail in the states.
3 Member states use of state aids controlled by Commission.	3 States aids can be modified or stopped by the Commission.	3 States are free to use state aids without federal interference.	3 States aids free from federal government modification unless state aids have a federal component.
4 Most public procurement contracts open to EU-wide competition but not in areas connected to strategic defence.	4 Limited access to some public procurement contracts.	4 States may restrict state procurement to companies based in the state.	4 State procurement can be restricted to state-based companies or affiliates.
5 Governance of company law and financial regulation of companies subject to complex interaction between national government and EU institutions.	5 Law governing pan-European companies very complex and regulations governing the means of raising finance and financial reporting requirements vary across the member states making use of EU-wide financial services difficult and expensive.	5 Federal procurement contracts (including defence equipment) open to US-wide competition.	5 All federal procurement contracts open to US-based companies.
		6 Company law and financial regulation of companies largely governed by federal law with no legal restrictions on pan-US companies.	6 Formation and development of pan-US companies face few legal obstacles and regulations on raising finance and financial reporting requirements permit easy use of US-wide financial services.

(Continued)

TABLE 2.2 (*Continued*)

Taxation frameworks			
The EU	**Implication for companies**	**The US**	**Implications for companies**
1 Attempts to harmonise taxation of sales and savings.	1 Prospects of significant changes to harmonise tax systems across the member states.	1 States free to set taxes on sales, income and savings.	1 No prospect of changes to harmonise taxation systems across the states – all harmonisation is based on decisions of individual states.
2 Systems to prevent difference in sales taxes from distorting trade.	2 Companies must have systems to record intra-EU exports and imports for tax purposes.	2 No system to prevent differences in sales taxes distorting trade.	2 No need to have record of intra-state trade for taxation purposes.
3 Shoppers for personal use pay sales tax (VAT and excise duties) in the place of purchase.	3 Cross-frontier shopping for personal use – incentive to buy in low VAT and excise duties member states.	3 Buyers for re-sale, inputs for other products and personal use pay sales tax in place of purchase - incentive to buy in low tax states.	3 Distortion of intra-state trade possible because of taxation differences.

Economic and social policies			
1 EU economic and social policies that seek to enhance effective free movement and promote a socially cohesive and environmentally sustainable economic system.	1 Significant differences in the extent of the use of social market approach across the member states.	1 States can adopt their own approach to many economic and social policies – a tendency towards a market-based approach.	1 A diverse range of economic and social policies across the state, some of them joint with federal schemes.
2 In many areas member states permitted to have higher standards than the minimum set by EU.	2 Minimum employment and working conditions and many aspects of environmental regulations set by EU law.	2 Many aspects of employment and working conditions and of environmental policy decided by the states as are policies to help poorer regions and social groups.	2 Limited influence of federal laws and policies that affect employment and working conditions but in area of equal opportunities federal laws and policies are very important, also a federal minimum wage.
3 Important funds available to help poorer regions and identified social groups but no	3 A multitude of EU funds available for agencies and companies to help poorer regions and to help	3 Federal laws and policies strong on equal opportunities, health, some aspects of environmental policy and	3 A multitude of state and state/federal government funds to help with identified social problems

(*Continued*)

TABLE 2.2 *(Continued)*

The EU	Implication for companies	The US	Implications for companies
competence in health, education or housing.	with social groups with identified problems.	some areas connected to education and housing.	and federal systems for health care have a significant impact on employment costs in some organisations.

Macroeconomic policy frameworks

The EU	Implication for companies	The US	Implications for companies
1 Common monetary policy and a single currency for Euroland countries.	1 For companies located in Euroland general economic conditions (inflation and growth) heavily influenced by common monetary policy.	1 Common monetary policy and a single currency for all states.	1 All US companies face the same general economic conditions and exchange rate conditions.
2 Some controls on fiscal policy via the Growth and Stability Pack.	2 For companies located in the EU but outside of Euroland possibility of volatile exchange rates with the euro and the dollar.	2 No controls of state fiscal policies - states can therefore amend fiscal policy to help to adjust to asymmetric shocks.	2 Companies faced with asymmetric shocks are helped to adjust by ability of states to alter fiscal policies and by automatic federal transfers to states suffering from asymmetric shocks.
3 No automatic transfer via EU tax/expenditure systems to member states suffering from asymmetric shocks.	3 Companies faced with asymmetric shocks need to take quick action to control their costs.	3 Automatic transfer via federal tax/expenditure systems to states suffering from asymmetric shocks.	

Political frameworks

The EU	Implication for companies	The US	Implications for companies
1 Implementation, monitoring and enforcement of EU laws and policies largely depends on national governments.	1 Companies face different implementation, monitoring and enforcement of EU laws and policies depending on the member state in which they are located.	1 Implementation, monitoring and enforcement of federal laws and policies is largely done by federal agencies and state laws and policies by state agencies.	1 Companies face well-defined and uniform procedures that govern the implementation, monitoring and enforcement of federal and state laws and policies.
2 The EU does not have its own implementation, monitoring and enforcement agencies.	2 Companies seeking to influence the development of EU laws and policies face a complex political environment that is not transparent	2 Well-defined political system to make and amend laws and policies - political parties are national and are organised at both federal and	2 Companies seeking to influence the development of laws and policies face a well-defined political system with clear division of competencies

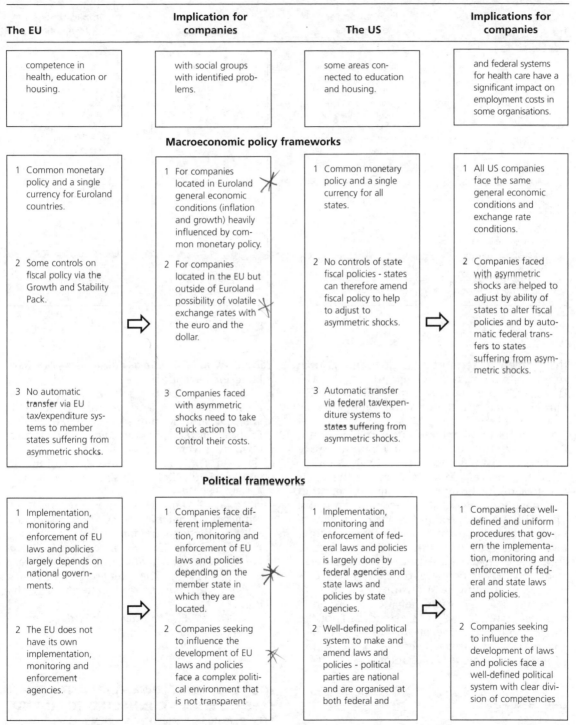

(Continued)

TABLE 2.2 *(Continued)*

The EU	Implication for companies	The US	Implications for companies
	and is a complex mix of national and EU institutions – political parties are nationally based and therefore do not have clear means to influence EU laws and policies.	state level into a coherent system.	and political parties and institutions that form a coherent system with clear means to resolve disputes between federal and state authorities.
3 Lack of a well-defined EU based political system (e.g. no European political parties) and complex interaction between EU institutions and national government agencies to make and modify EU laws and policies.			

that largely determine inflation and growth trends are more fully developed in the US. However, those member states that are part of Euroland face a similar macroeconomic policy system as in the US.

Companies that operate within the EU do not face the same type of a single economic space that US companies encounter in their domestic market. However, doing business in the EU is not like doing business in different countries that have their own distinct economic systems. The EU has a complex and evolving single economic space. Euroland presents yet another level of integration within the EU that further complicates the characteristics of the single economic space. Furthermore, the EU has deep economic and trading relationships with most of the countries of Europe that are not currently member states. These links extend parts of the single economic space of the EU such that it covers most of Europe. These issues are further explored in the next two chapters.

REFERENCES

Aisbitt, S. (2002) 'Tax and accounting rules: some recent developments', *European Business Review,* 14: 92–7.

Cairns, W. (1997) *Introduction to European Law.* London: Cavendish.

El Agraa, A. (2001) *The European Union: Economics and Policies,* London: Prentice Hall.

Mazey, S. and Richardson, R. (eds) (1993) *Lobbying in the European Community.* Oxford: Oxford University Press.

McDonald, F. (2000) 'The European Union and employment relationships', *European Business Review,* 12: 208–15.

McDonald, F. and Dearden, S. (eds) (1999) *European Economic Integration.* London: Addison-Wesley Longman.

Nugent, N. (2002) *The Government and Politics of the European Community.* London: Macmillan.

Pinder, J. (1995) *The European Community, Building the Union.* Oxford: Oxford University Press.

Swann, D. (1998) *The Economics of the Common Market.* London: Penguin.

JOURNALS THAT HAVE RELEVANT ARTICLES ON ISSUES CONNECTED TO EU AND THE BUSINESS ENVIRONMENT

European Business Journal
European Business Review

European Economy
Journal of Common Market Studies
Journal of European Public Policy

USEFUL WEBSITES

www.ecb.int
The website of the European Central Bank.

www.economist.com
The Economist – a site with limited free access (unlimited to subscribers) to articles and surveys on matters connected to european business.

www.eubusiness.com
A website on the effects on business of economic and monetary union.

www.euro-emu.co.uk
A website devoted to matters connected to economic and monetary union.

www.european – convention.eu.int
A website containing information on the proposed changes to the treaties of the European Union.

www.europa.eu.int
The website of the EU with access to all the institutions, policies and programmes of the EU.

www.ft.com
The *Financial Times* – a site with limited free access (unlimited to subscribers) articles and surveys on matters connected to european business.

www.libweb.uncc.edu/ref-bus/vibehome.htm
Virtual International Business and Economic Sources (VIBES) – a site that provides access to a wide variety of sites with data on economic and business issues covering all European countries and most other countries.

www.unece.org
United Nations Economic Commission for Europe (ECE) – a website with papers, reports and statistics on economic and business conditions in Europe.

3 THE POLICIES OF THE SINGLE ECONOMIC SYSTEM OF THE EUROPEAN UNION

The EU is in the process of developing a single economic system, which is outlined in this chapter. This area includes the member states, but also partly extends to much of the rest of Europe. The extension of the single economic system to cover much of Europe is explored in Chapter 4. This chapter considers the policies and programmes that are involved in the creation and development of the single economic system. The implications of these policies and programmes for business are also outlined.

The treaties of the EU have developed in a way that identifies the desired single economic system as an Economic and Monetary Union (EMU). The EMU of the EU is based on three major foundations:

1 The creation and development of a free movement area for goods, services, capital and labour to help companies to boost competitiveness and thereby to provide consumers with low-priced and high-quality products.
2 Monetary integration programmes to reduce distortions and transaction costs associated with different monetary, fiscal and exchange rate policies to provide the conditions under which the strategies and operations of companies are not hampered by unstable and uncertain macroeconomic environments.
3 Economic and social policies that allow effective free movement and the development of competitive companies that are compatible with a market-based economic system which provide acceptable economic and social outcomes.

The development of the EMU based on these foundations has led to nine major economic objectives that impact on the strategies and operations of companies.

1 Reducing transaction costs of conducting business by removing or reducing legal barriers (tariffs, quotas and non-tariff barriers) that restrict or distort the free movement of goods, services, capital and labour.
2 Reducing transaction and uncertainty costs by establishing monetary union, thereby lowering the costs associated with currency conversion and exchange rate risk.
3 Promoting economies of scale and scope by providing the conditions that permit companies to rationalise, relocate and evolve in response to the creation of a single economic space and thereby to reduce production and distribution costs.
4 Ensuring the development and maintenance of a competitive environment that provides consumers with low-priced and high-quality products and that also allows companies to successfully adapt to changing competitive and technological conditions.
5 Creating and developing institutional structures that encourage the development of effective pan-EU operations by companies by, for example, the development of European patent and European standards systems.
6 Developing governance systems in areas such as mergers and acquisitions, company law and auditing and financial reporting systems to permit effective pan-EU operations.
7 Creating and developing economic and social policies that help companies to achieve competitiveness whilst delivering social welfare objectives such as equal opportunities and the protection of workers rights and that the gains of competitiveness are not restricted to particular geographical regions or sections of society.
8 Promotion of environmental objectives in production, distribution and recycling systems that provide for the sustainable use of renewable and non-renewable resources.
9 Creating and maintaining stable macroeconomic conditions that reduce the uncertainty associated with inflationary or deflationary processes which reduce the incentive to invest

by companies and thereby undermine the short- and long-term competitiveness of companies.

Clearly, a single economic space based on this type of EMU is in essence the creation and development of a common economic system rather like those that exist in nation states such as the US. Indeed, one of the implicit objectives of the EU, at least for some of its major advocates, is to create a common economic system that would deliver the kind of benefits (such as economies of scale, critical mass of research and development (R&D) and innovation systems and the bargaining power in world economic forums) as is available to the US. Hence in economic terms the pursuit of EMU is an attempt to create the equivalent of an economic super state. However, the EU does not (yet) have the political equivalent of an emerging economic super state. Thus the EU is not a single economic space in the sense that the US is a common economic system (see Chapter 2). However, it is much more than a loose bloc of states linked together in some sort of free trade area. The EU is considerably more than a free trade area, but not quite a complete common economic system.

This means that companies that operate in the EU, or trade with it, are faced with a complex economic area that has elements of a common economic system but where there are also significant differences across the member states. The differences under consideration here are not the normal ones referred to in much of the business literature, for example, language and cultural differences. In the EU, many aspects of legal and institutional systems vary across the member states as do the approaches to economic and social policies that impact on companies. Moreover, even in areas where there is common EU laws and policies, their implementation and policing can vary across the member states (see Chapter 2). In some crucial areas such as monetary union not all member states are part of the common currency area and many of the Central and East European countries have partially adopted some of the aspects of the single economic space but are not yet full members of the EU. Companies that do business in the EU and in the wider area of Europe face a complex set of laws, policies, and economic conditions that make production, marketing and distribution different from what they faced in a nation state with a common economic system. However, there are sufficient commonalities to

make doing business in the EU and Europe more like doing business with a nation state than with a group of countries that all have distinct economic systems. Nevertheless, the differences make doing business in the EU and Europe rather more complex that doing business in the US. The implications on these similarities and differences for European business and marketing are explored in Chapter 2.

As the EU develops and expands, the commonalities of the economic system increase but there are still many areas where significant differences remain. This chapter examines these issues by looking at the three foundation policies outlined above.

THE FREE MOVEMENT AREA

The free movement area is based on two main programmes:

- the creation of a Customs Union; and
- the creation of a Common Market.

A Customs Union consists of an area with no barriers to trade in goods and services and the imposition of a common trade policy. The key aspects of the Customs Union are the elimination of tariffs and quotas and the erection of a common external tariff (CET). However, the Customs Union, as specified by the Treaty of Rome, also required the elimination of all barriers to trade that affect the movement of goods and services. This requires the removal of all non-tariff barriers (NTBs); these include technical regulations and standards, laws and other devices that prohibit or restrict the free movement of goods and services. The removal of such NTBs was one of the key goals of the programme to complete the Single European Market (SEM). The main aspects of the SEM programme to create a Single Market are outlined in Exhibit 3.1.

The Common Market requires a fully implemented Customs Union with the added dimension of free movement of capital and labour. The SEM programme removed many of the barriers limiting the free movement of capital and labour. However, there still remain barriers in these areas due to failure to agree to legislation in some sectors. There are also problems connected to implementing the new laws and rules relating to free movement of goods, services, capital and labour. These problems have been examined in the review of the Single Market (Monti, 1996).

EXHIBIT 3.1   THE SINGLE EUROPEAN MARKET (SEM) PROGRAMME

The SEM programme was based on the removal of non-tariff barriers in order to create a free movement area for goods, services, capital and labour. Three main types of barriers were identified by the White Paper 'Completing the Internal Market' (Commission, 1985):

- *Physical barriers*: the removal of frontier controls and customs formalities.
- *Technical barriers*: restrictions on economic activities caused by national rules and standards. These included technical specifications that hindered or prevented trade in goods and services, discriminatory public procurement rules that limited tendering for governments to domestic companies, and legal obstacles faced by companies in member states from setting up subsidiaries in other member states.
- *Fiscal barriers*: the need to adjust VAT and excise duties to allow goods to cross frontiers without frontier controls.

The general objective of the SEM programme was to create a market environment in which there were no legal barriers to the movement of goods, services, capital and labour. The main method of achieving such a market environment was to remove technical and standards barriers by mutual recognition of, and the development of, European standards by the Comité Europeen de Normalisation (CEN) and the Comité Europeen de Normalisation Electronique (CENELEC). This process, it was assumed, would lead to a more competitive market in the EU and would bring benefits by reducing prices and stimulating a more effective allocation of resources. It was in effect a large 'supply side' policy, with the hope of providing a one-off boost to the economy of the EU and a resultant reconstruction process that would lead to large-scale improvements in the efficiency of the company sector in the EU. The Cecchini Report 'The Costs of Non-Europe' claimed that an extra 7.5 per cent in the GDP of the EU could be achieved by implementing the SEM programme (Commission, 1988). This rosy picture was subject to criticism by economists from all political and ideological persuasions (see McDonald and Dearden (1999) for a survey of the criticisms).

THE REVIEW OF THE SINGLE MARKET

The review included a survey of 20,000 enterprises, a number of specific industy studies, investigation of particular issues (for example, public procurement, capital market liberalisation, price convergence, market concentration) and a number of studies on the growth and regional development effects of the SEM programme (see www.europa.eu.int/comm/internal_market). The review concentrated on three main economic effects of the SEM programme.

1 Allocation effects arising from improvements in the efficiency of the use of resources. These were supposed to result from increased competition leading to lower prices and improved quality of products. The SEM was also supposed to lead to economies of scale as the lowering of barriers allowed markets to be supplied from plant operating at high levels of output that could be sold without the burden of NTBs across the frontiers of the EU.

2 Accumulation effects or growth effects resulting from the increase competition and lower prices that permit the economy of the EU to increase its trend rate of growth as a result of the improvement in the efficient use of resources.

3 Locational effects that emerge from the rationalisation of production to take advantage of free movement. This would have implications for the geographical location of industries and firms. In particular, industries and firms relocating to take advantage of the new opportunities and challenges created by the SEM.

The review found evidence that some changes had occurred with industrial structures, trading patterns and market conditions from the SEM programme. The review did not indicate that the SEM programme had no significant effects, rather it suggests that these were less than was expected. Evidence was found that in many industries prices were converging across the member states, indicating that markets were becoming more competitive. Firm size had also increased on average but price–cost margins had not widened, indicating that economies of scale had been reaped and the benefits passed on in lower prices. Nevertheless, in some industries (in particular in areas were there were large governmental interests such as gas and electricity production and distribution) there was sparse evidence that markets had become more competitive. This evidence (based on examination of convergence of prices across the member states) was supported by surveys of industries that revealed in some cases that NTBs were still causing problems which hindered intra-EU trade. There was little evidence that the SEM programme had increased the trend rate of growth. However, the period covered by the review coincided with a recession in many of the member states. Some evidence that relocation was taking place was found, but it was not clear how much of this was due to the SEM programme. Those member states that have been members of the EU for a long time provided clearer evidence of increased competition. This indicates that it takes time for companies to rationalise and react to the pressures that emerge from the progress towards free movement.

The review highlights several areas where additional actions by the institutions of the EU and by national governments were needed to improve the effectiveness of free movement. These deficiencies in the legislative programme and the need for more effective policies to create and develop the conditions for effective free movement may be responsible for the relatively poor results that have followed from the SEM programme. The nature of these legal and institutional problems is discussed in Chapter 2.

The remaining legal and institutional obstacles have proved to be difficult to overcome and despite a multitude of reports from the European Commission and solemn declarations at European Summits there continues to be significant obstacles to free movement in areas such as gas and electricity production and distribution, and in many areas connected to public procurement. The free movement of capital is also hampered by failure to agree on deregulation of national rules governing many types of financial instruments. Nevertheless,

progress has been made, even in areas that had proved difficult to dislodge from national control, for example, telecommunication services and air travel.

The EU has not yet achieved a free movement area, in the sense that the US constitutes such an area. However, the SEM programme has achieved a considerable reduction in barriers to trade between the member states. This has had a significant impact on the structure of companies, by mergers and acquisitions, joint ventures and restructuring to achieve cost reductions from economies of scale and scope. Joint ventures, alliances and other types of collaboration to develop pan-European operations (or operations across several of the member states) are also growing. There have also been benefits from more competitive, and therefore lower-priced, business services in areas such as distribution, subcontracting and financial services. Major benefits in terms of lower prices and improved quality of service have emerged from liberalising telecommunications services and some progress towards this goal has also been made in the field of gas and electricity supplies. Nevertheless, the conditions to establish an effective single economic system have not yet been completed (see the website of the EU www.europa.eu.int/comm/internal_market for the most up-to-date information on the progress in removing legal and institutional barriers to free movement).

As the EU continues to reduce NTBs and develop other means to improve free movement, it is likely that an ever-larger number of industries will become subject to greater competition. This will lead to lower prices, pressures for improved quality of products and rationalisation and relocation among firms.

MONETARY INTEGRATION

One of the factors that adds to the transaction costs and uncertainty of intra-EU trade is the existence of different currencies. These costs arise from conversion costs when changing currencies and also the hedging costs of dealing with exchange rate risk. The EU has sought to promote monetary integration from its earliest years. This arose from the requirement in the Treaty of Rome for the removal of all impediments to the free movement of capital. The obligation to create free movement of financial services also meant that the EU had a strong interest in the promotion of monetary integration, at least with respect to the requirements for the creation of a free movement area for capital and financial services. However, very little progress was made in removing capital controls and allowing for the free movement of financial services until the SEM programme began to take effect in the late 1980s.

The system of floating exchange rates that prevailed in the 1970s proved to be harmful for the operations of the EU. Problems arose regarding transfers of income between the member states because of the volatility of exchange rates that led to dramatic fluctuations in the value of these payments in terms of domestic currencies. There was also dissatisfaction with the system of floating exchange rates because it did not deliver stable economic conditions and often led to rapid changes in the foreign trade prices of goods and services. These problems were deemed to be harmful to the creation of the common market because it made it difficult for companies to make long-term investments due to the uncertainty in general economic conditions caused by the high level of monetary instability among member states.

In response to these problems a system to stabilise exchange rates was launched in 1979 – the European Monetary System (EMS). This system was successful in stabilising exchange rates until the crises in 1992 and 1993 led to the effective abandonment of the system. This setback did not prevent the EU from pressing on with the plan to create a European monetary union with a single currency and a European Central Bank (ECB). The ECB is responsible for the monetary policy of the 12 member states (Euroland) that have joined the EMU. Euroland has a common monetary policy and one currency, the euro. Bonds and other financial instruments have been issued denominated in euro and many interbank and financial transactions between multinational corporations (MNCs) are already being conducted in euros.

The creation of monetary union eliminates transaction costs of currency trading and the costs of hedging to cover exchange rate risk for trade between the members of Euroland. The reduction in these costs has stimulated an increase in intra-Euroland trade and thereby should increase competition. Moreover, the use of one currency improves price transparency because buyers will notice differences in prices across EU markets. This will stimulate parallel importing and thereby promote a convergence of prices. However, the existence of a single currency does not mean that prices will converge to a single Euroland price for the same products. Differences in competitive environments across the members of Euroland as well as variations in taxes and transport and distribution costs are likely to lead to the continuation of significant price differences for the same products. Only those products that are faced with the similar tax conditions, competitive environments, transport and distribution costs across Euroland are likely to have the same price. Widespread parallel importing would help to establish the same or similar prices for the same products. However, many products face transport and distribution cost differences that limited parallel importing. Moreover, differences in legal, economic, social and cultural factors across Euroland mean that products often have to be modified to meet these conditions. Given these factors it is unlikely that all, or even many, products will experience the emergence of a single Euroland price.

Monetary union makes it easier for a single European financial market to emerge and thereby to reduce the prices of financial services. Companies that conduct considerable business across the members of the Euroland will also benefit from lower treasury costs because they will be able to conduct all of their intra-Euroland financial transactions and accounting procedures in one currency. However, this benefit may not be large because many MNCs already conduct the majority of these transactions in one currency – the dollar. The implications of the introduction of the euro for the use of the dollar in business transactions are further explored in Chapters 4 and 5.

The creation of monetary union tends to make EU markets more competitive and a lower-priced area for many goods and services. European monetary union may also reduce the long-term cost of capital for those members that have had high and unstable inflation. This will happen because countries with high and unstable inflation attract a premium on interest rates to compensate for the costs of uncertainty associated with unpredictable inflation rates. If the ECB succeeds in creating low and stable inflation, real interest rates for countries with a record of high inflation will decline, leading to a lower cost of capital.

Problems could emerge for companies based in member states that find it difficult to compete without use of deprecation of their currency to restore competitiveness. It will be impossible for national governments to ease monetary policy in times when demand is low in their domestic economies (Eltis, 2000). For Euroland, these decisions now rest with the European Central Bank (ECB). The ECB acts in the interests of Euroland as a whole. Therefore, if parts of Euroland are suffering from a recession while most of the other members are experiencing a boom, a so-called asymmetric shock, the ECB will act to curb inflation. This may mean that those countries facing recession will have to cope with monetary policy that leads to high interest rates and a strong euro during a period when lower interest rates and a weaker currency are required. The reverse of this problem will exist if a member of Euroland is experiencing a boom while most of the rest of the members are suffering from recession.

Monetary union implies a need for companies to be lean and more flexible such that they can rapidly adjust to control their costs in periods of inappropriate monetary and exchange rate policy. The increase in price transparency together with the reduction of the transaction and uncertainty costs because of the elimination of different currencies has also stimulated the need for leaner and more flexible company strategies and operations in response to the growth of intra-Euroland trade and the consequent increase in competition. However, these changes have also provided new opportunities for companies to expand their markets and to obtain lower-priced and better quality inputs. The introduction of the euro also has implications for the international monetary system and exchange rate stability with the dollar and the yen. For an outline of the main implications of monetary union for companies, see McDonald (1997). The international monetary issues connected to European monetary union are explored in Chapter 4.

ECONOMICS AND SOCIAL POLICIES

The EU has a variety of economic and social policies that affect a range of business activities (Andersen and Eliassen, 2001). Up-to-date information on legislation and programmes connected to economic and social policies can be found on the website of the EU (www.europa. eu.int). There are six main policy areas that have a direct impact on business activities:

1 Competition policy.
2 Industrial policy.
3 Social policy.
4 Environmental policy.
5 Public health and consumer protection.
6 Regional policy.

Competition policy

The competition policy of the EU is based on Articles 81 (Article 85, Treaty of Rome) and 82 (Article 86, Treaty of Rome) of the Treaty of Amsterdam. Article 81 prohibits companies from engaging in anti-competitive practices such as price fixing and market sharing. Abuse of market power by companies with such power is prohibited by Article 82. In 1990, the Merger Control Regulation came into force, enabling the EU to investigate and limit or prevent acquisitions, mergers and alliances that are deemed to be harmful for competition within the EU. To be subject to Articles 81 and 82, the Merger Control Regulation companies must operate in more than one member state. The Merger Control Regulation is only applicable for mergers and acquisitions over a certain size (see www.europa. eu.int for details). The competition policy also prohibits the use of state aids (the use of tax concessions, grants and other types of state subsidies) that distort intra-EU trade. State aids are permissible if they are to improve conditions in regions designated as underdeveloped, or in areas where there are problems with unemployment. The use of state aids to give competitive advantage for domestic companies is prohibited by the terms of the competition policy. The objective of the competition policy of the EU is to prevent companies and national governments from distorting competition between the member states by use of restrictive agreements, cartels, abuse of market power and state aids.

The competition policy is based on the assumption that any action that reduces or restricts competition within the EU is potentially harmful. However, it is recognised that restrictions of competition that leads to benefits such as economies of scale, increased choice of goods and services or improvements in the technical competence of companies may be permitted, providing that the benefits are greater than the costs associated with the decline in competition. The competition policy is based on a cost–benefit approach rather than a rules-based approach. Therefore, if a company breaches the conditions specified in the competition policy, it may not be found guilty if it can be shown that these actions lead to improved outcomes that outweigh the harm caused by the behaviour of the company.

The competition policy of the EU can be criticized because of the lack of firm rules to guide the Commission in the selection and examination of cases. The Commission does not follow a rules-based monitoring system for choosing cases to be examined, rather cases are selected because of widespread complaints, or specific complaints by national governments, or concern by the Commission, about the behaviour of companies. The examination of cases is usually based on investigations by the Commission, often working with the agencies in the member states, to ascertain whether the company is guilty of a breach of competition policy. Moreover, the operation of the Merger Control Regulation is restricted by the qualifying criteria for selection. These criteria exclude all but very large mergers and acquisitions because of these problems and there is, a campaign to restructure the conditions of the Merger Control Regulation. However, several proposals to reform the competition policy to correct these deficiencies have been put forward and some changes in the operation of the policy have already been made (Albors-Clorens, 2002).

Another criticism of the competition policy is that the boundaries are not clearly distinguished between those cases that should fall into the jurisdiction of national governments and those that should be examined by the Commission. The growth of global mergers involving the EU and the US has also led to a need for cooperation with the competition authorities in the US. This problem was clearly illustrated when the Commission prevented the merger of two US companies (General Electric and Honeywell) because it was considered to be harmful for competition in EU markets. However, the US authorities had approved this merger and the US government and the two companies expressed strong disapproval of the failure of the Commission to liaise with the relevant US authorities before making the decision. The Commission is also investigating the European operations of Microsoft, because it has been decided that there is a possible case that the company is breaching the competition policy. If the Commission finds against Microsoft it can fine the company and require changes in behaviour. In this circumstance, it is likely to lead to a reference to the European Court of Justice (ECJ) and possible conflict with the US. These cases highlight the power of the competition policy of the EU to have profound implications for company strategies even when the companies are not based in the EU (European Economy, 2001b).

Disputes over the decisions of the Commission in matters connected to competition, or in cases where it is not clear what the articles mean, are referred to the ECJ. The resultant case law that emerges from these referrals provides another important component of the competition policy of the EU. The ECJ has normally taken a pro-competition stance on the cases referred for judgment. However, the ECJ permitted perfume companies to restrict outlets of supply because a particular type of retailing associated with high-priced perfume was judged to be an integral part of the product. In other cases, the ECJ has upheld complaints from companies about retailers importing their products (sunglasses and Levi jeans) from outside of the EU and selling them at a lower price than was normal within the member states of the EU. In these cases the supplying companies have claimed that customers were being deprived of the full benefits of their products because the retailers were not providing the full range of services that should be associated with these types of products. These cases suggest that the ECB is prepared to accept anti-competitive behaviour on the grounds of intangible benefits to customers. However, these cases have been very controversial and retailers and consumer groups have expressed the view that the ECJ has been too soft on this type of anti-competitive practice.

The competition policy of the EU has a clear purpose to promote and protect a competitive market system while taking into account the possible benefits that can arise from cooperation or mergers and acquisitions between companies. However, the large amount of discretion given to the Commission in the operation of the policy calls into question the ability of the policy to achieve a balance between the interests of consumers and producers. Organisations with power and access to the Commission have the potential to influence decisions in their favour, while smaller and less powerful organisations may have less opportunity to influence the Commission. It is also seems that the Commission is unwilling to tackle state aids and other types of implicit support from national governments that are used to protect national industries, as this brings it into conflict with national governments. The review of the SEM in 1998 indicated that in many areas there is a lack of competition in some European markets often caused by national government intervention, for example, in the airline sector, energy (gas and electricity), telecommunication services and vehicle manufacture. In all these cases the

Commission has begun to take a tougher stand, particularly regarding state aids and protectionary practices by national governments.

Industrial policy

Industrial policy in the EU is mainly based on Article 130 of the Maastricht Treaty. Article 130 contains provisions for a series of policies and programmes to encourage an open and competitive industrial sector. This article has been clarified and developed in Article 157 of the Treaty of Amsterdam. The basis of the industrial policy has been focused on the promotion of a smooth adjustment to structural change, the encouragement of SMEs and the stimulation of cooperation in the area of R&D and other methods of stimulating technical development. The Masstricht Treaty also contains many articles that had the intention of stimulating cooperation in R&D, vocational education and training and the development of trans-European networks. The latter is a plan 'to contribute to the establishment and development of trans-European networks in the areas of transport, telecommunications and energy infrastructures' (Article 129b of the Treaty on European Union – the Maastricht Treaty). The Treaty of Amsterdam continues to support these goals, but has increased the emphasis on improving the competitiveness of companies.

The main methods proposed to achieve this outcome are the promotion of new technologies and the creation of a business environment that is conducive to entrepreneurial activities by encouraging the development of institutional frameworks such as venture capitalism, a European patent system and links between companies and R&D agencies (for example, universities) to promote innovative developments. The approval of a takeover directive to provide a framework for pan-EU mergers and acquisitions is also considered to be important to aid in the process of taking advantage of the new opportunities that have arisen from the creation of the single economic space. Obtaining approval for the takeover directive has proved to be difficult because of very diverse views on the benefits of allowing hostile cross-frontier takeovers. The European Parliament stopped the takeover directive and it is not clear, at this stage, how this directive can be moved forward. Similarly, the process of creating a European patent system is also stalled, as are many proposed directives and programmes connected to the creation of institutional frameworks that would aid the development of pan-European companies.

Clearly, the impressive number of policies and programmes aimed at improving and developing the industrial sector does not mean that the EU has a coherent industrial policy. Many of these measures lack concrete plans and proposals that would allow them to be implemented and many of the proposed directives are held up by failure to reach agreement among the member states about the type of business environment that is considered to be desirable.

There is heated debate about the type of industrial policy that should be adopted. One view is that the EU should have a strong competition policy backed by deregulation to open up industries that are sheltered from EU-wide competition. Policies to enhance productivity by promoting new technologies such as ICT (information and communication technologies), e-commerce and biotechnology are also often favoured by those that take this approach. The advocates of this view of industrial policy regard the globalisation process as not only a challenge but also an opportunity; hence they are not disposed to restrict EU policies to European-owned companies. Indeed, as many new technologies and products are centred in the activities of US-owned companies, encouraging transatlantic cooperation in industrial matters is considered to be good for the development of European industries. The alternative approach is for the EU to be less concerned with promoting competition within European markets and to be more actively involved in the process of restructuring the industrial base to develop a strong and vibrant economy based on European-owned champions that can successfully compete with US companies. The development of the European Airbus to compete with Boeing in the large civil aircraft market is a good example of this approach to industrial policy. Advocates of this view argue that deregulation would lead to the development of Anglo-Saxon type capitalism with the danger of not only increased dominance of European markets by US-owned companies, but also the emergence of US-type corporate structures and employment conditions that would be unacceptable to European citizens. These two competing visions were discussed at the European Summit in Lisbon in 2000 but there was failure to agree on the way forward. These issues continued to be discussed at European Summits and at the Barcelona Summit in 2002 there was some progress towards deregulation in the electricity supply market and in the moves towards creating an institutional structure that would enable the single financial market to develop effectively. However, there is still considerable opposition to an industrial policy based on deregulation and the creation of institutional structures that encourage entrepreneurial activity in a global setting. There is also heated debate as to the effectiveness on EU industrial policy in terms of creating and developing global competitiveness (McPherson, 2000; Daler et al., 2002).

Social policy

In the Treaty of Rome, social policy considerations were mainly concerned with issues connected to eliminating unfair trading advantages arising from discrimination in labour markets. Therefore, laws were passed on equal pay for work of equal value, and discrimination against migrant workers was forbidden. The European Social Fund (ESF) was established in 1961 to provide relatively small amounts of money to help to train disadvantaged workers and their dependants.

The creation of the SEM led to a considerable change in the rationale and potential scope of social policy. A fear arose that the SEM would lead to attempts by companies to reduce working and employment conditions to the lowest levels prevailing in the EU to reduce costs. This, it was argued, would lead to social dumping, that is, the increase in competition would force companies to adopt the lowest possible working employment conditions to ensure survival. If this were not possible, because of high minimum standards in some of the member states, the companies would move to other member states to reap benefits of lower employment costs. A downward spiral in working and employment conditions was predicted and pressure grew for a social dimension to be added to the SEM programme to stop such developments. This led to the Social Charter, a statement on basic social rights, and eventually to the Social Chapter of the Maastricht Treaty.

Concerns over social dumping and the commitment to the Social Chapter led to a raft of directives connected to employment and working conditions. These included: working time directive; parental leave directive; European works council directive; granting rights to a-typical workers (part-time and temporary workers); and a host of directives on safety and health at work. This legislation has had a considerable

impact on the development of employment conditions in the EU (McDonald, 2000a). The UK obtained an opt-out from the Social Chapter and was therefore exempt from most the directives in these areas. However, the Labour government, elected in 1997, dropped UK objections to the Social Chapter and committed the UK to the accepting the Social Dimension to the SEM.

The Treaty of Amsterdam includes a Social Agreement that granted power to the Commission to bring forward directives and policies in four main areas.

1 Improvements to the working environment and employment conditions.
2 Providing the means for workers to have access to information and consultation in matters connected to their employment.
3 Integrating excluded persons, such as the unemployed and the disabled, into the labour market.
4 Promoting equality between men and women in the workplace.

The Amsterdam Treaty included a section on employment that indicated that reducing employment was a high priority for the EU and that the promotion of competitiveness in companies was crucial to the achievment of this goal. Articles 125 to 130 relate to the objectives for employment. These objectives arise from a number of meetings of the European Council, particularly the 1994 meeting in Essen and in 1996 in Dublin. These meetings called for measures to promote investment in education and training, to reduce non-wage costs and to make labour markets more flexible. The tone of the debate on social policy appears to have moved away from legislation to protect the rights of workers towards policies to improve productivity to create more jobs. However, new directives covering rights to information in cases of redundancy, extension of the working time directive and on flexible working have either been approved or are in the pipeline. The Amsterdam Treaty also provided a treaty basis for legislation in the areas of discrimination on the grounds of age, sexual orientation and race. Legislation and policies in theses areas is likely to become an important element in determining employment conditions in the EU. Decisions of the ECJ in matters connected to employment and working conditions are also adding to the EU law in this area. Therefore, although the EU is becoming more concerned with promoting the conditions for more job creation by the private sector, legislation to promote employment rights and to enhance working conditions remains a high priority. This reflects the tendency of the EU to promote a 'social market' type of a single economic system (see Chapter 2).

Environmental policy

Environmental policy has become more important in the EU as a result of growing concern about the ecosystem. Reference to environment policy first appeared in the Paris Summit in 1972 and achieved treaty status in the Single European Act (SEA) in 1987. Its role and importance have grown since and the treaty basis for environmental policy was extended and strengthen in the Treaty of Amsterdam. The Treaty commits the EU to integrate into all of its policies and programmes the objective of promoting 'sustainable development' (European Economy, 2000a). However, the clear commitment to sustainable development by the EU has not been accompanied by a clear workable definition of this term.

Legislation is possible in the future to promote the use of life-cycle analysis. This involves the analysis of the environmental impact of products through all stages from inputs used, production systems, distribution and final disposal of the product. Effective life-cycle analysis would seek to impose the minimum level of environmental damage throughout the whole of the life cycle, not simply at particular stages, for example, at the production stage or the final consumption stage. Further legislation on emission levels from vehicles and on recycling of packaging materials have been proposed. Legislation requiring producers of cars and some types of consumer durables, such as refrigerators, televisions and computers and other types of electronic equipment, to provide the means of recycling their products at the end of their economic life has also emerged. These legislative changes have led to considerable changes in sales and distribution policies, as companies increasingly have to provide the means to recycle not only packaging but also what is left of the product when it reaches the end of its functional life.

Environmental policy raises some problems connected to the concept of fair competition. This is connected to the issue of environmental dumping. This problem arises when member states have differences in the standards set for environmental factors. There are very high standards in Germany, Denmark and The Netherlands and relatively low standards in Spain, Portugal and Greece. This leads to fears that companies will face an incentive to push for lower environmental standards throughout the EU, or they will move production to those countries with lower standards. It is likely that the proposed enlargement of the EU to include many of the countries of Central and Eastern Europe will intensify concerns about this problem.

The global implication of some types of pollution and the growth of global trade means that the EU is increasingly involved in international forums that are concerned with the physical environment (Welford, 2000). International agreements on new trading rules connected to the environment and the establishment of rules on new products such as genetically modified organisms (GMOs) involve the EU and its environmental policy. These issues are explored in Chapter 5.

Public health and consumer protection

The public health and consumer protection policy of the EU was once a minor, rather unimportant policy area that was mainly about technical issues connected to minimum hygiene standards for food, the provision of information to consumers on rights and entitlements and minimum contractual requirements for cross-frontier sales. However, disputes about food safety, the arrival of GMOs on the market place, the growth of cross-frontier trade in services and the development of e-commerce have transformed it into one of the most controversial and important policy areas in the EU (McDonald, 2000b). It is against this background that the EU is seeking to develop a public health and consumer protection policy that will enhance consumer confidence to enable the development of the SEM whilst facilitating good relationships between the member states and with the community's trading partners. Given the complex and politically sensitive nature of many of the problems that need to be overcome, the EU faces a difficult task in creating and developing such a consumer protection policy.

Articles 152 and 153 of the Treaty of Amsterdam provided a firm base for a strong public health and consumer protection policy. The Directorate General of the Commission for

Consumer Protection and Public Health is developing the system for public health and consumer protection to provide strong safeguards to reassure consumers about the safety of food and enhanced protection in areas such as misleading advertising, warranties and product safety. A new agency, the European Food Safety Authority (EFSA), has been founded to help to gather and disseminate information on food safety. More stringent inspections and reports are planned to improve adherence to food safety laws in the member states and in third countries that supply EU markets. Moreover, new laws on product liability for materials used in the food chain and clearer labelling of foodstuffs are being prepared to help to improve the confidence of consumers and national governments about the safety of food. It is hoped that these actions will help to overcome the objections of some national governments to the free movement of foodstuffs and to reassure customers who have been alarmed by the bovine spongiform encephalopathy (BSE) food scare. Plans are also being made to strengthen the rules governing GMOs and on the use of the Internet for commercial purposes. The rules on GMOs and the Internet are important as they provide the legal background under which these new technologies can be used in the EU. As many of the companies that use these technologies are MNCs (especially from the US), the direction taken by the public health and consumer protection policy of the EU will affect relationships with third countries that trade and/or have investments in the EU.

The new approach to public health and consumer protection has led to directives in food safety, trade in services and in areas of new technology such as GMOs and e-commerce. These new laws and the tougher approach to enforcing laws in these areas will affect companies by increasing the requirements to comply with new laws on safety and when passing on information to customers. Moreover, laws governing the sale of GMOs and the use of the Internet will also impact on companies. Laws that help to reassure customers and national governments without imposing undue costs on suppliers will help to expand and develop markets across the EU. However, laws that impose large costs may prove harmful to the growth of such market development. The task of the public health and consumer protection policy is to find the type of policies that reassure customers and national governments without imposing large costs on companies.

Regional policy

The main impetus to develop the regional policy of the EU stemmed from the Paris Summit in 1972. At this summit concern was expressed about pockets of relative poverty in some regions against a background of rising wealth for the Community as whole. Declining industries such as coal, shipbuilding, textiles and clothing were also leading to problems of high unemployment in certain regions. The enlargement of the Community to include Ireland and the UK also added to the regional problem of the EU. The second and third enlargements greatly increased these problems when Greece, and then Portugal and Spain, joined the Community. The process of economic integration that was at the heart of the European integration project was itself contributing to the problem as the reduction in the transaction costs of intra-EU business exercised a tendency for the concentration of business activity in the heartland of the EU (Amin and Thrift, 1994; Amin and Tomaney, 1995). This heartland – the Benelux countries, northern France, Germany, northern Italy and south-east England – became the centre of activity in the EU, leaving a periphery of regions and member states that had much lower levels of development and economic activity.

To counter the problems in the periphery and in regions with declining industries, the EU developed a regional policy that was centred on the use of structural funds – the European Regional Development Fund (ERDF), the European Social Fund (ESF) and the European Agricultural Guidance and Guarantee Fund (EAGGF). These funds were mobilised by a regional policy that would help the periphery and regions with specific problems to develop and to 'catch up' with the heartland. In the early 1990s, the structural funds were increased in size and they became a major source of funds to develop the poorer regions. Ireland, Spain and Portugal received large flows of funds to help to develop the infrastructure. In all of these countries, but especially Ireland, Portugal and the Barcelona and Madrid regions in Spain, large-scale improvements took place. Indeed, by the end of the 1990s, Ireland reached the position where its gross domestic product (GDP) per capita rose above that of the UK. However, there was also a large flow of funds to Greece and Southern Italy, but the relative position of these countries and regions did not significantly improve in the 1990s (European Economy, 2000b).

Some regions where there were problems with declining industries experienced improvement, for example south Wales, but other areas, such as north-east England and Northern Ireland, did not see significant improvements. It seems that the structural funds in themselves are not sufficient to enable the poorer region to 'catch up'. The case of Ireland illustrates that good government policies (low taxes and a business-friendly approach) together with high levels of direct foreign investment (DFI) seem to be more important than liberal application of help from the structural funds. Clearly, the regional policy of the EU may help poorer regions to 'catch up', but they are not sufficient on their own to achieve this goal.

The enlargement of the EU to include many of the countries of Central and Eastern Europe and possibly Turkey presents an enormous challenge to the regional policy. The level of economic development of these countries is considerably lower than the average for the existing 15 member states. The extension of the existing structural funds to cover the new member states is not possible because it would lead to a very significant increase in the size of the budget of the EU and large-scale transfer of income from the rich member states (especially Germany) to the poorer member states. To avoid this problem the EU is seeking to target the structural funds more closely to the poorest regions and areas and to develop policies that are not based on transferring large sums of money. This will mean that poorer regions and areas in the existing member states will receive fewer funds. Furthermore, the poorer regions in the new member states will not be treated as generously as the poorer regions were in the 1990s. It is likely that more emphasis will be placed on identifying the factors of success in countries such as Ireland and seeking to develop policies that will help poorer regions to emulate the success of Ireland.

IMPLICATIONS FOR BUSINESS

The creation of the EMU has a multitude of effects on the environment in which companies have to operate. The major effect of the creation and development of the Customs Union, the Common Market and the EMU is to reduce the costs of conducting intra-EU transactions. This happens as the creation of free movement and a single currency reduces or eliminates costs associated with tariffs, NTBs, currency conversion and exchange rate hedging costs. The economic and social policies of the EU impose costs by requiring organisations to comply with laws and regulations, but also benefits that arise from any improvement in the business environment that follow from these policies. The main implications for the business environment are summarised in Figure 3.1.

THE INCENTIVE TO CLUSTER AND TO DISPERSE

Companies are faced with a changing competitive environment as the development of a single economic space reduces the transaction, production and distribution costs of conducting intra-EU trade. The development of a single economic space also induces increased growth by stimulating growth of intra-EU trade and improving the allocation of resources. These factors encourage companies to relocate and rationalise their operations in response to the challenges and opportunities that arise from the growth of intra-EU trade and investment. In cases where local networks of suppliers and support services exist (or could be created) that confer proximity benefits, the incentive to form or join geographical concentrations (clusters) of companies in the same or related industries will grow as they provide competitive advantages (Porter, 1990; McDonald and Vertova, 2001; McDonald and Vertova, 2002). Clusters provide a fertile ground for spillover benefits such as pools of skilled labour, effective supply chain networks and networks of companies and other supporting agencies that aid the process of effective learning and innovation. These spillover benefits generate competitive benefits that have lower costs and/or higher quality of output than is possible in operations outside of clusters. Such clusters can be observed in, for example, information technology equipment (Silicon Valley), films (Hollywood), international financial services (London) and high-fashion goods (Milan). As the development of a single economic space reduces the costs of supplying the EU market it makes sense to locate in such clusters (to reap these competitive benefits) and to supply the European market from these sites.

Given the importance of transport costs and other benefits of being close to the main markets for your product, most clusters are close to

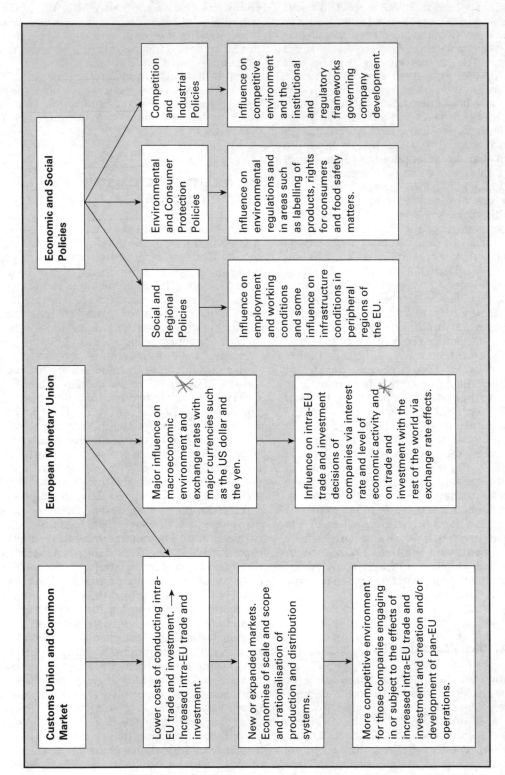

Figure 3.1   *The impact on companies of economic and monetary union*

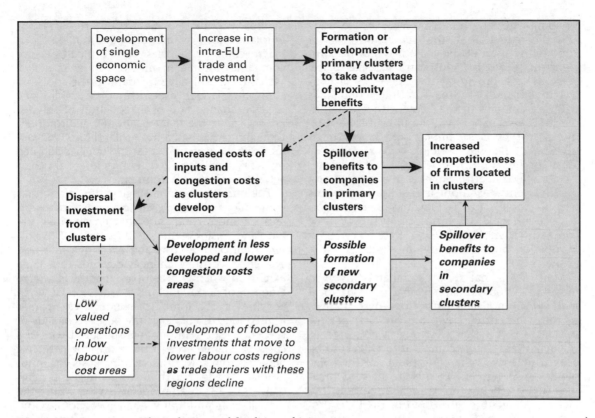

Figure 3.2 *Incentives to form clusters and for dispersal investment*

large markets (Krugman, 1991). However, as well as the incentive to cluster there are also pressures to disperse from clusters because of increases in the price of labour and property that result from the high demand for these resources in clusters. There is also a tendency for congestion costs to rise as clusters grow and develop. These cost increases encourage dispersal to lower cost sites, especially for those activities that do not benefit from location in a cluster. For example, a bank may wish to conduct its wholesale activities in international banking in London, but it could more cheaply and just as effectively carry out mundane paperwork connected to these activities outside of a high-cost area such as London.

Economic integration such as the EMU programme encourages clustering in those industries that can benefit from supplying all or large parts of the EU market from clusters. However, as the clustering process grows and develops incentives to disperse, lower-cost sites appear. Dispersal investment may lead to the development of new clusters in peripheral regions. However, dispersal

investment may be footloose if it is based on seeking low labour costs for mundane operations. In this case dispersal investment may only deliver low value added operation to peripheral regions and such investments may be easily induced to move to other, even lower cost labour areas. As the EU expands, the removal of trade barriers via the liberalisation process of the World Trade Organisation (WTO) and by bilateral trade liberalisation (see Chapter 4), the ability to disperse to lower labour cost areas expands. The ability to retain and develop high value added operations in these circumstances is mainly connected to the generation of spillover benefits and proximity to desirable assets such as large markets and technological knowledge that require companies to locate near such assets. This process of clustering and dispersal is illustrated in Figure 3.2.

Some industries will not be encouraged to engage in clustering in response to economic integration. This will happen when transport costs are high or if there is an absence of proximity and spillover advantages from clustering.

In some cases the removal of barriers to trade and the reduction in the transaction costs of conducting intra-EU business may not be sufficient to allow for clustering to take place. Nevertheless, providing that the costs of conducting intra-EU business decline, companies will face changes to their competitive environment. These changes will be brought about by increased exports and imports and direct foreign investment flows to develop and expand markets. The result of these activities will be to create a more competitive market in both price and quality terms. As more industries and sectors become subject to the lowering of transaction costs connected to intra-EU business, these competitive effects will be forced on a larger number of companies across most sectors of the economy.

Many SMEs that are predominately involved in supplying national, regional or even local markets will not be exempt from these changes to the competitive environment. That part of the SMEs sector that is strongly connected to the activities of large companies are likely to be caught up in the changing nature of the competitive environment in the EU. Large companies that are being forced to restructure in the face of changes brought about by the EMU programme will drag their supporting SMEs into the new, more competitive environment that is emerging in the EU.

EFFECTS OF EUROPEAN MONETARY UNION

European monetary union has created changes that have implications for companies. The introduction of a common monetary policy and a single currency means that the macroeconomic environment in which companies operate alters. The ECB may produce a macroeconomic environment that is conducive to low inflation and high growth, or low inflation but with low growth. Given the high priority for the ECB to deliver low inflation, it is unlikely that Euroland will suffer from high inflation. The euro exchange rate against the dollar and the yen may be high or low, stable of unstable (see Chapter 4). It is also possible that asymmetric shocks may occur within Euroland. These shocks emerge when shocks to the economy caused by, for example, decline in demand for products where the production is strongly centred in one of the member states lead to a need for different macroeconomic policies from the rest of Euroland. However, monetary union makes such macroeconomic policies very difficult. Hence companies located in member states that face such shocks will have to adapt to the shock by controlling labour costs without the cushion of a lower exchange rate or a reduction of interest rates. Clearly, the macroeconomic environment that companies based in Euroland face is uncertain. What is certain is that the policies adopted by the ECB will largely determine the main characteristics of this environment.

The introduction of a single currency requires companies to change over to the new currency, and for those companies that engage in intra-Euroland business there will be an end to currency conversion costs and exchange rate risk. The effect of these changes depends to a large extent on whether a company conducts a large amount of intra-Euroland business relative to activities in its domestic economy. Companies that conduct no or very little business outside of their domestic economy will be faced with the costs of change-over to the euro, but with few benefits from lower transactions costs for intra-Euroland trade. For these companies the main benefits of European monetary union will come, if at all, from an improved macroeconomic environment. The increase in intra-EU trade and investment induced by the monetary union and the enhanced price transparency will add to the growth of a more competitive environment. European monetary union has also stimulated the development of a more integrated European financial markets system that has implications for the development of financial services firms (Houston, 2000; European Economy, 2001a). The main implications for companies of European monetary union are illustrated in Figure 3.3.

EFFECTS OF ECONOMIC AND SOCIAL POLICIES

Many of the economic and social policies of the EU impact on companies whether or not they engage in intra-EU business. For example, directives on working time, parental leave, a-typical workers, health and safety, consumer protection and many areas connected to environmental issues are not restricted to companies that are involved in intra-EU transactions. All companies that are located in the EU must conform to such directives. In cases where there are no direct benefits from implementing these directives,

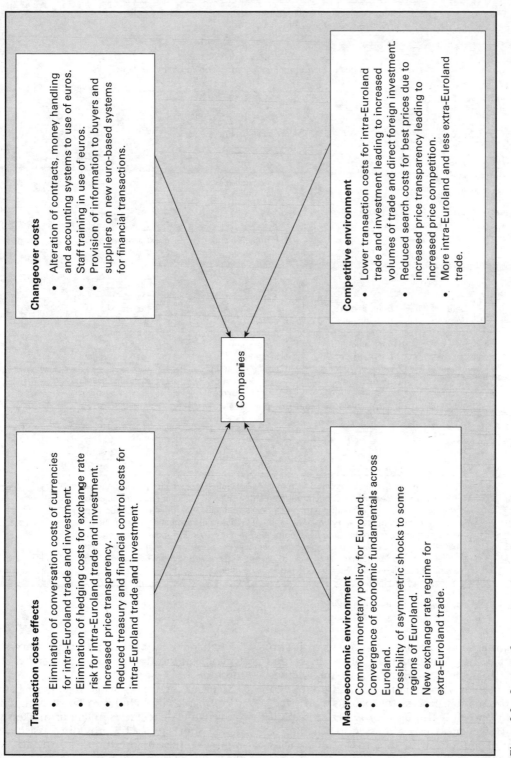

Transaction costs effects

- Elimination of conversation costs of currencies for intra-Euroland trade and investment.
- Elimination of hedging costs for exchange rate risk for intra-Euroland trade and investment.
- Increased price transparency.
- Reduced treasury and financial control costs for intra-Euroland trade and investment.

Changeover costs

- Alteration of contracts, money handling and accounting systems to use of euros.
- Staff training in use of euros.
- Provision of information to buyers and suppliers on new euro-based systems for financial transactions.

Companies

Macroeconomic environment

- Common monetary policy for Euroland.
- Convergence of economic fundamentals across Euroland.
- Possibility of asymmetric shocks to some regions of Euroland.
- New exchange rate regime for extra-Euroland trade.

Competitive environment

- Lower transaction costs for intra-Euroland trade and investment leading to increased volumes of trade and direct foreign investment.
- Reduced search costs for best prices due to increased price transparency leading to increased price competition.
- More intra-Euroland and less extra-Euroland trade.

Figure 3.3 *Impact of monetary union*

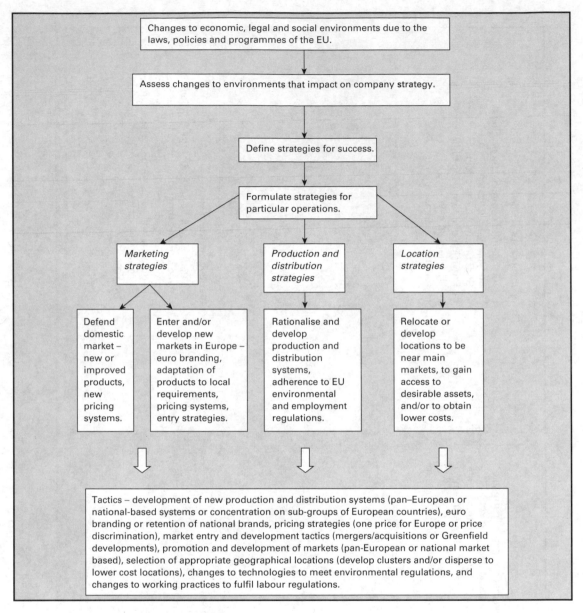

Figure 3.4   *European strategy and operations*

companies are faced with costs with no benefits. These policies may, however, confer benefit to society as whole, for example, environmental laws and regulations and policies to help the market process to operate in an effective way, possibly through consumer protection laws. However, as was discussed in Chapter 2, the implementation of directives and policies varies across the member states and across industries. Therefore, the effect for good or ill of

EU policies is not uniformly experienced, but depends on location in terms of member states and industry.

Some of these policies confer direct benefits to companies by helping to boost productivity to overcome deficiencies in labour markets such as skill shortages or by providing assistance to improve infrastructure by use of the structural funds. Policies to promote R&D and to help companies to adopt 'best practice' procedures also provide direct benefits to companies. Other policies such as competition policy only effect companies that engage in intra-EU transactions. However, the competition policy of the EU can be harmful for companies that are prevented or limited in their desire to merger or acquire companies. Competition policy confers benefits to the society as a whole by seeking to promote competitive markets that provide low-priced high-quality products. The problem with policies such as competition, environmental and social is that they may impose costs on companies that are greater than the benefits to society. The debate on this rages over such questions as directives that seek to improve employment and working conditions, or measures to improve the physical environment.

THE EMU AND STRATEGY AND OPERATIONS OF COMPANIES

The EMU project to create a single economic space is increasingly affecting the strategic and operational polices of the business sector in the EU. The creation of free movement, monetary union and economic and social policies is developing a single economic system that requires companies to react to economic, legal and social changes. These changes require companies to consider the need to defend their markets, enter new markets and to rationalise production and distribution systems. The EMU project also requires companies to make strategic decisions on operational issues such as pricing, branding and other marketing and business issues. An outline of the issues that are affected by the emergence of a single economic space in the EU is given in Figure 3.4.

CONCLUSION

The evolution of the single economic system of the EU is based on policies and programmes to create and develop the EMU. These are well developed in areas such as the free movement of goods, services, capital and labour. European monetary union has further increased the pressures for change to the competitive environment, at least for those countries that have joined Euroland. There have already been profound changes to the business environment because of the success of the EMU project. The

EU has also developed a series of economic and social policies that aid and in some cases hinder the development of competitiveness of companies based in the EU. However, there are still many sectors and industries that have not been significantly affected by the EMU project. As the project continues to evolve, more and more sectors and industries will be drawn into this new system. Furthermore, the links between the single economic system of the EU and the rest of the world are further altering the business environment of companies; these issues are explored in the next chapter.

REFERENCES

Albors-Clorens, A. (2002) 'The changing face of EC Competition Law: reform or revolution?', *European Business Journal*, 14: 31–9.

Amin, A. and Thrift, N. (1994) *Globalisation, Institutions and Regional Development in Europe*. Oxford: Oxford University Press.

Amin, A. and Tomaney, J. (1995) *Behind the Myth of the European Union*. London: Routledge.

Andersen, S. and Eliassen, K. (2001) *Making Policy in Europe*. London: Sage.

Commission (1985) *White Paper – Completing the Internal Market*, Brussels.

Commission (1988) *The Costs of Non-Europe*, Brussels.

Daßler, T., Parker, D. and Saal, D. (2002) 'Economic performance in European telecommunications – 1978–1998: A comparative study', *European Business Review*, 14: 194–209.

Eltis, W. (2000) *Britain, Europe and EMU*. London: Macmillan.

European Economy (2000a) 'Environmental sustainability', *European Economy*, 72.

European Economy (2000b) 'Regional dispersion and activity', *European Economy*, 72.

European Economy (2001a) 'The EU Economy: 2001 – Review of Financial markets integration', *European Economy*, 73.

European Economy (2001b) 'The efficiency defence and the European system of merger control', *European Economy*, 73.

Houston, J. (2000) 'European Financial Markets: Action Plan for the New Economy', *European Business Journal*, 12: 207–15.

Krugman, P. (1991) *Geography and Trade*. Cambridge, MA: MIT Press.

McDonald, F. (1997) 'European Monetary Union: Some Implications for Companies', *Journal of General Management*, 23: 47–64.

McDonald, F. (2000a) 'The European Union and employment relationships', *European Business Review*, 12: 208–15.

McDonald, F. (2000b) 'Consumer Protection Policy in the European Union', *European Business Journal*, 12: 39–55.

McDonald, F. and Dearden, S. (1999) *European Economic Integration*. London: Addison Wesley Longman.

McDonald, F. and Vertova, G. (2001) 'Geographical concentration and competitiveness in the EU', *European Business Review*, 13: 157–65.

McDonald, F. and Vertova, G. (2002) 'Clusters, industrial districts and competitiveness', in *Global Competition and Local Networks*, R. McNaughton and M. Green (eds) Aldershot: Ashgate.

McPherson, C. (2000) 'EU policy inconsistency, market concentration and satellite television: a specific case with pan-business implications', *European Business Journal*, 12: 100–109.

Monti, M. (1996) Review of the Single Market. London: Routledge.

Porter, M. (1990) *The Competitive Advantages of Nations*. London: Macmillan.

Welford, R. (2000) *Corporate Environmental Management: Towards Sustainable Development*. London: Earthscan.

JOURNALS WITH RELEVANT ARTICLES ON ISSUES ON THE EUROPEAN BUSINESS ENVIRONMENT

European Business Journal
European Business Review
European Economy
European Journal of Social Policy
European Urban and Regional Studies
Journal of Common Market Studies

USEFUL WEBSITES

www.ecb.int
The website of the European Central Bank

www.economist.com
The website of *The Economist* provides limited free access (unlimited to subscribers) to articles and surveys on the implications for companies of EU programmes and policies.

www.eubusiness.com
A website on the effects on business of economic and monetary union.

www.euro-emu.co.uk
A website devoted to matters connected to economic and monetary union

www.europa.eu.int
The main website for all matters connected to the EU.

www.ft.com
The website of the *Financial Times* provides limited free access (unlimited for subscribers) to articles and surveys on the implications for companies of EU programmes and policies.

www.unece.org
United Nations Economic Commission for Europe (ECE) – a website with papers, reports and statistics on economic and business conditions in Europe.

The EU is clearly the most important economic bloc in world. The member states include the four largest economies in Europe (France, Germany, Italy and the UK) and with the exception of Iceland, Liechtenstein, Norway and Switzerland all West European countries are members of the EU. Moreover, all countries in Western and Central and Eastern Europe (with the exception of the Russian Federation, Belarus and Ukraine) have close economic relationships with the EU. Most of the countries of Central and Eastern Europe, together with Cyprus and Malta, are likely to be full members in the near future. In the longer-term, Turkey may also become a full member. The EU together with the US and Japan compose what is widely known as the Triad. The Triad is responsible for the bulk of world trade, the majority of international capital flows and is the home base for most of the large multinational corporations (MNCs). The EU exercises a large influence on world trade as it is the largest exporter and importer in the world. Moreover, the EU has wide ranging economic and trading links with most of the developing countries of the world. European monetary union has led to the introduction of a major world currency (the euro) and consequently the EU is now one of the most important financial powers in the world. The importance of the EU to the world economy means that in trade and international monetary matters, the EU together with the US may be regarded as two economic superpowers of the world.

The influence of the EU on the global business environment stems from four main factors.

1   The Common Commercial Policy (CCP) that governs trading relationships between the EU and the rest of the world.
2   The economic and trading relationships between the members of the EU and the rest of Europe.
3   The importance of the EU in the Triad.
4   The possible emergence of the euro as a major world currency.

THE COMMON COMMERCIAL POLICY

Article 113 of the Treaty of Rome granted powers to the Commission to develop and operate a Common Commercial Policy (CCP). These powers give the Commission the power to implement policies approved by the Council of Ministers on tariffs and quotas between the member states and the rest of the world. A decision of the ECJ in 1978 interpreted Article 113 in a manner that gave the Community powers to include negotiations on trade liberalisation in goods and general matters connected to the governing of trade with third countries and with international trade agencies such as the World Trade Organisation (WTO). The Amsterdam Treaty extended the scope of Article 113 (new Article 133) to include negotiations on trade liberalisation of services and intellectual property. The Amsterdam Treaty confirms and extends the powers of the Commission, acting on the instructions of the Council of Ministers, to conduct nearly all aspects of external trade policy.

The Treaty of Rome envisaged a CCP that would promote a progressive movement towards free trade between the Community and the rest of the world. Indeed, the principles of the WTO are that members should not discriminate against each other. This requires the granting of the most favoured nation (MFN) treatment to members of the WTO. This means that members of the WTO should grant the type and level of trade concessions that it gives to the MFN to all countries that belong to the WTO. However, the EU discriminates against countries that are not members of the Community by

EXHIBIT 4.1   EU TRADING AGREEMENTS

The EU has three main types of trading agreements:

- *Preferential agreements*: these agreements allow for trade concessions, mostly on a reciprocal basis. The common external tariff (CET) is usually abolished or significantly reduced for industrial goods, except for textiles. Many types of agricultural goods are also exempt from trade liberalisation in these agreements. The Maghreb countries (Algeria, Morocco and Tunisia), the Mashreq countries (Egypt, Jordan, Lebanon and Syria) and Israel have such preferential agreements with the EU.
- *Association agreements*: these agreements grant considerable access to the EU market for industrial goods. They are often, but not always, the first step towards full membership of the EU. Association agreements have been signed between the EU and most of the countries of Central and Eastern Europe, but not with the republics of the former Soviet Union. These agreements are not fully reciprocal; the EU has granted trade liberalisation to these countries for industrial goods, with the long-term commitment from the countries to grant the EU full access to their markets. Most of these countries regard their association agreements as a stepping-stone to full membership. Many countries – Turkey, Israel, Cyprus and Malta – have long-standing association agreements with the EU. All of these countries, except Israel, have applied for full membership of the EU.
- *Trade relations*: between the EU and most of the former colonies of France, Italy, The Netherlands and the UK are covered by the Lomé Convention and the agreements between the EU and the African, Caribbean and Pacific (ACP) countries. These agreements grant freedom from the CET for industrial goods (but not textiles) and free access for agricultural goods not covered by the Common Agricultural Policy (CAP). Most of the other developing countries are subject to the Generalised System of Preference (GSP) of the WTO. This grants them preferential access to the EU market.

imposing a common system of tariffs, quotas and non-tariff barriers (NTBs) on imports from countries that are not member states. However, the countries of Western Europe that are not member states (Iceland, Norway, Liechtenstein and Switzerland) have special agreements that require them to abide by many of the EU laws on free movement of goods and services for most products, but not for agricultural products covered by the Common Agricultural Policy (CAP). These countries are therefore free from tariffs, quotas and NTBs for most industrial goods and for many services. In addition, the EU has a large number of trading agreements with countries that grant them special access to the markets of the EU for most non-agricultural products (see Exhibit 4.1).

As a result of these agreements only Australia, Canada, China, Japan, New Zealand, the US and the advanced industrialised countries of Asia encounter the full force of the tariffs, quotas and NTBs on their exports to the EU. The EU has agreements with the Australia, Canada, New Zealand and the US to develop the use of mutual recognition to reduce NTBs in trade

between the EU and these countries. A similar agreement is being developed with Japan. All countries confront very strong protection of EU markets for agricultural products and foodstuffs because of the CAP. The textile and clothing markets of the EU are also subject to special forms of protection under the auspices of the Multi-Fibre Arrangement (MFA). The MFA is being progressively dismantled as part of the Uruguay agreement on global trade liberalisation. The Uruguay agreement also provided for action to reduce the level of protection in agricultural products. However, summits of the WTO in the late 1990s and early part of the 2000s have not made much progress towards implementing policies that would dismantle the MFA and in reducing the protection of agricultural products. In both of these areas the EU has been a major obstacle to the successful implementation of the Uruguay agreement and in moving on to promote world trade liberalisation in other areas such as services and international investments.

The EU has, in principle, a strong commitment to the promotion of free trade not only

---

EXHIBIT 4.2   MEASURES USED TO PROTECT AGAINST UNFAIR TRADE

A variety of measures can legitimately be used by the EU to counter unfair trading practices:

- Anti-dumping duties are levied against imports that are deemed to be 'dumped' – sold at less than the cost of production.
- Countervailing duties are applied when an import is suspected of having received a subsidy that confers unfair advantage to exporters.
- Anti-dumping duties and countervailing duties are producer-specific and they normally lapse five years after their imposition.
- Surveillance measures allow the Commission to gather documents and other evidence from exporters that are suspected of engaging in unfair trading practices.
- Counterfeit goods measures allow the member states to confiscate imported goods that are counterfeit.
- The new commercial policy instrument allows the Commission to propose retaliatory measures against imports from countries that unfairly restrict access to their markets for EU exports.

Details of the measures available can be found on the website of the EU at www.europa.eu.int/comm/trade.

---

between its members, but also with the rest of the world. However, the large number of bilateral trading agreements that the EU has negotiated has led to a set of complex rules governing trade with the EU (Davison and Johnson, 2002). There are also questions over the commitment of the EU to multilateral trade liberalisation in WTO negotiations and in the creation of effective WTO trading rules and dispute procedures. There have been a number of serious trade disputes between the EU and the US (that have involved the WTO). For example, complaints from the US about privileged access for bananas to the EU from African, Caribbean and Pacific (ACP) countries and a EU ban on beef where cattle have been injected with hormones. The EU has also complained about tariffs placed on steel imports by the US and tax subsidies to US exporters. These actions call into question the commitment of the EU and the US to abide by WTO rules and trade dispute procedures. The EU is also blocking trade liberalisation in agricultural products because of problems connected to the reform of the CAP.

The CCP includes a set of trade protection measures to safeguard the EU from unfair trading practices (see Exhibit 4.2). These measures are meant to protect companies from unfair competition. However, they can be used to provide protection for European companies that are unable to compete with companies that have cost and/or quality advantages. For example, in 1991 the Commission secured an agreement with the Japanese Ministry of International Trade (MITI) for a voluntary export restraint that limited Japanese exports of cars until the end of 1999, after which the limits were removed. The Commission has also imposed a large number of anti-dumping/countervailing duties and surveillance actions against imports of mainly electrical and electronic goods from Asian countries, notably South Korea and China. Anti-dumping/countervailing duties and surveillance actions are also increasingly being levelled against India and Latin American countries.

The development of the CCP has given the EU significant influence in the various institutions that are concerned with world trade. This influence stems from the role that the institutions of the EU have in many of the important world trade and financial institutions. The EU is involved in four main areas:

1   EU–US transatlantic agenda.
2   EU–Japan framework.
3   Asia–Europe Meeting (ASEM).
4   The WTO and the IMF.

EU-US transatlantic agenda

The New Transatlantic Agenda (NTA) was established in 1995 to promote peace, stability and democracy and to encourage economic relations and expansion of world trade. The Transatlantic Business Dialogue (TBDC) component of the NTA enabled an agreement to be reached to develop a system of mutual recognition of testing and certification procedures for EU–US trade. This agreement is being developed with the objective of establishing a transatlantic marketplace – a type of a single market for EU–US trade (Coen and Grant, 2001). The NTA has also provided a variety of forums where problems connected to the liberalisation of trade in services and the establishing of rules on foreign investment can be discussed. This dialogue is increasingly setting the agenda for trade liberalisation throughout the world. The magnitude of trade and financial flows between the EU and the US mean that if they agree on standards or rules for trade, they exercise enormous influence in determining world standards and rules. Trade conflicts between the EU and the US also influence the ability of agencies such as the WTO to reach agreement on trade rules. In matters connected to new challenges for world trade such as trade in services, genetically modified organisms and e-commerce, agreements between the EU and the US often form the basis for wider agreements. In those areas where the EU and the US cannot agree, it is not normally possible to reach wider agreements.

EU–Japan framework

The EU–Japan framework was established in 1991 and covers political dialogue, economic and trade matters and global challenges (pollution and organised crime). The framework allowed the Commission to make a number of suggestions to the Japanese government on how the deregulation of the economy could be framed in ways that would facilitate attempts by EU companies to enter Japanese markets. As well as these market access issues, the framework has also facilitated the development of cooperation schemes in the areas of R&D and environmental protection issues. The framework is also being used to begin the process of establishing mutual recognition of testing and certification procedures to reduce NTBs in EU–Japanese trade. However, this arrangement is not as advanced as the EU–US system.

Asia–Europe Meeting (ASEM)

ASEM was inaugurated in 1996 at a meeting in Bangkok and includes all the Asian newly industrialised countries (NICs), China and Japan. It provides a forum for sharing information and for discussion on economic relationships, development issues, environmental concerns and educational and cultural matters. Much of the work of ASEM has involved establishing bodies to gather and disseminate information on economic, business, environmental and cultural conditions and problems in the ASEM countries. The economic and business forums, especially the Asia–Europe Business Forum (AEBF) has identified a number of problems associated with trading and are working on ways to reduce the obstacles to trade that arise from tariffs and NTBs. However, ASEM does not have the same type of practical agenda as the NTA. Nevertheless, ASEM is the beginnings of an institutional framework that could develop into a practical system of resolving problems connected to EU–Asian trade (Dent, 1999).

The WTO and the IMF

The Amsterdam Treaty established that the EU was responsible for nearly all matters that are within the remit of the WTO. Therefore, issues connected to trade liberalisation in goods, services and capital and dealing with the trade dispute procedures of the WTO are dealt with by the EU. Many important and controversial issues at the WTO, including attempts to overcome long-standing problems such as trade in agricultural products, textiles and clothing, are handled by the EC. New problems connected to the liberalisation of services, investments, genetically modified organisms (GMOs) and in e-commerce are also dealt with by the EC. The EC also handles negotiations on very contentious issues such as calls for WTO rules on competition policy and on labour and social conditions that affect trade. In nearly all matters connected to international trade, the member states have no direct role as these issues are dealt with at EU level. However, the member states retain their role in the International Monetary Fund (IMF) as each European country is a member and has a say in the running of the IMF. Consequently, in matters connected to international monetary issues, the EC has no real role. Collectively, the member states have potentially a larger voice in the IMF than the US because they have a larger tranche of the assets of the IMF than does the US. If the EU acts collectively, it could exercise considerable power at the IMF (Boles et al., 2002). European monetary union and the introduction of the euro is likely to influence the member states to act together at the IMF, and the European Central Bank (ECB) will be an important actor in the work of the IMF.

THE EU AND THE REST OF EUROPE

Austria, Finland and Sweden joined the EU in 1995 leaving only a handful of West European countries (Iceland, Norway, Liechtenstein and Switzerland) outside the Community. These countries have agreements for the free movement of industrial goods and the adoption of EU laws and some of the policies governing free movement of industrial goods. Free movement of services is increasingly being included in these agreements. In effect these countries are members of the single economic space of the EU with the major exception of the free movement of labour and of agricultural products. The Europe Agreements (see Exhibit 4.1) embrace most of the countries of Central and Eastern Europe and are likely to lead to a free trade area for industrial goods with the progressive adoption of EU laws and policies on free movement. Cyprus and Turkey have both started the process of establishing a customs union (a free trade area with a common external tariff) with the EU. Therefore, the EU will soon have established a free trade for industrial goods that encompasses all of Western Europe, most of Central and Eastern Europe, Malta, Cyprus and Turkey. This free trade area will also progressively adopt EU laws and policies that affect free movement for most goods, services and capital.

Most of the countries of Central and Eastern Europe have begun the process of negotiations and preparations to become full members of the EU. The first wave of countries for membership is Cyprus, the Czech Republic, Estonia, Hungary, Lativia, Lithuania, Malta, Poland, the Slovak Republic and Slovenia; they will become members in May 2004. Consequently, by 2004 the EU will have 25 member states with a combined population of approximately 500 million, but the addition to the GDP would be around 5 per cent. This illustrates the lower level of development of the prospective members compared to most of the existing member states.

The second wave is likely to include Bulgaria and Romania, with a planned accession date of 2007. Turkey may also join this second wave of enlargement, but there are many political and economic problems connected with Turkey's application to join the EU. The remaining countries of Europe (the Russian Federation, Belarus, Moldovia, the Ukraine and the former Yugoslavia – with the exception of Slovenia) are unlikely to join the EU in the foreseeable future. Iceland, Norway, Liechtenstein and Switzerland are not currently members of the EU, but they are nearly fully integrated into most of the economic aspects of the Union. Thus, the EU will have 25 members in 2004 and possibly 27 by 2007. If Turkey and the West European countries that are not members were to join, the EU would have 32 members. This prospect presents a tremendous challenge to the institutional, economic and political structures of the EU and will have significant implications for business operations in Europe.

The institutional challenge of enlargement

The institutional challenge stems from the need to reform the decision-making and political structures of the EU. The institutions of the EU are already finding it difficult to work effectively with 15 members. Each member state takes its turn at acting as President of the European Council, but the ability of the small member states to cope with the logistical and administrative pressures of the Presidency is open to question. A Commission and a Council of Ministers that was drawn from 21 or 27 or possibly 32 member states would be very difficult to run effectively, given the existing rules on vetoes and national government nominations for Commissioners. Currently, the institutions have to work with 11 official languages; with a possible membership of 32 countries the number of official languages could rise to around 27. The most serious political problem for enlargement would be to effectively make, implement, monitor and enforce EU laws and policies. The EU is already encountering difficulties with these problems with 15 member states, most of which have well-developed political and legal systems (see Chapter 3). The admission of countries with less well-developed political and legal systems would pose significant problems unless the institutional structures of the EU were streamlined and made more effective. The problem of the democratic accountability of the institutions of the EU is also of growing importance because the laws and policies of the Community increasingly affect a large range of economic, social and political areas. In the interests of good government it is important that these laws and policies are subject to the test of democratic processes.

Many of the applicant countries are developing new democratic systems to replace communist systems of government. This often involves radical change to political systems that have been entrenched in communist ideology for many decades. To satisfy the conditions for EU membership, political systems in the member states must be democratic and capable of implementing, monitoring and enforcing EU law and policies. Some of the countries in Central and Eastern Europe and Turkey will find it difficult to satisfy these criteria. In the case of Cyprus a solution needs to be found to the bitter division of the island into Greek and Turkish areas. Concern over human rights issues in Turkey and some of the Central and Eastern countries also pose serious problems for membership of the EU. Furthermore, enlargement to include most of the countries of Central and Eastern Europe and Turkey in the EU would also bring in countries with very different values and culturally-determined attitudes. This could significantly affect the problems of securing agreement on laws and policies.

The member states have struggled to agree on a viable plan for the type of radical change that is necessary to make the institutional system effective. The main problem is the reluctance of the member states to grant the European Parliament (EP) new powers to make the institutions of the EU more accountable. There is also a need to create workable and effective relationships between national governments and the institutions of the EU. The most radical solution would be the creation of a federal system with a well-defined constitution and a federal system of government based on European political parties. However, such a solution is unlikely in the foreseeable future. Therefore, the enlargement of the EU is likely to increase the problems of the effective government of the single economic space that will emerge from the enlarged EU. The EU will certainly become larger, but it is likely that it will not become more effective in the government of the single economic space. The EU is engaged in a process of negotiations to agree on institutional reform (see Chapter 3).

The economic and political challenges of enlargement

There are many economic challenges connected to the enlargement (Gower and Redmond, 2000). The level of development (in terms of GDP per head and other measures of economic welfare) of the applicant countries is considerably lower than the average for the current 15 member states. Moreover, many of the applicant countries are in the process of transforming their economies into market-based systems. This requires large-scale privatisation and the construction of new political and economic institutions. More importantly, new attitudes to work and to the way that business is conducted have to be developed. Moreover, new technologies and production systems have to be introduced and managers and workers have to learn how to use effectively these new systems. Given the large differences in levels of economic development, the granting of free movement of people to the applicant countries may well lead to considerable migration of people from countries with low levels of economic development to the heartland of the EU in north-west Europe. Such migration would bring economic, political and social challenges to the richer member states.

The EU defined, in a Summit in Copenhagen, a set of conditions that must be fulfilled before these applicants can be considered for membership. To prepare the EU for enlargement, an agenda (Agenda 2000) of major changes to institutions and policies was determined (see www.europa.eu.int for details of the Copenhagen Criteria and Agenda 2000 and the progress that has been made with the Agenda). Although negotiations have begun for the first wave of applicants, it is clear that the challenges set out in the Copenhagen Criteria and Agenda 2000 have yet to be fully resolved. This implies that the EU may be enlarged before the political and economic challenges of growth have been met. Consequently, the EU is likely to be faced with a group of member states that will have difficulty in adjusting to the political and economic demands of being part of the Union. Moreover, if the EU grants membership before it has agreed and implemented internal institutional change, the government of the single economic space of the EU is likely to be hampered by institutional log-jam and inertia.

The EU is set to become the largest market in the world, with 27 or possible 32 countries committed to creating a single economic space and in the long term a single monetary system with a common currency. In principle, this should present opportunities to establish European-wide business and marketing systems that would rival or indeed surpass the size and scope of the US economy. However, the existing single economic space of the 15 member states does not provide the same type of single economic space as the US and it has many unresolved problems (see Chapter 3). Enlargement to 27 or 32 member states with very different legal, economic, social and cultural systems will present considerabe challenges that are likely to delay the creation and maintenance of an effective single economic space. Therefore, most of Europe will become a type of a single economic space but it is likely that significant barriers and obstacles to free and effective movement of goods, services, labour and capital will remain for many years. Indeed, enlargement may slow the process unless solutions to the institutional, political and economic obstacles to good government of the single economic space are found.

Enlargement will increase the importance of the EU in institutions such as the WTO and the IMF because the Union will increasingly become the main agency for negotiations and developments for European countries in these institutions. The EU together with the USA will have significant power in the WTO and if European monetary union progresses in the IMF (Boles et al., 2002).

THE EU AND THE TRIAD

The trade and financial relationship between the US, Japan and Europe are often referred to as the Triad (Dent, 1997). The economic relationships between the members of the Triad have a strong impact on developments in the world economy. The combined share of world exports of the Triad in 1998 was 45 per cent, with the EU and the US accounting for 36 per cent (19.7 per cent and 16.3 per cent respectively) of this trade. The members of the Triad accounted for 83 per cent of the GDP of the Organisation for Economic Cooperation and Development (OECD), of which 34.5 per cent came from the EU and 35.3 per cent from the US (OECD, Main Economic Indicators, 1998, see their website for latest data at www.oecd. org). The mechanisms that link these economies are not fully understood, but trading, financial and investment links play a key role in the process. Links created by international financial markets that are centred in the US (New York and

Chicago), Japan (Tokyo) and Europe (London) yokes the EU to the US and Japan. Changes in stock, futures and exchange rate markets in one of these centres are quickly picked up by the other centres, and funds flow freely between these markets in response to these changes. This process is of great importance in the transmission of cyclical changes in economic activity.

Trading and financial links between the EU and Japan are not as well developed as those with the US, and the links to the Asian NICs are at an early stage of development. In terms of exports the largest market for the EU is the rest of Europe (33 per cent), then the US (22 per cent), with Japan taking less than Africa (4 per cent and 8 per cent respectively). The whole of Asia (including China, Japan, India and the Asian NICs) took 18 per cent of the EU exports (Eurostat: Foreign Trade Statistics, 1999; see the Europa website for latest data at www.europa. eu.int). In terms of investment flows, the main flows are also between the EU and the US and between Japan and the US. Clearly, Japan and the Asian NICs do not have strong direct economic links with the EU. However, Japan and the other Asian economies are strongly connected to the US and America has strong links to the EU. The major links between the Triad arise from the focal position that the US has in linking the three areas to the powerhouse of the world economy.

The Triad is also the home base for most of the large multinational companies (Dicken, 1998). In 2001, of the top 100 companies, measured by market capitalisation, 67 per cent were American, 29 per cent had their headquarters in Europe (3 per cent of which were based in Switzerland) and 3 per cent are Japanese. The US had 50 per cent of the top 500 companies, while the figures for the Europe and Japan were respectively 35 and 10 per cent (*Financial Times*, FT 500, 2001). Generally, US companies have a strong presence in a wide range of industries, for example, information technology products and services (Time Warner AOL, Cisco Systems and Microsoft), vehicle production (Ford and General Motors), oil (Exxon and Mobil), aerospace equipment (Boeing) and personal hygiene products (Proctor & Gamble and Colgate). The Europeans have a few world leaders such as Vodafone/Mannesmann in mobile telecommunication services, pharmaceutical companies Glaxo SmithKline, and oil companies BP Amoco and Royal Dutch Shell. European companies are also strong in a number of other sectors, for example, food and drinks industries (Nestlé, Diageo and Unilever) and vehicle production

(DaimlerChrysler, Volkswagen and Renault). The Japanese have world-class companies in vehicle production (Toyota and Honda), electronics (Hitachi, Matushita, NEC and Sony) and trading companies (Mitsubishi, Mitsui and Sumitomo).

Clearly, economic transactions within and between the members of the Triad are the main generators of the world economy. The US provides the pivotal role of linking the Triad because EU–Japanese links are considerably less important than EU–US and Japan–US transactions. The development of economic integration in Europe and the creation of the North American Free Trade Area (NAFTA) between the US, Canada and Mexico hold the prospect that the Triad may evolve into three trading groups based on NAFTA, the EU and Japan. As Japan has close trading and economic links to the Asian NICs, this would bring them into an extended Triad. Another possibility is the development of Asia–Pacific Economic Cooperation (APEC) as a free trade area that would include Japan, the Asian NICs, Canada and the US. The EU would have strong links to such a grouping because of its strong economic connections with the US. Given the strong trading and economic relationships between the EU and the rest of Europe and the many trading relationships that the EU has with developing countries, it is clear that the EU plays a central role in linking the economies of world into a type of a global economic system. The heart of this global nexus is EU–US relationships.

THE IMPACT OF EUROPEAN MONETARY UNION

The establishment of European monetary union is likely to have two main effects on international monetary issues:

- the introduction of a new currency that may become important for the finance of international business activities; and
- a change in the balance of power in the international monetary system.

Financing international business activities

The attraction of using a major world currency to finance international business activities follows from the lower transaction costs that are made possible by using such currencies. Buying and selling currencies to finance business activities involves transaction costs. If a large number of currencies are used, the transaction costs can be large. Furthermore, a measure of risk is involved when different currencies are used because of fluctuations in exchange rates. Using currencies that are widely traded and backed by a large economy can reduce these costs and risks. Currently, the US dollar and, to a much lesser extent, the euro and the yen are used as international currencies.

Much of international trade is invoiced and paid for in US dollars, for example, all trade in crude oil, most primary commodities and a substantial part of the trade of countries. The use of the dollar reduces the costs of invoicing and paying in a multitude of currencies. The dollar is also used as a vehicle currency in exchange markets. Therefore, instead of exchanging South Korean won for Brazilian real, won can be exchanged for dollars and the dollars are then exchanged for real. The size of dollar markets means that there are lower transaction costs when using the dollar in converting into these minor currencies rather than using direct conversion from South Korean won. Dollar-denominated assets are the most important way of providing the means by which capital is transferred (across frontiers) from savers to borrowers. Most financial instruments that are traded internationally (for example, bonds, derivatives, swaps) are denominated in dollars. Moreover, governments hold the majority of their foreign currency reserves in dollars. The dollar is, therefore, the most important currency in international capital markets and in the reserves of governments.

The introduction of the euro has led to a shift from the dollar in the invoicing and payment of international trade, as a vehicle currency and in international capital markets. There has also been some shift from the dollar in government holdings of foreign reserves.

Most intra-EU trade (except for crude oil and basic commodities) is likely to move to the use of the euro for invoicing and payment. Some of the countries that conduct the bulk of their trade with the EU may also move to the use of the euro in invoicing and payment. This will lead to a decline in the demand for dollars in Euroland. The introduction of the euro will eliminate the use of the dollar as a vehicle currency for third-party exchanges that involve members of Euroland and perhaps for those member states that do not enter the first phase of monetary union (for example, the UK). The euro may also be used as a vehicle currency for those countries that have significant trade with the EU (for example, Central and Eastern European countries). In the long run it is possible that the euro would be used as a vehicle currency all over the world. This is likely to happen if the euro develops deep and wide markets that lead to low transaction costs compared to the dollar. Such developments could only happen over a fairly long period because euro financial markets will have to develop before they can effectively handle large-scale trade in euro and euro-denominated assets.

The denomination of government and private bonds in euros is creating a very large euro bond market. The bond market could develop low transaction costs relative to the dollar markets and thereby lead to substantial movements from dollar asset to euro assets. Euro equity markets could also develop as serious competitors to the dollar-dominated equity markets. Euronex, a merger of the stock exchanges of Amsterdam, Brussels, Lisbon, Liffe (in London) and Paris has already created a prototype European stock exchange. The two largest stock exchanges in Europe (the London Stock Exchange and the Deutsche Börse in Frankfurt) are looking for partners to create another large European stock exchange. It is possible that Euronex could be expanded by membership of the two largest stock exchanges to create a very large European bourse. The introduction of the euro has stimulated the development of larger and more effective bond and equity markets that could help in the transition of the euro into a major world currency that could challenge the current dominance of the US dollar.

If the introduction of the euro leads to a small and gradual decrease in the use of the dollar, it is probable that euro–dollar–yen exchange rates will not be significantly affected by the shift to the euro. However, a large and rapid shift towards the use of the euro could have significant effects on the dollar exchange rate. In these circumstances euro–dollar–yen exchange rates could be very volatile and cooperation between the members of the Triad may become difficult to maintain.

New international monetary system

It is possible that the establishment of European monetary union will stimulate a greater degree of cooperation in international monetary and economic affairs. In particular, monetary union could lead to a bi-polar EU–US system of cooperation that could be more effective than the current system in terms of creating the conditions that would allow for a more stable international monetary order. In this system the dollar and the euro would be the dominant world currencies, with the yen playing a much smaller role. However, in the post-Second World War period the international monetary system has been dominated by the dollar. A large switch towards the euro may disturb this system and cause instability in the dollar–euro–yen exchange rates. This might lead to instability in the international monetary system and to a consequent period of turbulence in world trade and financial transactions.

The euro may be a strong and stable or a weak and unstable currency. Whatever happens, the euro exchange rate is likely to have different characteristics than existing relationships between national currencies and the dollar and the yen. This has implications for the development of the competitiveness of companies. The euro–dollar–yen exchange rate will reflect the conditions between the US, Japan and Euroland. These conditions may be different from those that prevail in the current dollar–yen relationship of the member states. This could lead to euro–dollar–yen exchange rates that are significantly different from the rate that prevailed in the dollar–yen exchange rates of the member states before they joined the EMU. It is possible that some member states could be faced with significant changes to their exchange rate against the dollar–yen. Such an outcome has important implications for companies that have large levels of extra-EU transactions.

IMPLICATIONS FOR BUSINESS

The relationship between the EU and the rest of the world influences business activities in three main areas:

- the creation and development of rules of trade and of trading relationships with the rest of the world;
- the emergence of a single economic space that embraces most of Europe; and
- the impact of the euro on extra-Euroland trade and investment.

TRADING RULES AND AGREEMENTS

The development of the CCP has led to the EU governing nearly every aspect of trading relationships, including trade rules and the development of bilateral trading agreements with third countries. Companies that engage in extra-EU trade can approach the Commission to complain about unfair trading practices because it has the power to levy trade protection measures against third countries. Voicing problems with access to the markets of third countries to obtain measures to open up the markets of third countries is also best dealt with by approaching the institutions of the EU. Moreover, companies that wish to influence the development of policies which affect extra-EU trade need to lobby the institutions of the EU.

The CCP requires that the EU take the prime role on behalf of the member states in international negotiations on agreements at the WTO and other international institutions. Consequently, companies that are interested in the development of trade rules which emerge from international agreements in areas such as rules for GMOs and e-commerce should lobby the institutions of the EU as well as their national governments. The importance of EU–US agreements on mutual recognition and other trading rules means that agreements between the EU and the US often form the basis of world trading rules. Businesses have direct access to EU–US discussions on these issues through the TABC of the NTA and specialist bodies such as the Transatlantic Consumer Dialogue (TACD).

The EU negotiates on behalf of the member states at the WTO in areas such as liberalisation of trade in goods (the General Agreement on Tariffs and Trades, or GATT) and in services (the General Agreement on Trade in Services, or GATS). The WTO is also the centre for negotiations on developing trade rules connected to trading problems arising from differences in industrial, competition, social and economic policies in the members of the WTO. The EU negotiates at the WTO on controversial issues such as developing rules to combating national industrial and competition policies that lead to unfair trading and restricted access to markets. Even more controversially, the WTO is the main area where talks take place on developing rules to prevent the use of child labour in developing countries and other social and economic policies that are deemed to lead to unfair trading conditions. The EU also represents the interests of the member states in WTO disputes procedures with other members of the WTO.

Clearly, the institutions of the EU are the main bodies responsible for the governance and development of the rules and agreements that shape the legal frameworks under which extra-EU trade take place. Moreover, the governance and development of the legal environment that shapes access to the markets of the member states by third countries are also largely the work of the institutions of the EU. These frameworks govern not only trade in goods but increasingly services. The growth of mutual recognition agreements between the EU and its major trading partners that is being developed is also reducing NTBs which companies that are not based in the EU face. This development is helping to integrate many of the markets of the EU into the global economy. This process has large-scale implications for the competitive challenges and opportunities that companies based in the member states are facing. Companies that wish to influence these processes need to effectively lobby the institutions of the EU.

The emerging European single economic space

The Europe Agreements and the prospect of enlargement of the EU to include most of the countries of Europe holds the prospects of a single economic space that would embrace most of Europe. The existing member states form a type of a single economic space that is gradually encompassing all of Western and most of Central and Eastern Europe (see Figure 4.1). In the near future the single economic space that is emerging may include up to 32 countries. However, this system covers countries with very different political, economic and social characteristics. Moreover, it is not clear if this single economic space will be an effective free movement area in the way that the US is a single economic system (see Chapter 3).

The EU faces many challenges to create and govern such a single economic system. Nevertheless, companies are likely to find that the NTBs they face when conducting business within this system are progressively reduced. Furthermore, the limitations on free movement within this area will also be reduced. The combined effect of these developments will be to induce a measure of integration of many European markets in the single economic space

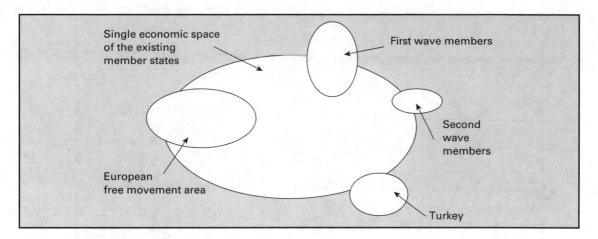

Figure 4.1   *The emerging European single economic space*

European free movement area: Iceland, Liechtenstein, Norway and Switzerland.

First wave member: Cyprus, Estonia, the Czech Republic, Hungary Latvia, Lithunia, Malta, Poland, the Slovak Republic and Slovenia.

Second wave members: Bulgeria and Romania.

Turkey, Cyprus and Malta have free access to the EU for most industrial goods, and Turkey and Cyprus are implementing a Custom Union with the EU.

that is centred in the EU. In those markets that have the economic and cultural conditions that are conducive to pan-European operations it is likely that the development of the single economic space will generate substantial cross-frontier mergers and acquisitions. New distribution and logistical systems are also likely to emerge to take advantage of the integration of the markets of the single economic system. However, such a European single economic space would include countries with significant differences in levels of economic development and in cultural conditions. These differences may lead to the bulk of business operations (especially those that cross frontiers) being located in the existing heartland of the EU with perhaps a few countries or regions managing to join this club.

The importance of the EU as a major player in the Triad means that access to the European single economic space by MNCs based in the US and Japan is likely to grow. Mergers and acquisitions, including mergers between MNCs in the different parts of the Triad, are also likely to grow. This process is already under way with mergers such as Renault/Nissan, BP Amco and DaimlerChrysler. Within the single economic space, new large MNCs are likely to arise to take advantage of the large markets in Europe. These MNCs are also likely to be key players in the global system that revolves around the Triad. This process is also under way with merger and acquisitions such as the Vodafone takeover of Mannesmann.

The impact of the euro on extra-Euroland trade and investment

The exchange rate between the euro and the US dollar and to a lesser extent the yen has important implications for extra-Euroland trade and investment. These exchange rates affect the price of the exports and imports of Euroland countries and also influence the strategies and operations of MNCs by altering the attractiveness of Euroland as a base for producing for Europe and the rest of the world. Therefore, DFI inflows and outflows from Euroland are influenced by these exchange rates. Moreover, these exchange rates affect global economic conditions as they act as one of the main conduits that transmit booms and slumps across the global economy, and also contribute to the stability or instability of the global economy depending if the exchange rates are stable or volatile. These issues are outlined in Figure 4.2.

Unstable exchange rates may not have a great influence on extra-Euroland direct foreign

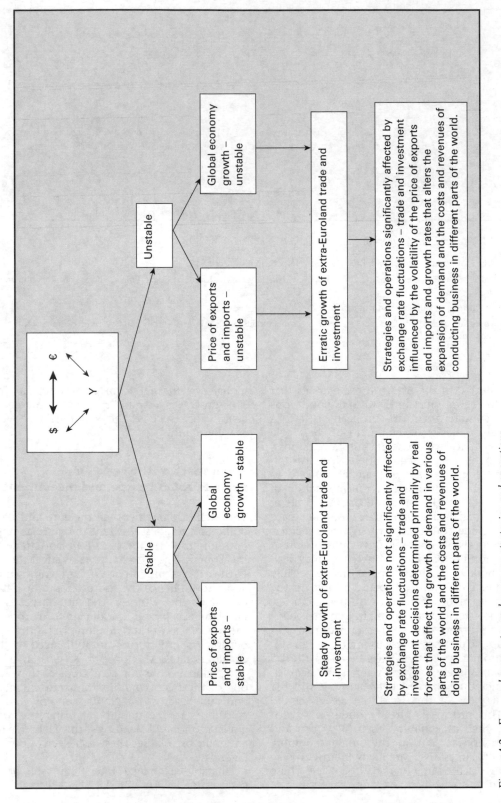

Figure 4.2 *Euro exchange rates and company strategies and operations*

investment (DFI) inflows and outflows because decisions about acquiring or expanding the ownership of real assets is normally not significantly influenced by short-run exchange rate changes. However, portfolio investments, particularly short-run investments, are strongly influenced by exchange rate changes because exchange rate changes are associated with changes (and expected changes) in macroeconomic variables such as inflation and interest rates, and these variables largely determine short-run international portfolio investments. Furthermore, changes in these macroeconomic variables have a strong influence on growth and thereby indirectly on DFI because erratic growth increases uncertainty about future costs and revenues and thereby tends to reduce investment. Clearly, unstable exchange rates between the euro and the US dollar and to a lesser extent the yen have a bad effect on extra-Euroland trade and investment. In this respect the creation and development of a new international monetary system that could limit harmful fluctuations in these exchange rates could be important for the steady expansion of extra-Euroland trade and investment.

A possible important affect of the euro for DFI inflows is the position of European countries that are not in Euroland. These countries are potential locations for DFI to supply all or large parts of Europe. As Euroland includes all of the large economies of the EU, with the important exception of the UK, supplying Euroland countries from European locations is likely to be important. However, if these locations are in the UK, for example, supplying Euroland from the UK entails the incurring of transaction costs and uncertainty associated with fluctuating exchange rates. It is possible that this would deter DFI inflows into countries such as the UK (Kewley, 2001; McDonald and Burton, 2002).

Thus far, there is little evidence that the UK has lost DFI inflows because of this problem. This may be because the UK is a large market and this therefore makes the UK an attractive location. The UK also has other advantages as a location for DFI inflows because of its desirable assets such as expertise in investment and corporate banking, technological knowledge in areas such as pharmaceuticals, information technology and telecommunications equipment and services. Moreover, the UK is English speaking (attractive for US and Asian investors) and has lower costs (than many Euroland countries) in areas such as hiring and firing labour and in many aspects of corporate governance. Nevertheless, the transaction costs and uncertainty disadvantages of not being in Euroland could be significant for DFI inflows that are not attracted by the size of the UK market and/or the type of assets outlined above. European countries that are not in Euroland and which do not have large domestic markets and lack the desirable characteristics that are currently helpful for the attraction of DFI inflows into the UK are likely to be less attractive for DFI inflows than countries in Euroland.

CONCLUSION

The development of the powers of the institutions of the EU to negotiate on behalf of the member states in matters connected to trade liberalisation and in the conduct of trade disputes has placed the EU in an important position in the development of the global trading environment. This role is becoming more important as trade liberalisation and the creation of new trading rules is emerging in areas such as services, capital and new products such as GMOs and computer and telecommunication based products. The moves towards global trade rules to govern the impact of competition, social and environmental policies on trade and investment has also placed the institutions of the EU at the heart of the negotiations on the development of the global trading and investment system. The evolution of the EU to encompass most of Europe into an emerging single economic space has also placed the Community, together with the US, as an economic superpower that can and does exercise considerable influence on developments in the global economy. The size and significance of the European economic space has also made the EU an attractive location for investments, and as both a source of goods and services for the rest of the world and as a market for exports. However, the European single economic space is still developing and even within its core there exists considerable differences in legal, economic, social and cultural environments (see also Chapter 2). Therefore, the business strategy and operations of companies located in, or doing business in, this economic space is complex and is also rapidly changing. The successful launch of the EMU has further added to this complexity because not all the members of the single economic space are currently members of

Euroland. Furthermore, the euro has altered the conditions of extra-Euroland trade and investment, thereby adding another layer of complexity to the evolving single economic space of Europe.

REFERENCES

Boles, K., McDonald, F. and Healey, N. (2002) 'The Euro: A Future International Currency?', in *European Integration in the 21st Century*, M. Farrell, S. Fella and M. Newman (eds). London: Sage. pp. 119–34.

Coen, D. and Grant, W. (2001) 'Corporate Political Strategy and Global Policy', *European Business Journal*, 13: 37–44.

Davison, L. and Johnson, D. (2002) 'Multilateralism, bilateralism and unilateralism: a critical commentary on the EU's triple track approach to the international dimension of competition policy', *European Business Review*, 14: 7–19.

Dent, C. (1997) *The European Economy*. London: Routledge.

Dent, C. (1999) *The European Union and East Asia*. London: Routledge.

Dicken, P. (1998) Global Shift. London: Sage.

Eurostat (1999) *Foreign Trade Statistics*. Luxemburg: Office for the Official Publications of the European Communities.

Financial Times (2001) *Top 500 FT Index Companies*. London: Financial Times.

Gower, J. and Redmond, J. (2000) *Enlarging the European Union*. Aldershot: Ashgate.

Kewley, S. (2001) 'Japanese automotive manufacturing investment in the UK and the euro debate', *European Business Journal,* 13: 167–76.

McDonald, F. and Burton, F. (2002) *International Business* Ch. 5. London: Thomson.

JOURNALS THAT HAVE RELEVANT ARTICLES ON ISSUES CONNECTED TO THE EU AND THE WORLD

European Business Journal
European Business Review
European Economy
Journal of Common Market Studies

USEFUL WEBSITES

www.bis.org
The website of the Bank of International Settlements provides information on the use of the euro in international markets.

www.ecb.int
The website of the ECB provides information on European monetary union.

www.europa.eu.int
The main website for all matters connected to the EU.

www.imf.org
The website provides details of the activities of the IMF.

www.oecd.org
The web site of the OECD provides information on many matters connected to international trade and business.

www.wto.org
This website provides details on trade regulations and liberalisation.

PART II: TACTICS AND IMPLICATIONS FOR THE EUROPEAN UNION

European marketing has similarities to international marketing in that it involves managing the multitude of decisions necessary when selling products (goods, services and combinations of goods and services) across frontiers. These frontiers lead to barriers that differentiate European marketing from domestic marketing. However, the strength of these barriers varies according to which European country is the focus of marketing activities. Thus members of the EU have fewer barriers that non-members, but there are still barriers (see Chapter 3). European countries with close connections to the EU, but that are not members, have lower barriers than those that have less links with the EU (see Chapter 4). Members of Euroland use the same currency – the euro – and therefore face zero barriers connected to exchange rate risk and currency transactions costs. This makes pricing and investment decisions within Euroland different from transactions with European countries that are not in Euroland.

Marketing in Europe involves managing activities that lie somewhere between domestic and international marketing. Countries that are integrated into the EU and Euroland face marketing management with these member states that closely resembles domestic marketing. However, even within the EU and Euroland, legal and economic differences exist that makes European marketing different from domestic marketing. Marketing to European countries that are not in the EU or Euroland involves larger legal and economic differences. Social and cultural differences also exist between European countries and these contribute to the differences between European and domestic marketing. Companies that are not in Europe but wish to engage in transactions with European countries face a complex type of international marketing because they are dealing with countries that have similarities but also significant differences.

This chapter begins with an overview of the key elements of the study of European marketing with an assessment of how it fits into the debates about Europeanisation/internationalisation. This is followed by sections on some practical aspects of European marketing. The first of these sections investigates the main methods that are used to assess the various market environments in which European marketing takes place. The practicalities of deciding on the characteristics of products, pricing, promotion and distribution are then considered.

THE CHARACTERISTICS OF EUROPEAN MARKETING

The essence of European marketing is not substantially different from international marketing in that it involves creating and developing the means to manage the differences in legal, economic, social and cultural conditions in the European countries that are selected for business operations. The main differences between European marketing and domestic marketing relate to barriers to cross-frontier trade. These barriers differ according to whether the European country is a member of the EU and of Euroland. Moreover, for those European countries that are not members of the EU, the level of their integration into the EU is the main determinant of differences between European and domestic marketing. Countries that are not in Europe but wish to conduct business in Europe face a complicated marketing environment with many legal and economic similarities but with differences according to which part of Europe is under consideration. Social and cultural differences exist even within the highly integrated countries of the EU and these factors are very different when considering the countries of North-west Europe compared with Southern Europe or Eastern Europe. Even within these regions, pronounced social and cultural differences exist.

European marketing can be viewed as a special type of international marketing but with some similarities to domestic marketing for those European countries that have few legal, economic, social and cultural differences. The established members of the EU and those countries in Euroland have the lowest level of legal and economic barriers between these countries. However, even these countries have some significant barriers in these areas (see Chapter 3). Those European countries that will soon join the EU have more legal and economic barriers and these will only slowly be reduced as they integrate into EU systems (see Chapter 4). Those European countries that are not members and which do not have close links with the EU have the highest legal and economic barriers (see Chapter 4). Companies not based in Europe face a complex international marketing environment, in terms of legal and economic barriers, because they face a set of countries that have different legal and economic conditions but some of them have relatively few significant differences. The social and cultural characteristics of Europe differ greatly, requiring considerable adjustments to European marketing strategies depending on which country is being considered. Clearly, Europe is a long way from being a single domestic market for European firms or a single foreign market for companies not based in Europe.

EUROPEAN MARKETING AND INTERNATIONAL MARKETING

The section above has argued that the distinction between European and international marketing depend largely on differences in legal, economic, social and cultural differences. However, the most important factors relating to international marketing have a bearing on European marketing. Therefore, the main literature and debates on international marketing have relevance for European marketing.

The essence of what constitutes international marketing emerged in the literature in the 1980s and the early 1990s (Cavusgil and Nevin, 1980, 1981; Douglas and Craig, 1989, 1992; Johanson and Mattson, 1986; Håkansson, 1982; Turnbull

and Valla, 1986) and two early works on the development of exporting (Bilkey and Tesar, 1977; Johanson and Weidersheim-Paul, 1975). This work identifies the strategic and managerial issues connected to internationalisation as the major focus of research work in international marketing. A number of key issues emerged from this literature:

- the process of internationalisation and the link to international marketing;
- the importance of networks in international marketing; and
- the decision on whether to segment or standardise products.

The process of internationalisation

The Uppsala Internationalisation Model suggests that internationalisation proceeds, by a process of learning, from exporting to the establishment of higher-level activities such as foreign production sites and product development facilities (Johanson and Vahlne, 1977). A similar developmental process is postulated in innovation-related internationalisation models (Bilkey and Tesar, 1977). Stage models of internationalisation stress the importance of learning, often originating from exposure to similar but slightly different cultural environments, that induce the development of internationalisation strategies on a steady path towards more complex and deep involvement with foreign markets. However, these models are rather mechanistic and suggest that companies follow a rigid linear development of internationalisation that is often not verified by empirical work (Andersen, 1993).

Theories based on the development of networks (Turnbull and Valla, 1986) sought to clarify the complex factors that appear to determine the internationalisation path of companies. These theories adopt a less mechanical view of the process of internationalisation. Notwithstanding the debate on how best to capture the many factors that influence the development of the internationalisation processes of companies, most of the theories and empirical evidence provides support for the view that internationalisation follows an evolutionary processes that develops over time. The time path and major characteristics of this evolutionary process seems to be influenced by a variety of factors, but in it seems that companies normally follow a progression from simple to more complex activities. However, this is not a straightforward or a linear development and appears to be strongly influenced by sector and characteristics of home and host countries.

In the context of European marketing, Europeanisation (internationalisation in the context of Europe) has similar implications to the impact of internationalisation on international marketing. Thus, the process of Europeanisation is likely to be complex and evolutionary and based on learning. This implies that European marketing strategies and activities adjust in line with the acquisition of information and its conversion into useful knowledge. In these circumstances, marketing strategies may begin with simple exporting; alternatively, more complex modes of entry such as direct foreign investment (DFI) may begin early in the Europeanisation process. The deciding factor is the knowledge that the company possesses on matters such as market conditions and the means of producing, promoting and distributing products in European markets. In the complex evolutionary view of the Europeanisation process, companies may start with a small number of countries to which they are geographically and culturally close or with a wide range of countries that are geographically and culturally disparate from the host country. Those countries that are members of the EU and Euroland are more likely to be at the heart of this process because the legal and economic barriers are low and the EU contains the largest economies in Europe.

It is likely that most companies will begin with simple marketing strategies and objectives but may rapidly move to more complex plans that miss out many of the intervening stages suggested in the more traditional models of internationalisation (Europeanisation). Therefore, the key to the development of European marketing strategy is the ability of companies to acquire knowledge about foreign markets and the supply conditions to these markets and to rapidly adjust their plans based on the acquired knowledge. This need not follow a linear path of development from exporting to more complex entry modes.

Networks and European marketing

The increasing focus on the importance of networks for international business activities is reflected in the international marketing literature. Research by the International Marketing and Purchasing (IMP) Group emphasised the importance of learning in uncertain and competitive environments that leads to sophisticated buying behaviour by companies, rather than the mechanistic approach that is expounded in traditional views of international marketing (Håkansson, 1982). In the IMP view of international marketing the main drivers of marketing strategy are the interactions between buyers and sellers as they seek to establish networks for production, promotion, distribution and after-sales service that deliver outcomes which are acceptable in an environment that is fast changing because of developments in the competitive and technology environments. This type of approach is also evident in the relationship approach to marketing where strategic alliances, partnerships and joint ventures are used to achieve desirable outcomes (Johanson and Mattson, 1986). The importance of networks for international marketing is also highlighted in the phenomenon of 'born global' companies and as a means to help small- and medium-sized enterprises (SMEs) internationalise (Madsen and Servais, 1997; Nielsen et al., 1999; Rennie, 1993). Clearly, networks and relationships within networks are important factors in European marketing for sales between companies and for arranging packages of products and distribution to final customers.

Segmentation or standardisation

The drive towards global standardisation was based on a view that the progressive removal of trade barriers plus the growth of global cultural values was creating a single economic system that could be supplied with global products and uniform marketing processes such as promotion and the use of common brand names (Levitt, 1983; Ohmae, 1995). The creation of a Single European Market (SEM) provides an even clearer example of the opportunities to create common European products given the removal of not only tariffs and quotas but also non tariff barriers (see Chapter 2). The advantages of mass production in terms of economies of scale and scope could be realised in the sort of world painted by Levitt and Ohmae. However, the case that a European economic system with very few economic, legal and cultural barriers is imminent has certainly been overstated (see Chapters 2 and 3). The persistence of economic, legal and cultural barriers to mass production generated an approach from many marketeers that markets should be segmented geographically according to cultural clusters and within countries by social and demographic groups (Czinkota et al., 1998; Halliburton and Hunerberg, 1993).

The focus on segmentation led in some cases to fragmentation of markets that were broken down into ever more complex and overlapping segments. Moreover, the use of continuous improvement by product development resulted in layers of production, sales and distribution systems with a consequent generation of a multitude of organisational systems. These developments added to the production and transaction costs often with little benefit it terms of extra sales. A study by McKinsey estimated that the costs of product differentiation and continuous improvement in the car industry for cars with limited demand amounted to $80 billion per year (Agrawal et al., 2001). Another example of the potential to waste resources by over-segmentation of markets is illustrated by Toyota when it reduced the product range by 25 per cent on discovering that 20 per cent of its range accounted for 80 per cent of its sales (Pine et al., 1993).

The solution to these problems is sought in build-to-order (BTO) systems where, by use of sophisticated information gathering, specifications from customers are matched to the supply chain to assemble the components to customer's specification. This type of an approach is being pursued by major car companies such as GM, Ford, Nissan and VW that are seeking to develop BTO systems which can deliver a car to the customer's specification in three days. White goods manufacturers in the US such as Whirlpool, General Electric and Maytag are also developing BTO systems to deliver products to customer's specifications (Economist, 2001). Operating BTO systems leads to lower production costs because of the reduced need for high levels of inventories of components, as BTO is a very lean and effective just-in-time (JIT) system. Moreover, by customising the product, premium prices can be charged. BTO systems based on the use of the Internet also offer the prospects of customised promotion systems by use of common platforms for advertising and information dissemination that are tailored to the groups or even individuals that are targeted by e-business systems.

Financial services companies have been operating BTO packages in areas such as personal savings plans and financial packages for leasing systems for companies for many years. However, financial services do not require the assembling of physical components and they have zero or low logistical costs of assembling the components of a financial package. The pioneer of mass customisation using BTO for manufactured goods was Dell Computers.

Dell's success was based on the use of standardised components that are slotted together according to customer's specification received via the Internet. The success of Dell Computers is largely due to the ability to use standardised components that can be assembled into different packages by fairly minor modifications to the basic platform of the PC. Furthermore, Dell is able to sell and promote online to people who are computer literate and therefore do not need sophisticated advice and after-sales services. Dell also does not face significant legal, economic or cultural differences that require significant changes to organisational system in order to use the standard Dell marketing model across a variety of countries. Using standardised BTO organisational systems for more complex products (which can be significantly different rather than have only minor changes to the same basic package and where there are legal, economic and cultural barriers) will present an altogether more challenging task. Moreover, some products can be successfully standardised to generate the ability to charge a price relative to cost of supply that leads to higher profit than a BTO system. This process of standardisation is well advanced in the commoditisation of components through e-auctions by companies that sell to final customers (McDonald and Burton, 2002).

BTO systems require the development of effective e-business and logistical systems that can deliver inputs and final products on very tight schedules. The problems of using such complex e-business systems for international business activities may hamper the use of this approach to mass customisation. Moreover, the cost of segmenting markets to this level, in terms of developing effective BTO organisational and logistical systems, may lead to similar results to the attempts by the car industry to mass customise by producing and marketing a myriad of different models, the costs of which was not covered by the extra revenue generated by the customisation. Economic, legal and cultural differences across countries may also limit the use of Europe-wide BTO systems because technical regulations and differences in rules and what is culturally and legal acceptable as means of promotion will require adaptation of the basic BTO marketing model. This will further complicate the organisational complexity of effectively operating BTO systems.

Clearly, the differentiation versus mass production debate has not yet been resolved and a judicious mix of standardisation to differentiation, including in some cases mass customisation, appears to be the way forward. The selection of

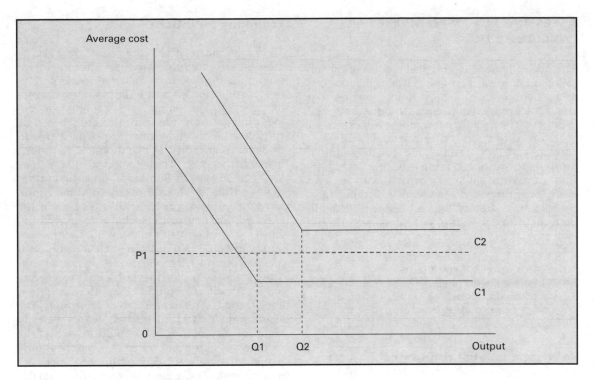

Figure 5.1   *Conditions for selecting BTO arrangements*

the appropriate approach is determined by the nature of the product, minimum efficiency scale, ability to easily adapt basic product platforms, the extent of legal, economic and cultural barriers and the ability to construct organisational systems that deliver the largest difference between a price which can be charged and the costs of differentiation.

The main issues connected to the choice of BTO arrangements are illustrated in Figure 5.1. The C curves represent the average cost of supplying countries 1 and 2 (C1 and C2) using a BTO system. These curves assume that average cost associated with operating a BTO arrangement falls until the minimum efficiency scale is reached – at Q1 in the case of C1 and Q2 in the case of C2. The falling section of the curves indicates that economies of scale can be reaped until minimum efficiency scale is reached. The flat section of the curves reflects an assumption that organisational systems can deliver BTO arrangements which can produce output at constant cost after the minimum efficiency scale is reached. The different positions of the curves reflect the higher cost of supplying country 2

using BTO arrangements. This could be due to higher information gathering and distribution costs and/or requirements for more adaptation of the basic platform when supplying country 2. If a price of P1 can be charged in both markets it would be profitable to supply country 1 using a BTO system, but losses would be made if such a system was used in country 2.

Figure 5.1 illustrates the main factors that are involved in deciding whether it is beneficial to use BTO systems and the conditions that need to be altered if BTO systems are to become profitable. Thus, to make it profitable to supply country 2 the price charged would have to rise above the curve C2, and/or the costs of supplying country 2 would have to be reduced such as to bring C2 below the price line. Clearly, the nature of the organisational system used to deliver BTO is also important as this affects the shape and position of the average cost curve. Differences in legal, economic, social and cultural conditions in countries 1 and 2 influence the position of the average cost curve and hence influence the decision on the wisdom of using BTO systems.

ASSESSING EUROPEAN MARKET ENVIRONMENTS

The beginning of the practical process of formulating a European marketing strategy is to assess market conditions in the various countries that companies may wish to consider for selling their products. The initial assessment involves screening markets to discover the potential of different countries. This process includes consideration of rates of growth of economies, technical changes that are creating new opportunities to sell and identification of long-term economic and demographic factors that are altering demand patterns. Four main types of assessment should be undertaken:

1   Political and legal conditions.
2   Economic conditions.
3   Cultural conditions.
4   Competitive conditions.

Political and legal conditions

Screening political and legal conditions requires examinations of factors such as the level of trade barriers, taxation rates and restrictions on foreign ownership, including repatriation of profits and restrictions on capital movements. Legal frameworks governing the protection of intellectual property, labour laws and other aspects of business law should also be evaluated. For most of Europe, legal and political differences are low, especially for members of the EU or for those countries with close ties to the EU. However, there are significant differences in taxation rates. Moreover, companies not based in Europe and those European countries with little integration with the EU will face a host of trade and other barriers (see Chapter 3).

The type of incentives available for DFI and the likelihood of being able to obtain exemptions from laws and policies that would hamper operations may also be considered. Risk assessment of the chances of political changes that could harm the firm must also be carried out. Failure to carry out such investigations can lead to costly mistakes, as was discovered by many of the companies that entered the Russian market on the mistaken belief that the fall of Communism and the introduction of markets had led to political and legal conditions that were similar to those in developed countries (Shama and Merrell, 1997).

Economic conditions

The economic health of countries should also be assessed to determine whether the macroeconomic conditions are conducive to stable economic conditions. Thus, inflation rates, balance of payments, exchange rate stability, government budgets and the record of growth will be considered to evaluate the prospects for growth of demand and on the likelihood of economic instability or crisis. These factors are likely to be very similar within Euroland and for countries that are integrated with macroeconomic conditions in Euroland (in effect all members of the EU and all countries seeking membership). However, the countries that are not members of Euroland could depart from such integration if macroeconomic imbalances were persistent. Moreover, even within Euroland macroeconomic conditions could be significantly different if these imbalances become strong. The assumption that Euroland will generate nearly identical macroeconomic conditions across the members of European monetary union will only happen if significant economic imbalances are not present. The more members of Euroland there are, the more likely it is that such imbalances will exist and that they will lead to differences in macroeconomic conditions (McDonald and Burton, 2002).

Demographic factors should be taken into account together with measures such as disposable income per head. These considerations enable appraisal of the strength of general demand. Microeconomic data, such as size and development of particular markets and price movements in these markets, is also needed. The level of development of financial, physical and supporting human resources infrastructures should also be scrutinised. This enables evaluation of the level and effectiveness of financial services and support that is available, for example, the state of transport, energy, water supply and logistical systems, and the support from educational and training agencies that can be expected. These conditions vary considerably in Europe and therefore need to be examined country by country or even region by region.

Data on these factors is often available from official agencies such as the EU, the Organisation for Economic Cooperation and Development (OECD) and various United Nations organisations. Private sector companies such as the Economic Intelligence Unit also provide this kind of information. The State Department of the US provides detailed information on some of these issues via its network of Commercial Sections in US Embassies. Many large multinational companies have their own research departments that can assess these types of issues. However, smaller companies are less able to gather and assess this type of information. They are often dependent on official sources such as the EU and OECD publications and the Commercial Sections of their government's Embassies.

Cultural conditions

Screening to assess cultural conditions is perhaps the most difficult of the market assessments that should be carried out. The complex and path determined nature of cultural values (McDonald and Burton, 2002) makes it very difficult for outsiders to assess accurately cultural values and how they affect norms for doing business. There is no shortage of airport lounge type of books that give often rather trite advice on rules of social interaction in various countries, but a more subtle understanding of how a culture operates and the impact on business behaviour is not easily learned other than by experience or the use of national partners that understand both home and host cultures. Failure to screen adequately for important cultural differences can lead to costly mistakes by using, for example, promotional techniques that are offensive or inappropriate to the home culture. Unfortunately, learning by making mistakes based on misunderstandings of cultural differences can be an expensive way to find out about the cultural values of countries. Making use of the Commercial Sections of Embassies and experts in national cultures in agencies such as Universities may be a useful source of information for screening cultural factors. However, securing access to good sources of information is often difficult. The use of networks and collaboration with individuals, companies and agencies that have experience of operating in selected countries can help to overcome the lack of good information.

Competitive conditions

Evaluation of competitive conditions in European markets requires detailed knowledge about which companies are already in the market and on those likely to enter. Information on the type of products sold by competitors and other information such as prices, quality of after sales and effectiveness of distribution systems of rivals helps to assess the prospects for capture of a sufficient share of the market to make entry worthwhile. Knowledge on technology used by main competitors and the effectiveness of their promotion, distribution and logistical systems provides a means to assess the prospects of successfully entering markets that are characterised by strong competition. In markets with low levels of competition, it is useful to know if potential competitors are planning to enter the market and to have some indications of their likely competitive advantages. However, gaining information of this type is very difficult because companies will seek to keep their plans and current operations secret. Information on these issues is normally obtained informally by observation of the activities of competitors. This can range from open observation to industrial espionage.

Evaluating information on European markets

After the process of screening European environments has been completed, companies need to analyse the information that has been gathered and processed. This can involve techniques such as PEST (political, economic, social and technological factors) and SWOT (strengths, weaknesses, opportunities and threats). A variety of models to formalise political risk assessment procedures may be used (Frank, 1999). Scenario building can also be used to assess how different policies of market entry and development might work out if political, economic, cultural and competitive conditions change. These models require significant resources and therefore smaller companies are often unable to utilise them. However, some of the large consultancy companies offer these services. Nevertheless, the reliability of such work may be questionable if the work depends upon sophisticated techniques of assessment and pay less attention to the quality of the information that is used by these techniques. Clearly, even many of the large multinational companies that entered Russian markets in the early days of the transition to a market-based economic system did not gather good information on the environment in Russia, although some did make use of techniques such as PEST and SWOT. The problems that companies entering the Chinese market encountered also indicated that prior assessment of new markets is often perfunctory (Osland and Cavusgil, 1996). Failure to undertake good quality assessment of these environmental conditions often leads to learning by mistake and, as many companies that entered China and Russia discovered, this can be a very costly outcome.

PRACTICAL ISSUES OF EUROPEAN MARKETING

The 4Ps of marketing (Product (standardised or differentiated), Pricing, Promotion and Place) have a place in European marketing, not as the cornerstones of marketing strategy, which as indicated above is centred on large issues such as the path of Europeanisation, but to establish the importance of networks and debates about segmentation versus standardisation. However, practical decisions have to be taken on the 4Ps.

Product

Whatever decision is taken about the differentiation versus standardisation choice, nearly all products require modification to fit in with legal, economic, technical and cultural conditions in the host country. Although the activities of the EU have reduced the need to modify products for legal reasons, they often need to be modified for economic, social or cultural reasons. Some products need very little modification and commodities normally need none. Products sold to other companies normally require very little modification because items such as computers, or fax machines or the components for cars are standard. Nevertheless, technical differences in areas such as electricity supply systems and health and safety rules differ across countries, even in the EU, and thereby require companies to modify their products. Companies that sell famous brand name products may be faced with a very limited need to modify their products. However, even some of the most famous brands are modified to satisfy local conditions.

Products sold to consumers often require more modification because of cultural differences. This is reflected in the extensive product differentiation undertaken by many of the companies involved in food products, for example, Campbells, Nestlé and Unilever. However, increasingly even food companies are standardising brand names, for instance, Mars the chocolate bar manufacturer uses the same brand name for most of its products everywhere in the world. Perhaps the most famous global brand name is Coca-Cola. However, in the case of Coca-Cola there are slight variations in the amount of sugar and carbon dioxide to satisfy local tastes. These modifications are made even with the countries of the EU. Differences in income also influence product differentiation, as higher income countries often demand higher specifications and better level of after-sales service than poorer countries.

Strategic decisions on the level of standardisation strongly influence marketing choices on product modification, but legal, technical and cultural differences across countries continue to require modification of products. The most important strategic decision is on the level of differentiation and the use of mass customisation that should be undertaken on top of essential legal, technical and cultural requirements.

Figure 5.2 can be used to illustrate the main points on the decisions connected to standardisation versus differentiation. The curve C1 and C2 represents (respectively) the average cost of supplying a country with a differentiated and a standardised product. The curves D1 and D2 represent (respectively) the demand curves for the differentiated and a standardised product. Assume that the price is set by an average cost plus mark up process: in both cases the price that can be charged leads to profitable operations as the mark-up above average cost is positive. The maximum mark-up possible would be at minimum efficiency scale (that is, either P1:Q1 or P2:Q2). In this case a choice would have to be made on either the option that leads to the higher profit or the one that delivers the best long-term advantages. The latter would be influenced by such criteria as development of the market and best-fit with the overall strategy of the company and other non-profit driven objectives. However, to satisfy the conditions that losses were avoided, the higher cost of providing a differentiated product would have to be at least covered by the price that could be charged. If this were not the case, cost reductions and/or product promotion (that was effective in boosting demand) would be necessary to reach at least a break-even point.

Pricing

Decisions on pricing are important because of the effect on revenues and hence profits. Pricing decisions in foreign markets are complicated by exchange rate risk and the possibilities to

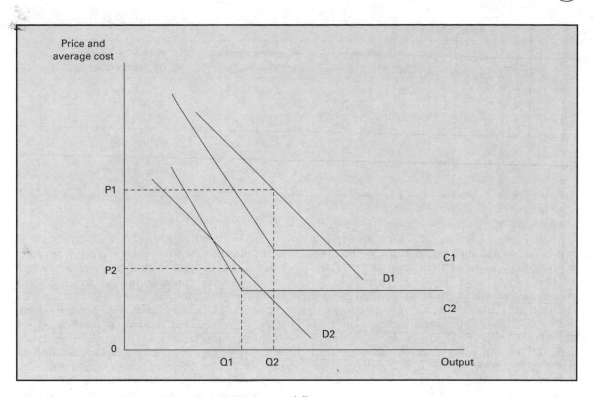

Figure 5.2 *Conditions for selecting standardisation or differentiation*

engage in transfer pricing to avoid taxes. However, exchange rate risk does not prevail in Euroland, but does to a greater or lesser extent in those European countries that are not members of Euroland, especially those such as Russia and the Ukraine which are not closely integrated into EU. Moreover, even countries that are members of the EU but not members of Euroland, such as the UK, can have significant differences in prices caused by exchange rate fluctuations relative to the euro.

Changes in the value of currencies also influence the price of exports (see Table 5.1). Mark-up pricing (the system used by most companies) requires careful estimation of costs and assessment of the level of mark-up that foreign markets can sustain and whether the strategy of the companies is to penetrate or skim markets. The accuracy of cost estimates and the wisdom of mark-ups that are applied may be difficult for the exporting or parent company to effectively monitor if agents or employees in the host country are given autonomy to set prices. If the exporter sets prices, it may not have good information on costs and appropriate mark-ups. The policy of host governments towards price

controls and to competition policy influences the pricing policy because skimming pricing may attract unwanted attention from government agencies.

Suppose a German exporter can supply a product at an export price of €20.00 and is going to export to France, Italy and Russia. As France and Italy are members of Euroland, the price will be in euros in both of these countries. However, the price in Russia will depend on the euro–rouble exchange rate. The price charged to final customers in France and Italy depends on the mark-up that is charged by importers and distributors into these countries. If these mark-ups are higher in Italy than in France (perhaps because of less competition among Italian importers and distributors compared to the situation in France), the final price will be higher in Italy (see Table 5.1). This example demonstrates that prices in Euroland for the same product need not be the same even although the same currency is involved. Differences in taxation could lead to further differences in price. The price charged in Russia depends not only on the mark-ups but also on the exchange rate (see Table 5.1).

Table 5.1 Pricing decisions

Country	Price charged by German exporter	Price after mark-up by importer	Price after mark-up by distributor
France	€20.00	€23.00 (mark-up 15%)	€27.60 (mark-up 20%)
Italy	€20.00	€23.60 (mark-up 18%)	€28.80 (mark-up 22%)
Russia (€1.00 = R1.05)	€20.00	R25.20 (mark-up 20%)	R31.50 (mark-up 25%)
Russia (€1.00 = R1.00)	€20.00	R24.00 (mark-up 20%)	R30.00 (mark-up 25%)

In the case of Russia, the German exporter would face a decision on what to do about the export price in euro if the exchange rate alters. In the example in Table 5.1, the German exporter could decide to keep the final price in Russia at R31.50. This would involve an export price of €21.00. This would increase the profitability of exporting to Russia. However, if demand for the product in Russia were price elastic (the percentage decrease in price was less that the percentage increase in the quantity sold) the reduction in price (in Russia) brought about by the change in the exchange rate would increase revenue from sales. Hence, the German exporter needs to assess whether profits will be higher by increasing the export price and leaving the price in Russia constant or by keeping the export price constant. If the product faces price inelastic demand in Russia, reducing the price in Russia by keeping the export price constant will lead to lower revenue. In this case, profitability can be increased by increasing the export price of the product.

In all three export markets, the size of mark-ups is crucial for the final price that will be charged and thereby for the level of export sales. If the exporter has little control over these mark-ups, this will further complicate the pricing decision as alteration of mark-ups will affect the final price and thereby the level of sales. This will influence the profitability of exporting (even with Euroland) and consequently has implications for the desirable export price of the product. In cases were the exporter has control over the mark-ups, it may be desirable to alter these to increase profits in countries with low profit taxes. This is connected to the problem of transfer pricing by multinational companies and is one reason why the EU is seeking to increase harmonisation of taxes. However, even within Euroland there is (currently) very little harmonisation of taxes (see Chapter 3).

Clearly, even in Euroland, pricing of exports is a complex process that involves consideration of price elasticities and mark-ups as well as government policies towards prices. Exporting to European countries that are not in Euroland, or exports to Euroland from other European countries, involves the added complication of exchange rate changes. For companies not based in Europe that are exporting to European countries, exchange rates will have a strong influence on pricing decisions. Although the dollar–euro rate will have the largest affect, exchange rates with European countries that are not members of Euroland will also have a strong influence on pricing decisions in those countries.

Promotion

Promotion involves the creation and maintenance or increase of demand for products. The major decisions taken in promotion are whether to use the same promotion methods everywhere or to adapt the methods to different markets. Together with the decision on the standardisation of products, this leads to the following possible combinations of product and promotion packages:

1 Same product and the same means of promotion.
2 Adapted product and the same means of promotion.
3 Same product and different means of promotion.
4 Adapted product and different means of promotion.

The first option, the European standardisation approach, is the least cost system and permits economies of scale and scope to be reaped. The fourth option has the highest cost and limits economies of scale and scope. The decision on which option to select will be influenced by strategic decisions on standardisation and on the need to adapt the product and the means of promotion because of legal, cultural and technical factors. Legal conditions influence promotion policies because laws on advertising and promotion activities vary across European countries. For example, what is permissible to state about the qualities of products and what is allowable in terms of social mores varies across countries. Cultural differences often require different types of promotion. Technical factors such as differences in the demographic and geographical coverage of newspapers and television and ownership of telephones and connection to the Internet also influence the ability to adopt the same promotion package.

The factors that affect the need to adapt products and promotion policies are likely to mean that hardly any products will have the same standards and the same means of promotion. Indeed, nearly all products will fall into the adapted product and different means of promotion category. However, depending on the marketing strategy selected and the extent of legal, cultural and technical barriers to standardisation the mix between product and promotion, standardisation will edge towards one of the first three options. Industrial products are more likely to edge towards the global standardisation option than are consumer goods.

Place

The means of distribution are influenced by transport and logistical systems and in the case of consumer goods by wholesaling and retailing systems. These vary across European countries for legal reasons, for example, transport laws and environmental rules on emissions and congestion and planning laws that restrict where production, distribution and retailing operations can take place. Although EU regulations in these areas are leading to convergence of legal conditions, there are still significant differences in some of these areas. Technical factors also affect distribution as transport networks often have different characteristics because of geographical and historical factors. Thus, European railway systems are not technically compatible because of the use of different technical standards. Moreover, European transport networks are nationally based (often focussed on national capitals), but economic considerations are pushing for European rather than national distribution systems (Cooper et al., 1994). Cultural

differences also affect distribution because in some countries retailing outlets sell a wide range of products, whilst in others retailers are more specialised. Some national distribution systems are closed networks of producers, transport companies, wholesalers and retailers. For example, access to UK supermarkets is a series of closed networks controlled by the big supermarkets. To gain access to these networks foreign companies must gain access to these distribution systems.

CONCLUSION

This chapter has examined the current debates on European marketing strategy and some of the practical issues connected to selling in European markets. Contemporary debates on international marketing strategy are centred on the process of internationalisation, the balance between segmentation and standardisation, and the role of networks. This literature provides the basic framework for examination of European marketing. The major differences between European and international marketing arise because although there are considerable similarities across European countries, there are also significant differences that make European marketing different from domestic marketing, even within the EU. These differences make European marketing a complex mixture of international and domestic marketing. Nevertheless, many of the debates in international marketing have important implications for European marketing.

The literature suggests that European/international marketing strategy is not primarily a rational measurement and calculation process but involves dynamic and evolutionary developments. Europeanisation/internationalisation does not always follow a linear path from exporting to more complex modes of entry such as DFI. Companies may miss sections of the linear path of European/internationalisation path or begin the process at different stages. Moreover, networks provide important means to overcome many of the problems of European/international marketing. Thus, European/international marketing strategy is increasingly focussed on companies as learning machines whose internationalisation policies evolve as companies learn and make new and hopefully more effective network connections.

Consideration of the practicalities of European marketing highlights the need for effective assessment of market environments to avoid the costly route of learning by making mistakes. However, obtaining and processing good information on political, legal, economic, cultural and competitive factors is difficult and probably beyond the reach of most small companies. Even large companies and consultancy companies are likely to find it difficult to obtain good information on these factors. Again, the use of networks of companies, agencies and individuals that have good knowledge on these issues holds the prospects of improving the flow of useful information.

Investigation of the 4Ps in European marketing reveals that strategic decisions on the mode of entry and about segmentation versus standardisation have important implications for marketing. However, differences in legal, economic, cultural and technical conditions affect selection of appropriate options for product, pricing, promotion and place.

REFERENCES

Agrawal, M., Kumaresh, T. and Mercer, G. (2001) 'The False Promise of Mass Customization', *McKinsey Quarterly*, 3: 12–22.

Andersen, O. (1993) 'On the Internationalization Process of Companies: A Critical Analysis', *Journal of International Business Studies*, 24 (3): 209–32.

Bilkey, W. and Tesar, T. (1977) 'The export behaviour of smaller Wisconsin manufacturing companies', *Journal of International Business Studies*, 9 (1): 93–8.

Cavusgil, S. and Nevin, J. (1980) 'A conceptualisation of the initial involvement in international marketing', in C. Lamb and P. Dunne (eds), *Theoretical Developments in Marketing*. Chicago, IL: American Marketing Association.

Cavusgil, S. and Nevin, J. (1981) 'State of the art in international marketing', in B. Enis and K. Roering (eds), *Review of Marketing*. Chicago, IL: American Marketing Association.

Cooper, J., Brown, M. and Peters, M. (1994) *European Logistics: markets, management and strategy*. Oxford: Oxford University Press.

Czinkota, M., Ronkainen, I., Moffett, M. and Moynihan, E. (1998) *Global Business*. London: Dryden.

Douglas, S. and Craig, C. (1989) 'Evolution of Global Marketing Strategy: Scale, Scope and Synergy', *Columbia Journal of World Business*, 24 (Fall): 47–59.

Douglas, S. and Craig, C. (1992) 'Advances in international marketing', *International Journal of Research in Marketing*, 9 (3): 291–318.

Economist (2001) 'Special Report: Mass Customisation', 14 July, pp. 79–81.

Frank, R. (1999) 'Political Risk, assessment and management of', in R. Tung (ed.), *The Handbook of International Business*. London: International Thomson Press.

Håkansson, H. (1982) *International Marketing and Purchasing of Industrial Goods: An Interaction Approach*. New York: Wiley.

Halliburton, C. and Hunerberg, R. (1993) *European Marketing: Readings and Cases*. New York: Addison-Wesley.

Johanson, J. and Mattson, L. (1986) 'International marketing and internationalization processes – a network approach', in P. Turnbull and S. Paliwoda (eds), *Research in International Marketing*. London: Croom-Helm.

Johanson, J. and Vahlne, J. (1977) 'The internationalisation process of the firm – A model of knowledge development and increasing foreign market developments', *Journal of International Business Studies*, 8 (1): 23–32.

Johanson, J. and Wiedersheim-Paul, F. (1975) 'The internationalisation of the firm – Four Swedish cases', *Journal of Management Studies*, 12 (3): 305–22.

Levitt, T. (1983) 'The Globalization of Markets', *Harvard Business Review*, 4 (May–June): 92–102.

Madsen, T. and Servais, P. (1997) 'The Internationalization of Born Globals: An Evolutionary Process', *International Business Review*, 6 (4): 561–83.

McDonald, F. and Burton, F. (2002) *International Business*. London: Thomson.

Nielsen, K. Pedersen, K. and Vestergaard, J. (1999) *Internationalization of SMEs*. London: Macmillan.

Ohmae, K. (1995) *The End of the Nation State: The Rise of Regional Economies*. New York: Harper.

Osland, G. and Cavusgil, S. (1996) 'Performance issues in US-China joint ventures', *California Management Review*, 38 (2): 106–30.

Pine, B., Victor, B. and Boynton, A. (1993) 'Making mass customization work', *Harvard Business Review*, 71 (Sept–Oct): 108–22.

Rennie, M. (1993) 'Born Global', *The McKinsey Quarterly*, 4: 45–52.

Shama, A. and Merrell, M. (1997) 'Russia's True Business Performance: Inviting to International Business?', *Journal of World Business*, 32 (3): 320–32.

Turnbull, P. and Valla, J. (1986) *Strategies for International Industrial Marketing*. London: Croom-Helm.

Durng the past two decades some of the most important developments in marketing practice and theory have been made in the two overlapping areas of what has come to be known as business-to-business and relationship marketing. The concepts developed in these areas have increasingly been applied in the public sector and not-for-profit markets and as a result have encountered a number of complex ethical and societal issues such as in political campaigning or public affairs work.

Relationship marketing has emerged as the lingua frança term for a wide range of marketing practices that have, as one common facet, a focus that goes beyond the single interaction between buyer and seller, supplier and purchaser, retailer and consumer or government and stakeholder. It is centred on interactions in the marketplace over time, earned trust and relational exchange.

It is now widely accepted that the notion of marketing as simply being about developing, selling and delivering products or that all communication should be propaganda is out of date. Marketing is increasingly more concerned with the development and maintenance of mutually satisfying long-term relationships between buyers and sellers and a two-way process of communication. Thus a number of important questions emerge around which the rest of this chapter is structured:

1   What is meant by a long-term buyer–seller relationship?
2   How did business-to-business marketing evolve and what is its impact upon the development of relationship marketing?
3   What is the definition of relationship marketing and how is it used in European markets?
4   What is the impact on political marketing and the special role of lobbying in public affairs management?
5   What are the future developments likely to be?

MARKETING AND RELATIONSHIPS

Fundamental to the notion of relationship marketing is the concept of relational exchange. The best way to think of this is as one end of a spectrum of possible behaviours. At the far end, as far away from relational exchange as it is possible to get, is the 'discrete transaction'. A discrete transaction is where an exchange occurs with the absolute minimum of communication between the buyer and the seller. It is a one-off event, and neither party to the exchange is concerned that they may do business with this person again, and at the other end of this spectrum is the regular transaction or 'relational exchange'. In its extreme, relational exchange describes a situation in which the buyer and the seller are tied together by social and economic 'bonds', where the act of exchanging goods for money is but a small part of the extended interaction between the two parties. Social bonds could be of various types, including friendship and kinship (belonging to the same extended family), or bonds of mutual esteem developed over a period of years transacting business together. Economic bonds arise where the two parties to the exchange are financially better off doing business with each other than with a third party.

In principle, all marketing exchanges can be conceived to lie at some point along the relational spectrum. Where exchanges typically lie more towards the relational end of the spectrum, a relationship marketing strategy should be adopted. Where exchanges are typically more of the nature of discrete transactions, a conventional 'marketing mix' approach using the 4P's can be applied. However, it is clear that many firms have concluded that strategic action to move customers along the spectrum more towards the relational end is desirable as a means of trying to enhance and strengthen customer loyalty and improve their own long-term profitability. Relationship marketing strategies can either be a response to the nature of the exchange or an attempt to increase the relational element in the exchange in order to achieve a competitive advantage and increased profit.

Relationships have been described from many different perspectives in marketing. One way to structure relationships is to describe their antecedents, contents and consequences. However, many concepts are simultaneously and highly interrelated in an ongoing relationship and it can be difficult to distinguish how concepts such as commitment, loyalty or trust can affect each other in an ongoing relationship. A further way of understanding relationships is to outline what activities and exchanges they encompass – tangible products, services or a combination of both. Human and eventual business interaction is the focus of the area and consequently relationships can be analysed from a socio-psychological or a political perspective by focusing on the individual or groups of actors involved. Relationships can also be understood in terms of their technical content and importance and constitute core elements in business-to-business markets. Alternatively, relationships can be approached from an economic viewpoint, which suggests describing the different kinds of economic costs and benefits stemming from the relationship. Temporality and the study of the relationships over time is increasingly seen as a crucial tool and has been used extensively by the Industrial Marketing and Purchasing (IMP) group of researchers to assess phenomena.

Definitions of relationships found in the interaction and network approach in business marketing see relationships often compared to marriages as opposed to more short-term 'affairs'. This corresponds to the definition advanced by Holmlund and Törnroos (1997), who define a relationship as 'an interdependent process of continuous interaction and exchange between at least two actors in a business network context'. A relationship therefore is based on the notion that actors are connected by ties that exist between them. This area of relationship and network marketing therefore has a particular direct relevance to Europe and the study of complex communities, joint ventures and strategic alliances. The overlap can be seen very clearly in Chapter 7 and the Broadcasting, EVC and Philips case studies.

Relationships in business networks have been studied mainly from a dyadic point of view (that is, encompassing two parties). However, relationships may also be approached from the viewpoint of three parties, triads and the number of involved partners, and relationships may be increased further to encompass chains of relationships or a network of relationships. This can be seen very clearly in the case studies on EVC1, EVC2, Gruppo Massone and Philips and is a feature of evolving global business where 20 per cent of world business activity takes place within strategic alliances.

The emergence of relationship marketing

Starting from the mid-1980s, the concept of relationship marketing originally applied by Berry (1983) to services marketing and by Jackson (1985) to industrial marketing emerged in the marketing literature. The traditional view of marketing as a specialist function was increasingly questioned as a proper basis for strategic and operational marketing planning. As an example, Gummesson (1987) argues for what he calls 'new marketing', an approach emphasising business relationships and interaction out of new theories of services marketing and industrial marketing, and also out of practical experience and observation. The old marketing concept based on the marketing mix is perceived as too transactional, functionalist and prescriptive as business moves from a structured manufacturing paradigm to a more service orientated and holistic approach. Gummesson (1994) perceived the future shift in the marketing paradigm to be more orientated to that shown in Figure 6.1.

He argues that 'the 4ps [product, promotion, price and place] and their extensions will always be needed, but the paradigm shift develops their role from that of being founding parameters of marketing to one of being contributing parameters to relationships, networks and interaction' (Gummesson, 1994: 9).

The observable weakness of existing business theories in predicting or discovering vital aspects of changing business reality can be pointed to as the major reason for a shift in approach to the study of business disciplines. The significance of the interaction approach (Häkansson, 1982) and network theories (Thompson et al., 1991; Kickert et al., 1997) in providing a new way to understand business disciplines can also be seen to apply to political lobbying and can be viewed in terms of the new theoretical and empirical assumptions approach.

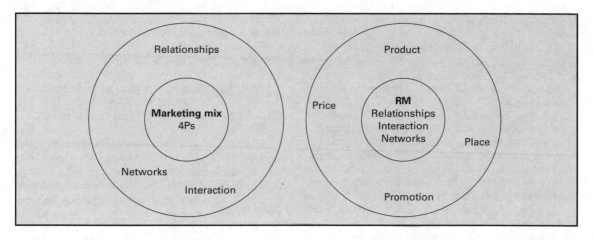

Figure 6.1   *The current marketing mix (4Ps) paradigm of marketing and the future Relationship Marketing (RM) paradigm*

Source: Gummesson (1994: 9).

Borg (1991) argues that the interactional approach to market relationships is one of several shifts in approach to markets which accommodate an understanding of business relationships, especially in industrial markets. The search for alternative business theory which interaction and network related theories represent can be regarded as a series of problem shifts rather than a change in fundamental aspects of market related theory building. The growing use of network theories in business-to-business marketing provides a relevant example of problem shifts in business research without at the same time abandoning a pluralist view of science. The observable weaknesses of existing business theories in predicting or discovering vital aspects of changing business reality can be identified as the major reason for a shift in approach to the study of business disciplines. Table 6.1 suggests examples of theoretical and empirical assumptions applying to business-related problem shifts.

It is for these reasons that relationship marketing is suggested as the area where lobbying and political marketing belong within the management discipline.

Core features of relationship and business-to-business marketing

The interaction, network and relationship marketing research shows that similar features of

relationships recur and are typically characterised by four core features: mutuality, long-term character, process nature, and context dependence.

Mutuality

According to Holmlund and Törnroos (1997), a number of factors may be at work within the feature of mutuality:

- *Degree of mutuality*: here, relationships continue because of different types of bonds between business actors. These include technical, economic, planning, social, knowledge and legal bonds. Mutuality between the partners may be expressed with concepts such as trust and commitment, as well as conflicts and conflict resolution.
- *Symmetry*: a relationship may be balanced in terms of the ability of each counterpart to be able to influence the relationship, or else one of the partners may dominate the relationship.
- *Power-dependence structures*: large and small firms may have distinct power positions, which change over time. However, no partner is assumed to have absolute control over their relationships, although their roles may differ.
- *Resource dependence*: firms develop some resources internally but most are gained through relationships with others in a business network. The resources might constitute financial, human or technological assets. Complementary skills and heterogeneous resources may be a major strength of business networks.

Long-term character

Two features emerge as long-term characteristics of a relationship (Häkansson and Snehota, 1995):

- *Continuation*: here, relationships evolve over time and therefore temporality is a vital component of a relationship. Relationships can be long-lasting, although it can take some time before a sequence of interactions can be labelled as an effective relationship. Both the past and future expectations related to business relationships influence the present state, and in this sense time is a relational factor. Continuity can also be a competitive tool, where creating long-term relationships becomes an asset. Clearly in the New Zealand Dairy Board case study this is a factor.
- *Strength*: this can increase over time as partners learn to work with each other and create bonds, make necessary investments and enhance the relationship through commitment between interacting actors.

Process nature

A further core feature of a relationship in business networks is its process nature, which can have a number of dimensions and include:

- *Exchange and interaction*: where relationships are composed of different interactions, consisting of a multitude of exchanges and adaptations between organisations. The content of this exchange can be products, personnel, money, social contacts or information. The map of Philips relationships in Chapter 6 is a good example of this.
- *Dynamics*: relationships are also characterised by change because of their dynamic nature. Processes and events within a relationship as well as in the surrounding network produce change and dynamics in relationships.
- *Use potential*: relationships are valuable to firms because they provide access to resources and may enable further opportunities. On the other hand, relationships may function as burdens for firms as they can also limit future options and entail large unexpected costs.

Context dependence

A fourth core feature of a relationship is that it is context dependent, with embeddedness (Granovetter, 1985) within the network a core factor.

The concept of embeddedness relates to the fact that economic action and outcomes, like all social action and outcomes, are affected by the actors' dyadic relations and by the overall structure of network relations (Strandvik and Törnroos, 1995). Relationships are embedded in a network and connected to other relationships in that particular network. Relationships are therefore highly context-bound, with their features dependent on their particular setting.

Although these four core features of relationships in business networks may go some way towards generating an understanding of a relationship, the notion of a business relationship still remains difficult to grasp (Halinen, 1997). There are many potential facets and elements to a relationship and the concept has rarely been defined explicitly in the literature. When considering what makes dealings with two companies in a market become a relationship, or what makes a relationship cease to exist, researchers have approached the problem in at least two different ways, using to a greater or lesser extent the four core characteristics outlined above. They have either tried to classify and characterise different relationships or have sought to identify the necessary conditions for a relationship to exist (Halinen, 1997).

'Network marketing' extends beyond a narrow definition of relationship marketing to encompass a much wider range of potential business relationships. This is akin to Morgan and Hunt's proposition that in order to compete successfully in global markets the firm must be a member of an effective network of partnerships, including supplier partnerships, buyer partnerships, internal partnerships and lateral partnerships (Morgan and Hunt, 1994). They developed a theory of relationship marketing using commitment and trust as the core concepts. They argued that to be an effective competitor in a global market requires the firm to be a trusted collaborator, which has given rise to the axiom 'collaborate to compete'. Global competition is conducted between networks of competing firms, and in order to succeed it is as important to build strong relationships within the network as it is to outperform the rival network. Relationship commitment exists where an exchange partner believes that an ongoing relationship with another firm is so important that maximum effort will be exerted to maintain it. Relationship trust is defined as having confidence in an exchange partner's reliability and integrity. Commitment is the glue that binds the relationship together. Trust is the key factor that enables commitment to develop. Where we trust an exchange partner we expect them to behave in a manner that promotes our interests. When we believe this to be the case, we can take the risk of making a tangible commitment to the relationship.

The emergence of political marketing

Only relatively recently has any significant research begun to address the interface between politics and marketing, with Nicholas O'Shaughnessy's work *The Phenomenon of Political Marketing* (1990), though this tends to be grounded primarily in the earlier political communication and political science literature rather than having a strong marketing and management science base. Newman and Sheth (1986), Newman (1994), Butler and Collins (1994, 1996), Wring (1997), Harris and Lock (1996), Newman (1999) and a growing number of others have begun to explore this difficulty and have applied marketing theory to explore consumer behavioural aspects of polling and so on. However, this research is limited as it tends to concentrate on the marketing issues associated with electoral politics, image, voter behaviour, promotion and some aspects of party management, especially media management or what has come to be known as 'spin doctoring'. It does not comment on commercial lobbying as it focuses on the marketing of politicians for elections and tends to concentrate on specific observable marketing tools that are being used within the political arena. In fact, until recently most writings in the area called 'political marketing' have concentrated on electoral and political communications and have not looked at the management of pressure on the legislative process as part of marketing. Nevertheless, it does supply a useful starting point from which to develop a conceptual analysis of where marketing and politics meet and there is growing evidence beginning to be published (Andrews, 1996; Harris and Lock, 1996; Harrison, 2000; Harris, 2001) that campaigning techniques are being directly adopted from the political electoral arena and used to influence the business environment for strategic corporate advantage.

Political scientists have a long tradition of writing in the psephological area, especially that relating to elections, party strategy, imaging of politicians and polling techniques. The Nuffield series of election studies in the UK carried out by David Butler and others since 1945 are well known and have been extensively added to by others, the most recent of which have begun to show a particular marketing emphasis (Jones, 1995; McNair, 1995; Kavanagh, 1995; Scammell, 1995; Marrek, 1995). The first text is rather journalistic, not surprisingly given that the author is the political correspondent of the BBC, but it does give some invaluable insights into modern party management and manipulation of the media, based upon first-hand experiences during the 1980s and 1990s. McNair (1995) gives a sound modern commentary on the use of all political campaigning techniques in both elections and pressure group campaigning in the UK. This is rather useful, as it is one of the few works that attempts to do this. Kavanagh (1995) in his work calls upon his knowledge of elections from the various Nuffield Election Studies; however, the text focuses very heavily on particular campaign techniques and is very communications orientated. Scammell (1995) in her argument can be criticised for similar reasons as the work focuses on image building in British electoral campaigning throughout the 1980s and 1990s, particularly Margaret Thatcher, although it does give a good historic commentary on the US origins of what has come to be called 'Political Marketing'. The last two authors are well known political scientists, but it must be argued that their understanding of the philosophical debates, theoretical underpinnings and breadth of marketing techniques and their use is still developing. Thus, although the texts by their respective titles and chapter headings would appear to embrace a managed marketing approach, they in fact only highlight one or two electoral techniques and, as in so much of the research, concentrate on the market communication aspects of politics.

Scammell (1999) has attempted to address this shortfall in her work and shows a considerable appreciation of how marketing theory has been broadening into service and not-for-profit sectors. She gave a chilling examination of how Margaret Thatcher was marketed in the UK in her 1995 work *Designer Politics*. The marketing of European politicians such as Tony Blair, Gerdt Shroeder and others has drawn heavily on this process. The development of appropriate political marketing models is one of the prime areas of current research and she suggests that the marketing concept appears to be the key to understanding political marketing. She further argues that one of the most fruitful paradigms for researching the area is that of 'relationship marketing', to explore the political and government business interface.

Functions of lobbying

Although lobbying was viewed as an alien concept in the UK and EU until recent recognition of its more overt forms by Nolan (1995) and the EC, the use of lobbying within the political system has been a common phenomenon ever since the birth of politics itself. However public policy is formulated, there will always be a tendency for those affected to influence the outcome.

Shaping the external environment by influencing government through lobbying activities or corporate campaigning is now typical of strategic marketing management practice, whether it is for business, public or not-for-profit sectors. The relevance of such activities stems, of course, from the fact that there is hardly an item of legislation passed through the UK Parliament or EU which does not in some way encroach upon business interests or impinges on organisational goals. The proposal to tax audio tapes (Harris and Lock, 1996), for example, would have affected a variety of organisations including educationalists and charities such as The Royal National Institute for the Blind (RNIB), not to mention a large number of consumers of blank tapes, and discreet organising via a commercial lobbyist company funded by the European Japanese Electronic Manufacturers Association resulted in the proposals being substantially amended. Changing the wording of a proposal or the insertion of a special exception in regulations can be worth millions of pounds or euros to commercial organisations and can be crucial to the survival of non-profit organisations' activities.

Former Chief Secretary to the Treasury in John Major's UK Conservative Government of 1992–97, Michael Portillo, observed that political lobbyists are 'as necessary to the political process as a thoroughly efficient sewage system is to any city' (*Marketing*, 1994). This might be seen as a backhanded compliment given that lobbyists have been described by some as unethical and against the public interest. There are two competing views on the legitimacy of lobbying. There is the view that lobbyists abuse the democratic system for their own selfish interests and that the growth in the industry, particularly in the use of political consultants, requires the imposition of greater controls over lobbying activities. The alternative position is that lobbying is genuinely an intrinsic part of the democratic process because it can create a counter balance to potentially ill-informed or badly thought out policy decisions. Moreover, in reality it can be argued that government liaison is necessary because the government, like the ruler in Machiavelli's *Il Principe,* cannot operate in a vacuum but depends on others for information and advice. After all, the nub of political marketing is having information and as Jordan (1989) argues, politicians are only as good as the information they receive. This equally applies to politicians and government officials across the US and Europe, whether they be in Berlin, Brussels, Dublin, London, Madrid, Strasbourg, Vienna or wherever, and their role in policy making and other parts of the legislative, executive and judicial process.

Growth of lobbying

Lobbying has grown considerably in the past 20 years throughout Europe and the UK; the reasons for this are outlined below. Precise information on the current scale of activity is hard to come by, the first Nolan Report notwithstanding, due to the difficulty of choosing what to measure and the general discretion in the way in which lobbying has to be conducted. However, there is substantial evidence of its dramatic increase (Jordan, 1989; Attack, 1990; Harris, and Lock, 1996). The growth of corporate lobbying and campaigning is a response to the complexities of modern business society caused by more pervasive government and increased need for competitiveness in a global market by companies. Harris and Lock (1996) reported estimates that expenditure on commercial political lobbying, both in-house and by independent lobbyists, in the UK was between £200–£300 million and that over 4000 people were directly employed in this activity. It was also estimated that expenditure at EU level was at least one order of magnitude greater than at national level. Recent evidence suggests that political lobbying in the EU is worth over £3 billion. The use of lobbying within the British political process, particularly lobbying by pressure groups (Alderman, 1984; Jordan, 1989; Richardson, 1993) or interest groups (Ball and Millard, 1986) is well documented. Corporate political lobbying, with the exception of major multinational campaigns which attract much media attention, has only recently begun to be published; one example was the UK brewers' lobbying to amend the UK Monopolies and Mergers Commission proposals on tied houses (Gallagher and Scott, 1994). In industrial markets, lobbying to obtain military contracts has always been of significance, though often conducted in secret; the recent highly visual lobbying by British Aerospace (BAe) of the Ministry of Defence to put pressure on the German Federal Government to continue to finance the development of the European Fighter Aircraft (EFA) is a prime example (Harris and Sherwood, 1994). Corporate lobbying, and consequently strategic public affairs management activity in the UK and the EU, has grown dramatically over the past 15 years (Attack, 1990; Hollingsworth, 1991; Nolan, 1995; Harris, 2002). The principal reasons for this growth appear to be:

1   Increased internationalisation and competition in business markets has increased the importance of government creating a competitive home business environment, resulting in increased deregulation and government adopting the role of market regulator.
2   Importation and influence of a more structured corporate lobbying system from the US, whose objective is to influence legislation affecting business markets, whether they be corporate, government or non-governmental organisation (NGO) interests.
3   Increased corporate acquisition, merger, strategic alliance and joint-venture activity as result of the development of trading blocs and globalisation.
4   A move away from consensual politics in the 1980s, and early 1990s, in the UK in particular. Those affected by proposals had to seek to ensure that their views were communicated as competently as possible or lose influence.
5   The growth of international and transnational government is generating substantial legislation affecting businesses, for example, on the environment (McCormick, 1991). It has been estimated that 70 per cent of environmental legislation is generated by the EU for member states. This has brought lobbying at national and European level to ensure business's voice is heard when proposals are being formulated.

The modern business literature barely recognises lobbying in the UK or EU, yet its impact over the past 15 years has been significant, as can be seen in the public affairs management activity on such cases as amending Sunday trading legislation in the UK (Harris et al., 1999), Chiquita and what has been termed the 'banana wars' (Pedler, 2002) and genetically modified organisms (GMOs) as outlined in the work of Huegens (2001) and Van Schendelen (2002). A good example of lobbying and public affairs management techniques can be seen in Leighton Andrew's (1996) account of the Devonport Naval Dockyard Campaign, a synopsis of which is outlined below.

The Devonport Naval Dockyard Campaign

This campaign won the Institute of Public Relations 'Silver Sword of Excellence Award' (IPR, 1994) for the most effective Public Affairs Campaign in 1993–94, for Rowland Sallingsbury Casey (RSC).

RSC, a government affairs company (part of the old Saatchi Group), was appointed by Devonport Management Limited (DML) to coordinate the political campaign for the MOD Trident Nuclear Submarine Refitting Contract. The contract was worth £5 billion and would ensure a future for the winning dockyard and safeguard thousands of jobs. 'For Devonport it meant 5200 jobs in the yard, 20,000 regional jobs and £540 million in annual regional income' (IPR, 1994).

RSC quickly found out through contact with politicians, officials and journalists that it was behind its competitor Rosyth, Scotland in gaining the contract.

Rosyth had its key supporters in strategic positions in government and parliament which was giving it a major advantage. The Conservative Government Defence Secretary, Malcolm Rifkind, was a Scot, whilst the south-west of England had no voice in Cabinet. The Scottish Secretary, Ian Lang, was a public and strong supporter of Rosyth. Not surprisingly Scottish Conservatives backed this position, which was in turn supported by all Labour MPs in Scotland. Dr Gordon Brown, the then Labour Party Shadow Chancellor, was very much to the fore of the Rosyth campaign as MP for Dunfermline East, which included the Naval Yard.

This position was changed by a very effective campaign that made the centre of its strategy three key points:

- Devonport as the right strategic location for Trident;
- the DML bid as the best value to the Royal Navy and the tax payer; and
- Trident in Plymouth as essential to the south-west Region's economic, and the Government's political, health.

To achieve this, an aggressive lobbying and media campaign was launched that would organise the community, workforce, MPs, business community and media. It was intended to show the Ministry of Defence specialists and political advisers, Cabinet ministers and parliamentarians, the strategic, economic and political case for Trident in Devonport.

Consequently, RSC worked with DML and produced the following during the campaign:

- lobbying material and literature;
- a detailed media audit to work out who was sympathetic and who was not;
- personal briefings for relevant MPs, civil servants and political advisers throughout the summer of 1992;
- lobbying at party conferences and Westminster;
- a 20,000 signature petition;
- amended proposals for the contract to make them more innovative and to increase local media awareness;
- trained staff to deal with various media and influencers;
- reviews of political events to see how they could be used to the advantage of the campaign; and
- regular monitoring of progress.

In 1993 DML won the contract.

Looking critically at the DML campaign, it can be seen that RSC's involvement broadened the approach from purely procurement issues. RSC provided a critical edge of political awareness, which before then DML had missed. It is also useful to note that the 1992 General Election brought significant Liberal Democrat Party gains in the Conservative dominated south-west, and fear of the impact of losing the Devonport contract clearly could have tipped the decision in the south-west's favour. However, this needed pointing out to many people.

Marketing situations in which lobbying plays a role

Key areas in modern strategic marketing where public affairs management techniques and particularly lobbying is used to influence government and relative importance has been developed by Harris and Lock (1995) in the following taxonomy:

1 **Government as purchaser or allocator**

- *Winner takes all*

In a number of situations, there is only one contract or opportunity to be bid for. A recent example is Camelot's successful bid to run the National Lottery (now Lotto). Commercial television franchises, the Channel Tunnel Consortium and certain military contracts have similar characteristics. Price is rarely the sole criterion. The public decision is usually very visible and lobbying is rife and the justice system invariably used as a tactic.

- *Large, infrequent contracts*

Defence and large public works contracts are typical of this category. Increasingly failure to obtain such contracts threatens the very existence of the company or a strategic business unit with a visible and politically delicate impact on employment. The situation of ABB's railway works interests in the UK is one example, the tactical closing of coal mines in the UK, France and Germany another. Lobbying plays an important role.

- *Regularly supplied items*

Apart from highly specialised items, these are usually supplied through standard purchasing procedures, notably by competitive tender. These procedures leave little scope for lobbying, except in so far as it may be necessary to qualify a supplier to be included in the approved list or to pass any other pre-tender hurdles.

2 **Government as legislator and promulgator of regulatory frameworks (that is, broadcasting, utilities and so on)**

Legislation on matters such as product safety, trademarks and intellectual property, and fair trading are obvious targets for business lobbying to ensure that legitimate interests are protected. However, it is easily forgotten that a great deal of matters that affect specific businesses are enacted through regulations under enabling legislation. Visible examples are vehicle construction and use regulations, and regulations affecting food and agriculture. Lobbying is important here to ensure that regulations are sensibly framed and represent an appropriate balance of business and other pressure group interests.

3 Government as initiator of action

There are a number of explicit circumstances in which the relevant Minister or Director state initiates action by a quango or similar body. The most familiar case is the Monopolies and Mergers Commission in the UK. In other examples, where a quango can initiate action itself, the government of the day exerts some influence in terms of matters that are taken up and is frequently the final arbiter in terms of action upon the recommendations it receives. Lobbying in terms of provision of information as well as persuasive communication can play an important role in shaping the progress of events.

4 Government and European legislation and regulation

With the increasing influence of European directives and regulations upon product markets, proper representation of manufacturers' and marketeers' interests have become critical in those areas that the EU is seeking to regulate. As well as direct lobbying of Commission officials and Members of European Parliaments (MEPs) and representation through pan-European business bodies, support from one's own national government through civil servants and the Council of Ministers is critical to success on significant issues. In these instances, lobbying at both national and EU level is an essential activity.

5 Government as decision maker

There are a range of other situations where the government has *de facto* or *de jure* powers to take decisions which affect business. Whilst the example is not directly a marketing one, the controversy over the decision to permit Shell to sink the Brent Spar platform (Thorsteinsson et al., 2001) in the Atlantic is a good illustration, both of convincing government of the correctness of a course of action and of a failure of a broader public relations campaign against a more well-organised but less well-funded opponent.

Recent research with parliamentarians and officials in the UK shows that organisations can be seriously disadvantaged if they are not providing information to support their long-term business positions or counter their national and international corporate competitors by providing information to relevant bodies. This may well sound very logical, but the reality is that a number of interests and companies do not know how or understand the various UK and EU government processes and their ability to develop policy and regulations that impact upon them and the markets in which they operate. This puts them at a serious disadvantage, particularly small- and medium-sized enterprises (SME's) that may not have the scale or time to lobby locally, nationally and transnationally to maintain its interests.

MODERN PUBLIC AFFAIRS MANAGEMENT

Increasingly, to be able to compete means being able to exert pressure on government to gain competitive advantage. A well argued case, which has been outlined before, is that it has been suggested that a number of German and French car manufacturers successfully lobbied the EU for them to adopt catalytic converters as their preferred vehicle emissions measures. This became compulsory legislation, to the advantage of Mercedes, Audi, VW, Peugeot and so on. At a stroke this wiped out £1 billion worth of investment by Ford in lean-burn engine technology and significant outlay by Austin Rover, who were also developing this technology. Both Ford and Austin Rover deemed this technology to be a lot cleaner than just using catalytic converters. They had opted to go for a higher specification system rather than the intermediate catalytic converters. Once the legislation was enacted across the EU, Ford lost its £1 billion investment in R&D and had to reinvest in catalytic converters to catch up. Austin Rover, as a result of this policy, lost its investment, could never catch up and went bankrupt. BMW subsequently purchased Austin Rover.

The second example is that of Philip Morris, who is protecting its interests by spending considerable sums of euros in Brussels trying to delay and defer national states and the EU bringing in similar measures for compensation to meet health care risks of cancer-infected tobacco smokers as are in place in the US. The money is being used to delay legislation, which leads to compulsory care and compensation for sufferers. In the US it is now almost mandatory for sufferers to get care for tobacco-related diseases. By delaying the legislation, Philip Morris benefit financially.

Other areas where one can exert pressure to lobby for advantage are:

- *Packaging*: which may use only particular materials across Europe to meet specifications. Clearly this disadvantages its competitive edge to certain processes and companies. (See EVC 1 and 2 case studies for Greenpeace activity.)
- *Broadcasting*: as broadcasting internationalises, the granting of licences or privatisation of public broadcasting can give strategic advantages. Look at Rupert Murdoch, AOL, Time Warner. (See the Broadcasting case study.)
- *Health*: delays in environmental protection, tobacco legislation or alcohol abuse have an effect both on the health care industry and on certain businesses.
- *Travel/ecology*: restricting travel and tourism may benefit the ecology – or may just mean that if you have the money then you can go there.
- *Resources*: clearly, the allocation of fossil fuels, emissions and scarce resources and their availability also impact on competitive edge. Reliable and renewable electricity can give competitive advantage. Erratic and hazardous energy systems can lead to decline. People do not shop in Chernobyl any more.

THE RISE OF REGULATION

Lobbying has grown as a result of business and non-governmental organisations wishing to influence government regulatory policy. As government has sold its ownership of control of various sectors of the economy – utilities, broadcasting and so on – so it has tried to shape the direction of these now private companies or organisations and their interests through regulation. In fact, the last part of the twentieth century and early part of the twenty-first century has seen government at every level develop the regulator and regulation. To influence that regulation leads to strategic gain for the organisation. If you can shape the market to your advantage, then you win, and lobbying is about shaping that regulation so that it suits you and your interests. To outline core issues in public affairs and lobbying two graphical illustrations can be used. Figure 6.2 shows that each time government increases regulation, lobbying public affairs activity increases to shape that regulation.

This can also be graphically shown in a 2 × 2 matrix, Figure 6.3, where the more government regulatory policy, the higher the level of lobbying, thus intense activity.

We can see this being developed further if we look at the ways in which business, lobbying and policies can be used to influence government; Figure 6.4 demonstrates how decision making is influenced at the national and transnational government levels.

CONCLUSION

Machiavelli in *The Prince* provides a useful guide to exploring government and where to exert influence. Perhaps we should consider political marketing's role in good governance! Political brand images, what are they? Could they be slogans, parties, politicians or policies, or even the desires of the consumer (citizen) in the modern EU? Perhaps we should consider the growth of the consumer electorate and the need for two-way communication. Should this be by focus group, the Internet, or even by referenda?

Political parties are in decline in most of the developed world. The emergence of the strong leader and their brand image is on the rise – what impact does this have on good governance? How do we develop a strong regenerating civic society? How do we deal with a sometimes partisan government meeting the needs of society? These are just a few of the issues that we need to address when we rejuvenate. And multi-headed media? Should we not apply the segmentation techniques to rather than reinvent government?

There has been a growth in lobbying because as government has withdrawn from its role of being owner in the economy it has attempted to regulate and set the business environment for companies to operate in. However, the more competitive companies and NGOs influence that regulation to their own competitive advantage. There are currently 28,000 NGOs registered in Brussels explicitly just to influence EU policy. I wonder why?

Lobbying is part of modern political communication. As politicians become increasingly isolated and short of quality information, effective lobbying fills up that vacuum and allows good decision making (and, of course, sometimes bad decision making). Globalisation is meaning that to gain competitive edge transnationally, lobbying is used to influence the EU, the WTO, NAFTA and so on.

Another trend is, of course, accountability and lobbying has to be seen to account like government and be of a high ethical standard with interests declared. As society has higher

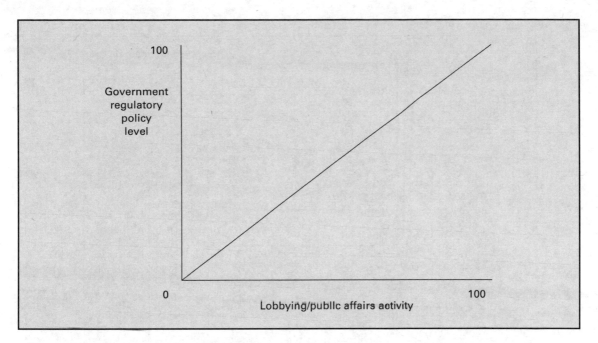

Figure 6.2   *The Machiavellian marketing graph*

Source: Harris, P. The Evolution of Strategic Corporate Lobbying, in the *Journal of Political Marketing*, 1 (1): 242.

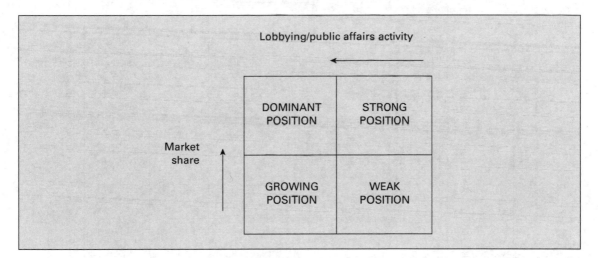

Figure 6.3   *The Machavellian marketing matrix*

Source: Harris, P. The Evolution of Strategic Corporate Lobbying, in the *Journal of Political Marketing*, 1(1): 242. The isotropic relationship between market share and levels of political lobbying: the maintenance of a dominant or monopolistic position in a market sector through political lobbying

demands, so it will want its voices heard and society will become more consumer driven and government will have to become more responsive to consumer needs. Perhaps consumer

needs in the EU are better roads, better health care, better education, rather than some of the things that politicians in the past have wanted. However, precise allocations of government

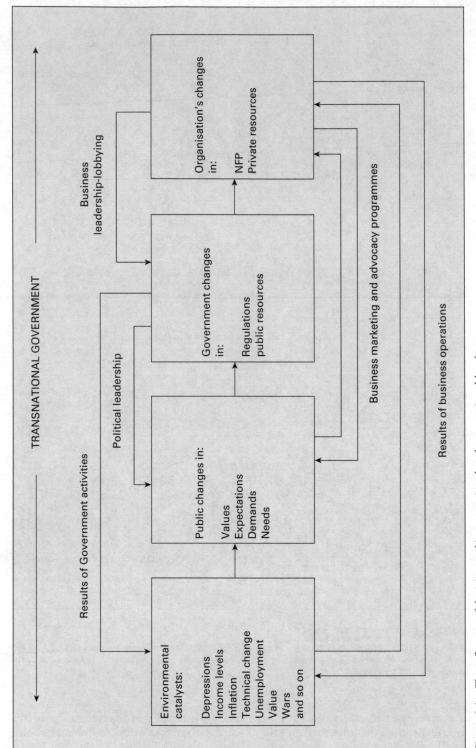

Figure 6.4   *The influence of decision making at national and transnational levels*

Source: Europen Journal of Marketing, 35(9/10): 1136–54.

funding to each of these areas will exercise public affairs management across Europe in the next decade. Consumers need to lobby for that quality of life and for resources to be spent on priority areas. All that we can say is that we can be sure of one thing, that as government increasingly develops a regulatory society, so lobbying will grow and the only way to counter this is to ensure that your voice is heard.

REFERENCES

Andrews, L. (1996) 'The Relationship of Political Marketing to political Lobbying: an examination of the Devonport Campaign for the Trident refitting contract in Special edition on Political Marketing' edited by P. Harris, *European Journal of Marketing*, 30 (10/11): 76–99.

Alderman, G. (1984) *Pressure Groups and Government in Great Britain*. London: Longman.

Attack, S. (1990) *The Directory of Public Affairs and Government Relations*. London: DPA.

Ball, A.R. and Millard, F. (1986) *Pressure Politics in Industrial Societies*. London: Macmillan.

Berry, L.L. (1983) 'Relationship Marketing', in L. Berry, L. Shostack and G. Upah (eds), *Emerging Perspectives on Services Marketing*. Chicago, IL: American Marketing Association.

Borg, E.A. (1991) 'Problem shifts and market research: the role of networks in business relationships', *Scandinavian Journal of Management*, 7 (4): 285–95.

Butler, P. and Collins, N. (1994) 'Political marketing: structure and process', *European Journal of Marketing*, 28 (1): 19–34.

Butler, P. and Collins, N. (1996) 'Strategic analysis and political markets, *European Journal of Marketing*, 30 (10/11): 32–44.

Curry, P. (1995) *Machiavelli for Beginners*. Cambridge: Icon Books.

Fisher, R., Kopelman, E. and Kupfer, Schneider, A. (1994) *Beyond Machiavelli: Tools for Coping with Conflict*. Cambridge, Mass: Harvard University Press.

Gallagher, J.C. and Scott, R. (1994) 'Scottish and Newcastle Breweries', in P. Harris and F. McDonald (eds) *European Business and Marketing: Strategic Issues*. London: Paul Chapman. pp. 231–236.

Gardner, J. (1991) *Effective Lobbying in the EC*. Deventer: Kluwer.

Granovetter, M. (1985) 'Economic action and social structure: the problem of embeddedness', *American Journal of Sociology*, 91 (3): 481–510.

Grant, W. and Sargent, J. (1987) *Business and Politics in Britain*. London: Macmillan.

Gronroos, C. (1994) 'From marketing mix to relationship marketing: towards a paradigm shift in marketing', *Management Decision*, 32 (2): 4–20.

Gummesson, E. (1987) 'The new marketing – developing long term interactive relationships', *Long Range Planning*, 4: 10–20.

Gummesson, E. (1994) 'Making relationship marketing operational', *International Journal of Service Industry Management*, 5: 5–20.

Häkansson, H. and the IMP Group (1982) *International Marketing and Purchasing of Industrial Goods*, Chichester: Wiley.

Häkansson, H. and Snehota, I. (1995) *Developing Relationships in Business Networks*, London: Thompson.

Halinen, A. (1997) *Relationship Marketing in Professional Services: a study of agency-client dynamics in the advertising sector*. London: Routledge.

Harris, P. (2001) 'Machiaveeli, political marketing and reinventing government', *European Journal of Marketing*, 39 (9/10): 1136–54.

Harris, P. and Lock, A. (1995) 'Machiavellian Network Marketing: Corporate Political Lobbying and Industrial Marketing in the UK', paper presented to the 11th IMP Conference, MBS/UMIST, Manchester, 7–9 September.

Harris, P. and Lock, A. (1996) 'Machiavellian marketing: the development of corporate lobbying in the UK', *Journal of Marketing Management*, 12 (4): 313–28.

Harris, P., Lock, A. and Rees, P.L. (eds) (2000) *Machiavelli, Marketing and Management*. London: Routledge.

Harris, P., Gardner, H. and Vetter, N. (1999) 'Goods Over God': Lobbying and Political Marketing – A Case Study of the Campaign by the Shopping Hours Reform Council to Change Sunday Trading Laws in the UK' in B. Newman (ed.), *The Handbook of Political Marketing*. Thousand Oaks, CA: Sage.

Harris, P. and Sherwood, R. (1994) 'British Aerospace', in *European Business and Marketing: Strategic Issues*, P. Harris and F. McDonald (eds). London: Chapman.

Harrison, S. (2000) 'Shouts and whispers: the lobbying campaigns for and against resale price maintenance', *European Journal of Marketing*, 34 (1/2): 207–222.

Heugens, P.M.A.R. (2001) *Strategic Issues: Implications for Corporate Performance*. Rotterdam: Erasmus Research Institute of Management.

Hollingsworth, M. (1991) *MP's for Hire: The Secret World of Political Lobbying*. London: Bloomsbury.

Holmlund, M. and Törnrous, J.-A. (1997) 'What are the relationships in business networks?', *Management Decision*, 35 (4): 304–309.

IPR (1994) *Sword of Excellence Awards*, London: Institute of Public Relations.

Jackson, B.B. (1985) 'Build customer relationships that last', *Harvard Business Review*, 63, (Nov. Dec.): 120–28.

Jay, A. (1994) *Management and Machiavelli* (revised paperback edition). San Diego, CA: Pfeiffer.

Jones, N. (1995) *Soundbites and Spin Doctors*. London: Cassell.

Jordan, G. (1989) 'Insider lobbying: the British version', *Political Studies*, 37 (3): 107–113.

Jordan, G. (ed.) (1991) *The Commercial Lobbyists*. Aberdeen: Aberdeen University Press.

Kavanagh, D. (1995) *Election Campaigning: The New Marketing of Politics*. Oxford: Blackwell.

Kickert, W.J.M., Klijn, E-H., and Koppenjan, J.F.M. (eds) (1997) *Managing Complex Networks: Strategies for the Public Sector*. London: Sage.

Mareek, P. (1995) *Political Marketing and Communication*. London: John Libby.

Marketing (1994) Michael Portillo, quoted in 29 September, London.

Mazey, S. and Richardson, J.J. (eds) (1993) *Lobbying in the European Community*. Oxford: Oxford University Press.

McAlpine, A. (1992) *The New Machiavelli*. London: Aurum.

McCormick, J. (1991) *British Politics and the Environment*, London: Earthscan.

McNair, B. (1995) *An Introduction to Political Communication*. London: Routledge.

Miller, C. (1990) *Lobbying*. Oxford: Blackwell.

Moodie, G.C. and Studdert-Kennedy, G. (1970) *Opinions, Publics and Pressure Groups*. London: Allen and Unwin.

Morgan, R.M. and Hunt, S.D. (1994) 'The commitment-trust theory of relationship marketing', *Journal of Marketing*, 58 (July): 20–38.

Newman, B. (1994) *The Marketing of the President*. Thousand Oaks, CA: Sage.

Newman, B. (ed.) (1999) *Handbook of Political Marketing*, Thousand Oaks, CA: Sage.

Newman, B. and Sheth, J. (1986) *Political Marketing: Readings and Annotated Bibliography*. Chicago, IL: American Marketing Association.

Nolan (1995) *'Standards in Public Life'*, First Report of the Committee on Standards in Public Life, Chairman, Lord Nolan, Volume 1. London: HMSO.

O'Shaughnessey, N. (1990) *The Phenomenom of Political Marketing*. London: Macmillan.

Pedler, R. (2002) *European Union Lobbying: Changes in the arena*. Basingstoke: Palgrave.

Richardson, J.J. (1993) (ed) *Pressure Groups*. Oxford: Oxford University Press.

Scammell, M. (1995) *Designer Politics: How Elections are Won*. London: Macmillan.

Scammell, M. (1999) 'The Development of Political Marketing', *The Journal of Political Studies*,

Scammell, M. (1999) 'Political Marketing: Lessons for political Science', *Political Studies*, 47 (4): 718–39.

Shea, M. (1988) *Influence: How to make the system work for you, a handbook for a Modern Machiavelli*. London: Century.

Strandvik, T. and Törnroos, J.-A. (1995) 'Studying relationships in Industrial and Services Marketing', Paper presented at the 11th IMP Conference, Manchester Federal School of Business and Management, 7–9th September.

Thompson, G., Frances, J., Levacic, R. and Mitchell, J. (eds) (1991) *Markets, Hierarchies and Networks: The Coordination of Social Life*. London: Sage.

Thorsteinsson, J., Harris, P. and Gardner, H. (2001) 'Eco-Warriors and the Seven Sisters: Environmental Pressure Groups and the Rise of Targeted Action Against Global Energy Companies', Academy of Marketing Political Marketing Conference, September, Dublin University Business School.

Van Schendelen, M.P.C.M. (2002) *Machiavelli in Brussels: The Art of EU Lobbying*.: Amsterdam University Press.

Wring, D. (1997) 'Reconciling marketing with political science: theories of political marketing', *The Journal of Marketing Management*, 13 (7): 651–64.

USEFUL WEBSITES

www.cia.gov/cia/publications/factbook
The CIA World Fact Book, one of the best sources of information on all countries and governments.

www.europa.eu.int
The prime EU government website with press releases.

www.henrystewart.com/journals
The home of the Journal of Public Affairs.

www.ukgovt.com
This site has links to all the UK government
websites and information.

CASE STUDIES

That can be read in conjunction with this
Chapter are:

American Furnishing
Broadcasting
BSE Crisis
Cooperative Bank
EVC1 and 2
Mannesmann Mobilfunk
Philips Electronics
Shell
Unilever

In the past two decades the growth of joint venture company formation as part of the process of developing strategic business alliances has been one of the key features of international markets. In Europe this surge of interest in forming joint venture equity companies,or cooperations as the EU calls them, has given birth to such transnational companies as:

- Iveco, the Fiat–Ford truck manufacturing and marketing operation;
- EVC, the Anglo-Italian PVC manufacturer; and
- Airbus, the EU-based aircraft manufacturer.

There are many forms of strategic alliance to consider besides joint venture company formation. These can include:

> ...formal and informal alliances; vertical, horizontal and conglomerate links; equity and non equity agreements; local, national, continental or transoceanic alliances, and so on. (Gugler, 1992)

In this chapter we aim to explore strategic alliances and particularly to focus on joint venture company formation in a European context, rather than look across all available options of acquisition, merger and so forth. It takes as its starting point an attempt to explain why there has been such growth in the formation of joint venture companies across Europe in the 1980s and 1990s. Is this just the latest corporate strategic fashion or is this in response to the trends and structures that are emerging in an increasingly competitive global market?

What particular reasons are there for a surge in growth in joint venture formation in Europe in the past 10 years?

How and why are joint ventures formed? What types of joint venture are there? What lessons can be learned for the formation of successful joint ventures?

What other methods of strategic alliance should be considered by companies wishing to compete in global markets?

FORTRESS EUROPE AND THE SINGLE EUROPEAN MARKET

In 1987, the Single European Act (SEA) came into force across the European Community, with the declared aim of achieving 'an area without frontiers, in which the free movement of goods, persons, services and capital is ensured' by the end of 1992. The urgent implementation of the SEA had been vigorously promoted by Paolo Cecchini's influential report, 'The European Challenge' (1988), which spelt out the dangers of a fragmented EU and the need to improve competition by increasing the macro-economic supply side of the Community by the following four policies being adopted internally:

1 The removal of border controls.
2 The opening up to competitive tender of public procurement markets.
3 Liberalisation of financial services.
4 The resulting benefits of business strategies being developed in a more competitive market, resulting from the above three reforms.

The competitiveness of the EU had been continually falling behind that of Japan and the US, the worlds leading trading nations. The loss of competitiveness could be seen in a slow-down in absolute output and high rates of inflation and unemployment, coupled to slow growth in investment and productivity. Europe was

TABLE 7.1   Changes in export market shares (%)

	1973–68	1979–73	1985–89
Industry, total			
Europe 10[a]	–1.83%	–0.24%	–1.44%
US	–3.36	–0.17	+0.73
Japan	+1.61	+0.85	+5.37
Strong demand			
Europe 10[a]	–3.43	–0.56	–2.54
US	–4.96	+0.57	+1.24
Japan	+2.21	+0.70	+7.14
Moderate demand			
Europe 10[a]	–1.19	–0.29	–2.54
US	–4.61	–0.99	+1.24
Japan	+2.85	+1.64	+5.66
Weak demand			
Europe 10a	–1.67	+1.70	+1.93
US	–1.55	–0.09	–1.05
Japan	–0.71	–0.40	+1.85

Source: European Commission (1991).

Note: Share of exports of a certain country or zone in total exports of all OECD countries (at current prices), including intra-EC trade.

(a) Europe a does not include Greece and Portugal and excludes intra-EU trade.

especially vulnerable in new emerging technologies, where much of the future of the world's economic business looked likely to lie. Table 7.1 shows this decline in competitiveness very clearly, from 1968 to 1985.

To address this specific problem, the SEA of 1986 saw as one of it's primary objectives 'to strengthen the scientific and technological basis of European industry and to encourage it to become more competitive at an international level'.

As a result, the EU adopted economic policies which fostered the development of strategic technologically-based industries, for instance, a viable microprocessor industry using such pan-community programmes as the European Strategic Programme for Research and Development Technology (ESPRIT).

European firms, unlike their Japanese and US counterparts, were restricted to their own smaller national markets. Any attempt to broaden their competitive scope by expanding into other EU nations was hampered by a broad array of barriers and rising costs, all undermining efficiency prior to the Single European Market (SEM). These barriers were largely national and restricted government support, contracts and business to indigenous companies.

Company ownership is also hampered by national boundaries and trading traditions, thus acquisition and merger in many EU states, most notably in France and Germany, is limited either due to state holdings in the former case or by the restrictions of a small elite equity owning groups in the latter. The *Practitioner's Guide to European Takeover Regulations and Practice* (Eurpean Commission, 1991) comments on the current encumbrances to acquisition and merger that:

Germany presents a paradox for the prospective foreign acquirer. On the one hand, no exchange control permission is required for a foreign take-over and there are no restrictions on the making of acquisitions and the carrying on of business by foreigners, except in relation to the defence industry. On the other hand, the structure of German business is such that there are comparatively few large targets and Germany is a difficult territory for hostile take-overs, even for German offerors. (1991)

By the start of the 1970s the EU had recognised this weakness and was commenting on the potential of takeovers within the community to bring about world-scale competitive companies.

> ... operations of mergers and absorption are virtually impossible between corporations of different nationalities, as the corporate laws of member states pose obstacles which are difficult to surmount. Apart from the legal possibility ... the fiscal cost of the operation constitutes in general a prohibitive obstacle. (European Commission, 1991)

Restrictions on mergers do not operate equally across the EU. In the UK, The Netherlands, Spain and Eire there are few restrictions on traditional takeover activity, thus ahead of the full introduction of the SEM. By 1993 many more companies in these countries had been acquired by Japanese, US or other European countries interested in gaining access to one of the largest trading blocks. A good example of the latter was in 1988 when the Swiss food group TNC Nestlé, in a contested takeover with the Swiss confectionery company Jacob Suchard, acquired Rowntree-Mackintosh, the UK-based confectionary and food company.

The Rowntree-Mackintosh takeover gave Nestlé a strong EC base to operate from post the full implementation of the SEM, a good portfolio of well-known brands and a strengthened European position in the chocolate market. Thus Nestlé was able to compete more effectively against its main global rival, the US MNC-Mars. This acquisition eventually forced Suchards to withdraw from the chocolate market, as it no longer saw itself as a viably large enough company to compete on equal terms in an enlarged market.

As has been outlined, the development of international companies prior to the establishment of the SEM in Europe was restricted, giving a competitive advantage to economic rivals like Japan and the US. Leading European industrialists were openly raising these issues, for instance in 1988, ICI's, Chairman, Sir Denys Henderson, concluded in an address on the EU 'that some European companies are not viable world-scale competitors'.

Under this pressure and with growing recognition of the need to change, the EU has adopted a policy to foster the formation of European joint ventures as a way of building world-scale strategic companies. Jacobs and Stewart-Clark (1990) have commented that joint ventures are often seen as major contributors to the economic objectives of the EU:

> They may, for instance, be very useful in a field of research and development; when companies need specialisation of another or of each other; for the development of an important new product which would be too expensive for one company to produce; to facilitate undertaking risky investments, to develop a new market to reduce costs for the benefit of users; or to increase competition and in that role to help small and medium-sized firms which might otherwise not be able to penetrate a particular market. (1990: 87)

The EU has also recognised that alliances can avoid duplication and may even help to rationalise the manufacture of the products involved, and has therefore positively fostered the development of joint venture companies as a way of putting together strategic companies to compete in world markets. A good example was the formation of the electrical generating equipment manufacturer GEC-Alsthom from UK and French-based parent companies. This collaborative joint venture has built up a European company that can compete on an equal basis in competitive world markets against major transnational companies like the General Electric Company of America (GEC) and the Swiss–Swedish multinational ABB.

In fact, GEC-Alsthom makes a powerful argument for the advantages of synergy derived from a product and marketing fit between two former operations, for GEC's traditional power-station market has been in the UK, China, the Far East and South Africa, whereas Alsthom's has been France, North Africa and the Middle East. GEC has been strong in middle-size transformers, Alsthom in big and small machines. The UK arm brought switchgear with vacuum technology, Alsthom the more costly, but more sophisticated gas technology. In gas turbines, the GEC-Rushton turbine company had machines ranging from 1.6MW to 52MW. Apart from the strategic fit, the success of the company will be measured in profits, merging cultures and the accruing benefits from pooling the best resources.

The formation of joint venture companies is not restricted to technology-based company formation, but covers the whole spectrum of economic activity and has included retailing (electrical retailing joint venture, E and S Retail), Services (Visa card) and food manufacturing and marketing, where General Mills and Nestlé agreed, over 11 days in November 1989, to set-up a joint venture company, Cereal Partners Worldwide, to market ready-to-eat cereals in the fast growing but Kellogg-dominated markets of continental Europe.

During the period 1980–89, of the 520 equity and non-equity joint ventures formed by UK firms with Western European, US and Japanese partners announced in the *Financial Times*, 13.7 per cent were in financial services, 11.4 per cent in telecommunications, 10.6 per cent in Aerospace and 14.0 per cent were in other manufacturing sectors (Glaister, 1991).

Government has also directly fostered joint venture formation for Community economic and technological gain on a grand scale. The EU stimulated the development of the joint venture Airbus Industrie, a response to a global market characterised by a necessity for large-scale production. It was an attempt to break down the domination of the world commercial aircraft market by airframe makers – Boeing, Lockheed and McDonnell Douglas. In 1967 a consortium was formed by the British, French and German governments to develop the Airbus aircraft – the A 300 Airbus Industrie was initially composed of Aerospatiale (France), British Aerospace (Britain), Construcciones Aeronauticas (Spain) and Messersschmitt-Boelkow-Blohm (Germany). By 1991 the European collaborative project had six models under production or development and had increased its share of the world market from 5 to 30 per cent. This success led to Lockheed withdrawing from the civil aviation market and increased competitive pressures on Boeing and McDonnell Douglas.

Government has also been a stimulus in other technological programmes, with the EU using its programmes like ESPRIT and BRITE/EURAM (Basic Research in Industrial Technologies for Europe/European Research in Advanced Materials) to foster the effective development of European-based R&D; this was used to great effect in establishing a European-based semiconductor industry in the 1980s.

Military projects have also been stimulated by governments to be joint ventures developed on a European-wide basis. This has resulted in the development of the all-European fighter the Jaguar and its eventual replacement, the European Fighter Aircraft (EFA), although the scale of involvement and partners commitment to the project is yet to be finalised as Europe goes into deeper recession and partners reassess the need for sophisticated weaponry in a post-Iron Curtain world.

Many joint ventures alternatively are market led, for instance, the linkage between Volvo and Renault in car and vehicle manufacture was in response to competitive pressures from the market forcing two national companies to pool research and production facilities to maintain competitive edge or be forced out of this business individually. Of course, the relationship broke down and Volvo decided to sell its motor car vehicle operations to Ford.

Market-led change stimulating the birth of joint ventures is not just restricted to the automotive industry, but good examples can be seen in the petrochemical and plastics chemical industry – European Vinyls Corporation (EVC), the ENI–ICI joint venture company that was formed in response to the need to rationalise the PVC industry. In the pharmacuctical industry the formation of SmithKline Beecham to create a global-based drug supplier out of US and UK parents produced one of the world's largest companies in that industry, the scale and cost of R&D in drug development being a crucial factor in bringing about what was an agreed merger.

EASTERN EUROPE

The joint venture has played an essential part in the industrial and commercial development of post-Second World War Eastern Europe. Before the liberalisation of Eastern Europe, the breakdown of the Soviet empire and the ultimate symbolism – the pulling down of the Berlin Wall in November 1989 – was frequently used as a tool to link the command economies of the East with the technical and commercial skills of the West. Paliwoda (1989) explored this area in depth with regard to Polish joint ventures and has written a detailed case study on Massey-Ferguson's cooperation with the state tractor manufacture Agromet-Motoimpor. More recent researchers have updated this area of study in the light of political and economic development, whilst others have looked at the complexity of setting up joint ventures in the old USSR and its satellite countries.

Sterch Control is a good Russian state example of a joint venture between the old Soviet organisations Org Minudobeniya and OKB Mineral, of the USSR Ministry of Fertilizers and the US-based company Honeywell. Using its Austrian subsidiary, Honeywell GmbH, the US parent was able to effectively combine with its Soviet partners to form a company whose basic objectives are to deliver to the Soviet market, as well as to developing world markets, Honeywell products. The US parent company is the world leader in manufacturing control systems, instrumentation and hardware and their implementation in various industries (chemistry, oil processing, power, pipeline transportation, pulp and paper, glass and so on), construction and non-industrial application (housing, public health, education and so on).

The importance of joint venture activity to the former USSR and now CSSR can be seen in the fact that by 1991, 1200 East–West joint ventures were operating in the Soviet Union. Interestingly, Austrian and Finnish companies were very much at the forefront of this wave of activity, paralleling their historical involvement in being brokerage centres for commercial trading with the Eastern block. Ironically the major provider of consultancy information and expertise on setting up joint ventures in the CSSR is the Soviet–Finnish joint venture management consultancy Vneshconsult.

The complexity and difficulty of setting up commercial ventures in the old USSR and new CSSR can be seen in the following commentary on barter trade in the last months of the reformist Gorbachev Government:

> The Soviet Government has placed extreme restrictions on the sale of raw materials to the West, insisting that value-added manufacturing/processing occur before the product leaves the country. The Soviets are extremely worried about the opportunists trying to make a 'quick buck' without reinvesting into long-term growth of the infrastructure. The laws of the past 18 months also require joint venture partnership as a virtual prerequisite for barter trading in the market. (Sovtec, 1991)

This rigidity does not seem to have lasted, the need for hard currency having negated this tough stance, however, it is quite clear that the drive for investment through joint venture companies is preferred.

One of the most ambitious cooperations for CSSR investment is the American Trade Consortium, a joint venture of major US multinational corporations (MNC's)–Chevron, Archer-Daniels-Midland, Eastman Kodak, RJR Nabisco, and Johnson & Johnson (the Ford Motor company was involved but pulled out) – led by the Mercatator Corporation, an investment bank created for the enterprise (Hertzfield, 1991). The rationale for the company is that the CSSR needs consumer goods and is prepared to give Chevron the rights to develop a particularly promising

oilfield 'if the parties to the oil venture agree to share their hard currency earnings with various consumer goods joint ventures that simultaneously open plants to serve the market'. Hertzfield asks, 'Is the ATC a model to be emulated?' It certainly appears so as it is a strong model for dealing with the CSSR, for the partners split the cost and reduce their exposure in trading in a restructuring and volatile state, rather than being one external company taking all the potential risk. As one sees the painful development of the CSSR as it moves towards a market economy, one can see even more reasons for joint venture operations.

As the old Eastern block emerges from its isolation, so there are signs that the use of the joint venture is changing to become a more useful way of forming strategic alliances to gain access to markets, technological transfer or new capital. The evidence is that most new joint ventures within Hungary, Czechoslovakia, Poland and the Baltic states are more reflective of Western models for strategic alliance formation, although in the East they are still trying to come to terms with market forces and reform (Carr, 1991), whilst those joint ventures being formed within the CSSR are still very bureaucratic, mirroring the highly-centralised nature of state government as a partner. The Russian Entrepreneurship, Shell, Skoda, Unilvever and Starobrno case studies deal with a number of the complex issues relating to Central and Eastern European transition economies, especially corruption, environment, building markets and state bureaucracy.

STRATEGIC RATIONALE FOR FORMING ALLIANCES

The development of the SEM has fostered a surge in the growth of joint ventures by European companies, but other forms of strategic alliance have also grown dramatically as part of the process of gaining competitive advantage in an increasingly global market. Gugler (1992) has commented that 'in the 1980s, US firms formed over 2000 agreements with European Corporations. The number of US international joint ventures (i.e. the creation of a new entity) established annually increased six-fold from 1976–87.'

Much recent research on strategic alliances is dominated by joint ventures and mergers, however, there is also much that can be said about marketing agreements and acquisitions in looking at corporate competitive edge. The reader who wishes to examine this area in more depth is urged to look at McCall and Warrington (1984), Young et al., (1989) and Bleeke and Ernst (1993) as starting points, as this chapter can only briefly introduce the reader to the area and concentrates on strategic alliances and especially joint venture company formation.

To comprehend realistically what strategic alliances are, we need a reasonably robust definition to encompass fully what has become a very broad international corporate term. Borys and Jemison (1989) make a good starting point in categorising strategic alliances; they see them as hybrids and define five main types of inter-company agreements:

1 Mergers are the complete unification of two or more organisations into one entity.
2 Acquisitions involve the purchase of one organisation by another, enabling one buyer to assume control over the other.
3 Licence agreements involve the purchase of a right to use an asset for a particular time and offer rapid access to new technology and product innovations.
4 Supplier arrangements (of which partnering is one specific example) represent contracts for the sale of one firm's output to another.
5 Joint ventures result in the creation of a new organisation that is formally independent of the parents; control over and responsibility for the venture varies greatly among specific cases.

These points all warrant different levels of organisational commitment from the acquisitive or alliance forming organisations; for instance, a merger can stretch management to the limit as they are forced to grapple with building a new organisational structure, merging the two businesses and developing a single corporate direction and culture to name but a few issues. The failure rate of corporate acquisitions has been well documented, particularly in the UK in the study by Booz Allen and Hamilton who estimate that on a sample of all industries, 49 per cent are net winners, 39 per cent losers and the rest in between.

Davidson (1987), in denigrating the effectiveness of many acquisitions, quotes the Industrial Performance Analysis of the ICC, 'Too many acquisitions are based on an attractive-looking balance sheet and earnings statement plus a quick trip to the plant'. Haste in corporate acquisition policy is seen as a poor developer of businesses and indicative of a lack of commitment by management to the business. One should always question: Why was it up for sale in the first place? Why is it available now? Was it run badly? What were its earnings per share?

As the SEM approaches, so merger and acquisition activity has increased in the EU as firms position themselves to take advantage of or defend themselves from the consequences of 1992. Ward et al. (1991), in their useful analysis of corporate restructuring and management buyouts in Europe, point out that in 1989 there were some 5682 acquisitions in Europe by European companies for a total value of £70.6 billion and that this figure was rising as 1993 drew closer.

TOWARDS A DEFINITION – JOINT VENTURES

To understand the use of joint ventures as a major part of strategic alliance formation, we need a working definition that will explain realistically current corporate understanding of what one is. In assessing joint ventures it is usual to differentiate between equity joint ventures and non-equity joint ventures.

Killing (1982) and others see equity joint ventures as 'traditional joint ventures', which are created when two or more partners join forces to create a new incorporated company in which each has an equity position. Thus each partner expects a proportional share of dividends and representation on the board.

Harrigan (1991) in her analysis sees joint ventures as 'separate entities with two or more active businesses as partners', with the emphasis being on the development of the child – a corporate 'entity created by partners for a specific activity' and normally over a fixed renewable period. Equity joint ventures can thus be defined as involving two or more legally distinct organisations (the parents), each of which invests in the venture and actively participates in the decision-making activities of the jointly owned entity (Geringer, 1991).

The use of the parent–child metaphor for understanding joint ventures and their development is a good one, which is widely used and can be extensively developed to make sense of what is a difficult concept to comprehend. Using the atomic family as a metaphor one can explore and assess the corporate relationship and its direction. Is it a marriage of convenience? Have the partners entered into a formal contractual relationship, perhaps an equity joint venture (marriage) which could result upon consummation and other partnerings in the birth of a number of other joint ventures (as children)?

Or is the joint venture just the result of one brief alliance between the two parents which gave birth to an unwanted new corporate child? It was good at the time but is not wanted now, as the partners do not get on. Could it be adopted or fostered by somebody else?

If the relationship is a stable one, how is the child nurtured, educated and developed?

Is it starved of funds and good staff, or given these freely in quantities that will enable it to make its own way in the world and achieve full independence from its parents?

Will it be allowed to enter adulthood and be responsible for its own actions, rather than the parents controlling it and restricting its independence?

Will the child eventually grow and challenge the parents' actions?

Contractor and Lorange (1988) explore the development of non-equity joint ventures and see them as agreements between partners to cooperate in some way, but do not necessarily see them leading to the separate legal corporate entities. In non-equity joint ventures, like for example the Eurotunnel contractor Trans-Manche Link which was made up of four partners, the norm is to have carefully defined contracts setting down rules, regulations, formulas governing the allocation of tasks, costs, penalties and revenues. Contractor and Lorange give three examples, which involve different levels of risk and return for the partners:

- *Exploration consortia*: often involves the sharing of costs out of the venture once a successful formula has been developed and marketed. Many offshore oil exploration ventures adopt this risk/profit sharing approach.
- *Research partnerships*: in contrast, costs may be allocated by an agreed mechanism, but the revenue of the company is dependent on what each partner does with the formulation. This is commonly used as a mechanism for effective shared pharmaceutical research; the cost of such activity can be very punitive and the outcomes not always marketable.
- *Co-production agreements*: each partner's costs are a function of its own efficiency in producing its part, while revenue is a function of the successful sales of the major partner. This has frequently been used in co-production agreements in automotive and aerospace markets.

With non-equity joint ventures, rewards for each firm are dependent upon the level of profits earned and there is a reasonable degree of inter-organisational dependence, much as there is with equity joint ventures. In terms of financial benefits, it can also be seen that the use of joint ventures offers much scope for parent companies to keep borrowings, losses and returns on capital off the main balance sheet and thus trigger asset and profit growth.

All other types of cooperative agreements, such as contracting, franchising and licensing, may be considered as contractual arrangements where reward is determined by profits generated and inter-organisational dependence is low to negligible.

Thus the term 'joint venture' is frequently used as a catch-all to define a number of commercial arrangements and relationships, some fairly loose, whilst others are characterised by formal equity stakes and linkages to third parties. Christelow (1987) suggests a very broad definition of joint-ventures: 'Joint ventures are cooperative forms of organisation between independent parties who could otherwise engage in competition or have competitive potential.'

This definition does not specify the necessity for creating a separate entity and can therefore include marketing agreements and teaming arrangements. Lyons (1991) suggests in analysing strategic alliances that there are four potential domains; technological, industrial, commercial and financial. Thus cooperations and joint ventures can be formed on the basis of any combination of these domains.

The ability to do more through synergy is also a factor, as organisations need to pool resources to compete and meet the needs of the global customer. Joint ventures can be a very effective way of putting two or more organisations together to create something greater than the sum of the two parts by synergy. The development of Airbus Industries, a result of four partners pooling their expertise and resources to create a world-class EU-based commercial aircraft supplier from a much smaller base, shows the great benefits of synergy. Technology, engineering, marketing, finance and modern management have been put together from various countries and industries into one group that, through synergy, has grown this business.

The benefits of synergy are difficult to bring about and test managers to the full in many cases. The experience of acquisitions and mergers is not good because there seems to be little benefit from synergy in many cases as very often the two or more organisations do not fit together very well and they are certainly not complimentary. This can result in failure on a grand scale, as can be seen in the poor results and declining profits of merged groups which have attracted corporate predators who then acquire them and dismember them.

The prevailing management style has been decentralisation in the last two decades to counter poor mergers. However, synergy, through putting together companies to make something more successful on a global scale, is now becoming a necessity of international business life. Crompton (1990) observes that some organisations are now too decentralised to benefit from the synergy of their product portfolios, and as a result competitive advantage in their industries is being lost. He argues that some businesses need restructuring 'to exploit potential shared resources, where these give competitive advantage (for example by creating a distribution company or upstream component manufacturing unit).'

GLOBALISM

One of the most significant developments in the global economy in recent years has been the growth and spread of strategic alliances that have developed in response to the changes which have been happening to the world economy: acceleration of technological change, increased costs of developing, producing and marketing new products. Collaborative ventures between firms across firms is not knew, as Kindleberger (1969) has pointed out. What is different is the scale, which has dramatically increased, with many firms forming not just one alliance but networks of alliances. These relationships Dicken (1992) has highlighted 'are increasingly polygamous rather than monogamous'.

Companies assessed in a *Business International* study (1987), showed that 'few companies have only a single alliance. Instead, they form a series of alliances, each with partners that have their own web of collaborative arrangements, like Toshiba, Philips, AT&T and Olivetti who are at the hub of what are often overlapping alliance networks which frequently include a number of fierce competitors.'

Global competition is frequently found as a key feature in why alliances are formed. Devlin and Bleackley (1988) state that 'Probably the greatest stimulus to alliance formulation has been the emergence of global competitors and those corporations wishing to become global.' This view has been echoed by Ohmae (1989), who has commented that 'To compete in the global arena, you have to incur and defray – immense fixed costs. You need partners.'

Thus the necessity to effectively compete in the new global market is driving companies into forming strategic alliances, and the most competitive companies in the new global market have a network of alliances covering all aspects of their business. An excellent example of the network of alliances can be seen in Gugler's (1992) work on alliance networks in the semi-conductor industry, which can be seen in Figure 7.1 taken from the same work on Philips' international network. These diagrammatically outline the complex network of alliances, joint ventures and dependencies that are in operation in these ultra-competitive and interdependent electronics and information technology markets.

Lorange and Roos (1991) argue that 'For many multinational firms, strategic alliances have become increasingly important tools for ensuring speed and flexibility in arguing out multinational strategies.'

RISK REDUCTION

A commonly quoted factor stimulating the drive to the formation of strategic alliances and particularly joint venture formation is risk reduction. Lyons (1991) states that 'one motivation to form joint ventures is frequently to reduce risk. The sharing of risk helps some organisations to follow new or innovative paths.' Lynch (1989) further suggests, 'Given the riskiness of a start up subsidiary, US companies should consider forming cooperative ventures as the first strategic step into the European Market place.' This clearly holds true for any company seeking to enter a foreign market and not just the EC. Another stimulus often referred to is structural change in a particular industry or market. Typical of this view is Lyons (1991), who observes that 'Joint ventures as well as acquisitions and mergers, are the response of many organisations to pressure prompting structural change.'

This can be seen in the responses of many of the basic commodity businesses, like coal, steel, petrochemicals, plastics and even vehicles, that having reached maturity and market saturation

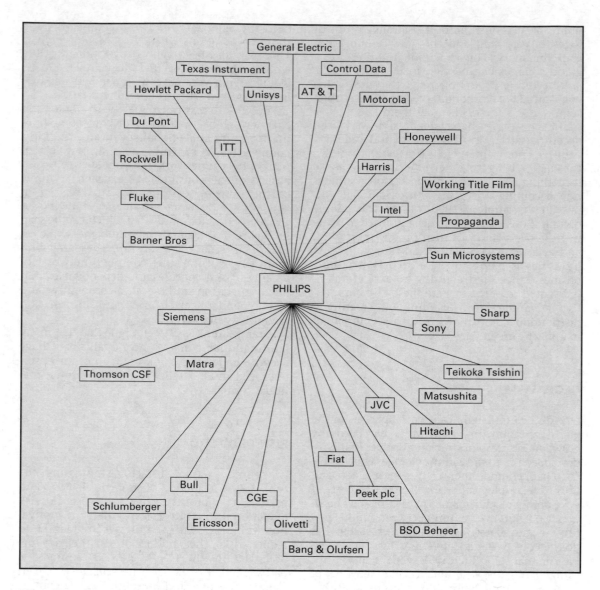

Figure 7.1   *International network alliances of Philips*

Source: Gugler, P. (1992) 'Building transnational alliances to create competitive advantage', *Long Range Planning*, 25 (1): 97.

on certain products restructure frequently using strategic alliances and joint ventures. Historically, this need to restructure resulted in rationalisation in the immediate post-War period through nationalisation, state owner-ship, state equity holding and has more recently been followed by joint venture com-pany formation.

If we look at mergers and acquisition activity it can be seen that there are four great waves of energy this century (de Jonquieres and Fidler, 1990). Each successive wave has been pushed by

distinct pressures and corporate objectives, and each has wrought important transformations in the structure of the world's industrialised economies. The latest wave is seen as reaching full flood in the late 1980s (Nabisco, the Imperial Group and so on, all of which have been broken up as groups subsequently), with the main impetus being generated by the fol-lowing three factors:

- to strengthen existing positions in core business (including divestments);

- financial deregulation, which has made capital increasingly mobile; and
- global competition.

As has been explained, merger and acquisition is not always possible and there has been a marked growth in the development of strategic alliances. Selwyn (1991) sees five main reasons for companies responding in this way:

- penetrating new markets;
- entering new businesses;
- sharing R&D costs;
- eliminating wasteful competition; and
- avoiding predators.

Corning Glass Works, the US-based MNC, is involved in a number of technology-intensive businesses and has used joint ventures extensively to open up markets that would not have normally been accessible to the firm. The company operates 23 joint ventures and more than half its operating profits come from these alliances. In the television glass business, Corning used joint ventures with Asahi Glass of Japan and Samsung of Korea to provide it with new technology. This was essential as Corning's traditional US customers gave up manufacturing and the industry became dominated by Japanese and Korean companies. J. Houghton, the Chief Exceutive Officer (CEO) of Corning, gives five reasons why Corning see joint venture formation as an important part of their corporate marketing strategy:

1 To gain access to markets.
2 To 'leap downstream'–vertical integration.
3 To apply technology they have already developed.
4 To gain access to new technology.
5 To overcome barriers in national or international markets.

This final feature as has previously been discussed has contributed much to the growth of joint venture. Formation by EU companies and non-EU companies wishing to have access to that market stimulated much of the growth in the adoption of the joint venture as a standard way to operate within Eastern European markets.

CRITERIA FOR STRATEGIC SUCCESS

There are many factors that influence success in alliances. Lynch (1989) argues that 'underpinning all successful alliances are several core

elements. First there must be a spirit of trust, cooperation, and integrity reinforced by a "Win–Win" commitment by both parties. Second, both strategic and operational synergy must prevail among partners. Ideally the strengths of one partner should complement the weaknesses of the other, and vice versa. Third, as the venture matures sponsoring companies must be willing to address new risks' and be prepared to change the structure of the organisation in response to changed operating considerations. Devlin and Bleackley (1988) put forward a four-stage process to ensure success:

1 Clearly define the goals and objectives, of the alliance/venture.
2 Identify potential partner's attributes.
3 Assess potential partners and what they bring to the planned venture and to your own organisation.
4 Negotiate an alliance agreement that has senior management commitment to it.

Figure 7.2 shows a framework of paths to consider and is also very useful in understanding the successful development of a joint venture diagrammatically.

The freedom to make decisions and operate as a separate entity from the parents is often raised as a critical success factor. Too much interference from parents and not enough operational responsibility given to the joint venture are often cited as reasons for failure. For the secondee from a parent company who needs to challenge in order to gain responsibility, this can present a major conflict of interests and a situation that cannot be resolved, especially as many secondments of employees into joint ventures can be for only two years.

Other success factors frequently highlighted are mutual dependence and growth within the joint venture and the growth of trust. This can be fostered by a sharing of knowledge either about products, markets or parents' organisation and generally operate alongside one another to achieve agreed objectives. Trust is incremental and builds up over time, so it is essential in the early stage of the venture that agreements are adhered to while people and the organisation settle down to their respective roles.

Another factor contributing to success is often seen as the growth of an independent culture for the organisation. Its parents may be highly structured MNCs who do not have the flexibility in fast-growing markets. This may mean that the joint venture has to develop a more

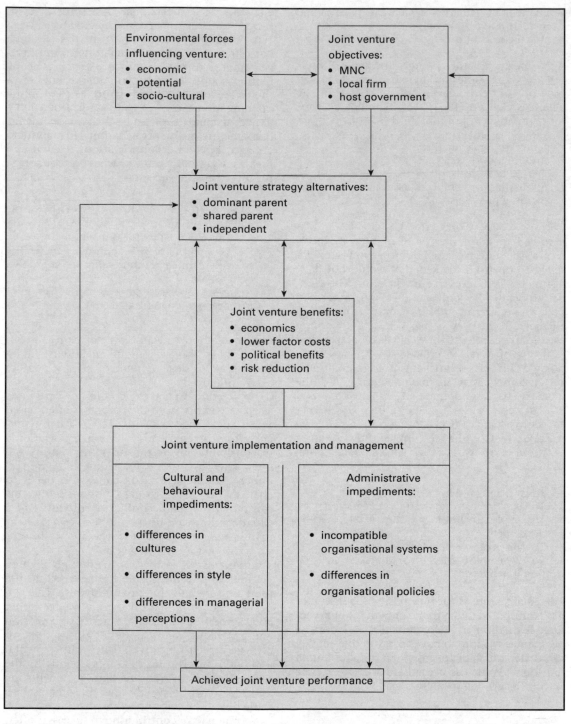

Figure 7.2   *A framework of paths in joint venture development*

Source: Datta, D.K. (1988) 'International joint ventures: a framework for analysis', *Journal of General Management*, 14 (2): 81.

independent entrepreneurial style in order to succeed. It may have to develop a more flexible culture to deal with changing circumstances or rapidly respond to a changing market. A culture may have to be developed to encompass the parents' employees effectively within the new organisation. What happens if it is two national groupings coming together? How do they communicate? And in what language? How are staff allocated or seconded to the venture? What conditions do they have and how is status and rank agreed? How will customers respond to the birth of this new organisation? What will its attitude be to the market place? Will it be short term or is the organisation going to be around for some time?

All these are crucial questions in developing a sustainable corporate culture. Main (1990) has commented that 'Sheer human incompatibilty causes more failures than anything else. You have to surpass the ego.' The importance of developing a culture for the venture can therefore be seen as being critical for success. Quite rightly, Batchelor (1990) has commented that 'differences of culture, language and accounting procedures still pose formidable obstacles to cross-border takeover despite the imminent creation of the Single European Market.' Guy de Jonquieries (1990) has made a similar comment, 'Picking a suitable target or partner in a foreign country and integrating its business smoothly with one's own is a hazardous obstacle course, riddled with national differences in business practices, management culture, laws, regulations and language.'

A plan for an amicable dissolution of the alliance should also be developed otherwise any divorce could be potentially violent and detrimental to the marketplace in which the business is operating. How would customers perceive a rapid break-up? Who owns what? If a procedure or protocol is developed ahead of any such eventuality, this will ease any transition arrangements. There are some horror stories of break-ups of US–Italian joint ventures in the oil and petrochemicals industries during the 1970s. Some Italian nationals have related to the author how they came in to find their offices totally empty and devoid of all furniture and equipment on the Monday morning, as the joint venture had collapsed the Friday afternoon when the US parents had notified their employees to pull out and take everything away during the weekend. Amicable dissolution rules forestall these disastrous situations and even allow for partners to withdraw on good terms.

For a small company, enhanced status can be derived from being part of a bigger joint venture that has major international parent company links. As an example of this, Cheeseright (1989) quotes a Mr Craig of Brookmount, who commented on this benefit from his alliance: 'The tie up with Trafalgar and Blue Circle gave us a status we would not otherwise have had.'

Lyles (1988) conducted a study into learning among companies who had knowledge of joint ventures and concluded that 'The experience of joint venture sophisticated firms provides a window of opportunity for their increasing competitiveness. It creates competitive advantage for them by establishing their presence worldwide, by giving them information about operating in various countries and about environmental events, and by the development of a skill base that has prior knowledge of the likelihood of certain events.'

Clearly the use of joint ventures to build up operating experience in overseas markets and gain access to national markets where there are barriers to entry is of major significance to the modern global company. The experience gained by both staff and the organisation in developing knowledge via this process is significant.

That all the benefits of an alliance cannot be quantified in financial reward has been well put by Ohmae (1989), 'most of the time, the financials do not capture the real benefits of alliances'.

The disadvantages associated with strategic alliances have been well shown by Devlin and Bleackley (1988) who state that:

> In choosing a company with which to form a strategic alliance, senior executives must be aware that what may seem to be a short-term operational benefit arising out of the alliance may, in fact, lead to the eventual loss of the company's strategic position, either to its alliance partner or to one of the company's competitors.

Reich and Mankin (1986) and more recent commentators have highlighted that US companies forming a joint venture with a Japanese partner may be giving away part of their market, as they rely on the Japanese company for manufactured products and technology; the firm unknowingly brings in a Trojan horse and encourages new competition. This is so because the indigenous partner's contribution is in the area of sales and distribution, which has little concrete value and is potentially replaceable. The dispute between the independent car distribution company Nissan (UK) and its Japanese manufacturing parent Nissan and its desire to operate its own sales and distribution company in the UK is a clear example of this.

Equity issues between the parents of a joint venture can also become a major issue. Who has the largest stake to lose? Is control given to the partner with the largest equity stake? How are royalties, fees and dividends paid? If it is a marketing operation, then what about ownership and control of the manufacturing and development aspects of the organisation? Are they controlled by the parents or jointly operated? Will these assets eventually be owned by the venture? The area of control is an important one. Who makes the decisions, the joint venture or the parents? Are the best staff put in to run the venture or is it a repository for staff no longer wanted by the parents and therefore not fully motivated? Are the partners in the venture of equal size or is one more powerful than the other?

All these are issues that impact upon the success of the alliance, and handled without forethought can lead to its failure. With the right planning joint ventures can be a major success, but the opposite is also true. There is still the need for further research on why joint ventures fail or cease to operate, as there is only limited data in this essential area.

Joint ventures and strategic alliances are not always seen as the best method of internationalising one's operations. Porter (1990) has commented: 'Don't collaborate, compete'. He believes the current wave of mergers and alliances prevalent in Europe in response to the SEM will undermine their competitive advantage. He states that 'The secret of competitive advantage is to compete'.

Buckley and Casson (1988) have shown their scepticism, commenting that 'A joint venture may be merely a subterfuge, luring partners into making commitments which leave them exposed to re-negotiation under duress. It may be a device for enhancing collusion.'

Clearly the EU, in monitoring the formation of joint ventures, has one eye on whether they lead to increased competition or not and has not been frightened in the past to stop some joint ventures being formed on the grounds that they can sometimes be against competition policy. Gomes-Casseres (1987) highlighted the fact that 'The requirements of global strategy often conflict with the interests of local partners' and therefore some joint ventures may be in conflict with their parents' actions.

The (UNCTC) has developed a useful check-list as a guide to establishing effective joint ventures, and this has been developed by Young et al. (1989) into the following:

1 The major goals of the partners.
2 Their contributions, responsibilities and obligations.
3 The equity share of each partner.
4 Means of financing each partner.
5 Products, customers and markets to be supplied.
6 The composition of the board of directors.
7 Procedures for selecting senior and middle management.
8 Provisions for technical training and management agreements which may be part of the joint venture.
9 Provisions for safeguarding patents, trade marks and technical secrets.
10 Duration of the agreement and ways of modifying it.
11 Management processes, including strategic and operational planning.
12 The control and information system.
13 Sources of supply for raw materials, intermediates and components.
14 Accounting standards.
15 Reporting requirements.
16 The audit and review of financial statements.
17 Means of settling disputes.
18 Policy regarding the declaration and distribution of dividends.
19 Procedures for dissolving the partnership and the distribution of assets.

CONCLUSION

Joint ventures and strategic alliances are here to stay as a complex web of interests is developed by the truly global company. It has recently been reported (Forbes, 2001) that over 20 per cent of global business activity is by strategic alliances. In the EU they have been fostered both by government and the desire to break down artificial barriers. Joint ventures can be very successful but the divorce rate is very high, with many partners taking over and squeezing out those with only a small stake holding. To run a successful joint venture takes senior management commitment, forward planning and special skills, but if successful the rewards are high.

REFERENCES

Batchelor, C. (1990) 'Partnership: a taste for Cooperation', *Financial Times*, 24 July.

Bleeke, J. and Ernst, D. (1993) *Collaborating to Compete*. New York: John Wiley.

Booz, A. and Hamilton Inc, (1987) *New Product Management for the 1980s*. Internal publication cited in H. Davidson, *Offensive Marketing (2nd edn)*. London: Penguin.

Borys, B. and Jemison, D.B. (1989) 'Hybrid arrangements as strategic alliances: theoretical issues in organisational combinations', *Academy of Management Review*, 14 (2): 234–49.

Buckley, P.J. and Casson, M. (1988) 'A theory of cooperation in international business, *Management International Review*, 28: 19–38.

Business International (1987) *Competitive Alliances: How to Succeed at Cross-Regional Collaboration*. New York: Business International.

Carr, S. (1991) 'The guide to a sockful of zlotys', *Independent*. p. 20.

Cecchini, P. (1988) *The European Challenge*, Brussels: European Commission.

Cheeseright, P. (1989) 'Joint ventures a key asset to growth', *Financial Times*. p. 14.

Christelow, D.B. (1987) 'International joint ventures: how important are they?', *Columbia Journal of World Business*, 22 (2): 7–13.

Contractor, F.J. and Lorange, P. (eds) (1988) *Cooperative Strategies in International Business*. Lexington, MA: Lexington Books.

Crompton, R. (1990) 'The return of synergy', *Long Range Planning*, 23: 122.

Datta, D.K. (1988) 'International joint ventures: a framework for analysis', *Journal of General Management*, 14 (2): 81.

Davidson, H. (1987) *Offensive Marketing*, (2nd edn). London: Penguin.

Devlin, G. and Bleackley, M. (1988) 'Strategic alliances guide-lines for success', *Long Range Planning*, 21 (5): 18–23.

Dicken, P. (1992) *Global Shift*. London: Chapman. p. 213.

European Commission (1991) *A Practitioner's Guide to European Takeover Regulation and Practice*, Woking: Westminster Management Consultants.

Forbes special issue (2001) 'On alliances', from *Thomson Financial*, May 21.

Geringer, M. (1991) 'Strategic determinants of partner selection criteria in international joint ventures', *Journal of International Business Studies*, March, Vol. 22 (1).

Glaister, K. (1991) 'UK joint venture formation in Western Europe, USA and Japan: 1980–89', University of Leeds, School of Business and Economic Studies discussion paper.

Gomes-Casseres, B. (1987) 'Joint venture instability: is it a problem?', *Columbia Journal of World Business*, 22 (2): 97–101.

Gugler, P. (1992) 'Building transnational alliances to create competitive advantage', *Long Range Planning*, 25 (1) pp. 90–9.

Harrigan, K.R. (1991) 'Strategic alliances and partner asymmetries', *Management International Review*, 28 (3): 53–71.

Hertzfield, J.M. (1991) 'Joint ventures: saving the Soviets from perestroika', *Harvard Business Review*, (Jan.–Feb.): 80–91.

Houghton, J.R. (1991) 'Corning cultivates joint ventures', *The Strategist*, 3 (2): 15–16.

ICI Roundel Magazine, (1988) *ICI Roundel Magazine*, 5: London.

Jacobs, D.M. and Stewart-Clark, J. (1990) *Competition Law in the European Community*. London: Kogan Page. p. 87.

de Jonquieres, G. (1990) 'Corporate alliances: the path for career couples?', *Financial Times*, 2 April.

de Jonquieres, G. (1990) 'Expansion strategies, the oddson approach', *Financial Times*, 28 September, p. 15.

de Jonquieres, G. and Fidler, S. (1990) 'International mergers and acquisitions', *Financial Times*, 18 Otober, pp. 33–7.

Killing, J.P. (1982) 'How to make a global joint venture work', *Harvard Business Review*, (May/June): 120–7.

Kindleberger, C.P. (1969) *American Business Abroad*. Newhaven, CT: Yale University Press.

Lorange, P. and Roos, J. (1991) 'Why some strategic alliances succeed and others fail', *The Journal of Business Strategy*, 25–30.

Lyles, M.A. (1988) 'Learning among joint venture sophisticates firms', *Management International Review*, 28: 85–9.

Lynch, R.P. (1989) *The Practical Guide to Joint Ventures and Corporate Alliances*. New York: Wiley.

Lyons, P. (1991) 'Joint-ventures as strategic choice – a literature review', *Long Range Planning*, 25 (1): 90–9.

Main, J. (1990) 'Making global alliances work', *Fortune*, pp. 75–8.

Mazzolini, R. (1974) *European Transnational Concentrations*. New York: Mcgraw Hill. p. 19.

McCall, J.B. and Warrington, M.B. (1984) *Marketing by Agreement*.Chichester: Wiley.

Ohmae, K. (1989) 'The global logic of strategic alliances', *Harvard Business Review*, (March/April): 143–54.

Paliwoda, S. (1989) 'Massey-Ferguson-Agromet-Motoimport (Poland)', in L. Moutinho, (ed.) in *Cases in Marketing Management*. Wokingham: Addison-Wesley. pp. 262–84.

Porter, M. (1990). 'Europe's companies after 1992: don't collaborate, completion', *The Economist*, pp. 23–6.

Reich, R.B. and Mankin, E.D. (1986) 'Joint ventures with Japan give away our future', *Harvard Business Review*, (March/April): 78–86.

Selwyn, M. (1991) 'Making marriages of convenience', *The Strategist*, 3 (2): 9–12.

Soviet Trade Association (1991) *Sovtech 1991*. Moscow: Century Press.

Ward, M., Wright, M. and Robbie, K. (1991) 'Corporate restructuring and the development of management buy-outs in Europe', *European Business Journal*, 3 (1): 26–40.

Young, S., Hamill, J., Wheeler, and Davies, J.R. (1989) *International Market Entry and Development*. Hemel Hempstead: Prentice Hall.

CASES STUDIES

Case studies that can be read in conjuction with this chapter are:
Broadcasting
EVC1
EVC2
Mannsmann Mobilfunk
Philips Electronics
Shell
Stena
Unilever

As businesses and marketing evolves and pupates in this relatively new millennium, it is becoming increasingly urgent to have at least an awareness, if not a deep understanding, of corporate and national culture in order to be a successful trader. It is no longer sustainable to have a purely Amerocentric, British, French, German or Spanish business culture in the increasingly global business world; it may be acceptable if you are operating purely within your national marketplace but is increasingly difficult to sustain if you are transnational and competing across different trading blocs.

For the European manager, if indeed such a person or groupage exists, this is strengthened further by the certain knowledge that the EU will admit new members from Central Europe and the Mediterranean (Cyprus, the Czech Republic, Estonia, Hungary, Poland and Slovenia) over the next few years. All with their own customs, history, religions, ethnic mixes, languages, media, geographic locations and even local weather. There has been much debate about whether there is a distinct European style of management emerging, stimulated by the need for cross-border collaboration and cooperation that, it has been argued, has developed distinct collaborationist abilities and skills. However, even the term 'manager' does not have one definition in the EU: in the UK it is all embracing, but in Italy it is defined more precisely 'quadric', which refers to middle-ranking managers, whilst 'dirigenti' covers senior ones. In addition, there is still a great deal of evidence that French stakeholders or German equivalents prefer one of their own nationality running major national champions, such as French Telecom and BMW for example, rather than a transnational foreigner, no matter how well qualified. A number of US companies also contradict stereo-typical perceptions of Amerocentric management styles in that they often employ European national managers within the US, and may have a positive policy on employing the talents of a range of nationalities in senior management such as that applied by the US white goods manufacturer Whirlpool. So a standard senior manager, whether European or American, is very difficult to sustain as an argument, although one that has an increasing awareness of culture management is.

The world has become a much smaller place and business today is conducted in a global market (Schuster and Harris, 1999). Business activities, however, still take place through and with people, whether it is by having field engineers travelling to another country providing technical assistance, customers purchasing globally branded products, executives crafting a strategic alliance or setting up a joint venture equity company transposing borders and, of course, salespeople travelling to another country to call on a potential customer. Each of these people has a particular view of the world based upon the culture of their ethnic group, country, organisation, religion, home town, region or family. These perspectives do not often overlap when doing business across borders. Doing business effectively in the EU requires the understanding of other cultures and the ability to adapt successfully.

Managers, and especially those with a marketing background, ask questions about the beliefs, values and attitudes of customers in any market because understanding the customer is the foundation for successful marketing. Thus understanding cultural similarities and differences is a critical part of effective marketing and sales within Europe as it is in other parts of the globe. When customers or business partners live in another country, asking these questions in greater depth is important because the variance is generally greater across borders than it is within borders. Only by relying on the similarities and adapting to the differences can products be developed that will appeal across borders and in local markets, can distribution be organised efficiently, can prices be determined competitively, and can effective promotions be developed. Not only do cultural similarities and differences affect the development of global or localised strategies, but also the execution of those strategies, which involves, for instance, the behaviour of marketing executives who must work with other marketing executives across borders.

In Europe, Geert Hofstede and Fons Trompenaars have developed major theories on culture that have significant implications for business activities. In the US, Edward T. Hall, John Graham, Camille Schuster and Michael Copeland have also developed theories of culture that have significant application for business activities. In this chapter we assess the European and US approaches on cultural understanding, the overlapping contributions of the European and US theoretical perspectives, and identify issues that need further study/resolution. A good example of this is that it is quite a common occurrence to be asked to brief or coach a new US-based senior executive who has been transferred to Europe on how the different European business cultures work as they are having problems understanding it.

THE EUROPEAN PERSPECTIVE

Hofstede's impressive body of work began with a major data collection project involving questionnaire responses by 116,000 IBM employees in over 72 countries, collected between 1967 and 1973 (1980a, 1980b). Analysis of the data for 50 individual countries, and 13 more grouped into regions, revealed that they differed along four dimensions. These were:

- The power distance dimension which 'expresses the degree to which the less powerful members of a society accept that power is distributed unequally'.
- The individualism versus collectivism dimension is the 'degree of interdependence a society maintains among its members'.
- The masculinity versus femininity dimension describes 'the way in which society allocates social roles between the sexes'.
- The uncertainty avoidance dimension 'expresses the degree to which the members of a society feel uncomfortable with uncertainty and ambiguity'.

At a later date the Chinese Value Survey was administered to 1000 students in 22 countries and the data gathered revealed a fifth dimension (Hofstede and Bond, 1988).

- Confucian dynamism represents the extent to which a society holds a pragmatic future-oriented perspective rather than a normative historic or near term point of view.

All of these dimensions reveal attitudes, values or beliefs that individuals hold regarding social relationships or decision making. Each of the 50 countries and three regions received a numerical score on each dimension identifying the importance of the specific dimension, generally, to that cultural group.

Subsequently, this data has been compared, contrasted and analysed regarding the implications of these attitudes, values, or beliefs for various business activities. For instance, Hofstede and Usunier (1996) discuss the influence of these dimensions on international business negotiations. Usunier (1996) also examines the relationship between Hofstede's dimensions and management theories to support the argument that management theories are culturally relative.

Similarly, Trompenaars (1993) collected data on a number of attitudes, values and beliefs regarding people, relationships and decision making. The topics investigated were:

- Universalist versus particularist;
- Individualism versus collectivism;
- Neutral versus affective;
- Specificity versus diffuseness;
- Achievement-oriented versus ascription-oriented, sequential versus synchronic; and
- Internal control versus external control.

The data revealed a range of responses on each topic with each country receiving a specific numeric value, allowing for comparisons across countries. In addition, the implication of country positions for business behaviour and decisions were examined by Trompenaars (1993).

While some of the topics differ between Hofstede and Trompenaars, they have a similar approach to the study of culture. First, it is important to identify the attitudes, values and beliefs of people in different cultural groups by collecting data that can be statistically analysed to reveal scores on specific dimensions. These scores can be used to analyse the impact of the dimensions of business behaviour and to compare differences or similarities across cultural groups. Empirical data used to ascertain scores on attitudes, values or beliefs that are fundamental to particular cultural groups is the foundation for studying the affect of culture on business practice from a European perspective. It is also worth noting that the EU especially, post the creation of the Single European Market (SEM) in 1992, has stimulated a growth in qualitative research from a phenomenological perspective. Examples of work in this area are Guy and Mattock (1993), Randlesome (1993), Hampden-Turner and Trompenaars (1993), Harris and McDonald (1994) and Lewis (1996) from a linguistic perspective. One can even see nascent signs of that age-old debate between North American and European academic researchers emerging yet again, quantitative versus qualitative data analysis and validity – *vive la difference*!

AMERICAN PERSPECTIVES

For many years, Edward T. Hall was involved in the selection and training of Americans to work in overseas countries for both business and government. As a result of what he observed, read and talked about with these people, with in-country employees and academics, Hall (1969, 1981) developed theories on the use of time and language in different cultures. For instance, Hall's (1969) approach to time was to discuss the three ways in which people used time:

- formal time (everyone in a culture knows it and takes it for granted);
- informal time (involves situation or imprecise references); and
- and technical time (different system used by scientists and technicians).

Hall's (1981) approach to language was to develop a continuum of how it is used by classifying languages as either:

- high context versus low context; or
- explicit versus implicit.

Both theories of time and language are based upon empirical (not necessarily statistical) data and focus on differences in behaviour.

John Graham and his associates studied negotiation processes in 11 countries and identified 4

steps of international negotiation (Graham 1981, 1983, 1984, 1985a, 1985b, 1987; Graham and Andrews 1987; Graham et al., 1992; Graham and Lin, 1986; Graham and Sano, 1984). Much of the data gathered was quantifiable and statistically analysed. However, content analysis of the videotapes of the interviews as well as Graham's observations of and discussions with members of the culture were also an important part of understanding the process. Analysis of the data revealed that not only do international negotiations involve four processes:

- non-task sounding;
- task-related exchange of information;
- persuasion; and
- concessions and agreements;

but that specific cultural groups emphasise different parts of the process. The emphasis of this theoretical development is on the behaviour of participants in business activities.

Schuster and Copeland (1996) created two models based upon over 25 years of experience, research and empirical observations. The Culture Classification Model illustrates how cultural groups vary in the way they value tasks and relationships and devote time to each. Descriptions of historical events, language and assumptions regarding everyday activities are used to describe the classification of each cultural group in terms of time, tasks and relationships. The Global Sales and Negotiation Matrix illustrates how each of these cultural groups views the importance of different parts of the Global Sales and Negotiation Process based upon the way they use time, tasks and relationships. Again, this approach focuses on behaviour in business situations.

DIFFERENCES AND RECONCILIATION

In general, the European approach has been to gather data that can be statistically analysed to determine the attitudes, values and beliefs that form the basis of a particular culture. Since the objective is to examine information that may be at a level which is not always consciously considered by members of the culture, responses to questionnaire items are used to infer attitudes, values and beliefs. By translating the questionnaire, similar data can be collected across countries and compared to determine the inherent nature of the culture in a particular country and differences between and among cultural groups.

The advantage of this approach is that one can better understand a particular culture by becoming familiar with its view of the world and assumptions about how the world operates. The implications of this world view for business activities can then be articulated quite well.

The approach in the US is more behaviour-oriented, focusing on what people do and say using what processes. Whether focus is on the way people use time, the process and stages of negotiation, the way people use language, or the importance of various stages of negotiation, behaviours are the primary subject of investigation. The emphasis is action-oriented: what can business people do and say to be more effective during the process of business activities?

Understanding cultural differences is pursued not as a goal in itself, but as a means of determining how to effectively adapt to the differences in order to ensure greater success. The European approach leans more toward gathering responses to questionnaire items that will be analysed to make inferences regarding the attitudes, values and beliefs of a group of people. The US approach leans more to investigating behaviour in specific situations and identifying what influences that behaviour so that appropriate action can be made.

The theories proposed on both sides of the Atlantic have important implications for understanding cultural differences and becoming more effective business people or even managers. Behaviours are more effectively understood when one is familiar with the attitudes, values and beliefs behind the behaviour. Information regarding attitudes, values and beliefs is more useful for business people when their implications for business behaviour are explicated.

CORPORATE CULTURE: EUROPEAN AND US EXAMPLES

Just as every individual has a unique personality, so every company has a unique identity – its corporate culture. Corporate culture can be defined as the shared experiences, stories, beliefs and norms that characterise an organisation.

Consequently, a corporate culture assists in focusing employees' efforts, helps colleagues and suppliers to work toward the same goals, and stimulates newcomers to learn accepted behaviours. It gives each organisation its own identity, much the same way that personalities do to the people. In fact, it's shaped by the values held by the top management, by the firm's history, by stories and legend, like Walt Disney (the spirit lives in the businesses: quotations from Disney are affixed to portraits of him throughout the company's studios). Clearly, the corporate culture influences management philosophy, style and behaviour. The entrepreneurial flair, spirit of adventure exemplified by hot-air ballooning exploits amongst others of Richard Branson have done much to underpin Virgin's persona whether it be their insurance business, mobile phones, airline, railways or whatever. Anita Roddick and her strong environmental stance helped gell the corporate culture of Bodyshop, which became perceived as a corporate champion of environmentalism and those on the margins of captivity.

It is also the way we manage that determines many of the key differences between the American and the European corporate cultures. Why do these differences between the US and Europe exist? And what are the consequences for management styles? In order to answer these questions, we define what corporate culture is, then identify the core differences between the US and Europe, and even between European countries, and give some examples.

Corporate culture is a system of shared meaning, a pattern of beliefs by members of an organisation that produce norms and rules for behaviour that powerfully shape the operation of individuals and groups in the organisation. It is 'the way we do things here'. Corporate culture is not only in employees' minds, but also in each procedure or working method. Corporate culture is not just a question of apparent symbols and signs such as the organisation's logo, it is more a question of spirit or the soul of the organisation that operates at a preconscious level and drives behaviour in strategic ways.

FACTORS INFLUENCING CORPORATE CULTURE: HERITAGE, SIGNS AND SYMBOLS

Thanks to its logo, its institutional advertisements or its buildings, the firm shows its differences. That is why in France we can see that Saint-Gobain has an an image of a diversified and profitable company, whereas Paribas appears as a professional institution, well-known for its discreet luxury.

There are also special ritual behaviours, especially as regards the integration of the new employees (is it done on a hierarchical basis or is it informal?) or the meetings of the board of directors (are they collegial, hierarchical, formal, open, short or long in duration?). And thanks to these signs and ritual behaviours, it is possible to assess and define beliefs, codes and values and put a meaning to an organisation's activities.

The founders

Founders play a very significant role in the development of a corporate culture. But what have in common Edouard Leclerc (Leclerc supermarket chain), son of a Breton grocer, and Marcel Fournier (Carrefour), who studied in the US? Nothing but the fact that they are symbols of their companies, especially because they have given their firms guidelines and principles. Interestingly, Leclerc has been likened to Astrix the Gaul, and his son has recently led a campaign against Macdonaldisation of French cuisine. This strong pervading influence is why an analysis of a corporate culture has to take into account the family background of founders, their flair and originality (for example, their capacity to apply and or develop new technologies) and the values they have set.

History

It is essential to point out the historical guidelines and logic that underlie the development of firms and organisations. Throughout recent time, various national and ethnic cultural environments have influenced the elaborations of corporate cultures. The success of quality rings in Japan can be easily perceived as reflecting the social cohesion and stability of that society. The growing concern over the environment also has an influence on corporate culture – that is why the institutional advertisements and campaigns of BP, Rhone-Poulenc and so on as regards their custodianship and protection of the natural environment have partly modified and updated their corporate culture, which now seems increasingly to include these factors.

At Saint-Gobain, executives learn the history of their company in order to have an overall vision underpinning long-term strategies. Such a method helps employees of Saint-Gobain (diversified French manufacturer) to have the feeling that they belong to a prestigious institution and reinforces corporate culture.

It is essential to distinguish and understand the history of the different activities, products and the social structures of companies, because the evolution of these factors can have significant influence on the evolution of corporate culture.

CORPORATE CULTURE AND 'CORE SKILLS'

The specific know-how of a firm will undoubtedly make the firm different from other companies, including its competitors. The 'core skills' of the company play a great role in the elaboration of corporate culture; for instance, the 'core skills' of Bic, which focuses on mass-produced low-cost plastic consumables, explains the way the French firm has managed to develop its activities from disposable lights through pens to razors. Like every society, a firm creates its own system of values that enables employees to distinguish what is good or not for the company. Values represent a type of reference point that provide guidance for the employees.

Culture makes the company: Levy Strauss

As Chairman and past CEO of Levy Strauss, Bob Haas has inherited a dual legacy. Ever since its creation in 1850, the San Francisco-based apparel manufacturer has been famous for combining strong commercial success with a commitment to social values and its workforce. Achieving both goals was relatively easy throughout much of the post-War era, when the company's main product – Levy's jeans – became an icon of American pop culture and sales surged on the demographic wave of the expanding baby boom. Here we can see that the 'core skills' of Levy Strauss has definitively influenced the way the firm is managed. But during the uncertain economic climate of the 1980s, Hass and his management team had to rethink every facet of the business – including its underlying values.

Since his appointment as CEO in 1984, Haas redefined the company's business strategy, created a flatter organisation – including the painful step of cutting the work force by one-third – and invested heavily in new product development, marketing and technology. In 1987, he oversaw the development of Levy Strauss Aspirations Statement, a major initiative to define the shared values that guide both management and the workforce. This initiative is mainly based on the fact that the company's most important asset is its people's aspirations. This is a similar view held by Cooperative Bank and LEGO and can be seen in the respective case studies.

Many CEOs talk about values, but few seem to have gone to the lengths that Haas has in order to bring them to the very centre of how he runs the business. The Aspirations Statement has shaped how the company defines occupational roles and responsibilities, conducts performance evaluations, trains new employees, organises work and makes business decisions. The result is a flexible and innovative company, despite its age and size. The company has stayed true to its traditional commitment to social issues, even if it has updated that commitment to reflect the economic and social realities of a new era. Moreover, the fact that Haas himself was one of the foremost corporate spokespeople on the responsibilities of business in the AIDS crisis is one of the main symbols of Levi Strauss' corporate culture.

Reinventing the Levi Strauss' heritage has a particular meaning for Haas. He is the great-great-grand nephew of the company founder, and his uncle and father all led the company before him. He joined Levi Strauss in 1973 and has contributed to the history of the San Francisco company, which has considerably influenced corporate culture.

EUROPEAN AND US CORPORATE CULTURES: DIFFERENCES

As far as the reasons for distinct differences between corporate cultures is concerned, we should remind ourselves of the prime factors that constitute corporate culture. Among these factors two throw particular light on the origin of these differences: the ethnic and national environment, and the socio-cultural environment.

The US is a country built on the merging together of very different racial ethnic groups that can compete together within their own culture, with different ways to think and consequently it can stimulate distinct corporate cultures. For instance, UPS – a staid, conservative parcel-carrying giant – has succeeded in its

change due, in part, to a strong corporate culture that stresses commitment and quality service. Indeed, UPS's corporate culture has been described as a 'cross between the Mormons and the Marines' and a 'half Marine Corps and half Quaker meeting'. Drivers must keep their hair short and their pants properly creased. Beard and flowing moustaches are not allowed, nor is drinking coffee or other beverages at your desk. However, executives and mail sorters share a cafeteria at company headquarters.

The social cultural environment

In the US one of the most important factors that moulds the mind of the American people is the 'conquest of the West'. It gives people a special state of mind – a 'mind of frontier' – and the need to open up new areas. The man or woman who really wants to succeed in a business can do it. The mind of competition, of mobility (from the conquest of the West), of experimentation is strongly fostered by the American system, whereas in Europe the values are historically more settled, more routine, more moderated. Moreover, European people and Americans are individualist, but very differently: the American praises individualism and freedom at any price; the European believes in another form of freedom based on a certain solidarity, or even a need for societal assistance. This can be seen clearly in non-Anglo-Saxon Europe and explains some of the tension between the UK and other EU member states.

The other continents see Europe like a whole 'country' with inner frontiers not particularly well defined. But there is a real heterogeneity inside Europe, and consequently a significant heterogeneity in the corporate cultures. Italians and French often communicate with an implicit method where motions, gazes and non-verbal emotional proofs are at least as important as the explicit speeches. At the opposite end of the spectrum, Germans do not really know implicit communication, they tend to explain their ideas to the utmost, without resorting to allusions or in an 'analogical way' (non-verbal method). In The Netherlands, a lot of arrangements and coordinations are made simply and verbally, whilst across Europe those cultures that are rich in irony can be seen as distinctly different from those that do not have it.

Italian or French management culture can cope with a number of items at once, which they may see as part of a number of programmes; they can be latitudinian on delays and schedulings, but can also react rapidly when they are faced with a crisis or opportunity. On the contrary, Germanic corporate cultures tend to define, structure and respect programmes and schedules and can perceive clear purposes and focus on precision. They are not concerned by immediate feedback, but they prefer to have the time to respect all the defined stages (this can lead to the risk of a lack of flexibility by firms in responding to change). This style of deep, long analysis can be seen in the commentaries on German television before a Bundesleague football match – they are sometimes longer than the game itself.

CONSEQUENCES FOR MANAGEMENT STYLES

European corporate cultures are heavily moulded by the religious and cultural differences of each country. There are two fundamental features that determine corporate cultures across Europe, belonging to the 'Latino-Catholic' countries or to the 'Germano-Protestant' countries – The Lutheran–Rome split.

Consequently, the management styles are very different and this can be further strengthened by climate. The pace of an Andalusian afternoon, especially in the summer, much like that in large parts of Southern France, Italy and Greece, is dominated by the equivalent of the siesta. Whilst in Northern Europe and particularly in Anglo-Saxon countries the lunch break is increasingly disappearing.

In The Netherlands and Sweden, management styles are based on coordination and are transnational in nature, marked by an open style. Thanks to their social consensus, Germany and Belgium foster the monochromic approach of operations where the processes (time control, precision of the stages and long-term planning) are seen as the most important parts of management. France and Italy are particularly different through the importance of hierarchy and elites. In France the alumni of *grandes écoles* dominate government and business, the importance of the social laws, and polychronic behaviours (reactivity, simultaneous actions) is the style of management.

As a result, countries are either 'Latino-Catholic' or 'Germano-protestant', and as a result corporate cultures are built differently and reflect two very different ways of managing.

THE MARKET ENVIRONMENT: THE IMPORTANCE OF INTERNAL CULTURE

Each organisation faces a different reality in the marketplace depending on its products, competitors, customers, technologies, government influences and so on. To succeed in its marketplace, each company must carry out certain kinds of activities very well. In some markets that means selling (see the Gruppo Massone case study); in others, invention (see the Philips case study) and in others an emphasis on the management of costs (see the EVC2 case study as a good example of this). In short, the environment in which a company operates determines what it must do to be a success.

This business environment is the single greatest influence in shaping a corporate culture. Thus, companies that depend for success on their ability to sell an undifferentiated product tend to develop one type of culture that keeps its sales force selling. Companies that spend a great deal of research and development money before they even know if the product will be successful or not tend to develop a different culture, designed to make sure that decisions are thought through before actions are taken.

Values

These are the basic concepts and beliefs of an organisation, as such they form the heart of the corporate culture. Values define 'success' in concrete terms for employees and establish standards of achievements within the organisation, and those with strong cultures all have a rich and complex system of values that are shared by the staff. Managers in these companies talk about these beliefs openly and without embarrassment, and invariably have little tolerance for deviance from the company standards. But what happens when the business environment changes? One of the most serious risks of a strong system of shared values is that economic circumstances may change while shared values continue to guide behaviour in ways no longer helpful to the organisation's success in the changed environment. An example is British Airways (BA) concentrating on supplying premium-priced business travellers across the Atlantic and in Europe at a time when consumer purchase patterns changed and low-cost, no frills air operators such as GO, Easyjet and Ryanair grew by meeting increasing demand for low-cost travel in Europe. In fact, a past chairman of BA was cited as saying that he did not want the backs of his aircraft cluttered-up with 'back-packers', incidently one of the core growth segments in international travel. This could help explain why Ryannair in September 2002 was worth more on the stock market than BA. When a company with strongly held values finds that it has lost marketplace or economic relevance, it generally has great difficulty in adapting to a new competitive marketplace. We will detail this problem later.

Heroes and heroines

These people personify the culture's values and as such provide tangible role models for employees to follow. Some heroes are born – the visionary institution- builders of American business – and some are 'made' by memorable moments that occur in day-to-day corporate life. Smart companies take a direct hand in choosing people to play these heroic roles, knowing full well that others will try to emulate their behaviour. Strong culture companies have made heroes. At General Electric, for instance, the heroes include: Thomas Edison, the inventor; Charles Steinmetz, the complete engineer; Gerald Swope and more recently Jack Welch, the CEO entrepreneurs; and a legion of lesser-known but equally important internal figures: the inventor of the high-torque motor that powered the electric toothbrush; the chief engineer of the turbine works; the export salesman who survived two overseas revolutions; the international manager who had ghosts exorcised from a factory in Singapore; and many others.

The hero figure is the great motivator, the magician, and the person everyone will want to lead them when the going gets difficult. Heroes are symbolic figures whose deeds are out of the ordinary, but not too far out. They show, often dramatically, that the ideal of success lies within human capacity.

The rites and rituals

These are the systematic and programmed routines of day-to-day life in the company. In their mundane manifestations, which we call rituals, they show employees the kind of behaviour that is expected of them. In their extravaganzas, which we call ceremonies, they provide visible and potent examples of what the company

stands for. Strong culture companies go to the trouble of spelling out, often in copious detail, the routine behavioural rituals that they expect their employees to follow. Without expressive events, any culture will die. In the absence of ceremony or ritual, important values have no impact.

The cultural network

As the primary (but informal) means of communication within an organisation, the cultural network is the 'carrier' of the corporate values and mythology of the organisation. Storytellers, spies, priests, cabals, gossips and even whispers form a hidden hierarchy of power within the company. Often being able to work the network effectively is the only way to get things done or to understand what's really going on. The network is actually the primary means of communication within the organisation; it ties together all parts of the company without respect to positions or titles. The network is important because it not only transmits information, but also interprets the significance of the information for employees. In a strong culture, the network is powerful because it can reinforce the basic beliefs of the organisation and enhance the symbolic value of heroes by passing on stories of their achievements, sets a new climate for changes and provides a tight structure of influence for the CEO.

MERGERS AND ACQUISITIONS

A core trend in modern business has been the rising number of mergers and acquisitions, and more recently joint ventures and strategic alliances. An acquisition is simply the case of one firm purchasing another whether by agreement or not. In contrast, a merger is a consolidation of two firms. Joint ventures and strategic alliances are fully explored in Chapter 6. In the case of an acquisition, one firm (usually the larger) buys the other (the smaller). In a merger, on the other hand, the firms are usually more similar in size and the arrangement is more collaborative. A merger is somewhat akin to an agreed relationship.

After a merger or acquisition, three things can happen. One possibility is that the actual company will continue to operate as a separate entity (see EVC2 case study). Another possibility is that the actual business will be absorbed by the other and simply disappear. Finally, the two companies may form a new company.

In this case there may be strong variations in the behaviour of different parts of the company. For example, different divisions will have different cultures; these are called subcultures. Several subcultures can cause troubles for an organisation.

Subcultures

If there is no regular formal or informal commerce among subcultures, they can become ingrown and begin to work to the detriment of the company as a whole. A clear sign of subcultures becoming too strong is when they publicly try to undermine each other. A healthy tension among subcultures is desirable, but when the tension becomes pronounced and destructive it can signal a problem. A sure sign of problems arising is when subcultures take on the perquisite of exclusive clubs – restrictions of memberships, arbitrary exclusion of individuals and rituals for members only. Companies work best when all employees pull together, not when some place their own collective interest over others.

In an organisation with a robust culture any employee at any time can tell you what the company stands for or believes in. Balancing the legitimate differences of subcultures with the core elements of the company's culture as a whole is one of the most difficult tasks for management. As a minimum, managers must know what is happening in existing subcultures and be alert to new ones that may emerge.

When facing a problem of various subcultures within the same firm, the manager will have to resolve and, in fact, re-consign differences among subgroups in a culture. Rather than be afraid of subcultures falling apart, the manager will seek to strengthen each subculture as an effective group within the overall culture. Thus he or she will often attend functions called to celebrate a particular subculture, and generally endorse the subculture's existence and meaning within the larger culture. The manager will try to focus subcultures and cabals on understanding the problem of other subcultures and cabals. A typical ploy of a manager confronted with an issue of possible cultural clash will be to assign teams – each drawn from one of the subcultures in conflict – to study the problem of the other and formulate recommendations. By setting each subculture tasks that force it to understand and cope with the problems of the others, the manager will benefit both by educating the members of each team to the problem of the other subculture and by the fresh perspectives that each team – conditioned by its own experience – will bring to the problems of the other subculture.

So, having a strong culture can be a strength but a source of problems too in a merger. However, a weak culture is not a solution for this problem of subcultures. Indeed, a company with a weak culture lacks some or all of the characteristics of their stronger counterparts, specifically:

- Weak cultures have no clear values or beliefs and subsequently direction or targets about how to succeed in their business.
- Weak cultures have many beliefs but cannot agree among themselves on which are the most important.
- Different parts of the organisation have fundamentally at variance beliefs.
- Leaders of the culture are destructive or disruptive and do not foster any common understanding about what is important to the organisation.
- The rituals of day-to-day life are disorganised, with staff carrying out their own agenda and broadly one side of the business does not know what the other side of the company does or is doing. In fact, it is a dysfunctional organisation.

It seems that to re-engineer a new culture is the best solution in a merger or in an acquisition to avoid the problem of confrontation between cultures. However, it is essential to stimulate the growth of a vigorous and dynamic culture, as a weak version will damage the interests of the organisation and be vulnerable to competitive attack. There are signs of this in the Mannesmann Mobilfunk case study, which gives an insight into why this vast German group was successfully acquired by Vodaphone. The EVC 1 and EVC2 case studies in turn give an outline of how vigorous cultures can be developed within a new joint venture company.

Entry into a new market

The main problem for the company is to adapt to the new national culture it meets. There exist a number of standard psychological and social processes that can be used to gauge successful international market entry. The foreign company usually experiences some form of culture shock. Our mental software contains basic values. These have been acquired early in our lives, and they have become so natural as to be almost subconscious. These underpin our conscious and more superficial manifestations of culture rituals, heroes and symbols.

The company has to try to learn and mix with its own culture all those elements. If not, there will be a gap that will increase more and more and the market entry will be a failure.

CONTRASTING CORPORATE CULTURES: FOUR FRENCH EXAMPLES

Michelin

Michelin has a poor social image. It has a strong persona of being based on paternalism and being old-fashioned because its managers have never cared a lot about what they call popular fads, and they give priority to daily usage and reliability before fleeting trends. Unlike many other companies, Michelin has managed to link the company with the family, while managers remain in the background. Francois Michelin is not a media manager, and he will never be like Bernard Tapie or Francis Bouyges are or were. Michelin's identity is not built on the chief, but rather on the product and their reputation.

Michelin is a quiet company (the stress is put on the product and the quality, instead of publicity) and it defines itself as the opposite (paternalism and social archaicism) of other companies. Rather than talking about the importance of human resources, the company keeps silent and recognises it through its uses. On the one side, the individual takes great pride in belonging to the company, and on the other side, he withdraws behind the firm.

What actually shows Michelin's soul is the way human resources are managed, particularly recruitment. Recruiters follow very precise proceedings, and the three most important values are the man/woman, the client, the firm, and the coherence between them.

What is hard for recruiters is being able to resist departmental pressure on recruitment, so those selected are compatible with the company's soul and not just with the department's requirements. A few basic principles guide them:

- *Homogeneity principle*: ethical criteria (internal values of the company) are more important than technical criteria.
- *Integration principle*: the recruitment department is charged with the whole process, without any external interference.
- *Long duration principle*: every appointment made is on a permanent contract.
- *Experience principle*: each member of the recruitment team must have had considerable and long experience in the commercial or technical function that they are recruiting for.
- *Career principle*: external mobility is not what recruiters look for, but internal career development (inside the company) is closely thought through and planned.
- *Humanism principle*: the candidate for a particular post must benefit from the interview/recruitment process, even if they are not hired.
- *Personality principle*: recruitment is based more on personality than on technical skills.
- *Projective principle*: candidates who will be able to progress inside the company are hired.
- *Individual principle*: the candidate is not recruited for a precise appointment, but for his own personal qualities.
- *Independence principle*: recruiters do not overheed technical or commercial department needs, instead their criteria follows the company's long-term direction and goals.

As far as recruitment policy is concerned, Michelin is a conservative company. The principles held by Michelin are long-term oriented in order to preserve the firm's soul and culture. In fact, the recruitment principles highlight the company's soul, which is centered on the three values of the Man/Woman, the Client and the Firm.

Euro-Disney

New employees hired at Euro-Disney, Paris are taught some basic corporate principles during their two days' induction before they start formally working for the company. Walt Disney's life is the first and main point of this teaching; pictures of him are present everywhere in the park, restaurants and hotels, as well as his successful creations such as Mickey Mouse.

The Disney smile that is taught to employees has a very precise definition:

- You do not smile with your teeth but with your eyes.
- There are 'no problems, only solutions'.
- You must be patient, to listen, to calm a person so that every problem ends with a smile.
- You must enable people to dream – you are the Disney magic ambassador.

Rituals

On a daily basis staff follow a few rules of behaviour:

- *The uniform*: each department has its own costume.
- *The vocabulary*: translation into French is not allowed for some phrases such as 'break', 'phone-room', 'babycare'. When a machine does not work, you must say '101' (referring to the *101 Dalmatians*), then say '102' when it works again.
- *The greeting*: every morning, the manager shakes everybody's hand and you have to say 'Hello' to everyone.

Hierarchical barriers are not strongly felt in the relationships between employees. The *'vous'* form of address is not used and employees call one another by their first name. There remain some slight differences in costume quality and decoration depending upon position and status within the hierarchy.

Internal promotion is relatively easy to obtain. Employees' recognition is given much weight, so that efficiency and motivation is stimulated. A company newspaper is regularly issued, and every month there is an election for the employee who has been particularly efficient. A picture and article on them are published and prize awarded for the achievement.

(Prize-giving for targets achieved or met are frequently used to promote sales or finance targets in such organisations as Canon, Xerox and so on.)

Decathlon

Decathlon, the French sporting goods business, defines its culture by what it argues are six values and six main objectives. The values are:

- vitality;
- pleasure;
- brotherhood;
- natural products;
- a genuine and sincere organisation; and
- a responsible company.

The objectives of the company are seen as:

- business satisfies sportsmen and women;
- a genuine company;
- personal enrichment through responsibility;
- efficient and profitable teams;
- an international company in the making; and
- acting in harmony with nature.

How values and objectives are reflected in everyday operations

Decathlon perceives itself as an international school of employment and careers ('Ecole Internationale des Métiers'): 8 per cent of salaried staff are on training at any one time. Employees are employed and empowered to progress, so that there is significant mobility in each shop; no person keeps the same function for a significant time. All staff are encouraged to move jobs and develop.

The image of the company is achieved through a sportive look amongst employees. Staff are allowed to be casually dressed, but significant make-up is not allowed. Brotherhood and fraternity should be expressed towards buyers and a relaxed, natural and gentle attitude is recommended. This rule is also true for the use of vocabulary: a letter to a client always ends with 'sportively ...'. Team spirit is based on this kind of brotherhood, everybody is called by their name, there is no 'Mr' or 'Mrs', and the *'vous'* is not used. Furthermore, activities to foster team spirit and morale are organised by managers through sports like mountain biking, jogging, and so on.

The team has to be genuine. During training, the employee is taught to say always what is wrong and what is right.

Finally, the employee is taught to give rewards in order to meet that virtuous spiral: rewards produce job satisfaction, which allows vitality, which calls rewards. This spiral is pasted to the wall of the break room so that everybody can be reminded of them.

IKEA

IKEA started as a small mail-order business in 1947; in 1989, sales were approximately $2.68 billion. Behind this growth is IKEA's unusual approach to furniture retailing. IKEA's wares include not only furniture from beds to sofas to tables, but also a wide range of furnishings such as plants and housewares. Each IKEA store offers a large children's playroom and features its own low-priced restaurant, so that customers shop longer, stay longer in the store and take time to consider what they have seen and decide what to buy.

IKEA's culture and management are guided by some principles that have been set up by the experiences of the company:

The management system

- The true IKEA spirit: enthusiasm and search for innovation.
- Waste is a sin.
- Simplicity, efficiency virtue.
- Dare to be different to evolve.
- Those that sleep make no mistakes.

Action principles

- The client is a producer and a consumer at the same time.
- Achieve high-usage value rates (another name for the quality–price ratio).
- Work with partners (if they can produce high returns).
- The store in the country and in the suburbs.
- The pleasure is to be found in the way of buying, as well as in the purchase (the store is a place for relaxation).
- Sell a way of life (the range of products corresponds to a perceived lifestyle segment).
- The best salesperson is the catalog.

The main idea developed by IKEA's culture is savings. Savings for the company and for the client were introduced by the founder Ingvar Kamprad with the concept of furniture in kit form.

Contrasting Michelin, Euro-Disney, Decathlon and IKEA

In the four examples of corporate culture we can see some similarities between Euro-Disney's and Decathlon's culture; both develop positiveness (Disney smile, Decathlon's salesmen's attitude towards buyers). Hierarchical relationships tied to salary are limited so that employees feel that they are working in a flat structure and that they can take more responsibility, feel greater job satisfaction and are thus efficient

(Decathlon's spiral). In both Decathlon and Euro-Disney, rewards for achievements are given greater importance since stimulating employee satisfaction and internal mobility and promotion are very common.

Is Decathlon, the French group, influenced by a form of American corporate culture? Similar to that utilised by Euro-Disney? No. It seems that the prime reason is that both companies sell a product that is pleasure oriented and have positive images (Decathlon's sport items linked with health and pleasure, and Euro-Disney's rides linked with a magic world) and that having outward-going staff is the best way of supporting this type of sale.

Michelin's culture seems to be the opposite of Decathlon and Euro-Disney as it is a discrete, large conglomerate, which is very stable and consequently staff are given a strong internal career structure within an agreed area and have limited functional mobility. Positive-mindedness and an ability to engage with the customer does not seem to be a pre-requisite for most staff within Michelin as in the two other companies, reflecting the nature of its core activity, the development, manufacture and sale of vehicle tires (the latter being predominantly through agents).

These four companies can be divided into two types. In the first one, Decathlon and Euro-Disney, we see a corporate culture oriented towards the external users of the company, who are paying customers for predominantly recreational/leisure products. Internal elements within the company are aimed at developing a group spirit between the members of this kind of friendly family and its customers. In the second group, Michelin and IKEA, the culture seems to be more oriented towards the company, as salaried staff are considered more as individuals and not as a group. Careers of staff are not controlled by the company but are allowed to be individualistic and reflect the specific talents and skills of the employee concerned.

CULTURE AND EUROPEAN BUSINESS

Culture in business has many meanings. An appreciation and awareness of the richness of language and the national and regional cultures that flow from them is essential for the modern business manager in Europe. Whether it be the richness of Shakespeare in English, Cervantes in Spanish, Goethe in German or Dostoyevsky in Russian, Erasmus and so on, all reflect national cultural heritages and the way one can perceive the world and experience it. The fact that German is a very precise language and is widely used by engineers and scientists, whilst English is the international commercial language, gives some insight into the importance and complexity of language. A working knowledge of a language can give a powerful insight into not only its culture but also it can help practically in negotiations.

A definition for corporate culture is: all the elements around which an organisation defines itself and relates to its stakeholders. This can include the way it organises its employees, allows them to express themselves and imparts its values. Corporate culture can be influenced by the founders of the company and their lives, by the company's own life and its history. The differences between the American and the European political, social and cultural environment help explain the main differences between American corporate culture – high risk, immediate feedback, hands-on style management – and European corporate culture – which is more based on proceedings and rules.

The need to cohabitate, or at least cohabitate amongst European states, has stimulated a softer and more cooperative style of management, which at times can appear grey rather than have a black and white direction. Religious and cultural differences between European countries create differences between their corporate cultures, such as the work rhythm and the planning of activities and production. However, today these general tendencies – which are more or less theoretical explanations for differences that run deep – seem to be in decline, as there are more and more multinational corporations operating in Europe and the sole national champion organisation is in decline. Yesterday, differences in corporate cultures used to be due to geographic and political reasons; different countries would mean different corporate cultures. In more recent years it seems that American business culture is invading European corporations, and there is a growing homogenisation between Europe and America. Of course, some core differences still remain, but they are becoming less over time, and what is increasingly the main reason for corporate culture differences is the levels of activity of the organisation.

We can observe that the globalisation of the world economy is also beginning to globalise company culture in transnational organisations. The Greenpeace campaign manager in London is equally at home in Buenos Aires or at the WTO talks, whilst the equivalent at BP may have a similar educational background, geographic location and meeting agenda. In SME's this cultural internationalisation has had less of an impact, although in the past five years the web and its easy access to global markets and consumers has meant that the global marketing culturalisation process has begun to steadily increase even in the small business sector.

REFERENCES

———. (1996) 'Developing Global Managers' *Seminar presented by ITM*, 7–8 December, Chicago, IL. In P.N. Ghauri and J-C. Usunier (eds), *International Business Negotiations*. New York: Elsevier. pp. 119–30.

Graham, J.L. (1981) 'A hidden cause of America's trade deficit with Japan', *Columbia Journal of International Business Studies*, (Fall): 5–15.

Graham, J.L. (1983) 'Brazilian, Japanese and American business negotiations', *Journal of International Business Studies*, 14 (1): 47–61.

Graham, J.L. (1984) 'A comparison of Japanese and American business negotiations', *International Journal of Research in Marketing*, 1 (2): 51–68.

Graham, J.L. (1985a) 'Cross-cultural marketing negotiations: a laboratory experiment', *Marketing Science*, 4 (2): 130–46.

Graham, J.L. (1985b) 'The influence of culture on business negotiations', *Journal of International Business Studies*, 15 (1): 81–96.

Graham, J.L. (1987) 'Deference given the buyer: variations across twelve cultures', in P. Lorange and F. Contractor (eds), *Cooperative Strategies in International Business*. Lexington, MA: Lexington Books. p. 473–84.

Graham, J.L. and Andrews, J.D. (1987) 'A holistic analysis of cross-cultural business negotiations', *Journal of Business Communications*, 24 (4): 63–77.

Graham, J.L., Evenko, L.I. and Rajan, M.N. (1992) 'A comparative study of soviet and American business negotiations', *Journal of International Business Studies*, 23 (3): 387–418.

Graham, J.L. and Lin, C.Y. (1986) 'A comparison of marketing and negotiations in the Republic of China (Taiwan) and the United States', in S. Tamer Cavusgil (ed.) *Advances in International Marketing*. Greenwich, CT: JAI Press.

Graham, J.L. and Sano, Y. (1984) *Smart Bargaining: Doing Business with the Japanese*. Cambridge, MA: Ballinger.

Guy, V. and Mattock, J. (1993) *The New International Manager*. London: Kogan Page.

Hall, E.T. (1969) *The Silent Language*. Greenwich, CT: Fawcett.

Hall, E.T. (1981) *Beyond Culture*. New York: Doubleday.

Hamden-Turner, C. (1991) *Corporate Culture*. London: Economist Books.

Hamden-Turner, C. and Trompenaars, F. (1993) *The Seven Cultures of Capitalism*. New York: Doubleday.

Harris, P. and McDonald, F. (1994) *European Business and Marketing*. London: Chapman.

Hofstede, G. (1980a) 'Motivation, leadership and organisation: do American theories apply abroad?', *Organisational Dynamics*, 9 (1): 42–63.

Hofstede, G. (1980b) *Culture's Consequences: International Differences in Work-Related Values*. Beverly Hills, CA: Sage.

Hofstede, G. and Bond M.H. (1988) 'The Confucius connection: from cultural roots to economic growth', *Organisational Dynamics*, 16 (4): 4–21.

Hofstede, G. and Usunier J-C. (1996) 'Hofstede's dimensions of culture and their influence on international business negotiations', in P.N. Ghauri and J-C. Usunier (eds), *International Business Negotiations*. New York: Elsevier. pp. 119–30.

Lewis, R. (1996) *When Cultures Collide*. London: Nicholas Brealey.

Randlesome, C. (1993) *Business Cultures in Europe*. Oxford: Butterworth.

Schuster, C.P. and Copeland, M.J. (1996) *Global Business: Planning for Sales and Negotiations*. Fort Worth, TX: Dryden.

Schuster, C.P. and Harris, P. (eds) (1999) *Newer Insights into Marketing: Cross-cultural and Cross-national Perspectives*. New York: International Business Press.

Usunier, J-C. (1996) *Marketing Across Cultures*, (2nd edn). New York: Prentice Hall.

CASE STUDIES

Case studies that can be read in conjunction with this chapter are:

Boutinot Wines
Broadcasting
BSE Crisis
Cooperative Bank
EVC1 and 2
LEGO
Mannesmann,
Philips
Russian Entrepreneurs
Unilever

USEFUL WEBSITES

www.airbus.com.
The European aircraft manufacturer.

www.eurodisney.com
The Paris-based operation of Disney Corporation.

www.michelin.com
The French tyre manufacturer.

www.wto.org
The World Trade Organisation.

PART III: CASE STUDIES

CS1 EVALUATING EUROPEAN POTENTIAL AND EXPANSION POSSIBILITIES FOR A US FURNITURE COMPANY*

CAMILLE P. SCHUSTER

Furniture Distributors, a privately-held US corporation, has been a successful domestic company since 1973 with 30–35 per cent growth every year. A major portion of their business is distributing household furniture to retailers. Products are sourced from the US and international markets. Furniture Distributors is vertically integrated, however, and can manufacture selected products for themselves. Sales in 1998 were approximately $100 million.

Furniture Distributors sells everything needed for furnishing a house, except porcelain. The best description of the company's business is that they sell a 'house in a box'. Their job is to create a complete package of furniture and accessories for a room or a whole house so that the major furniture pieces, occasional tables, lamps and upholstery fit together, creating a unified 'look' for the room or home. 'Rooms to go' are available at three price-point levels, but they all focus on creating a 'one-stop package' for the customer.

As Furniture Distributors has expanded operations beyond just distribution, they have become involved in a number of different kinds of business relationships. For instance, upholstered furniture and goods are primarily manufactured in the US and Furniture Distributors owns two upholstery plants in the US. They are 50 per cent owner of a bedding company that has 14 manufacturing plants in the US. Dining room and occasional tables are manufactured in the US and many other countries. Most Furniture Distributors' imports come from Asia, where sourcing may be in the form of buying products directly from manufacturers, contracting with manufacturers for specific products, or having a partnership with a manufacturer whereby 100 per cent of their capacity is purchased by Furniture Distributors.

---

*This case is based upon a real company, but facts have been changed to protect the anonymity of the company and its owners.

INTERNATIONAL INTEREST

Over the past few years, a number of customers from other countries have purchased items from Furniture Distributors. These occasional orders have resulted in 66 accounts outside the US, spanning the continents of Asia, Africa, Europe, and Asia. At the semi-annual furniture show in High Point, North Carolina, during April 1998, Furniture Distributors made a conscious attempt to attract customers from outside the US. In a two week period, $275,000 worth of merchandise was sold to non-US customers. During the following year, over $1,000,000 worth of merchandise was sold to non-US customers. This kind of response indicated the potential of more growth outside the US, but no one could answer the question as to what market or region outside the US had the best potential for investment and/or growth. Therefore, a study was conducted to determine what potential existed in the furniture markets of Latin America, Europe, Africa or Asia.

Evaluating every country in each of these regions was not considered to be a good use of resources, so a decision was made to choose those countries with existing accounts, countries that have been identified as good markets for US products in general, and any countries in those regions with a large market. After an initial assessment, Europe was identified as a particularly attractive region, but management wanted a more specific evaluation of individual countries. As a result, the following countries were compared in a second phase of the project:

Europe: Belgium, Denmark, England, Finland, France, Germany, Greece, Ireland, Italy, The Netherlands, Norway, Portugal, Scotland, Spain, Sweden and Wales.

SCALE DEVELOPMENT

The research team gathered information on economic, demographic, political, social and cultural variables for each country. After analysing the gathered information, 12 distinct categories were created for comparing market potential across these countries. Each category consisted of a 3-point scale.

- *Housing:* If strong social and cultural influence to establish separate housing existed, if evidence of strong housing starts to exist, if second home owner-ship was prevalent, or if increasing divorce rates were prompting the estab-lishment of independent households, then 3 points were awarded. If these conditions did not exist, 1 point was awarded for this category.
- *Human development index (HDI):* A country's HDI reflects the level of access to health care, education and economic prosperity affording people opportu-nities and choices in their lives. An HDI approaching 1.0 indicates a high level of economic and social development. One point was awarded if the HDI was

less than 0.60. Two points were awarded if it was between 0.61 and 0.87. Three points were awarded if it was above 0.88.

- *Gross domestic product (GDP) per person employed*: To determine more accurately the amount of income available as discretionary money in each country, the GDP was modified to include only the working population:

$$\frac{GDP \text{ in adjusted US\$}}{1 - \% \text{ unemployed} \times \text{number in 15–64 population segment}}$$

One point was awarded if the GDP per worker was higher than $15,000. Two points were awarded if the GDP per worker was between $15,001 and $20,000. Three points were awarded if the GDP per worker was higher than $20,001.

- *Distribution channels:* The existence of good channels of distribution that are easily accessible by companies outside the country resulted in a score of 3. If the channels were accessible but not efficient or if they were efficient but not easily accessible by foreign companies, the country received a score of 2. If the channels of distribution were neither efficient nor easily accessible by foreign companies, the country received a score of 1.

- *Barriers to entry:* If major barriers to entry existed, the country received a score of 1. If some barriers would create a significant problem for entry into the market, the country received a score of 2. If the existing barriers were minor and/or manageable, the country received a score of 3.

- *Free trade membership:* A country was either in a free trade agreement or it was not. Therefore, a country received a score of 3 If It was a member of a free trade agreement and a score of 1 if it was not.

- *Banking:* The average rate of exchange rate/currency stability over the last three years was an indicator of economic stability and demonstrated a country's purchasing strength against the US dollar. If a country's exchange rate fluctuated more than an average of ten percent over the last three years, the country was given a score of one. If a country's exchange rate fluctuated between six to nine per cent over the last three years, the country received a score of two. If a country's exchange rate fluctuated at a per cent less than six over the last three years, it received a score of three.

- *Urbanization:* Urbanized areas were viewed positively since consumers living in these areas would be more likely to be earning a steady income and buying furniture for new households that were being established. Therefore, countries with over 70 per cent of their population living in urban areas received a score of three. Any country that had an urbanization rate between 41 and 69 per cent received a score of two. Any country with less than a 40 per cent rate of urbanization received a score of one.

- *Political risk/government stability:* To invest money, time, and resources into developing a new market, companies are interested in being able to know, understand, and predict government decisions. If regulations are created and changed in an arbitrary manner, investments are difficult to protect. If the political risk and government instability were high, a country received a score of one. If either the political risk or government instability were high while the other factor was low, the country received a score of two. If the political risk and government instability were both low, the country received a score of three.

- *Gross domestic product:* If the gross domestic product is high, then the country has money to spend on education, manufacturing, telecommunications, or infrastructure. Countries with a high Gross Domestic Product received a score of three. Countries with a moderate Gross Domestic Product received a score of two. Countries with a low Gross Domestic Product received a score of one.

- *Inflation:* If a country's inflation rate is exceptionally high in relation to the US rate, then that country's currency will suffer downward pressure, making US goods more expensive to purchase. If the adjusted Gross Domestic Product is rising but the inflation rate is rising more rapidly, then the longevity of that economic expansion is suspect. Therefore, a country received a score of 1 if the inflation rate was high, a score of two if the inflation rate was moderate, and a score of three if the inflation rate was low.
- *Infrastructure:* Transportation, power generation and distribution, postal or package services and telecommunications are important requirements for being able to deliver goods on time and in good condition. A country with an excellent infrastructure received a score of three. Lack of infrastructure resulted in a score of one. Countries with some weaknesses in their infrastructure system received a score of two.

While the research team agreed upon these variables, it was not possible to find data on all twelve categories for all of the 59 countries being investigated. Appendix A contains a table for each of the countries based upon the available data.

Challenge

The report containing the tables in Appendix A and supporting documentation was presented to the owners of Furniture Distributors. A meeting has been scheduled to evaluate the information in the report and consider the feasibility of expanding into specific European countries. At the proposed meeting the following decisions will be discussed:

1   Should Furniture Distributors choose to concentrate on the European market?
2   If a decision is made to concentrate on the European market, which country or countries offer the best potential?
3   If a decision is made to concentrate on the European market, should the effort begin by targeting one country or a group of countries?
4   In which country should the company begin its expansion efforts?

INSTRUCTOR'S DISCUSSION GUIDE

This case is roughly based upon a distributor of furniture in the US Midwest. The information presented here generally describes the situation at the time the research was requested. Implementation of the decision is in progress, so no results are known at this time. A group of MBA students were the research team that gathered and analysed the secondary data.

Owners of Furniture Distributors were unfamiliar with the furniture market outside of the domestic US market. While some shipments had been made to accounts outside the US, no active sales or marketing campaign had been directed to these markets, goods were priced and paid in US dollars, and no one from the company travelled outside the US to call on potential customers. When an effort was made to focus on international sales, the first attempt resulted in revenues of $275,000 in two weeks at a trade show. Revenue from non-US sales had increased to over $1,000,000 at the end of the year. While this was only 1 per cent of the company's total revenue, it was enough to make the owners begin to ponder the possibilities of growth outside the US domestic market.

The research project gathered secondary information on the economic, political, demographic, social and cultural characteristics of 57 countries. The comparisons across countries highlighted those regions of the world in which consumers had money, in which household furniture was an important product, in which the furniture market either was growing or had potential for growth and in which the political structure justified investment. Decisions for the following year include a commitment to consciously pursue growth outside the US.

The market potential for furniture in Europe is high and predictions are that the European market will grow slightly in 1999. Therefore, a decision was made to begin investigating the possibility of using agents and/or distributors in this market. Company representatives will attend a European furniture fair to begin intensive assessment of the market and potential business partners.

QUESTIONS FOR DISCUSSION

1 How best to conduct a screening analysis?
2 The choice of variables?
3 The definitions of categories?
4 Reliability and/or validity of scoring system?
5 Analysis of potential?
6 International versus global orientation of company?
7 Choice of regions for market entry?
8 Choice of countries for market entry?

Appendix: Comparison table – furniture market assessment*

	Housing	Human Development Index (HDI)	GDP per person employed	Distribution channel	Barriers to entry	Free trade access	Banking
Asia							
Thailand	3	2	1	2	3	3	2
Pakistan	1	1	1	1	1	1	1
India	1	1	1	1	1	1	3
China	3	2	1	2	2	3	3
Singapore	3	3	3	3	3	3	3
Taiwan	3	3	3	3	3	2	2
Indonesia	3	1	1	2	2	3	1
Japan	3	3	3	3	3	2	1
Korea	3	2	2	3	2	3	1
Vietnam	3	1	1	1	1	3	1
Malaysia	3	2	1	3	2	3	1
Australia/New Zealand	3	3	3	3	2	3	3
Latin America							
Argentina	2	3	2	3	3	3	3
Brazil	N/A	2	1	3	2	3	2
Chile	N/A	2	2	3	3	3	3
Columbia	N/A	2	1	3	2	3	1
Costa Rica	1	2	1	1	2.67	3	1
Dominican Republic	N/A	2	1	2	1	3	2
Ecuador	N/A	2	1	2	3	3	1
Honduras	1	1	1	1	2.33	3	1
Mexico	2	2	2	2	2.25	3	1
Nicaragua	1	1	1	1	2.33	3	1
Panama	N/A	2	1	3	2	1	3
Peru	N/A	2	1	2	2	1	1
Puerto Rico	N/A	N/A	2	3	3	3	3
Uruguay	2	2	1	2	1.75	3	1
Venezuela	2	2	2	2	1.75	3	1
Africa							
Cote d'Ivoire	1	N/A	1	2	2	3	2
Zambia	2	1	1	3	2	3	1
Kenya	2	1	1	2	2	3	2
Ethiopia	1	1	1	2	1	1	2
Ghana	1	1	1	1	3	1	1
Mozambique	1	1	1	1	2	1	1
Senegal	1	1	1	1	3	1	2
Republic of South Africa	2	3	2	3	2	3	3
Zimbabwe	1	1	1	1	2	2	1
Zaire	2	1	1	1	2	1	1
Cameroon	1	1	2	3	1	2	3
Nigeria	1	1	2	2	1	1	1
Central African Republic	1	1	1	1	1	1	1
Europe							
England	3	3	3	3	3	3	3
France	3	3	3	3	2	3	2
Ireland	3	2	3	3	3	3	3
Portugal	3	2	3	2	2	3	3
Scotland	3	3	3	2	3	3	3
Spain	3	2	3	3	3	3	3
Wales	3	3	3	2	3	3	3
Sweden	3	3	3	3	2.33	3	3
The Netherlands	3	3	3	3	3	3	3
Germany	3	3	3	3	3	3	3
Belgium	3	3	3	3	3	3	3
Greece	3	2	2	3	2	3	3
Italy	3	2	3	3	2	3	3
Finland	1	3	3	3	3	3	2
Norway	3	3	3	3	2.5	1	3
Denmark	3	3	3	3	3	3	3

Appendix (continued): Comparison table – furniture market assessment*

	Urban	Political risk/ government stability	GDP growth	Infra-structure	Inflation
Asia					
Thailand	1	3	3	2	2
Pakistan	1	1	3	1	2
India	1	1	3	1	1
China	1	2	3	2	3
Singapore	3	3	3	3	3
Taiwan	3	3	3	3	3
Indonesia	2	1	1	1	2
Japan	3	3	1	3	3
Korea	3	2	3	3	3
Vietnam	1	2	3	1	2
Malaysia	3	3	3	3	2
Australia/New Zealand	2	3	2	3	3
Latin America					
Argentina	3	3	3	3	3
Brazil	N/A	2	2	2	2
Chile	3	3	3	2	2
Columbia	3	1	2	2	1
Costa Rica	1	2	1	1	2
Dominican Republic	N/A	2	3	2	2
Ecuador	2	2	2	2	1
Honduras	1	1	3	1	2
Mexico	2	2	2	2	1
Nicaragua	1	1	3	1	2
Panama	2	2	2	2	3
Peru	3	1	3	1	2
Puerto Rico	3	3	3	3	2
Uruguay	2	2	2	2	1
Venezuela	2	2	3	2	1
Africa					
Cote d'Ivoire	1	2	N/A	2	3
Zambia	2	2	2	2	1
Kenya	1	2	3	2	1
Ethiopia	1	3	3	1	2
Ghana	1	3	3	1	1
Mozambique	1	2	2	1	1
Senegal	1	2	3	1	2
Republic of South Africa	3	3	3	3	2
Zimbabwe	1	1	1	1	1
Zaire	1	1	1	1	1
Cameroon	1	2	2	2	3
Nigeria	2	1	2	1	1
Central African Republic	1	1	1	1	1
Europe					
England	3	3	2	3	3
France	3	3	2	3	3
Ireland	3	3	3	2	3
Portugal	3	3	3	2	3
Scotland	3	3	3	1	3
Spain	3	3	2	2	3
Wales	3	3	3	1	3
Sweden	3	3	3	3	3
The Netherlands	3	3	2	3	3
Germany	3	3	2	3	3
Belgium	3	3	2	3	3
Greece	2	3	3	2	2
Italy	3	3	2	3	3
Finland	2	3	3	3	3
Norway	3	3	3	3	3
Denmark	3	3	2	3	3

*These variables and calculations were prepared by MBA students in a Multinational Marketing class, based upon their research.

CS2 WHAT'S YOUR BEEF? THE ROLE OF THE MEAT AND LIVESTOCK COMMISSION AFTER THE UK BSE CRISIS*

PAUL R. BAINES AND PHIL HARRIS

The Meat and Livestock Commission (MLC) was established under the 1967 Agriculture Act with the aim of promoting greater efficiency in the livestock and livestock product industries of Great Britain whilst caring for the interests of the consumer (MLC, 1999: for more information access their website listed in the Reference section at the end of this case study). The MLC raises a statutory levy on animals slaughtered or exported in order to fund its activities. The levy is supplemented by commercial income from the livestock industry. The MLC has been trying to reduce its dependence on statutory levies and raised £6.6million from the EC and the beef industry in 1996, during the bovine spongiform encephalopathy (BSE) crisis.

The MLC has concentrated on trying to restore consumer confidence in beef products, as well as trying to ensure that lamb and pig meat products capitalise on the opportunities offered as substitute products. The MLC launched a minced beef initiative where prime minced beef cuts displayed a rosette to illustrate its quality. This initiative arose out of the realisation that consumers were more worried about minced beef than they were about steaks. This was typified by a comment from a consumer in a focus group who, when asked what minced beef was made of, stated 'it's the ears, tails and eyelids and anything else they can't sell' (Irvin, 1999).The result was a campaign by the MLC, which sought to reassure consumers that prime cuts of beef used in mince production were safe to eat; thus they launched their rosette quality kite mark on mince with the words 'offal-free'. This initiative boosted domestic sales of minced beef by 18 per cent. One of the key performance indicators used by the MLC is the uptake by meat processors (and others in the beef industry) of its blueprint techniques for production and distribution. These blueprint techniques are designed to ensure that meat quality is optimised prior to its distribution. The MLC has had a consistent target of trying to ensure that 60 per cent of its target companies comply with its procedures (MLC, 1999).

*This case study is intended to be used as the basis for class discussion and not as a guide to good or bad management practice. Please do not contact the MLC, or any other organisation mentioned in this case study, since the case study is intended to provide sufficient informational content for teaching and learning purposes. However, students in need of contextual information should visit the websites listed in the Reference section at the end of this case study.

Table C2.1   Chronology of the events leading up to the BSE crisis

Date	Events
~1985	Clinical signs of bovine spongiform encephalopathy (BSE) are found.
June 1986	UK government scientists make first official diagnosis of BSE.
August 1988	The government orders the slaughtering of BSE-infected cattle with compensation provided for farmers.
November 1989	Specified bovine offal (material most likely to contain BSE-infected tissue) from cattle over six months of age banned from human food.
April 1990	British Government chief veterinary officer criticises Russian ban on British beef.
March 1993	First human death of Creutzfeldt-Jakob Disease (CJD).
March 1996	UK Health Secretary admits possible link between BSE-infected cattle and CJD.
March 1996	EU imposes worldwide ban on British beef.
April 1996	EU Agriculture Minister, Franz Fischler, and EC President, Jacques Santer, both state that they would personally eat British beef.
	The British Prime Minister refers the ban to the European Court of Justice, insisting that the ban is operating on political rather than public health grounds.
May 1996	The UK government initiates its Over Thirty Months Scheme (OTMS) where cattle over the set age (those most likely to have contracted BSE) are destroyed.
August 1999	Worldwide ban on British beef lifted.
October 1999	French continue to operate ban on British beef despite EC ruling, provoking UK consumer boycott of French products led by leading UK supermarket groups, including Budgens, leading itself to port protests by French farmers.
October 1999	EC scientific committee considers new French evidence, ruling that removal of the trade ban on British beef is still justified, paving the way for the re-establishment of its export markets.

THE BSE CRISIS IN BRITAIN

BSE was caused by polluting cattle feed with infected tissue. By 9 September 1998 (Jenkins, 1998), 27 human deaths had been attributed to Creutzfeldt-Jakob Disease, (CJD) the human equivalent of BSE, considered by scientists to have crossed the species barrier through the food chain. The key problem, and the surrounding furore, could be considered to be the result of the failure of the communication of scientific information to the public. After all, previous food scares such as those associated with salmonella in eggs (late 1980s) and e-coli (early 1990s) had not produced the same public hysteria, although in the case of eggs it took many years for the market to recover its lost ground. Jenkins argues that the root cause of the crisis was that a group of UK scientists changed the risk of contracting CJD through eating beef from 'an inconceivable risk' in 1995 to 'a very small one' in 1996. The timeline of the events leading up to the BSE crisis are represented in Table C2.1.

The impact of the crisis, and the subsequent ban, has been considerable. Estimated costs to the UK taxpayer vary depending on the time of reporting, but press reports estimate the cost of the crisis to have been approximately in the range £3–£3.5billion, with a further cost to UK exporters of between £1–2billion. The cost to the government represents payments to farmers to destroy cattle over 30 months old (the OTMS scheme) and which had cost the UK government £1.2billion in payments up to the end of July 1999 (MAFF, 1999). A further scheme, the calf processing aid scheme, was also introduced, though ended in July 1999, in order to provide farmers with support for their sudden loss of markets. Nevertheless, at least in the UK, consumer confidence in beef had risen considerably. Total GB household beef consumption for the four-week period ending 31 July was only 6 per cent down on the same period in 1998, and 2 per cent down on the same period in 1995. Similarly, the number of UK homes purchasing beef during the same four-week period dropped from 47 per cent to 46 per cent, 14 per cent down on 1998 and only 2 per cent down on 1995 (MAFF, 1999).

The BSE crisis has effectively become a global issue. Japan, which has not allowed imports of UK beef since 1951 out of fear of foot-and-mouth disease, has announced plans for the banning of all UK beef products including pet food. Taiwan has announced a ban on canned beef, sausage and ham to supplement its original ban placed on British and Irish beef in 1990. In the Middle East, Iran and Egypt have both turned away Irish beef shipments (USMEF, 1999).

The MLC has developed plans for a worldwide marketing campaign to promote British beef and is expected to focus on quality breeds such as Aberdeen Angus. It is expected that, in the short term, only small quantities of British beef are likely to be exported, aimed at the catering trade rather than supermarket shelves (The *Independent*, 1999). The beef export scheme for the UK (excluding Northern Ireland, which has a computer tracking system and has been able to demonstrate that its herd has been BSE-free for more than a year) imposes restrictions on the preparation of the meat. The meat must be de-boned from the 1 August 1996 (when the meat and bone meal feed restrictions that were argued to be the source of the infected meat came into place) and has to be aged between 6 and 30 months. UK politicians now argue that British beef is the safest meat in the world as a result of the considerable restrictions it faces in its production.

THE MARKET FOR BRITISH BEEF

The ban on British beef and the erosion of consumer confidence in its safety has ensured that domestic sales fell heavily. This was particularly pronounced after McDonalds and other high street food retailers announced their own boycott of British beef, with some retailers sourcing their beef from as far away as New Zealand. In 1995, total beef consumption in the UK was 901,000 tonnes. By 1998, after a significant initial drop, it had risen back up to 884,000 tonnes. Safeway plc, however, continued to sell its Heritage beef range, launched in 1994, with confidence since it had full control over production protocol and

Table C2.2   Beef exports (tonnes) for 1990 and 1995

Destination	1990	1995
France	67,000	80,000
Italy	4,000	42,000
The Netherlands	9,000	17,000
Spain	1,000	7,000
South Africa	3,000	27,000
Other EU	16,000	45,000
Other non-EU	14,000	28,000
Total	114,000	246,000

Source: Harris and O'Shaughnessy (1997)
Note: *Figures rounded up to nearest thousand.

traceability back to individual farms, and could be confident that it was selling meat sourced from animals aged under 30 months (Robertson, 1999).

Prior to the BSE crisis, France and Italy represented substantial markets for British beef, exports representing almost 50 per cent of the total exports in 1995. However, since 1990, significant growth had been achieved in exports to South Africa and Italy over the five years between 1990 and 1995. Table C2.2 illustrates UK beef exports.

Table C2.2 illustrates a substantial increase by tonnage over the five years with exports increasing 116 per cent. However, in 1999 this export trade had been completely eroded as a result of the EU's worldwide ban on British beef exports.

Table C2.3 illustrates the substantial loss of revenue to the UK beef industry as a result of the ban on exports, with significant proportions of this loss coming from outside the EU. The combined revenue lost represents £520million at 1995 prices. Potentially significant non-EU markets include South Africa, Australia, the US and Japan. However, the US has banned British beef since 1991 as a reaction to BSE and in retaliation for the European ban on American meat treated with hormones. Japan, which has traditionally only imported Aberdeen Angus for sales of sushi, also stopped its limited imports.

THE UK BEEF INDUSTRY AND ITS SUPPLY CHAIN 'STAKEHOLDERS'

Shaoul (1999) argues that the food industry is 'generally fragmented' and controlled by a few large vertically-integrated companies. The market has seen a lack of growth, with changes of ownership in this mature market occurring as companies refocus on their core food businesses. The beef supply chain consists of several major components comprising farmers (who raise and maintain beef herds), the meat processing industry and within this, the slaughtering and rendering industries, and the knackers yards (see below for further detail).

The beef farming industry is highly fragmented, with farmers maintaining herds of relatively small sizes over a wide range of locations (Shaw and Gibbs,

Table C2.3   Revenue obtained from UK beef exports by country

Importer	1995 value (£m)	1999 value (£m)
France	179.0	0
Italy	126.0	0
Ireland	52.0	0
The Netherlands	49.4	0
Spain	17.4	0
Denmark	12.0	0
Belgium	10.0	0
Portugal	7.0	0
Sweden	3.0	0
Greece	0.6	0
Germany	0.6	0
Finland	0.0	0
Austria	0.0	0
South Africa	23.8	0
Mauritius	4.0	0
Ghana	2.5	0
Angola	1.5	0
Malta	2.2	0
Saudi Arabia	1.7	0
Hungary	1.8	0
Philippines	1.5	0
Gabon	1.7	0
Hong Kong	1.8	0
Other non-EU	20.5	0
Total	520.0	0

Source: Meat and Livestock Commission (1999)

1995). Farmers have the option of either selling their cattle to meat processors (which often buy at a set dead-weight cost) or selling them via auction markets (where prices fluctuate), which can allow farmers to obtain significantly higher prices per head of cattle. Since the switching costs from maintaining a relationship with the meat processor to auction houses is low, farmers often alternate between the different sources of income.

The meat processing industry has been characterised by defensive horizontal mergers between companies and vertical integration between the slaughtering and the wholesale meat market (Shaoul, 1999). Sainsbury's operates abattoirs to supply its own beef through one of its subsidiaries, Newmarket Foods, whilst the Sims Food Group, a leading British meat processor, operates its own abattoirs for beef processing, supplying European retailers with pre-packed, added-value products (Shaw and Gibbs, 1995) and supplying Safeway with its high-quality 'Heritage' beef from selected farmers with whom it had fostered strong mutually-reinforcing relationships.

The slaughtering industry in the UK comprised around 491 abattoirs in 1992, though this had declined to around 402 by 1996. Their role is to kill the animals and ensure that certain aspects of the carcass are removed prior to the despatch of cuts to the meat processor. Many of these abattoirs had not altered their procedures and practices sufficiently to comply with existing EU directives. The Meat and Hygiene Service (MHS), set up in 1996 to police the BSE controls and modifications to procedures in slaughterhouses (which had previously been regulated by Local Authorities' Environmental Health Departments), has the power to close abattoirs for non-compliance with the new regulations. The slaughter industry is responsible for the removal of specified bovine offal (SBO) – the material most likely to contain BSE-infected tissue – and the MHS was set up to ensure that this is conducted satisfactorily. Shaoul (1999) states that while 55 per cent of the bovine carcass passes into the human food chain, 45 per cent must be disposed of, by law, within 48 hours by either incineration, burial or rendering. Since the first two options incur costs, rather than profits, abattoirs deliver bovine carcasses to operators in the rendering industry who pay a fee to the abattoirs for each carcass.

The bovine carcass, however, contributes a number of by-products which include material for pet food, gelatine, sausage skins, animal feed, and material for use in the production of glue, soap and fertilisers. Renderers ensure that the material required for the manufacture of these by-products is removed from the animal carcass. It is as a result of material sold to the animal feed industry that the BSE crisis is said to have originated, since infected tissue is thought to have been sold by the renderers to bone meal manufacturers who in turn sold this to farmers who fed it to cattle.

Knackers yards are responsible for the disposal of diseased and dead animals from farms by incineration and burial. However, this role was also being played by officially-approved rendering plants with the responsibility for the separation of pathogenic material (in this case BSE-infected tissue) from the carcass prior to the carcass being sent to operators in the rendering industry. It is likely that this unclear definition of the roles between government-approved renderers and knackers and the lack of – and enforcement of – government regulation contributed significantly to this crisis.

THE POLITICAL NATURE OF THE EUROPEAN BEEF MARKET

The production of beef in the EU is largely governed by the political and administrative arrangements of the EU and the General Agreement on Trade and Tariffs (GATT) and by competition policy in both the UK and the EU. It is also affected considerably by the value of the pound within and outside the EU. Thus, when the pound is strong, UK beef exports become expensive to our European partners, making domestic supply more profitable. In the UK, Sainsbury's, Asda, Tesco and Safeway control more than 60 per cent of the food retailing industry (Wrigley, 1992), with considerable implications for the balance of power of supermarkets concerning their suppliers. Shaoul (1999) states that, under the Food Safety Act 1990, companies could avoid conviction for safety offences if they could demonstrate that all reasonable precautions had

CS3 BLENDING ETHICS AND MODERNITY THE CO-OPERATIVE WAY

MONICA GIBSON-SWEET

The size of a banker's heart, by some estimates, is smaller than a rosary bead but there is one bank that seems to make some of its customers feel on better terms with their moneylender: the Co-operative. Such customers tend to be found in the genteel classes of suburbia; relatively well-off and versed in the skills of preparing fettucini with basil. They also tend to be overwhelmingly in favour of the profit motive and welcome the fact that Co-op profits filter through a system originally designed to ease the historic perils of exploitation. But the biggest pull of all is the Co-op's stance on ethical issues...

Lindsay Vincent, 1995

In 1997, the UK's Manchester-based Co-operative Bank reported record profits and an excellent return on capital. Profit before tax had increased by 21 per cent to £55 million, and earnings attributable to its equity shareholder, the Co-operative Wholesale Society, had increased by 35 per cent to £30.7 million. The Bank's Chairman, Alan Prescott, attributed these results to the continued development of 'its distinctive market position based on its ethical and ecological policies, innovative products and superior customer service' (The Co-operative Bank Financial Statements, 1997).

The Co-operative Bank's 'modernity', that is, its forward looking approach to all aspects of its business, was acknowledged in 1997 by a leading UK consumer magazine when its personal current account was singled out as 'best buy'. Its market position on ethical and ecological policies was applauded in the same year with the presentation of the Corporate Conscience Award for Global Ethics from the Council on Economic Priorities. This case study reviews this blend of ethics and modernity, tracing the Bank's repositioning strategy from the publication of its Mission Statement in 1988, its Ethical Policy in 1992, its Ecological Mission Statement in 1996 and its Partnership Report in 1998. The four different dimensions of the Co-operative's brand proposition are examined, that is, its ethical stance, access, product innovation and customer service. A detailed profile of the Bank's customers is presented along with a synopsis of its promotional strategy from the early 1990s through to the present day. The Co-operative Bank's Partnership Approach, particularly in relation to its suppliers, its employees and its local community, is outlined.

Finally, some conclusions about the Bank's strategy and its future challenges are reached.

FROM CO-OPERATION TO PARTNERSHIP: BACKGROUND TO THE BANK'S ETHICAL STANCE

The image of banks in the UK has been shaped by their history. During the 1920s and 1930s, great architects were commissioned to design impressive marble halls to attract the rich and prosperous who were the only stratum in society likely to use the banks' services. The banks had to present a strong image to reinforce the customers' psychological need to feel that their money was safe. These buildings have helped to form the relationship between the banks and their customers ever since. In the 1960s and 1970s, when banks were forced out of their up-market niche to develop mass-marketing, they found it difficult to come to terms with new types of customer. The traditional master–servant relationship was no longer appropriate and the new relationship generated many problems. Banks, in general, developed a poor reputation that plagued them throughout the early 1980s as national headlines constantly exposed customer complaints. The Co-operative Bank traded off this well because it was a small bank that was perceived as providing good customer service. Between 1973, when it achieved clearing bank status, and 1985 the Co-operative Bank grew from 0 per cent market share to 2.5 per cent on the back of price differentiation such as free banking and the payment of interest on current accounts.

By the mid 1980s, developments in the banking world meant that the Co-operative Bank faced a very different and challenging competitive environment. Perhaps the main reason was that the 'big four' (National Westminster, Midland, Barclays and Lloyds (now Lloyds TSB)), who had traditionally concentrated on the corporate sector, where the greatest profits were to be found, began to turn their attention to the personal banking sector. This was largely as a result of heavy losses in the third world and in the property market, as well as the rising consumer boom. Added to this, the 1986 Building Societies Act led to building societies moving away from their traditional areas of business, that is, savings and mortgages, to offer current accounts and personal loans. Furthermore, the 'Thatcherite era' was very hostile to the Co-operative Banks' basic values and the values of the co-operative movement in general.[1] Ten years ago, the Co-operative Bank was under serious threat and the image that it presented to the marketplace was personified by its turquoise and white block logo:

> At that time, the Co-op lozenge and all the baggage that came with it implied corner shop; down market; left of centre; old-fashioned. In other words, not the sort of brand image to expect customers to aspire to.
>
> Jim Sinclair, Group Marketing Manager, 1998

Against this background, the Bank executive had to seriously think about what the nature of the bank should be in the years ahead and to find a position that would give it a long-term competitive advantage in the marketplace. The mission statement that resulted from this process in 1988 aimed to define how the principles of the co-operative movement could underpin the business in the modern context. The Bank concluded that the interests of a wide range of parties should be taken into account in all business transactions, and this notion of inclusivity was the central theme of the mission statement (see Appendix 1).

The Co-operative Bank then engaged in research to establish why customers had joined the Bank. In addition to the usual reasons such as 'parents' bank', 'personal recommendation', 'the nearest bank to home', 'the nearest bank to work', 20 per cent of customers said that they had joined the Co-operative Bank because it was ethical! This surprised the Bank's management; they had never really come across this sort of statement before, nor had the Bank promoted itself in this way. Further research convinced the Co-operative Bank that ethical banking did have a degree of credibility and in 1992, after close consultation with its customers, the Ethical Policy was announced (see Appendix 2). The policy sets out who the Bank will or will not do business with:

> The important thing in all of this was customer involvement because when the bank is asked and challenged by external bodies, which we are, when taking a position on the environment or the arms trade, we cannot be accused of 'playing god' as it is not 'the bank' or one individual within the bank. The [ethical] policy is agreed by the customers who are consulted regularly, in fact, every three years. Last time we consulted 1.2m customers in a huge ballot and we received a resounding endorsement of our ethical policy.
>
> Jim Sinclair, Group Marketing Manager, 1998

Fortunately for the Bank, when it ran its corporate customer book against the statements espoused in its ethical policy, it found that only five small organisations (one associated with foxhunting) had to be asked to leave as a result. This almost seems to suggest that the approach had been staring the Bank in the face all along, and perhaps today the strategy appears obvious. This was not true at the time and the notion of ethical banking in 1992 was almost bizarre.

Initially, the Co-operative Bank adopted a negative approach to the selection of its business customers, that is, it would not do business with partners which it viewed as unethical. This contrasts with the selection policies of other banks; Lloyds TSB, for example, positively look to encourage those large companies that have created the most environmental damage but who are doing the most to rectify it. At the Co-operative Bank, customers are asked to suggest new issues which the bank should incorporate into its strategy. The results of the latest customer survey will be published in January 1999. Previous ballots have revealed that human rights is the most important issue; 84 per cent of customers in 1991 and 96 per cent of customers in 1994 placed human rights at the top of their list. This evidence suggests that as more customers have been recruited to the Bank, the proportion of customers supporting the ethical stance has grown. Indeed, whilst only a tiny percentage of banks' overall customers cite political or ethical reasons for choosing their bank, over one-third of the Co-operative Bank's customers cited this as the main reason for their choice (Mori, February 1998).

In 1996, the Co-operative Bank published its *Ecological Mission Statement* (see Appendix 3), which went much further than the Ethical Policy in respect of environmental issues and set out four rules that represent the Bank's under-standing of the minimum conditions required for an ecologically sustainable society:

> The ecological considerations that make up the Mission Statement are essentially non-negotiable facts of life. Therefore, it is not anticipated that the statement will require constant revision'
>
> The Co-operative Bank Partnership Report, 1998, p. 3

In the year 1997 it was the Co-operative Bank's 125th anniversary and also the year in which it announced its Partnership Approach. In 1998, it published its first Partnership Report in which it identified seven partners: shareholders; customers; staff and their families; suppliers; local communities; national and international society and past and future generations of co-operators (with the natural environment encompassing all seven partners). The Bank sees its approach as a new model for managing a successful business in the 1990s and beyond. The Partnership Report is the result of a scrutiny of the bank's commitment to managing its business in a socially responsible and ecologically sustainable manner in relation to all seven partners. The report was externally audited by ethics and so on[2] and The Centre for Tomorrow's Company[3] both pioneers of social auditing techniques.

ETHICS IS NOT ALL: THE THREE OTHER DIMENSIONS OF THE CO-OPERATIVE BRAND

Although the Co-operative Bank's customers and potential customers are very interested in the ethical dimensions of the brand, they also need to be convinced about the Bank's credentials as a service provider before they join. Generally, the customer places greatest value on the hygiene factors of the brand and the ethical dimension will only ever be considered in a tie-break situation. The Co-operative Bank sees its brand as the totality of everything it does and believes that a myriad of factors influence customer perceptions of the brand including: customer letters; community support; telephone calls; statement inserts; brand advertising; staff communications; bank branches; media coverage; political relations; the Customers Who Care scheme; corporate identity; its partnership approach and ethical policy implementation and development. These elements can be categorised into the four dimensions of the Co-operative Bank's brand proposition: its ethical stance; access; product innovation and customer service.

In 1989, when First Direct first launched telephone banking, the Co-operative Bank recognised that this provided the way to achieve its ambitions of growing and gaining a national customer base. Within nine months, it had transferred all its existing customers onto the telephone banking system. The Bank now has three call centres in Skelmersdale, Stockport and Salford, all in the north-west region of England within close proximity to the head office in Manchester. The initial operation was staffed by less than 100 people, but rapid expansion has led to approximately 1300 people being employed in the call centres. The Co-operative Bank is now considered to be the UK's leader in this field. This 'anytime, anywhere' principle has recently been extended so that the Bank provides its services throughout the UK via the Post Office network and worldwide via the Internet.

Product innovation is a vital ingredient of the Co-operative Bank's success. One example is the Bank's gold card market, which has grown from a 0 per cent presence in 1991 to become the market leader in Europe in 1998. This growth was on the back of a 'free for life' proposition in a market that was charging between £60 and £70 per annum for the privilege of having a card. During the 1970s and the 1980s, the Bank gained competitive advantage through product innovation, which is a vital element of the brand that customers and the outside world now expect. A recent example of product innovation has been the replacement of the PVC credit card. Highly toxic dioxins are released from PVC when it decomposes and the Bank was committed to developing an alternative. This involved extensive lobbying on a number of committees to bring about a change in the international visa regulations, substantial investment in research and development and the persuasion of manufacturers to invest in production systems to produce relatively small quantities. A real partnership was required and success was achieved when biopol was produced as the raw material for future credit card production at the Co-operative Bank.

The final part of the brand proposition is service excellence, and the Co-operative Bank now offers a customer service guarantee whereby the customer will receive £10 if they score against this guarantee. Service is at the core of the customer relationship and the Bank has found that customers have taken the guarantee at face value and not attempted to abuse the system. Mori (February1998) found that 51 per cent of other banks' customers are very satisfied with their level of service, compared with 73 per cent of the Co-operative Bank's.

The Co-operative Bank sees itself as a modern bank that conducts its business in an ethical manner. In this context 'modernity' includes issues of innovation, professionalism, up-to-date attitudes and behaviours and elements of fashionability; 'ethical manner' includes both the implementation of the bank's ethical policy and its attempt to maintain high levels of integrity in its dealings with partner groups:

> If the bank had adopted a public face like Neil from 'The Young Ones': long hair, afghan coat and lentils … the bank would not have been taken seriously by the media, the city or our customers. The blend of ethics and modernity is very important: how we speak, how we look and what we say is very important.
>
> Jim Sinclair, Group Marketing Manager, 1998

TABLE C3.1 Co-operative Bank customer profile

	Measure	Index	%*
Middle-aged	45–54	162	26
Hard-working	Take work home	144	23
Wine-drinking	Heavy user	141	17
Prudent	AVC Contributions	139	43
Upmarket	AB	128	27
Educated	Term. Age > 21	126	15
Home-owning	Own/buying home	112	82
Working	Full-time worker	111	41

Source: BMRB, TGI, September 1998
Note: *Percentage of Co-operative Bank personal customers that fit the description.

TABLE C3.2 Co-operative Bank Customers' Views

	Index	%
I am a vegetarian	137	9
I'm not too concerned about my appearance	136	21
I check food labels for additives	124	39
I read the financial pages of my newsletter	123	24
Friends ask my advice about gardening	121	23
I loathe doing housework	117	31
I never buy animal-tested products	114	52
A car is only to get from a to b	111	42
A real man can down several pints of beer	90	6
I judge a person by the car they drive	87	11
I like to stand out in a crowd	82	12
A woman's place is in the home	74	7
Real men don't cry	63	5
Designer labels improve one's image	56	6

Source: BMRB, TGI, September 1998

Unlike Anita Roddick of the Body Shop who talked about 'pin-stripe dinosaurs' in her overt challenge of the UK financial systems (Gibson-Sweet, 1994), the Co-operative Bank appears to have worked within the constraints of the city and conformed in many ways. The difference between the Co-operative Bank and other banks is that an ethical policy has underpinned its strategy.

THE CO-OPERATIVE BANKS' CUSTOMERS: FETTUCINI AND BASIL?

The Co-operative Bank has a national market with deeper penetration in the north-east, south-west and midlands regions of England. Manchester, home to the Head Office and traditionally considered to be the heartland of the co-operative movement, has always been one of the lowest areas in term of market share. Penetration in the London area was traditionally weak, but over the last five

TABLE C3.3   Co-operative bank customers' newspapers

	Index v UK Pop.
Guardian	318
Observer	211
Financial Times	205
Independent on Sunday	189
Independent	173
The Times	148
Sunday Express	127
Express	117
Mirror	117
Daily Telegraph	116
Sunday Telegraph	112
Star	112
Mail on Sunday	106
Sunday Times	105
Sunday People	103
Daily Mail	94
Sunday Mirror	93
Sun	86
News of the World	82

Source: BRMRB, TGI, September 1998

years it has become an area of extensive growth as it has a larger proportion of people with sympathetic attitudes as well as a larger proportion of people interested in direct/telephone banking. Table C3.1 summarises the Co-operative Bank's customer profile.

The Co-operative Bank's customers are typically conservative (with a small c!), ethically minded and 'unshowy' as Table C3.2 illustrates:

Unsurprisingly, the Co-operative Banks' customers prefer broadsheets, particularly left-of-centre titles as illustrated in Table C3.3.

THE CO-OPERATIVE BANK'S PROMOTIONAL STRATEGY: FROM CO-OP LOZENGE TO LANDMINES

Following the publication of its ethical policy in 1992, the Co-operative Bank faced the challenge of communicating it to the general public. Its first stab at television advertising in 1992 has been dubbed the 'House that Jack Built' approach. It was largely focused on environmental issues and aimed to educate customers about the fact that their money is recycled. This fairly mild approach was followed, in 1994 and 1995, with another two television advertisements, which were far more direct and unsettling. The first of these black and white advertisements featured a male presenter who asks the viewer 'What's the difference between the Co-op banks and other banks?' The benefits of 24-hour telephone banking, 6000

TABLE C3.4 **Co-operative Bank's competitor spend-UK bank advertising 1997–98**

£ million	1997–98	As % of total
Barclays	32.9	· 19.5
Lloyds TSB	22.0	13.1
Abbey National	18.9	11.2
Alliance & Leicester	16.2	9.6
Halifax	14.5	8.6
National Westminster	13.1	7.8
Nationwide	10.5	6.2
Royal Bank of Scotland	7.8	4.6
Midland	7.3	4.3
First Direct	6.4	3.8
Bank of Scotland	4.9	2.9
Bristol & West	3.4	2.0
Woolwich	3.1	1.8
Northern Rock	2.9	1.7
Co-operative Bank	2.5	1.5
Britannia	1.9	1.1
Total	168.3	

Source: Mori, February 1998

linked cash machines and so on were outlined as the footage flashed between the presenter and snatched images of travesties of human rights. The advertisement ended with the presenter asking 'Or is it that we promise never to invest our customers' money in countries with oppressive regimes?' The second advertisement followed the same pattern, except that the benefits of the Co-operative Bank's service were interspersed with footage of environmental disasters, ending with the question 'Or is it that we promise never to invest our customers' money in companies which needlessly pollute the environment?' The earlier campaign tried to describe the fundamental proposition of the ethical policy whilst ensuring that customers understood that their money is not simply deposited in a little box in the bank. People quickly bought into the ethical concept but almost immediately went on to ask about the quality of the other services available. Hence the second campaign, which attempted to convince the customer about the benefits of Co-operative brand as well as its unique ethical stance.

The television advertising campaign has been successful over the years and the correlation between advertising and new accounts has been high. The Co-operative Bank's spend on advertising has been fairly modest (see Table C3.4) compared with other banks. Awareness amongst the ABC1 21–45-year-old target audience is high, but the Co-operative Bank has identified the need to target a younger audience and higher advertising spend is planned.

The Co-operative Bank's promotional tactics have become more political in recent years with the adoption of cause-related themes. The first example was in 1996 when it ran a campaign against the arms trade and supported the international campaign to ban landmines. The campaign told the true story of how 9 million landmines, at a cost of £30 each, were sourced by a UK arms broker from an Italian manufacturer and then shipped via Singapore through the back door to Northern Iraq. The Bank ran a UK press campaign in the *Financial Times* on the day of the publication of the Scott Report (1996), which investigated the sale of arms to Iraq scandal. At the same time, they wrote a letter to the heads of all British banks asking them to join the campaign. This was followed up with a cinema campaign aimed at young people whereby the people in rows A–G were told that standing on a landmine (or its lengthy trip wire) would completely tear them apart, rows H–L would be maimed beyond all recognition and the rest critically injured. The advert ended with the statement 'Certain regimes in the world borrow millions of pounds in order to plant landmines indiscriminantly, which is why one bank never has and never will finance the supply of arms to oppressive regimes'.

The Co-Operative Bank's Customers Who Care Programme guarantees that for every £100 a customer spends, the Bank will donate 2.5p to charitable causes. Instead of just giving a cheque, the Bank aims to build up a more meaningful relationship with a charity, giving both its time and expertise. The first project was inspired by the 1996 National Disabilities Act. As both an employer and service provider, the Bank was keen to embrace the spirit of the legislation and not just comply with the letter. It worked with a range of charities on three fronts. One was a conference for fund raisers that examined the use of negative imagery in the media portrayal of people with disabilities in bids to raise funds. The second was a national cinema campaign that ran in September 1997. The third was targeted at the opinion-formers and a specially compiled video was sent to every head of production at the BBC, ITV and Channel 4 as well as to heads of advertising agencies and heads of marketing. The Bank originally aimed to run a different campaign each quarter and other projects included work with the UK's Royal Society for the Protection of Birds and a safe food campaign. However, the continuing relationships that have developed with campaign partners has meant that campaigns are now only run bi-annually. The current campaign (1998), on which the Bank is working closely with Amnesty International, marks the 50th anniversary of the Declaration of Human Rights.

As well as striving to meet the needs of the wider world, the Co-operative Bank aims to be a good neighbour in the local communities in which it operates. A significant proportion of the Bank's community support has been focused on urban regeneration (30 per cent), ecological projects (28 per cent) and educational initiatives (29 per cent) (the Co-operative Bank's Group Public Affairs Unit 1998). One example is the donation of four community woodlands covering 250 hectares in the north-west of England for recreation, sports, education and as a new habitat for wildlife. This 'birthday present' to mark the Bank's

125th anniversary was opened to the public in 2000. The Bank acknowledges that satisfying 'the community' can be problematic as it consists of different groups with varying and often conflicting aims. In 1997, the Co-operative Bank contributed a total of £1.95 million to charitable causes and almost one-third of this was allocated to the community.

THE CO-OPERATIVE BANK'S ECOLOGICAL MISSION: FROM PAPER TO PEOPLE

The Co-operative Bank aims to make concern for the environment central to everything it does, recognising that the earth is a closed system with a finite number of resources. The Bank's Ecology Unit applies the natural step methodology (see The Co-operative Bank's Partnership Report, 1998: 42) to all business decisions and high priority has been given to: ensuring that the bank has an effective ecological management system; reducing energy consumption; accounting for global warming; utilising information technology effectively to reduce ecological impact; ecologically sound paper purchasing and disposal and minimising the impact of transport on the environment. Attention is also being paid to chemicals that have a tendency to persist in nature and sustainable waste disposal. An audit of its activities in this area was conducted and reported in the 1998 Partnership Report. Comparisons could only be made against the National Westminster, which is the only other UK clearing bank to release similar information. As a result of the audit, the bank was commended for its serious and systematic approach to its environmental impact, with attention to recycling being the one main area for concern.

A crucial element to this ecological management is the fostering of positive supplier relationships as the Co-operative Bank believes that interdependence can work to mutual advantage. However, it recognises that there are risks in adopting such a strategy, for example, the possibility of being let down by a critical supplier or, on the supplier side, over-reliance on one large customer. Since 1995, all suppliers have been screened against the principles outlined in the Ethical Policy and the Bank looks at the 'ecological profile'of the products and services purchased. In particular, the Bank aims to source fair trade products and services and it is one of the largest consumers of fair trade coffee in the UK. The Bank introduced its Partnership Approach to building mutually beneficial relationships with its suppliers in 1997, which formally recognises that both sides must want a relationship and that there must be trust between the two parties. Research revealed that 65 per cent of suppliers felt that 'each party gets the best out of the relationship' (The Partnership Report, 1998: 36), but whilst research has confirmed that the vast majority of suppliers share a belief in partnership, many of them were unaware of the detail of the Bank's partnership approach. This is something to which the Bank will have to pay more attention in future.

Fundamental to all the Co-operative Banks' activities are the commitment and enthusiam of its staff. The Bank has a total of 3776 employees, with over 60 per cent based in the north-west region of England. It is interesting to note that staff *and* their families are identified as a partner. In line with developments in business generally, the Bank has evolved a much flatter organisational structure that, it believes, has minimised bureaucracy and aided flexibility. Staff now work in 'cross-functional' teams on projects. The Co-operative Bank was the first UK clearing bank to achieve the Investor in People Award and 89 per cent of employees reported that they feel proud to be an employee of the Bank (Co-operative Bank Staff Survey, 1997). The Bank aims to measure its performance in relation to its employees in terms of the salary package, job security, employability and equal opportunities. Staff are informed about the ethical policy in the 'Heritage, Culture and Values' training programme that every member of staff has undertaken in recent years. Furthermore, staff are surveyed on their attitudes towards the ethical policy and partnership approach and almost all staff are satisfied with the Bank's decision to promote and implement the ethical policy (97 per cent), and the vast majority feel that it has had a positive effect on customer service (82 per cent), customer recruitment (97 per cent) and customer retention (89 per cent). Worryingly, however, almost one-fifth of employees felt that the ethical policy had had a negative impact on the way the Bank manages its staff, and the Bank acknowledges the need for initiatives that support and help staff to understand the ethical policy and partnership approach (see Partnership Report, 1998: 32).

CONCLUSION

Critics of the Co-operative Bank may feel that its ethical policy is simply another means of marketing the bank to 'a well meaning but naïve public' yet the Co-operative Bank is quite blunt about its use of the ethical issues as a marketing tool: 'We are a bank and have to make a profit … the ethical policy is a way of differentiating ourselves from other banks' (Thompson, 1994). The Co-operative Bank, by its own admission, strives to be modern, which implies fashionable. It could be argued that its approach is simply timely and once fashions change, customers will also change and move on to the next trend. However, the Bank is resolute about the importance of ethical issues and believes that they are no longer tangential to mainstream business. There is increasing evidence to suggest that there is growing pressure on business to act responsibly towards a range of stakeholders and to act transparently in terms of this responsibility (see, for example, Gosling, 1994; Welford, 1997; McDonagh and Prothero, 1997). Whilst this is not yet enshrined in British company law, many believe that the UK will follow the example of other countries, such as Germany and France, and force business to acknowledge responsibility beyond the shareholders (Thal Larsen, 1996).

Perhaps one reason why the Co-operative Bank has been so successful is its small size, which has allowed it to remain unchallenged by the big four who view it only as an irritant. It may be that the Co-operative Bank has influenced its sector and there is growing interest in some of the issues, particularly in relation to the environment. If the approach does become more widespread the other banks could beat the Co-operative Bank at its own game, but it is questionable whether they could ever afford to loose major accounts in order to follow this strategy. At the same time, however, the Co-operative Bank's size must be a hindrance as they lack the resources to fund expansion and its stance will detract many large investors. Hence a vicious cycle that will always result in low market share.

The Co-operative Bank faces many challenges, not least the rise in supermarket banking and the constant threat of new entrants. Deregulation has increased competition and, in 1999, the American MBNA Bank, with its massive resources, is set to penetrate the UK market. New entrants tend to cherry pick and compete in the most profitable sectors. In future, changing technology will make it far easier for customers to switch banks. In such an environment, the importance of branding will grow in significance and banks will have to strive to compete across the full range of hygiene factors. Currently, the Co-operative Bank's ethical stance is only ever considered in a tie-break situation, but if economic conditions worsen, customers may place more value on other aspects of the product offering.

The recent trend of demutualisation of several UK financial institutions, including Halifax plc and Norwich Union, must be a threat to the Co-operative Bank. Closer to home, its shareholder, the Co-operative Wholesale Society, has recently fought off a hostile takeover bid claiming that the CWS 'is not for sale to anyone at any price' (Potter, 1997). However, perhaps it is only a question of time before it is taken over (Cope, 1997), and if the Co-operative Bank finds itself with a new owner then clearly its stance may be threatened. Similarly, rumoured mergers with the Co-operative Insurance Society may also pose a challenge to current activities.

Terry Thomas, the Co-operative Bank's Chief Executive between 1988 and 1997, was a powerful force in the adoption of the bank's ethical stance. The Bank now has a new Chairman, Mervyn Pedelty, and it will be interesting to see whether he continues to bolster the ethical approach to business, particularly as his reign commences in a period of economic downturn when companies classically resort to cost-cutting tactics.

Whether or not one remains sceptical, the Co-operative Bank's financial performance has gone from strength to strength in recent years. It strongly denies that its social and ethical positioning is simply a gimmick and claims that it is not altruism. As Simon Williams, Head of External Affairs comments:

> We are not seeing this as philanthropy or do-goodism or a marketing ploy. There is a deep-rooted belief that there is a business purpose to this – that if we do all these things, better profits will result.

> (Graham, 1998)

QUESTIONS FOR DISCUSSION

1 Why do people bank with the Co-operative Bank?
2 How has the Co-operative Bank managed to be successful in the face of banking norms and strategies?
3 Has the Co-operative Bank contributed to a new business paradigm for the banking industry?
4 Can the Co-operative Bank sustain its stance and grow in the new millennium?
5 Consider the differences between the Co-operative Bank's communication strategy and more conventional strategies used in the industry.

NOTES

1 The traditional forms of co-operation that existed in rural Britain were weakened or destroyed during the Industrial Revolution when almost everything, even human labour, was viewed as a commodity to be bought and sold as part of the market society. The Co-operative movement was a conscious attempt to rebuild the bonds of social solidarity and to invent systems of mutual support in an attempt to overcome the newly-found depths of poverty witnessed in Britain during the 1820s, 1830s and 1840s. William King was the first advocate of 'practical Co-operation' and in 1828 he could point to several working examples of Co-operative societies largely based on shopkeeping. The Welshman, Robert Owen, provided the underlying philosophy of the Co-operative movement. He believed that the right to full humanity should be available to all and he valued kindliness, toleration, co-operation, respect for youth, the creation of a non-competitive environment and so on and he came up with the concept of co-operative communities. The real birth of the Co-operative movement, as described in the case study, was the rise of Rochdale Pioneers. The Society was formed in 1844 and became an effective and efficient retailer and producer whose members not only benefited from their dividend payments but from other ideals such as open membership, cash trading, pure and unadulterated goods, education and political and religious neutrality. From Rochdale, these principles travelled the world and provided a foundation for the Consumer Co-operative Movement. (For further reading please see Bichall, J. (1994) *Co-op, the People's Business*, Manchester University Press, Manchester.)
2 *ethics and so on* was set up by Richard Evans and Traidcraft Exchange in 1997 to help companies develop systematic and auditable reporting of their performance against their wider social and ethical objectives and values. *ethics etc* is a member of the Institute of Social and Ethical Account Ability.
3 The Centre for Tomorrow's Company was founded in 1996 to inspire and enable UK businesses to compete with the world's best through the inclusive approach.

ACKNOWLEDGMENTS

Grateful thanks are extended to Jim Sinclair, Group Marketing Manager at the Co-operative Bank for his insight and time to be interviewed, to Phil Harris for his continued support and to Chris, Harry and Cassie Gibson for their stoicism.

REFERENCES

BMRB (1998) British Market Research Board, TGI Report, September: London.
Co-operative Bank (1997) www.co-operativebank.co.uk/ethics/partnership1997/97_chief-exec-overview.html

Co-operative Bank (1998) www.co-operativebank.co.uk/ethics/partnership1998/introducing_partners.html

Cope, N. (1997) 'Co-op to press for hefty damages: CWS threatens legal action as Regan returns boxes of confidential information to the High Court', *Independent*: Business, 24 April.

Gibson-Sweet, M. (1994) 'The Body Shop International: An Ethical Success' in P. Harris and F. McDonald, *European Business and Marketing: Strategic Issues*, London: Paul Chapman.

Gosling, P. (1994) 'Corporations call in Ethics Police', *Independent on Sunday*, 14 August.

Graham, G. (1998) 'Holier-than-thou bank's ethical audit: MANAGEMENT CO-OPERATIVE BANK: The Co-op's first 'Partnership Report' will put its ethical and ecological claims up for scrutiny', *Financial Times:* INSIDE TRACK, 15 April.

Levitt, T. (1960) 'Marketing Myopia', *Harvard Business Review*, July/August: 45–56.

McDonagh, P. and Prothero, A. (eds) (1997) *Green Management: A Reader.* London: Dryden.

Mori (1998) cited in www.co-operativebank.co.uk/ethics/partnership1998/introducing_partners.html

Potter, B. (1997) 'Judge Slams "Disgraceful" Co-op Raid', *Daily Telegraph*: CITY, 26 April.

Scott, R. (1996) *Arms to Iraq Report*. London: TSO.

Sinclair, J. (1998) www.co-operativebank.co.uk/ethics/partnership1997/97_national_deliver.html

Thal Larsen, P. (1996) 'Stakeholding: stakeholding fails to pin companies – the ide of stakeholding companies: a warm thought for a cosier Britain, or a blueprint for the way companies should really run themselves? Either way it faces a tough reception', *Investors Chronicle*, 27 September.

Thompson, R. (1994) 'Moral maze for ethical investors', *Independent on Sunday*, 28 August.

Welford, R. (1997) *Hijacking Environmentalism*. London: Earthscan.

Vincent, L. (1995) 'The Co-op Crusader – Terry Thomas', *Observer*, 9 April.

APPENDIX I   MISSION STATEMENT

We, the Co-operative Bank Group, will continue to develop a successful and innovative financial institution by providing our customers with high-quality financial and related services whilst promoting the underlying principles of co-operation which are:

- **Quality and excellence**

    To offer all our customers consistent high quality and good value services and strive for excellence in all that we do.

- **Participation**

    To introduce and promote the concept of full participation by welcoming the views and concerns of our customers and by encouraging our staff to take an active role within the local community.

- **Freedom of association**

    To be non-partisan in all social, political, racial and religious matters.

- **Education and training**

    To act as a caring and responsible employer encouraging the development and training of all our staff and encouraging commitment and pride in each other and the Group.

- **Co-operation**

    To develop a close affinity with organisations which promote fellowship between workers, customers, members and employers.

- **Quality of life**

    To be a responsible member of society by promoting an environment where the needs of local communities can be met now and in the future.

- **Retentions**

    To manage the business effectively and efficiently, attracting investment and maintaining sufficient surplus funds within the business to ensure the continued development of the Group.

- **Integrity**

    To act at all times with honesty and integrity and within legislative and regulatory requirements.

APPENDIX 2   ETHICAL POLICY

Following extensive consultation with our customers, with regard to how their money should and should not be invested, the Bank's position is that:

- **It will not invest** in or supply financial services to any regime or organisation which oppresses the human spirit, takes away the rights of individuals or manufactures any instrument of torture.

- **It will not finance** or in any way facilitate the manufacture or sale of weapons to any country which has an oppressive regime.

- **It will actively seek** and support the business organisations which promote the concept of 'Fairtrade' i.e. trade which regards the welfare and interest of local communities around the world.

- **It will encourage** business customers to take a pro-active stance on the environmental impact of their own activities, and will invest in companies and organisations that avoid repeated damage to the environment.

- **It will not speculate** against the pound using either its own money or that of its customers. It believes it is inappropriate for a British clearing bank to speculate against the British currency and the British economy using deposits provided by their British customers and at the expense of the British taxpayer.

- **It will try to ensure** its financial services are not exploited for the purposes of money laundering, drug trafficking or tax evasion by the continued application and development of its successful internal monitoring and control procedures.

- **It will not provide** financial services to tobacco product manufacturers.

- **It will not invest** in any business involved in animal experimentation for cosmetic purposes.

In addition, there may be occasions when the Bank makes decisions on specific business, involving ethical issues not included in this Policy. We will regularly re-appraise customers' views on these and other issues and develop our ethical stance accordingly.

APPENDIX 3   ECOLOGICAL MISSION STATEMENT

We, the Co-operative bank, will continue to develop our business taking into account the impact our activities have on the environment and society at large. The nature of our activities are such that our indirect impact, by being selective in terms of the provision of finance and banking arrangements, is more ecologically significant than the direct impact of our trading operations.

However, we undertake to continually assess all our activities and implement a programme of ecological improvement based on the pursuit of the following four scientific principles:

1. Nature cannot withstand a progressive build-up of waste derived from the earth's crust.
2. Nature cannot withstand a progressive build-up of society's waste, particularly artificial persistent substances which cannot degrade into harmless materials.
3. The productive area of nature must not be diminished in quality (diversity) or quantity (volume) and must be enabled to grow.
4. Society must utilise energy and resources in a sustainable, equitable and efficient manner.

We must consider that the pursuit of these principles constitutes a path of ecological excellence and will secure future prosperity for society by sustainable economic activity. The Co-operative Bank will not only pursue the above path itself, but endeavour to help and encourage all its Partners to do likewise.

We will aim to achieve this by:

- **Financial services**
  Encouraging business customers to take a pro-active stance on the environmental impact of their own activities, and investing in companies and organisations that avoid repeated damage of the environment (as stated in our Ethical Policy).
- **Management systems**
  Assessing our ecological impact, setting ourselves clear targets, formulating an action plan and monitoring how we meet them, and publishing the results.
- **Purchasing and outsourcing**
  Welcoming suppliers whose activities are compatible with both our Ethical Policy and Ecological Mission Statement, and working in partnership with them to improve our collective performance.
- **Support**
  Supporting ecological projects and developing partnerships with businesses and organisations whose direct and indirect output contributes to a sustainable society.
- **Legislation**
  Adhering to environmental laws, directives and guidelines while continually improving upon our own contribution to a sustainable society.

KEVIN BOLES

Boutinot Wines Limited is a wine company based in the north of England. A small- to medium-sized enterprise with 52 employees, the company has a turnover of just under £40 million per year. It is a business that has grown, driven by one man's passion, from a hobby into an international company that produces and distributes wine not only to the UK, but also throughout the world. Paul Boutinot, founder, owner and Chairman of Boutinot Wines, has played a significant part in bringing about a cultural revolution in the British way of life. Although born and brought up in Manchester, being of French parentage Paul often visited his father's family in the Loire region of northern France. There, surrounded by terraces of vines and enjoying the classic food – that is, the everyday fare of provincial France – he learned 'how wine ought to taste'.

In the early 1980s he began working in his father's restaurant; wine drinking then had not become the cultural, social and everyday occurrence that it is today. In the UK many restaurants provided reasonably good food, but Boutinot recalls his frustration at not being able to obtain a bottle of good basic wine at a reasonable price. The wines sold in restaurants were often over-priced and generally of very poor quality, with the more popular being the cheap, slightly sweet bland white wines imported from Germany and Eastern Europe. At that time good wine was only available through specialist wine shops and was not the core product that is now widely available in supermarkets and multiple retailers. Consequently, Boutinot began importing small amounts of inexpensive wines from France, which he sold from the back of his father's restaurant to other restaurateurs. As interest grew, Boutinot realised that he had identified a gap in the market for inexpensive, well-made wines 'that tasted like wine' and offered 'value for money'. These two phrases were to become the common currency of the UK wine industry.

Owners of local restaurants and bars were among Boutinot's first customers, but the business soon expanded to include most of the independent wine shops and restaurants dotted around the north of England. Social habits were changing rapidly, dining out was becoming more commonplace and home cooking, driven by popular how-to-do-it television programmes of the Delia Smith variety, was enjoying a renaissance. The company established a firm reputation as a wine specialist, with a solid portfolio of French wines. Having begun with inexpensive, but good table wines, Boutinot began to add what he calls 'boutique' wines to the product portfolio. These were wines of higher quality produced in small quantities by little-known wine-makers in the south of France. Such wines were in great demand from restaurant clients for their quality and value for money. A good wine list was, and still is, an effective way to differentiate one restaurant from another. Boutinot established an office in Julienas in the Beaujolais region of France to source and organise the bottling of wines. A small warehouse in Stockport became the centre of all UK operations and many high street names were numbered among the company's customers, including Marks and Spencer, Victoria Wines and Sainsbury's.

GROWING THE COMPANY

Paul Boutinot decided that he needed greater control over the production and distribution process, and it was not a big step to take from buying other people's wine to producing his own. In partnership with winegrowers in France, Paul began by blending wines from different regions and he developed a series of wines especially for the UK market. The first range was named after his eldest son, Jean Paul, and included a red, a medium white and a dry white. A second range of a slightly superior blend was developed for the restaurant trade and named after his second son, Louis Alexander. These were to become the company 'house wines' and one of the few examples of successful brand development in the UK wine business. A great deal of mystery and lack of understanding still surrounds wine, but in the 1980s consumers understood very little indeed and many considered wine-talk pretentious. 'Good wines sell themselves', is still Boutinot's message to the sales team, 'but the client has to taste the wine first.' The marketing strategy was very simple: if the owners and managers liked the products, they in turn would recommend the wines to their customers. In developing a simple brand Boutinot offered clients an assurance that his wines were carefully chosen and offered value for money. Paul Boutinot refused to consider any advertising or promotional support beyond encouraging his own customers to try the products. 'Word of mouth has always been the most effective marketing tool. If people like a wine, that is the wine they ought to drink. The more often people taste wine the more experience they gain, but it comes back in the end to personal choice and in selling good wines at affordable prices we do give the consumer a real choice.'

GOING GLOBAL

Vertical integration has continued, with the company now owning vineyards in France and South Africa and with Paul making and advising on wine production in every major wine producing country in the world. Many clients and their customers demand a wider variety of wines and Boutinot expanded the company portfolio to include wines from Spain and Italy, Portugal and Germany, and has now added New World wines from Chile, Argentina, South Africa and Australasia. The product portfolio is constantly being updated, but the benchmark remains the same: quality at an affordable price. New additions include Boutinot's own sparkling wine, Cremant de Loire from France, Riojas from Spain, blended whites from South Africa and varietals from Argentina.

MARKETING IN THE UK WINE INDUSTRY

Indeed, Boutinot wines are sold in almost every major multiple retail outlet in the UK including Sainsbury's, Tesco, Asda, Safeway, Oddbins. They are distributed through major pub chains and are on sale in prominent cash-and-carry outlets, corner shops and most restaurants. It is very likely that any regular wine drinker has enjoyed Boutinot's value for money, well-made wines. Considering the market penetration he has achieved, Paul Boutinot is not a household name – at least not yet. This is very typical of the wine industry and it is a common feature of most suppliers to the food industries and of small businesses in particular. There are two significant reasons why this is the case. The first one is the nature of the industry, which is essentially a business-to-business activity. The second reason is the difficulty of developing and sustaining a brand image in a fast moving consumer goods (FMCG) business.

THE WINE INDUSTRY IN THE UK IS A BUSINESS-TO-BUSINESS ACTIVITY

Very few retailers and restaurants, the end-sellers of wine products, ever source wines directly from producers. Almost all use a variety of intermediaries who either produce wine themselves or act as agents for producers. In fact, many of the growers of grapes are not wine makers, but sell their produce to a winery where the wine is made. Wineries in turn sell wine in bulk to wholesale agents who blend, bottle and label the wine before shipping it to the country in which it is to be sold. The wines that appear on the retailer's shelves have often been bottled and labelled for that retailer, but the same blend of wine may well be on sale in another retailer's under a different label. Boutinot Wines directly manage most of this process and is very much the exception among UK wine companies.

BRANDS IN THE WINE INDUSTRY

Of the thousands of wines that are available on the supermarket shelves, in restaurants, bars and corner shops, very few are 'brands'. The market is characterised by a huge diversity of suppliers and products and no one brand has more than 2 per cent of the market by volume. There are some that are known by their place of origin, producer's name or because of heavy advertising support. Famous champagnes such as Moet et Chandon and Tattinger for example, or Blue Nun and Le Piat Dor can be considered identifiable brands, but branding in the wine market is a difficult concept to define. A 'brand' may refer to a particular vintage from one vineyard, such as Chateau Petrus 1947, or it might include a 'classic' range of wines, both reds and whites, from various countries and be produced under an own label, such as Tesco's Bordeaux, or Sainsbury's South African Varietals. While branded wines in general have accounted for a very small proportion of sales, some market research predicts that they will take a larger market share as more products are tailored to consumers' tastes. It is anticipated that the market share of own-label products will continue to grow beyond the 58 per cent market share reached in 2001.

THE CONSUMER

Across Europe consumption of wine has been falling, except that is in the UK where wine sales continue to expand. Habits have changed dramatically in recent years, with the bulk of consumers switching from cheap white wines to medium-priced reds. While interest in and knowledge about wine has developed, for many consumers it is the grape variety or the country of origin that fulfils the role of brand name. According to research undertaken for the Boutinot company, most consumers make their wine buying decision when they are actually in the supermarket or shop. Most consumers admit to having a preference for red or white, but several other factors influence their choice. After colour and grape variety, price is the most important, and then possibly country of origin. Faced with the abundance of choice many consumers choose supermarket own-label products, relying on the reputation of the stores for quality at the right price. These variations in choice have influenced the way Boutinot's now market their products. Until very recently, Paul Boutinot resisted any attempts to develop a marketing policy beyond the reliability of the product, good packaging and personal selling. He has always considered marketing as everybody's job and that includes the sales representatives, the office support staff as well as brand managers and buyers. Boutinot recognises that the industry has undergone a transformation in the last decade. When most wines were sold through wine shops and wholesalers it was possible for him to know many of the clients personally, to meet with them regularly and more importantly to know what they needed to add to their shelves to complete their portfolios. Now with over 55 per cent of wine products sold through supermarkets, marketing strategies have had to change to meet consumer needs.

MARKETING AND THE WINE BUSINESS

Perhaps the most significant change to marketing wines in Europe has been the arrival of large quantities of inexpensive new world wines from Australia,

New Zealand, South America and South Africa. Along with the changes in social habits of drinking at home, rather than in bars and restaurants, high alcohol 'fruity' Australian wines were to give a significant boost to wine drinking particularly in the UK. Australian red and white wines offered the consumer more flavour than the popular but bland Germanic wines. They also tended to be less dry and more approachable than the more traditional wines of France and Italy and therefore had more appeal to the still inexperienced palate of the British public. The Australians not only introduced the British public to a wide range of different wines, but they also introduced the industry to a highly proactive, marketing-led strategy. Prior to this, marketing strategies were almost unheard of in the wine business. There was very little advertising or product support and personal selling was more or less the only recognised marketing method in use. The Australians recognised the potential that the UK market offered, negligible home production, a growing consumption and interest, and they therefore established a generic body called 'Australian Wines' to effect a single awareness-raising campaign. Unlike their European counterparts, Australian wine makers did not have to meet a complex array of restrictions that applied to the type of grape to be used in wine making, the minimum and maximum alcohol levels or what information could or could not appear on the label. Added to the brash approach of the newcomers, both television and the popular press began to offer distinctive wine features among food programmes and in cookery columns.

FAVOURABLE MEDIA COVERAGE

Much of the mystique that surrounded wine and wine drinking has been stripped away as consumers have been encouraged to taste and enjoy the experience. National and regional newspapers and magazines have a wine column and some have their own wine clubs. There have been several television programmes aimed at informing the public about wine, often as a feature on a cookery or holiday programme. While these offer opportunities to promote particular wines or knowledge about wine producing countries, the true value to the wine industry is the promotion of the culture of wine drinking, reinforcing the idea that wine is fashionable and that knowledge of wine is a desirable social attribute. Having a wine featured in a television programme or in a wine column can significantly increase sales. The result has been an onslaught of 'concept' wines packaged with eye-catching labels and striking names, such as Big House Red, Old Block and Jacob's Creek. Although still very much committed to providing good quality wine at value for money prices, Paul Boutinot knows he has to keep up with the times. Building brands that can become household names is the way forward and while a French name once helped establish a reputation for reliability, the company now focuses on developing concept wines for the European market. Names like Old Git, Italia and Fruits of France are set to lead the company into the twenty-first century, but Paul Boutinot's passion is just as it was when he began his hobby: it is possible to make good wine available at a reasonable price for everyone to enjoy.

QUESTIONS FOR DISCUSSION

1 To what extent can Boutinot Wines' success be attributed to Paul Boutinot's personality and entrepreneurial flair?
2 What of the future, how will the management grow the business?
3 New product development (NPD) or innovation, how are these realised at Boutinot's?
4 How has vertical integration developed?
5 Are our attitudes to products and lifestyle shaped by or reflected in the media?
6 To what extent is Boutinot Wines targeting niche markets?
7 Many small businesses develop around an entrepreneurial figure; how can such businesses be developed, grow and be sustained over the long term?

CS5 EVC (1986–94): THE EUROPEAN PVC INDUSTRY AND THE CREATION OF THE EUROPEAN VINYLS CORPORATION (EVC)

PHIL HARRIS AND MATT DODD

In October 1986, ENI of Italy and ICI of the UK combined their polyvinyl chloride (PVC) businesses to form the European Vinyls Corporation (EVC), a 50:50 joint venture company. The strategic rationale was simple: by joining forces they would be able to reduce their overall production capacities and thereby more readily meet the needs of their European customers. They would also restore profitability to their impoverished PVC businesses.

BACKGROUND TO THE MARRIAGE

PVC markets and technology

PVC was first developed over 50 years ago, as a material for the insulation and sheathing of electrical cables. PVC has come to be one of the world's most widely used plastics, with a wider range of uses than any other comparable product – since polymer can be compounded with a variety of additives to produce both rigid and flexible end products. Table C5.1 outlines the main applications of PVC in Europe during 1990.

Despite the fact that certain PVC polymers are highly specialised and are able to demand substantially higher margins, over 80 per cent of the market is for general purpose (bulk) polymer.

PVC is produced from a combination of ethylene and chlorine in a two-stage process that is outlined in Figure C5.1. First, ethylene is combined with chlorine to form vinyl chloride monomer (VCM). Then the VCM is processed to produce PVC.

FORMATION OF A JOINT VENTURE COMPANY – BACKGROUND TO PARTNERS

EniChem

EniChem is the chemicals division of Ente Nazionale Idrocarburi (ENI), the state-owned energy conglomerate. ENI acts under the aegis of the Italian Ministry for

Table C5.1   Estimated demand for PVC in Western Europe by application, 1990

Rigid PVC applications	%
Construction (pipe, profiles inc. windows)	45
Film	8
Sheet	2
Containers	7
Vinyl records	2
Miscellaneous	1
Flexible (plasticised) applications	%
Cable	10
Film	8
Floor covering	5
Hosepipe etc.	4
Coatings	3
Miscellaneous	5

State Holdings and was established in 1953. Since then ENI has grown to become one of the largest industrial corporations in the world, with interests in exploration, mining, metallurgy, mechanical manufacturing, textiles, process engineering and chemicals.

EniChem was formed in 1983, as part of the Italian government's restructuring of its chemical industry. The previously separate companies Anic, Societa Italiana Resine, Liquichimica, Enoxy and Montedison were all brought under the EniChem umbrella. EniChem's activities were grouped into eight clearly defined business sectors, including: base chemicals; plastics; synthetic rubber and latices; synthetic fibres; detergent intermediates; pharmaceuticals fine chemicals; engineering polymers; and agricultural chemicals. As a result of these developments, EniChem became the second largest producer of PVC in western Europe, its core markets being Italy, Central and Southern Europe.

ICI

Imperial Chemical Industries (ICI) plc was established in 1926 through the merger of four manufacturers: Brunner Mond, Nobel Industries, United Alkali and British Dyestuffs.

Since the 1980s, ICI followed a policy of 'globalisation'. By 1990, over four-fifths of its revenues came from sales outside the UK. At the same time, the group has concentrated its efforts on developing strategic businesses that create 'added value' such as paints, pharmaceuticals, films, and speciality chemicals. In 1993, the company split itself into two, Zeneca becoming the specialist business producing pharmaceuticals, paints, films and speciality chemicals, whilst ICI retained the traditional core chemical businesses which included petrochemicals, chlorine derivatives, plastics and other bulk products.

In 1985, ICI's Petrochemical and Plastics business was it's largest, with a worldwide turnover of £2.7 billion of which 80 per cent was generated from EU countries. After the second oil crisis of 1979, ICI reassessed its strategy in relation to

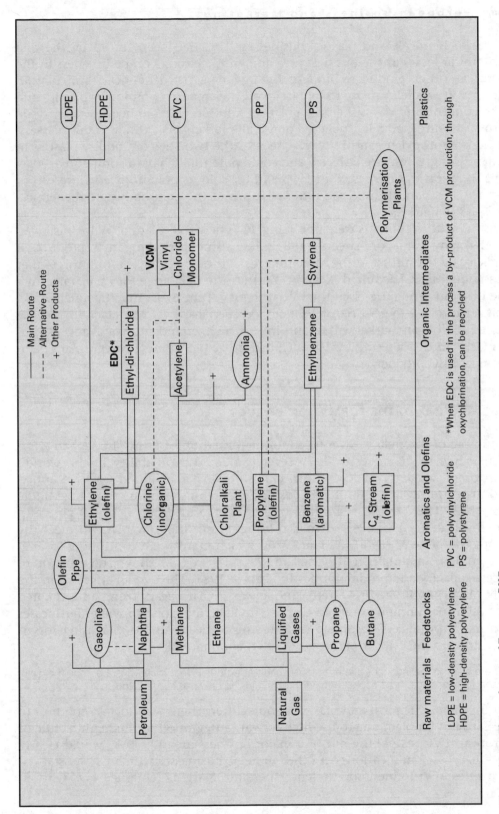

Figure C5.1 *The production of European PVC*

Source: Author's own research

it's petrochemicals and plastics businesses. This had been forced by the first substantial losses in the business area and an increasing competitiveness in the sector as other producers brought on line new petrochemicals and plastics capacity. It was felt unwise to remain in all the areas of commodity plastics and that 'concentration' was the only practical solution to avoid being stretched too thin and being gradually squeezed out of all markets. As a result of this reassessment, polypropylene and PVC were seen as the two key commodity plastics in which ICI's greatest strengths lay and could potentially have a competitive edge. This situation was reassessed in 1993 and ICI sold its polypropylene interests to Bayer AG as part of increased rationalisation in the commodity petrochemical and plastic markets.

As these developments were unfolding, ICI's new PVC plant at Wilhelmshaven in Germany came on stream (1981), increasing the company's production capacity by two-fifths. At the same time, as part of a rationalisation process that was going on, ICI acquired BP's PVC business (in exchange for their polyethylene interests) and purchased the PVC interests of the Swiss manufacturer Lonza. This enabled ICI to gain access to increased specialist PVC manufacture and the Central European market with plants in Sins, Switzerland and Waldshutz, southern Germany. As a result, by 1985 ICI had moved to number three in Europe in terms of PVC production.

BACKGROUND TO THE FORMATION OF EVC

A number of interrelated events led to the formation of EVC. The second enormous surge in oil prices in 1979 severely dented profitability in the world's petrochemicals and plastics industries. Businesses had acquired stocks in anticipation of shortages as a result of feedstock restrictions resulting from the Middle East crisis. Then at the beginning of 1980 demand dropped by 20 per cent. Moreover, many producers were also bringing on line new plant to meet the unprecedented growth of the late 1970s, which many were continuing to forecast would be maintained into the late 1980s. Figure C5.2 shows the situation of excess capacity and production for PVC up to 1981. The overall effect upon the bulk plastics industry in western Europe was that it began losing an estimated $2 billion per annum on its PVC, polyethylene and polypropylene businesses and many producers began slowly bleeding to death under increasing losses. The industry journal *Chemical Week* (1984) commented:

> The prevailing feeling among international chemical experts is that more must be done if overcapacity is not again to become a major problem in the next business downturn.

But for major chemical and plastic manufacturers there was no easy solution to the capacity problem due to the high forward integration in the manufacture of European PVC, as pulling out of a major business area like PVC would clearly have had cost ramifications for other strategic businesses which use substantial quantities of chlorine and ethylene. Therefore margins remained low, with all

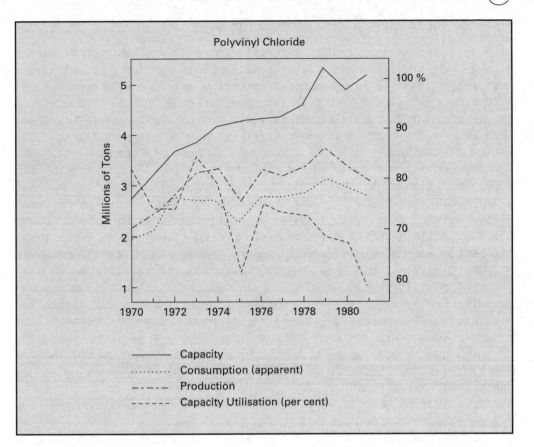

Figure C5.2   *The consumption, production and capability utilisation of PVC (in million tons)
1968–81.*

Source: Adapted from J. Bower (1986)

the major manufacturers experiencing substantial losses and it was very difficult
to see change in the market place.

At the same time as these events were unfolding, ICI were themselves reorganising their European operations. ICI Europa was set up in Brussels to coordinate its
European businesses and develop ICI into a more European-minded/focused
organisation. In 1982, as part of ICI's corporate restructuring programme, it's
petrochemicals and plastic divisions were merged and the PVC interests combined
into the new Vinyls and Plasticisers Group which moved to Brussels in the latter
part of that year. It became clear that there was a need for rapid action to stem
losses and chronic overcapacity or be gradually forced to withdraw from the business area. As a result potential partners were assessed to bring about a restructuring of the loss-making PVC business and the one prepared to develop a
commercial relationship was EniChem.

Reasons for forming a joint venture company

In terms of market coverage the two organisations was a good strategic fit. ICI was strong in the UK and Northern Europe and EniChem was strong in Italy, central and southern Europe; there was a minimal overlap in France and Germany.

Moreover, ICI was a marketing-led outfit, whilst EniChem was a production-led organisation and thus each brought particular strengths to the new joint venture. This improved geographic coverage would enable the new joint venture company to streamline its sales and marketing activities and improve logistics and customer service. This was an important factor in the bulk PVC commodity business, which offered the opportunity of market advantage to the lowest cost supplier. Clearly the nearer the bulk commodity supplying plants to the main concentrations of customers, the lower the distribution costs. This would be especially so in the highly competitive rigid PVC and cable markets, where prices were ultra-competitive as a result of producers wishing to obtain a share of this substantial volume business to keep their manufacturing plants loaded up.

Furthermore, both ICI and EniChem were multi-site, multi-plant companies and thus it was possible to close some plants/sites and still be able to meet the market's overall requirements. Other European producers were not in such a fortunate position since they only had one, or possibly two, sites and were therefore reluctant to sacrifice any of these through amalgamation. In addition, the joint venture could be structured in such a way that the ethylene and chlorine could be purchased in similar quantities from ICI and EniChem, thus ensuring secure outlets for parent companies' ethylene and chlorine production and allowing the development of dual sourcing.

The closure of older, less efficient plant and the reduction in unutilised capacity (300,000 tonnes) and a shedding of 1200 staff enabled significant cost savings to be made. However, given the political, economic and social landscape in Italy, the rationalisation of the Italian PVC producer was only possible as part of an international joint venture.

Finally, almost overnight EVC would leap-frog over Solvay of Belgium to become the largest European producer of PVC and VCM with over 20 per cent market share. Most importantly, EVC would set a an example to its European counterparts that the only way to meet market demand is to streamline capacity and avoid future overcapacity by debottlenecking and making technical improvements to existing plants.

The formation of the joint venture company was formally announced to the press on 13 February 1986. Professor Reviglio, the Chairman of ENI, commented:

> For too many years commodity chemicals in Europe have operated in a restricted field, without taking account of the wider European market of 300 million people. If the ICI/EniChem venture takes the PVC industry further out of the kind of nationalistic power-play which characterises the European steel industry, it will be a vital contribution. (*Financial Times*, 1986)

Although there was some concern expressed by existing customers at the merging of the Italian and UK companies, the predominant view was that the joint venture was essential for the continued survival of a viable PVC industry. Even competitors privately expressed their welcome to the realignment. The national government view was that it meant the development of sustainable businesses rather than ones which were vulnerable to the vagaries of a highly cyclical market.

State and European Commission approval

To allow the joint venture to formally get off the ground, both EniChem and ICI needed to obtain approval for the new venture from their respective governments and the European Commission (EC). The UK and Italian governments, competition and trade departments readily agreed, the only proviso on the part of the Italian government being that the plant in Calgari remain in operation, given the employment situation in Sardinia. (The partners have since been given permission to shut down the plant.)

The Directorate Generales' (DG) approached for approval within the EC were DG III and IV: DG III being responsible for internal markets and industrial affairs; and DG IV the Commission's regulator for European competition policy. The EU eventually approved the venture in principle as 78 per cent of the EEC's plastics vinyls market was supplied by competitors of Enichem and ICI. Final approval would only be witheld if interested third parties could prove that it harmed the competitiveness of the industry within the 12 EEC member states. Initial clearance from the EU took longer than expected, due to the complexity of the business and the size of the company, and delayed the official start-up by six months.

Formal approval was eventually given by the Commission in late 1987 for the company to trade for five years (this was subsequently extended indefinitely). However, given that EVC now had such a significant share of the European market and could be considered a 'dominant supplier' under EC competition policy, its actions within the EC market are limited. Thus the company would find it particularly difficult to grow via acquisition within the EC countries, unless of course this was seen in the interests of the EC competition policy. In the case of single-supply type agreements with large European buyers, EVC also had to allow its customers the freedom to select another supplier at least every two years. The two companies also agreed to close some of their vinyl production facilities. EniChem announced it would close three plants in Italy, whilst ICI would close one in Britain and one in Germany. This would represent over half the excess PVC capacity in the EU market.

However, given the recent reported return to losses by much of the commodity chemical and plastic businesses of Europe in the early 1990s, some commentators wonder how long EU restrictions on restructuring to maintain a viable European chemical and plastic businesses sector can be allowed to continue. The industry as a whole is beginning to look for support from across Europe and especially the EU to maintain it's viability, through grants for infrastructure investment and producing appropriate environmental legislation.

Pressure has mounted as the highly profitable German traditional chemical and plastic producing companies Bayer, BASF and Hoechst AG have gone into significant loss-making as a result of European recession and the high exchange rate of the Deutsche Mark.

A Child is Born

On 1 October 1986, EVC was formally launched to the world marketplace at a press conference in Paris. The birth of the new joint venture company was widely welcomed as part of long needed restructuring of the PVC industry.

The new executive board drew upon experienced managers from both ICI and EniChem. A chief executive officer (previously general manager, ICI Europa and ICI Vinyls group); a commercial director (previously head of planning group, ICI Corporate Planning); a technical director (previously president of EniChem Deutschland); a corporate resources director (previously commercial services manager, ICI Europa Ltd); and a finance director (previously manager, Agip SpA overseas crude oil exploration and production affiliates).

Representing the interests of the parent companies on the board were a very senior EniChem executive, who had been nominated chairman, and the equivalent from ICI.

This top management structure was at the behest of the new CEO, who having witnessed a number of joint venture failures because of the problem of dual leadership, insisted that there should be only one person with full executive responsibility for the new enterprise. Where dual leadership was attempted and tried it was found difficult to work, and was subsequently amended and resulted in the appointment of one executive with overall responsibility.

The core features agreed at the start up of the joint venture company and incorporated in the reported heads of agreement between ENI and ICI at that time were as follows:

1 Ninety per cent of raw materials (ethylene and chlorine) to be purchased from the shareholders at an agreed transfer price.
2 A common sales and marketing organisation to be set up in Brussels.
3 Parents to have the option (subject to unanimous agreement) either of taking profits out of the venture in dividends or they could agree to reinvest.
4 EVC to have the freedom to acquire downstream businesses.
5 Initial ownership of the assets to remain with the parent companies with the provision for EVC to gain control at a later date.
6 Core staff to be seconded on an equal number basis from the parent companies: 50 per cent ENI and 50 per cent ICI.
7 Six operating companies to be set up to act as sales and operating companies in the six core markets.
8 The commercial language of all parts of EVC to be English.

The holding company is officially registered in The Netherlands and at its start was serviced with publicity and public relations materials from a specialist company in Geneva.

THE PROCESS OF INTEGRATION AND ORGANISATION DEVELOPMENT

The process of integration has been achieved by a careful mix of equity and utilising the strengths of either partner. This is clearly demonstrated in the decision to locate the HQ in Brussels at the transnational government centre of Europe. Neither partner could have this on their own soil for fear of one partner dominance and the restrictions this would place on the development of an independent self-sustaining company culture. In addition, siting the new ventures HQ in Brussels would enable EVC managers to adopt ICI Vinyls' Management Information Systems (MIS) and Communication Systems, which were at a far more advanced stage of development than EniChem's existing systems.

In many other areas the process of integration has taken far longer to achieve; this is clearly seen in the area of improving technological efficiency and development work. The company's first seven years have been a period of consolidating over 10 different relatively complex PVC technologies. It needs to be remembered that EniChem was formed out of six separate Italian companies and that ICI has acquired a number of PVC producers itself. Merging of interests, especially on the technology side of an operation, can take a great deal of time and effort to achieve maximum benefits and the digestion process can be a slow one. Moreover, EVC has been busy on the acquisition front, acquiring several standalone fabrication companies (from ICI in Sweden, Germany and the UK) and PVC compounding businesses (from IPW, Maxichem, BICC and several others in Italy). More recently the heavily focused wallpaper and coverings business has been the first management buyout (MBO) from the organisation.

The development of an EVC culture has also been a gradual process, given the natural individual peculiarities of each partner, as can be seen in two areas of the organisation's life; career development and decision making. In the early stages of the joint venture, a senior manager was responsible for facilitating the development of a corporate culture. At EniChem career development, as in many organisations, was characterised by the importance of political and personal contacts. Decision making was concentrated at the top, with meetings allowing everyone to have their say, the senior manager would then go away and come back with a decision. At ICI, career development is based upon seniority and loyalty. The decision making processes being highly formalised, with meetings having a specific purpose and agreed actions arising from them following a style reflecting management by objectives.

It took some time to balance these differences and rather than force one style upon the other, the EVC senior management attended a specialist French business school course to aid the process of developing a common corporate culture. From these courses EVC formulated its own programmes for developing an effective synergy of group processes.

In terms of the EVC manager, the aim has been to develop multi-cultural, highly skilled and mobile managers who can gain the respect of their partners. These managers it is hoped should reflect the distinct culture of EVC and see themselves as being representatives of that company rather than being former employees of the parent company.

In the past seven years this has been reinforced by the direct recruitment of staff into EVC and the creation of EVC's own identity. This has been achieved by the development of its own, separate, communications and MIS systems and own brand names. In 1991, EVC acquired all of ICI's and EniChem's PVC and VCM assets. These are predominantly manufacturing plant, offices, patents and R&D facilities. The next step will be to convert those working on these sites into EVC personnel. The financial results of EVC are not published as it is a private company, however, the results for the first two years of operation have been made available.

The results of EVC post the start up of the organisation were much better than expected due to a resurgence in European demand and the reduction in capacity restoring profitability to the loss-making area. It was reported that EVC made operating profits of DM 153 in 1987 on sales of DM 1860, whilst by 1988 profits had trebled on increased sales volume. These early profits on the new business lifted spirits and helped galvanise the development of a separate corporate culture. The market was growing fast and margins were steadily improving as a result of restructuring.

RELATIONS WITH THE PARENTS

Examination of the joint venture agreement reveals how dependent the new child is on its parents, both in terms of raw material supply and the withdrawal of profits. For example, during the boom years the parents could harvest all EVC's profits, but given the difficult world trading conditions they could be unwilling or unable to risk funding EVC's future strategic capital expenditure plans.

Moreover, the joint venture's early success may have put back EVC's own development, as the parents do not know how to respond to this young virile child they have created, which may want to go its own way.

To survive and thrive EVC needs to match the best PVC businesses in the world with their low cost bases, those of the US. This has been reported as being a corporate priority. EVC's strategy is clearly to do this by: upgrading its retained plants, improve plant efficiency and asset productivity; acquire low cost stand-alone downstream businesses; and to obtain technical advantage in all its products and processes.

THE FUTURE

EVC's future in the turbulent 1990s, like most, was uncertain. Both shareholders are now looking at their own strategies in relation to their own chlor-alkali business. EniMont's new chief executive (EniChem having merged with Montedison in 1987) has let it be known that he might sell EniChem's stake in EVC. And EniChem's future is also likely to fundamentally change as it is one of the key state assets that will be soon privatised by the new Italian Government.

ICI has announced that it would like to reduce its heavy chemical interests or pool some of the overall operating costs in alliances or joint venture operations. This has been further highlighted as a senior executive of ICI was reported as saying that they were looking for partners to share the costs and output of their major ethylene cracking facility on Teeside. However, as yet it is too early to know exactly what effect this will have on EVC.

Whatever either partner decides to do with its PVC businesses, EVC's development has gone far enough down the line to ensure that the effect upon the company would be minimal. EVC could always acquire ethylene and chlorine from the marketplace and maybe benefit in raw material costs from market trading. There is also the possibility that another PVC operator may follow Occidental's lead and make an offer for the venture. However, as the Economist has pointed out, '... in any big organisation corporate habit is a powerful enemy of radical change' (*Economist*, 1990).

EVC has proved itself a success. It has provided much needed leadership in an industry that was seemingly incapable of climbing out of loss. It has also shown others how to form a successful pan-European joint venture company. Given the cyclical nature of the bulk commodity chemicals and plastics industries, this is forcing others to follow EVC's lead.

Hoechst AG and Wacker-Chemie GmbH announced in July 1993 that they were forming a joint venture company to produce, market and develop PVC. This was in response to a dramatic drop in German demand and prices fell over two years from DM 1.75 to DM 1 per kilo for PVC polymer. The appreciation of the Deutsch Mark and a dramatic rise in imports into the German market, which increased by 70 per cent to 550,000 tonnes over the period 1987–91, have put further pressure on the industry to restructure or companies to withdraw from the market. As an analyst, Deutsche Bank commented on the European PVC producers: 'The consolidation has to come. There is just too much output and it's now too unprofitable. The only chance is for them to arrange joint ventures. In principle, everyone is on the prowl for a partner' (*Reuter News*, 1992). Perhaps the EU needs to look more favourably on this industry as it restructures, just as it has supported the various steel industry restructurings.

The first joint venture company in the turbulent PVC business was EVC. It has grappled with difficult structural problems in the business area and appears to have succeeded in producing a dynamic, slim and effective organisation for its parents, ICI and ENI. Given the amount of structural change in this industry sector, cheap Middle East, Eastern European and Asian production becoming available, environmental pressure and the need to generate profits, it looks as though EVC will be in for increased change and opportunity in its markets.

However, if EVC addresses the issues the way it did in its first seven years of existence and benefits from its own corporate management culture, it might give some more much needed leadership to the European PVC industry as it restructures. Or will it be up to its parents?

QUESTIONS FOR DISCUSSION

1 Why do DGIII and IV take such an interest in the setting up of certain joint venture companies, mergers and acquisitions in the EU?
2 The restructuring of the EU petrochemical and plastics industries has taken more than 10 years to show significant results. Why is this? Is there a parallel with other industries?
3 What are the advantages and disadvantages commercially of setting up a joint venture company?
4 Outline the differences between a joint venture company and a strategic alliance.
5 Outline how you could develop a common corporate culture in a joint venture company made up of two different national partners.
6 Why has the formation of joint venture companies become so popular within the EU in the last decade?

REFERENCES

Bower, J. (1986) 'When Markets Quake'. Cambridge, MA: Harvard Business School Press.
Chemical Week (1984), 25 January.
Economist (1990), 28 April.
Financial Times (1986), 14 February.
Reuter News (1992), 8 December.

CS6   EVC (1995–2002): JOINT VENTURE, THE AMSTERDAM STOCK MARKET FLOTATION AND ACQUISITION BY INEOS

PHIL HARRIS AND IRENE HARRIS

The chemical and plastics industry in Europe throughout 1980s and through to the new millennium has undergone dramatic change and fundamental restructuring. This has been driven by increasing cost factors, internationalisation and global industrialisation impacting upon the industry. A number of major companies of the 1980s, such as UK's ICI, have restructured, de-merged and sold off assets and businesses to re-engineer their focus of activities. Many large chemical and oil groups have moved significantly out of building block bulk chemicals and strengthened downstream product businesses, such as in ICI's case its paint business worldwide. A further example of ICI's corporate restructuring in the sector was that in 1993 it de-merged its pharmaceutical division to float on the stock exchange as the company Zeneca; this subsequently, through an agreed merger in 1999 with the Swedish group Astra AB, has emerged as the major pharmaceutical group AstraZeneca.

During the 20-year period from 1982 to 2002, 40 per cent of Western European chemical and associated industry production has migrated to lower-cost areas outside the EU and the numbers employed in these industries has dramatically declined. ICI's workforce, for instance, worldwide shrank from over 175,000 in 1979 to 38,000 by 2001, the bulk of this reduction being in Europe. This restructuring impacted upon private and public sector financed operations throughout Europe and has been similar to that experienced in other industries, such as coal and steel production.

EVC FORMATION

EVC was formed in October 1986 as a joint venture equity company that comprised the vinyl chloride monomer (VCM) and polyvinyl chloride (PVC) resin and compounds businesses of Italy's EniChem and England's ICI, which were at that time Western Europe's second and fourth largest PVC producers. The EVC joint venture was created against a background of consolidation of the Western

European PVC industry, where both parent companies had been making substantial losses along with most of their competitors. The formation of the joint venture established EVC as Europe's largest producer of PVC. Much of this background is outlined in more detail in the 'EVC 1986–94' case study by Harris and Dodd. In 2001, EVC had a turnover of €1.2 billion, employed 3100 staff and had capacity to produce 1.1 million tonnes of VCM and 1.4 million tonnes of PVC. Its core trademarks are EVIPOL (PVC resin), EVICOM (PVC compounds), EVICAS (build-up suppressants) and INOVOL (PVC additives).

Between 1986 and 1994, EVC underwent a process of rationalisation, closing down some older and less efficient plants, rearranging distribution and supply lines and acquiring new downstream subsidiaries while selling off other non-core businesses.

In November 1994, EVC floated its stock and became a public company listed on the Amsterdam stock exchange. Key dates in EVC's development and eventual acquisition by INEOS in 2001 are listed below, with some of the pivotal issues impacting upon the company internally and externally.

1986　EVC formed through a 50:50 joint venture between ICI and EniChem.

1987　Greenpeace International launch a major campaign on the phasing out of organochlorines. They argue that PVC plastic uses the largest proportion of chlorine produced (30 per cent) and is a major source of hazardous substances in the environment, both during manufacture and disposal. This position is, not surprisingly, vigorously countered by PVC manufacturers and much scientific evidence but becomes a mainstream activity of Greenpeace campaigning throughout the 1990s.

1988　Acquisition of VKW rigid film operations from ICI and of the PVC compounding assets in the UK and Italy, which allows the company to move into more downstream manufacture.

1989　Acquisition of the vinyls technology and licensing business of the Stauffer Chemical Company of America. This acquisition again enhances the companies' downstream activities

1990　Acquisition of Mazzucchelli Vinyls and Savinil. Transfer of production assets from ICI and EniChem.

1994　EVC is floated on the Amsterdam Stock Exchange.

1996　Acquisition of the VCM plant in Runcorn, UK from ICI, to be rejuvenated and expanded.

1997　Acquisition of the packaging film plant at Weißandt-Gölzau, Germany and of a majority shareholding in the Indian PVC film producer, Caprihans.

1998　Reports a net profit of NLG 32.6 million for 1997. Acquisition of BSL's PVC assets at Schkopau, Germany.

Enters into discussions with Norsk Hydro on combining vinyls and petrochemical businesses. Talks break down over strategic direction. Norsk is an upstream producer, whilst EVC is increasingly looking down the production chain for margins, thus, it is suggested, not a good match. PVC prices continue to deteriorate and EVC anticipates making a loss of NLG 50 million.

1999   In February it reports a net loss for 1998 after exceptional items of NLG 230.5 million.

In June following an accidental release of VCM into the atmosphere at its plant in the Veneto at Port Marghera (near Venice), it is closed down by the Italian Minister of Environment. In July manufacturing is recommenced following the implementation of a more vigorous environmental plan.

In July Greenpeace International maintains its attack on the PVC industry. It issues its report 'Chlorine and PVC restrictions and PVC free policies' in July. This lists actions being taken by government and organisations to reduce consumption and use of these products. It argues that some companies and organisations such as IKEA and LEGO have virtually ceased using PVC, whilst others such as Nike have recently initiated a phase-out. This is countered by the industry, which outlines the everyday usefulness of the product to the consumer and society and its relative low cost. Recycling and reprocessing facilities are increasing across the industry.

2000   EVC reports net loss of €46.9 million in 1999 against a previous year's loss in 1998 of €104.6 million.

In July announces discussions on merger with Vestolit GmbH (Degussa-Hüls AG PVC interests). Following worsening trading conditions as result of declining PVC prices and rising oil prices, it announces that the talks are off. EVC anticipates making a significant loss for 2000 and will seek additional finance to fund its operations. It announces the intention to make major cost reductions.

The 300,000-tonne VCM facility at Runcorn in the UK becomes fully operational and the new 180,000-tonne PVC facility at Schkopau in Germany is brought on stream in the third quarter of the year.

In November the management board of EVC is restructured and strengthened to turn round the business and arrange refinancing. A special meeting of shareholders is to be called in January 2001.

In December an INEOS affiliate agrees to put in €75million into EVC in exchange for a majority holding of shares.

2001   INEOS acquires a majority shareholding in EVC in March 2001. EVC becomes part of the INEOS Group.

2002   EVC reports a 2001 loss of €86.5 million (2000: €84.6 million). In August INEOS purchase EniChem's holding of EVC ordinary shares and now holds 75.35 per cent of the company.

TURBULENT TIMES

The PVC business across Europe has been faced by falling prices, increasing costs and environmental attack for more than a decade. Yet it seems to have survived well and its products are as common today as they were 20 years ago, with growth having been seen particularly in building products and specialist films. Producers have been rationalised and are being re-managed to ensure profits. Many of the traditional integrated chemical and plastic producers have broken up their operations to compete in the more global market and specialist capital groups with quality management skills have been established to run these commodity businesses.

EVC is still registered on the Amsterdam stock market but is now owned by INEOS.

BUILDING AN EVC CULTURE

Employees at EVC were originally seconded from the parent companies EniChem and ICI.

These employees were eventually transferred to new company contracts if they had not moved back to their original organisation. Many ICI or EniChem employees who had been seconded held company shares or future options, holiday rights, pensions and other entitlements from their former employers. From 1990 employees were recruited by EVC only; these employees increasingly saw themselves as dependent on that organisation rather than others. The development of a company culture has not been aided, however, by the fact that many of the works and operations around EVC sites are run or controlled by their former parents. In addition, the constant restructuring has meant that change has been constant throughout the last 10 years and consequently more has gone into surviving than developing a designed corporate culture. This nevertheless has stimulated much personal growth as entrepreneurialism, and competitive spirit has been rewarded within the smaller company, making EVC staff very loyal. Interestingly, INEOS states that its management philosophy is to operate a simple and decentralised organisational structure, coupled with programmes intended to incentivise its employees. This should suit EVC employees well.

INEOS

INEOS is a relatively young company, being formed in 1998. It has grown through a series of related acquisitions to become a medium-sized international company with sales of about €5 billion. INEOS is a significant global manufacturer of specialty and intermediate chemicals and comprises six businesses, each with a major chemical company heritage. It has 60 manufacturing facilities and operates in 16 countries around the world. Many employees are from major chemical and oil companies such as Dow, ICI, BP, Degussa and so on that have restructured, and bring experience and skills to the core business. Businesses that INEOS own in addition to EVC include acrylics, chlor chemicals, ethano-limines, silica and phenol amongst others.

REFLECTIONS ON A JOINT VENTURE

EVC is a classic example of how a joint venture company emerges and its stages of life; for instance, it was born in 1986, grows-up and is allowed to leave home in 1994 when it was floated on the Amsterdam stock exchange, survives on its own for 6 turbulent years in difficult markets until it has to be managed by another INEOS (2001) because it cannot fund its activities on its own through marketplace activity. However, it has clearly succeeded in developing and forming a coherent PVC business that has stimulated restructuring in that area in Europe.

QUESTIONS FOR DISCUSSION

1 What are the prime reasons for losses amongst PVC manufacturers in Europe?
2 Is further restructuring necessary in the industry?
3 Why has ICI shrunk so much as a company over the last decade?
4 Why do environmental campaigners pick on one business area at a time, that is, PVC, in the plastics industry? Is this a tactic of campaigning or is it purely conviction and opportunism?
5 Will the EU be able to maintain and sustain a position as a producer of commodity plastics ?

CS7 FULHAM FC*: CLUB–SUPPORTER RELATIONSHIPS 'COME ALL YE FAITHFUL'

SUKHBINDER S. BARN AND PAUL R. BAINES

'Harrods, The Ritz ... and now run-down Fulham Football Club. Hardly in the same league, but yesterday [29th May 1997] Mohamed Al Fayed paid about £10 million for this homely club by the banks of the Thames which has seen better days but few more inspiring than this.' (*Guardian*, 1997). Thus had begun another chapter in the turbulent history of Fulham FC. The club's supporters are now in a situation where the near future may preclude the need to be constantly searching the annals of history for memories such as: 'the day that the flood-lights failed and Haynes still picked out Chamberlain, locatable only by his fag end, loitering on the wing.'

Al Fayed's purchase of the ground and the promise of the injection of millions of pounds to take the football club into the Premier Division within the next five years has altogether given the die-hard supporters of the club a future to look forward to. Amongst many fans there was a reluctance to see Al Fayed as the 'knight in shining armour'. Indeed, many saw this as the opportunity for the Egyptian millionaire to purchase a valuable plot of land with river views in the desirable 'yuppiedom' of Fulham.

It was expected that the appointment of Kevin Keegan would certainly inspire a renewal in supporter interest, which would translate itself in the form of larger gates and attendance. While Craven Cottage initially saw new supporters coming to watch out of curiosity, a large majority of fans remained ambivalent to the immediate cure that Keegan might prescribe. There has certainly been much talk of the indecent haste with which Micky Adams (the former manager) was dispatched to make way for the new partnership. Indeed, many fans expressed anger at the treatment received by Adams, whom many regarded as the most successful manager that Fulham has had over the last 15 years.

*This case study was prepared by Sukhbinder S. Barn and Paul R. Baines, both at Middlesex University Business School. It is intended to be used as a basis for class discussion and not as an example of good or poor management practice. © Sukhbinder Barn and Paul Baines, 1999. Please note that Fulham Foolball Club cannot respond to enquiries related to this case study.

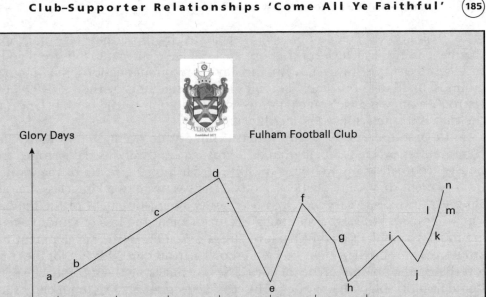

a – Relegated for the first time to Third Division (South).
b – Return to the Second Division as Champions, scoring 111 goals.
c – Win Second Division Title to reach the First Division for the first time in history.
d – Finish tenth in the First Division, highest ever league position.
e – Relegated in successive seasons to the Third Division.
f – Reach the FA Cup Final when in the Second Division, lose 2–0 to West Ham.
g – Suffer their worst defeat, 10–0 to Liverpool in the League Cup.
h – Threatened by bankruptcy and eviction. Stave of proposed merger with Queen's Park Rangers.
i – Secure tenancy of Craven Cottage for 10 years.
j – Relegated for the seventh time.
k – Clinch promotion from the Third Division with four matches remaining.
l – Al Fayed purchases Craven Cottage from the bank and promises £30 million cash injection.
m – Kevin Keegan and Ray Wilkins sign for Fulham.
n – Fifth round of the FA Cup with Manchester United at Old Trafford.

Figure C7.1   *Events at Fulham FC and their impact upon the club's support*

Now, almost 19 months into the relationship, Fulham are on top of the Second Division and have a fifth round FA Cup draw with Manchester United at Old Trafford, conceivably the best thing that has happened to the club since they reached the Final of the Cup in 1975. Figure C7.1 charts the high and low points of the club over the course of the last 70 years.

BACKGROUND

The involvement of Al Fayed with Fulham FC is seen by many as a typical indulgence of the rich and further testimony to the money culture that is all pervasive in football and the creation of leagues separated by those that have and those that have not. Yet such cash injections are essential to prevent clubs from going into receivership. However, with the Taylor recommendations that football grounds, in all divisions, must become all-seater stadiums by the year 1999, the Harrod's money is a welcome, and necessary, addition to the bank balances of the club if it is to achieve Premiership status.

In the past, football has seen its roots firmly within traditional working-class communities, where football grounds flourished amidst industrial factories and houses. Football teams were inextricably woven into the fabric of the locality from which they came, where football heroes were working-class heroes. However, in recent years there has been an embourgeoisement of the football supporter base. Whilst the traditionalists may lament the loss of atmosphere at grounds as a result of a conversion to all-seater stadiums, the development has attracted a new breed of supporter who shows a greater predilection for the comfort that stadia now offer. The middle classes are hijacking the sport for the new-found fashion ability that it offers. The causal effects are that glamour clubs such as Chelsea are much preferred to the nameless and not so continental players that grace Craven Cottage.

Fulham FC has seen the gentrification of its immediate environment, which once provided the bulk of its support, and further, witnessing actions by residents who are not only hostile to football, but to the development of the club since it would have a major impact upon the local environment through increased car and pedestrian traffic during match days. In addition, since the local community may wish to hinder developments at the ground through planned resident group opposition, particularly aimed at local council planning departments, it is important to keep this essential stakeholder 'on side!'.

It is also important for the club to realise that the Al Fayed and Keegan partnership is likely to be a success. This factor, along with the aura of romance that surrounds Fulham Football Club, may be the spur to attract local residents.

AN ANATOMY OF THE FOOTBALL 'PRODUCT'

In order for football clubs to understand fully that the nature of their supporters extends beyond traditional marketing considerations, they must have an understanding of what football *really* means to the football fan and to integrate this understanding into the products and services that they make available. The core product can be defined as: 'The level of a product that provides the perceived or real core benefit or service'. In footballing terms, the core product would quite simply be the game itself. Some games may naturally be more important than others, for instance, matches involving promotion, relegation and cup ties. However, the level of importance the supporter places upon the core product will vary according to the factors that affect attendance in the first instance. It is in this area that there is a need to understand what motivates a supporter to 'buy' the core product.

In many respects, it is the *actual* product that many customers are buying. As in traditional consumer goods marketing, it is the enhancement of the core product that adds to the appeal, and with football there is little difference. It is the manner in which the core product is adapted that is the key. Extremely loyal and dedicated supporters do not need the same enhancement of the core product compared with the incidental, occasional supporter. This may be illustrated through an individual's attitude towards the facilities at the stadium.

The uncertainty of the outcome of a game adds to the supporters' interest and desire to consume. This implies that there is an inconsistency in the consumption of the product from one occasion to the next. The marketeer cannot influence the outcome of the game and, therefore, emphasis should be placed upon those elements that can be influenced by the marketeer such as product extensions. This illustrates the fact that supporters (consumers) need to be provided with an offering that goes beyond the game itself and extends to an overall package built *around* the game. By enhancing the overall experience of the dedicated and casual supporter, marketeers engender a desire on the part of the supporter to return and consume the product again. However, the extent to which the product extensions are successful are dependent upon the attractiveness of the core product. Through an understanding of the different reasons for attendance, marketeers are able to provide a range of services that will meet the needs and wants of their supporter base. The cultural aspect of football emphasises the established tradition of the club, family, the socialising process and identification with the symbolic and ritualised artefacts associated with a club.

SUPPORTERS AS CUSTOMERS

Essentially, the football game and its associated features are more related to a services marketing perspective than a product marketing perspective due to the intangible nature of the core football offering. However, the football 'product' differs from a traditional commercial product and service in the sense that supporters display intense loyalty to the football brand and brand switching as a phenomenon occurs less frequently by football supporters. Football supporters are socialised into the purchasing decision (principally, by family, friends and the local community) to a far greater extent than are commercial consumers.

It is not unreasonable that many supporters feel alienated from the clubs that they support and follow. Certainly the wealthier clubs of the Premiership have courted the attention of corporate clients and attracted large sums of money from television coverage and thus found straightforward means of generating revenue. However, supporters have been expected to follow without comment or criticism, accept higher gate charges, numerous changes of strip during the season and unreasonably high prices for club merchandise. Indeed, many supporters will pass this test of 'loyalty' and take on these costs because the football team they follow plays an important role in their lives. Witness the complete sell out of Newcastle United season tickets (around 33,000) with a waiting list of

12,000 at the last count. Differing viewpoints either see the waiting list as a positive affirmation of the level of support and loyalty that exists within the region or 12,000 dissatisfied customers.

THE NATURE OF FULHAM FC

Prior to the arrival of Al Fayed's millions, the club had been involved in a number of issues regarding ownership of the ground and possible mergers with Queen's Park Rangers; the supporters, while not being neglected, felt that the club no longer 'belonged to them'. The recent changes have had the effect of attracting supporters, both new and lapsed, to come and watch out of curiosity. Furthermore, there have been tangible improvements to the ground and stadium that undoubtedly contribute significantly to the 'experience' of the game and the overall satisfaction felt by supporters.

Perhaps the most important changes that have occurred are actually less tangible but more important from a marketing point of view. Harrod's retailing and business experience have added a new impetus and dimension to the club's business outlook with the addition of Neil Rodford as General Manager. Previously, the marketing function was somewhat more fragmented, with fewer employees and a sole Commercial Manager who played a variety of roles (including fundraising and publicity) with limited support at the director level. Marketing operations now exist with a separate budget and the team comprises a Marketing Director and Marketing Manager with a team of support staff. There is now increased scope to understand the nature of the Fulham supporter. Fulham FC have always been interested in the needs of the supporter and actually initiated supporter research prior to the Harrod's ownership.

MARKET SEGMENTATION

Undoubtedly, one of the greatest attractions that Fulham FC offers is its excellent setting overlooking the Thames coupled with an aura of romance and tradition. The club finds itself labelled as the 'quaint, friendly club' and, thus, has been very much overshadowed in recent years by its Premiership neighbour, Chelsea, due to the low profile that Fulham has experienced in the past and a media and public concern with Premiership teams.

Although the football product is very diverse, opportunities do exist to offer and meet the differing needs of the various supporter groups. One such opportunity is the availability of supporters from other teams, in particular Chelsea. The historic ties between the two clubs allows supporters from either team to watch the other as their respective home matches are played on alternative weekends. The opportunity for Fulham lies in the prohibitive costs of attending Chelsea matches and the relative ease of accessibility and cost of attending Fulham FC matches.

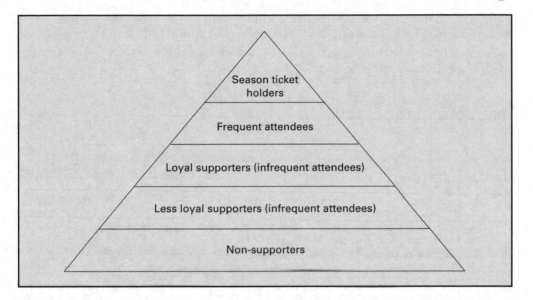

Figure C7.2 *Pyramid of supporter loyalty*
Source: Woodford, Baines and Barn (1998)

Fulham FC regularly attracts crowds of around 12,000 supporters, although the current ground capacity is around 18,000, with approximately 3000 Season ticket holders in January 1999. Season ticket holders represent a large section of the crowd attending any one particular game. However, although the season ticket holder represents the most frequently attending supporter, there are other types of supporter as indicated in Figure C7.2. The pyramid indicates that other types of supporter also exist and contribute to attendance figures.

For instance, whilst some supporters are frequent attendees, others are infrequent and some supporters are non-attendees (preferring to watch the match at home on television or follow the results in the papers, radio or the club's premium rate results line). There are also supporters who attend (either frequently or infrequently or somewhere in between) who are also supporters of another major football club. Similarly, as the pyramid indicates, whilst some attendees are loyal, others are less so and may defect to another club if an opportunity arises.

RESULTS OF RECENT FAN SURVEYS

In September 1997, Fulham FC commissioned independent market research to determine the nature of the season ticket holder (CEFM, 1998). Approximately 1000 questionnaires were sent out to season ticket holders by assigning random numbers to names on the season ticket holders' database, containing approximately

1500 names, thereby assuring a simple random sample. Of those, 584 questionnaires were returned and represented at that time over one-third of the entire season ticket holders' database. Appendix 1 contains some of the results to the answers of the questions contained within the survey.

QUESTIONS FOR DISCUSSION

1 Write a marketing plan to illustrate how Fulham FC should go about increasing its football match day attendance figures.
2 How can Fulham FC enhance its football 'product'? To which segments should these be directed?
3 What other considerations did Fulham FC take into account to achieve its Premiership status within five years?
4 Describe how market research can test the validity of the recommendations that you have suggested in your answer to question 2.
5 What would be the benefits to Fulham FC of gaining entry to a major European football competition?

REFERENCES

Centre for European Football Management (1998) 'Football Fan Survey', commissioned by Fulham FC, March 1998. Unpublished Consultancy Report, Middlesex University Business School, Hendon and London.

Guardian, The (1997) 29 September. p. 9.

Woodford, J., Baines, P.R. and Barn, S.S. (1998) 'Football Relationship Marketing: Can Football Market the "Sizzle?"', proceedings of the 27th EMAC Conference, 17–20 May, Stockholm School of Economics, Stockholm.

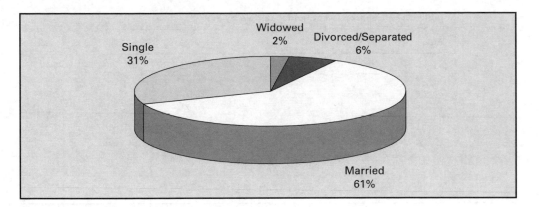

Figure C7.A1 *Season ticket holder by martial status*

Table C7.A1 **Season ticket holder by martial status**

Marital Status	%
Widowed	2
Divorced/Separated	6
Married	61
Single	31

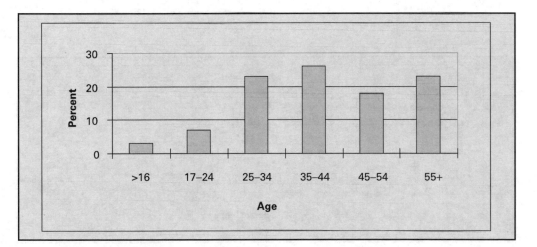

Figure C7.A2 *Season ticket holder sample by age*

Table C7.A2   Season ticket holder sample by age

Age	%
>16	3
17–24	7
25–34	23
35–44	26
45–54	18
55+	23

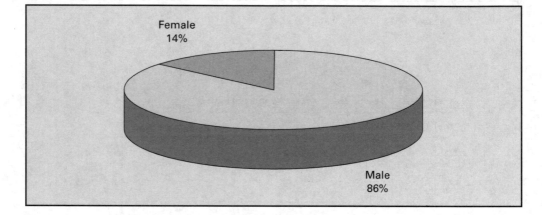

Figure C7.A3   *Season ticket holder sample by gender*

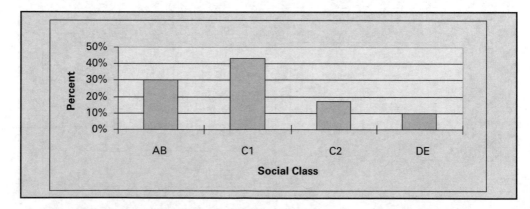

Figure C7.A4   *Season ticket holder by social class*

Table C7.A4   Season ticket holder by socical class

Social Class	%
AB	30
C1	43
C2	17
DE	10

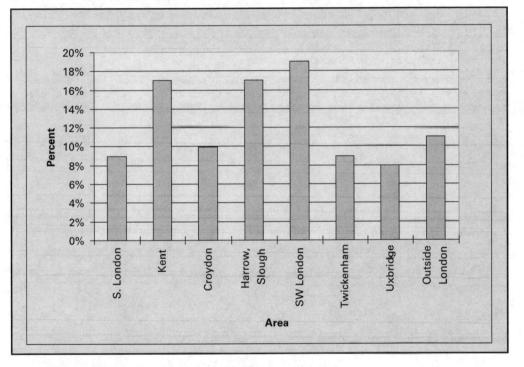

Figure C7.A5   *Distribution of season ticket holders*

Table C7.A5   Distribution of season ticket holders

Area	%
South London	9
Kent	17
Croydon	10
Harrow, Slough	17
South-West London	19
Twickenham	9
Uxbridge	8
Outside London	11

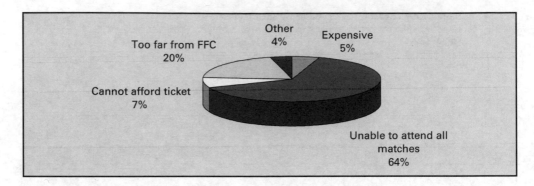

Figure C7.A6 *Reasons for not buying a season ticket*

Note: This above figure draws data collected from a different sample of supporters, Fulham 2000. This was an independent supporters' association, numbering approximately 3,500 members. The survey was conducted using mail survey methodology and a simple random sample in September 1997.

CS8 GRUPPO MASSONE: ACQUISITION VENTURE INTO THE UK

CLAUDIO VIGNALI

This case study takes the format of a report to the Managing Director of Gruppo Massone, the leading Italian supplier to the catering market in Italy. Gruppo Massone intended to enter the UK market and required basic information before carrying out extensive research.

BACKGROUND TO THE UK

After 18 years of Conservative government, restrictions and direct taxation levels have been consistently lowered and removed. The following list summarises those factors that we have identified as significant to Gruppo Massone in 1997 and Table C8.1 a shows key performance indicators of the UK as a whole:

- Corporation tax on profits is 33 per cent.
- One-third of all EU inward investment in 1993 went to the UK.
- Low labour costs and relaxed employment laws.
- Standard rates of income tax at 23 per cent and 40 per cent.
- No exchange controls or restrictions on sending profits overseas.

CONTRACT CATERING MARKET

Definition

Food service management includes catering for people at work in business and industry; catering in schools, colleges and universities; hospitals and health care; welfare and local authority catering; and other non-profit making outlets.

Table C8.1   UK Key performance indicators

	1993	1994	1995	1996	1997
Growth in gross domestic product (GDP)	4.1%	3.3%	1.3%	N/A	N/A
GDP per capita ($US)	16,289	17,515	18,846	N/A	N/A
Interest rates (base rate)	6.0%	5.4%	6.9%	5.2%	5.7%
Inflation (retail price index)	3.0%	2.3%	2.9%	2.5%	3.0%
Inflation (basic fuels and materials)	4.5%	2.6%	9.6%	3.4%	3.5%

Source: Details from the Mintel Report 2000 'food market' London.

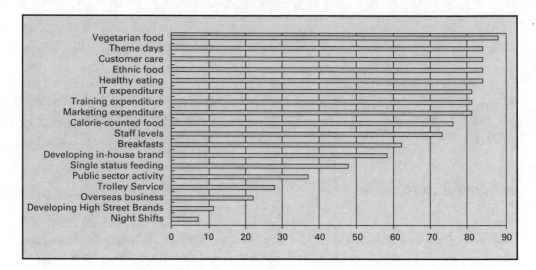

Figure C8.1   *Businesses expecting to increase their activities*
Source: Keynote 2000 "Food Market"

Recent developments

Definitions in this sector have become blurred as contract catering companies move into other areas, including catering for members of the public in such outlets as leisure centres, department stores, airports, railway stations, public events and places of entertainment. As a proportion of the total market, this commercial sector is important and will continue to expand in the long term.

Support services

Contractors are also providing a range of other support services, such as housekeeping and maintenance, reception, security, laundry, bars and retail shops. Figure C8.1 illustrates those activities which are expected to increase. Those activities that have been identified as particularly relevant to Gruppo Massone have been highlighted in red.

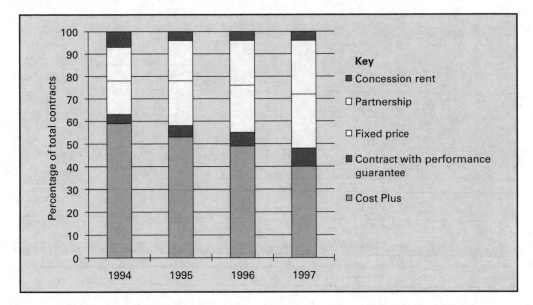

Figure C8.2 *Types of contract*

Source: Details from the Mintel Report 2000 'food market', London.

Contract types

Contract types within the industry can be categorised as follows:

- *Cost-plus:* in which all costs plus a management fee are passed on to the client.
- *Performance guarantee:* which guarantees that costs will not rise above a certain level.
- *Fixed price:* which establishes a total cost within which the caterer will work.
- *Partnership contract:* where the client and caterer are partners in the operation, sharing costs and revenues.
- *Concessionary rent:* in which the caterer pays a rent to the client, perhaps on a percentage of turnover and/or profit (typically used in airports, shops and so on).

As illustrated in Figure C8.2 the number of cost-plus contracts declined during the year, with a 30 per cent increase in the number of fixed-price and performance guarantee contracts. The trend is moving towards contractors becoming more commercially-minded in their approach and increasing their amount of risk.

Turnover

As Figure C8.3 shows, annual turnover in 1997 (the sum total of all billings to the client, including wages, food purchases and management fee) eased by 1.3

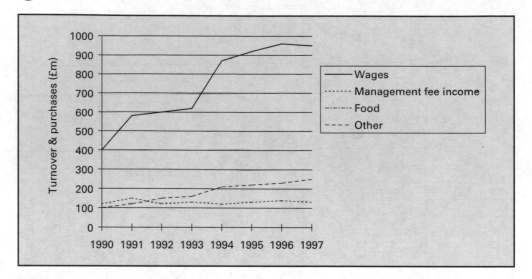

Figure C8.3   *Turnover and purchases*

Source: Details from the Mintel Report 2000 'food market', London.

per cent. This reflects the 2.4 per cent reduction in wages and a 2.3 per cent reduction in food purchases. However, there was a significant improvement in management fee income of £24 million (1.0 per cent), indicating that profitability was well sustained during the year.

Wage costs as a percentage of turnover reduced marginally from 42.5 per cent to 42 per cent. However, as the average wage per employee rose marginally in the year, the drop in the total wage bill is the result of a smaller total workforce and not of lower wages.

Management fee income increased from 10 per cent of turnover to 11.4 per cent, indicating real growth in income brought about by greater efficiencies and, in particular, the more productive use of employees and the continuing introduction of information technology.

Food purchases declined by 2.3 per cent, reflecting a 4.8 per cent drop in the average number of meals per contract and a 1.3 per cent drop in total turnover. This clearly indicates that contractors are putting greater pressure on their food suppliers. Although contractors produced more meals during the year, much of this increase was in the health care and state education sectors where there are tight cost controls. Food inflation during the period was under 3 per cent.

Turnover from overseas operations more than doubled, from £1,097 million to £2,365 million. Overseas turnover is not included in the UK figures but, as a percentage of total turnover, it has risen from 33 per cent to 52 per cent. The majority of this increase comes from the activities of two companies, both having consolidated their position as global food service management groups.

Future Issues and Trends

Downsizing by companies affects the growth of the business and industry sector along with the Ministry of Defence contracts. Coupled with the increasing use of automation in some industries (such as banking, insurance and oil exploration), fewer major construction projects were in hand during this year compared with last year. To a certain extent, the contract catering industry reflects the buoyancy of the sectors of the economy it serves.

This said, as contracting is seen as successful with cost-saving opportunities and because of the encouragement from the government for competitive tendering, the industry should continue to grow at something like its current levels or higher.

The future trends and issues surrounding the industry can be summarised as follows:

- The sector will continue to grow through the expansion of the industry into sectors such as education, health care, leisure and consumer catering.
- Business and industry will remain a key sector, fluctuating according to the state and structure of British industry generally.
- Contractors will grow due to mergers and acquisitions as well as from organic development.
- Contractors continued expansion into overseas markets.
- Increasing number of contracts awarded on a commercial basis, that is, with some guarantee, investment or risk on the part of the contractor.

MAJOR PLAYERS

Overview

In recent years major competitors have been expanding into Europe and the US, with some looking further afield to Asia and the Far East. Table C8.2 details the four leading competitors in the UK.

Table C8.3 compares turnover and profit of the significant players in the industry. It must be noted, however, that several acquisitions have taken place since the data was collated, which would remove several of the lower players.

Gardner Merchant Ltd

Gardner Merchant has recently become part of the Sodexho Group, which has transformed them into the largest contract catering business in the world. With contracts in over 25 countries worldwide, their main operations are within the UK, continental Europe, North America and Australia. This mainstream income

Table C8.2   UK contract catering: major players

	Coverage				UK market share
	UK	Europe	US	Other	
Gardner Merchant Ltd	√	√	√	√	26.7%
Compass Group plc	√	√	√	*	20.9%
Sutcliffe Catering Group plc	√	√	*	*	18.6%
Aramark plc	√	*	*	*	4.9%

Source: The Institute of Grocery Distribution Report 1999 'Grocery Market', London.

Table C8.3   Comparison of industry turnover

	Year end	Turnover (£m)	Pre-tax profit (£m)	Profit margin
Gardner Merchant Ltd	31/01/94	1,015.0	46.9	4.6%
Compass Group plc	02/10/94	917.9	55.7	6.1%
Sutcliffe Catering Group Ltd	01/10/94	405.0	31.0	7.6%
Aramark plc	01/10/94	116.0	5.7	4.9%
Catering & Allied Services Ltd	31/12/93	51.3	0.6	1.2%
BET Catering Services Ltd	02/04/93	40.0	1.3	3.3%
Russell & Brand Ltd	31/12/93	20.5	0.3	0.5%
Brian Smith Catering Services	25/03/94	15.6	0.2	1.3%
Shaw Catering Company Ltd	31/12/93	12.1	0.2	2.0%
Sodexho Services (UK) Ltd	31/08/94	11.8	0.3	2.5%
Bromwich Catering Ltd	31/03/94	11.8	0.3	2.5%
Leiths Ltd	31/03/94	5.9	0.5	8.5%
Summit Catering plc	22/04/94	6.1	0.2	2.6%

Source: The Institute of Grocery Distribution Report 1999 'Grocery Market', London.

is allowing Gardner Merchant to penetrate new markets in less developed countries such as Asia and the Far East.

Compass Group plc

Compass is an international catering company trading mainly in the UK, Continental Europe and the US. Compass is the third largest catering business in the world, and second in the UK. It is divided into subsidiaries that specialise in specific areas such as business and industry or health care and education. These divisions include Compass Catering, Bateman Catering, Chartwells, Lethby & Christopher, Compass Commercial Services and Travellers Fare.

Sutcliffe Catering Group plc

Sutcliffe are part of the Granada Group, which acquired the company in 1993 from the P&O Group. The company's main contracts are with the Ministry of

Defence, Marine Caterers and the NHS, which is a growth area of the market. The company is well organised, with regional sales divisions that cover the individual accounts on a new centralised computer programme.

This is enabling them to become more competitive within the market as they have become more efficient, accurate and faster. They are also looking towards the developing area of franchising with a recent deal with Burger King, but still remain behind Compass.

Aramark plc

Aramark is a subsidiary of the US company ARA Group Inc. Within the UK it operates in five main divisions: catering, vending, contract cleaning, office clubs and offshore services. The company has its own food brands that are taken from its parent company; these brands include Find Dining, Deli Corner, Salad Garden, Treat Yourself Right and Cafe Feature (all American brand names). Aramark is considerably smaller than its main rivals but still holds a strong fourth position with a share of just over 5 per cent.

Other competitors

World wide, other competitors hold 28.9 per cent of the market. As a few large companies such as Gardner Merchant and Compass dominate the market, the rest of the competition is highly fragmented with several hundred companies (not necessarily competing against each other). Many smaller companies cater for the niche market or concentrate their efforts on speciality services.

FRANCHISING AND BRANDING

There has been a significant move recently to develop a brand in the contract catering market. One such example is Compass Commercial Services, its new division that concentrates on the Famous Food Brands. The new trend in the industry is towards the franchising of branded famous foods such as Burger King, Pizza Hut, Harry Ramsdens and the move to in-house branded outlets such as Dixie's Donuts, Le Croissant Shop and Frank's Deli. Within the last year Compass have gained exclusive rights to operate Burger King franchises at particular non-high street sites. This has made them the biggest franchisee of Burger King in the UK.

SWOT ANALYSIS

The contract catering industry has been through many changes during the past decade. The SWOT analysis shown in Figure C8.4 tries to summarise these changes, issues and expected trends to present the opportunities and threats that exist.

Strengths	Weaknesses
• Increasing competition due to the contract caterers' expansion into other complementary services. • Contract catering is a fast expanding industry within the UK. • Recent trends towards the famous-names foods franchising sector. • The move towards outsourcing non-core activities, so that business can maximise efficiency and reduce costs.	• Poor consumer research within the market, which means that consumer needs are not satisfied. • Health conscious image which is overlooked by the branded fast-food products. • Overcrowded dining areas and long queues in schools make an uncomfortable atmosphere for children to dine in. • Market entry is relatively hard due to three established companies who control over two-thirds of the market. • The governments' tightening of health and environmental regulations. • The tendering of local authority contracts that are not given to the lowest bidder is creating a loss of faith in the whole tendering process. • Poorly-marketed school dinners, bad reputation amongst children.
Opportunities	**Threats**
• More emphasis on fresh foods rather than prepared foods. • Catering for leisure complexes will grow with the increasing number of people who frequent these facilities. • Expansion into prison management by provision of catering and other facilities. • New technology in the field, that is, new kitchen automation, to improve speed of service. • Less than half of all school children do not eat school meals, so there is great potential for growth. • Cashing in on youngsters buying sweets, carbonated drinks and crisps who snack through the day rather than eat proper meals. • Ability of the sector to react easily to preoccupation regarding healthy eating and the environment. • Preference towards fresh and home cooked meals, which encourages higher standards of quality and healthier eating. • Broadening of the consumers' tastes towards ethnic foods. • The projected increase in tourism will result in a rise in demand for catering at transport establishments. • Opportunities for smaller companies, since the larger competitors are concentrating their efforts in the US rather than the UK. • Diversification of methods of distribution, that is, drive-through's, home delivery and mobile units.	• Provision of ready meals. • Flexible working hours. • General decrease in the average expenditure on meals. • Companies withdrawing completely from the provision of food for employees, or returning to in-house catering. • Reduced corporate entertaining concentrating on quality. • Sandwich operators looking to expand business into contract catering sites. • Move towards vending machine snacks and away from conventional meals. • Closure of companies who use contract caterers. • A decrease in the subsidy on meals in the workplace will cause a drop in the number of meals consumed, so the consumer will have to pay an increased price. • The administrative burden of the attainment of BS EN ISO 9000 is too much for the smaller companies. • An increasing trend of working from home instead of the office. • Cost of raw materials for kitchen equipment is steadily increasing.

Figure C8.4 *Opportunities and threats in the contract catering industry: a SWOT analysis*

FOOD MANUFACTURING MARKET

Overview

Domestic companies dominate the food manufacturing market, with imports making up only 10 per cent of the total. Generally, there is a wide variance between sectors and companies and profit margins are low, averaging 1.7 per cent in 1995. Return on capital employed stands at around 7.6 per cent on average. It should be noted, however, that the largest companies in the industry have profit and returns well above these averages.

The retail market is worth approximately £4.6 billion a year at present and the catering market within it around £1.5 billion. Differences between the types and quality of food supplied to the retail and catering markets are becoming less obvious. A growing trend, copied from the US, is for caterers to provide branded foods on their menus, giving the customer reassurance on quality and encouraging them to spend more on their meals.

Recent changes and trends

The British market has undergone some important changes in the past few years. Over 90 per cent of UK homes have freezing facilities, either separate or as part of a refrigerator, and around 70 per cent of homes have a microwave oven. Recent changes and trends affecting the industry include:

- *Power of supermarket chains*: their bargaining and buying power continues to increase, as does their use of own-label brands. The diversity of these brands has increased, including the addition of luxury own labels, competing against premium manufactured brands. The top four supermarket chains, Safeway, Sainsbury's, Tesco and ASDA, make up around 40 per cent of the UK groceries market (1995).
- *Trends towards demanding more convenience*: due to demographic and lifestyle changes – more women and young mothers working, as well as increasing ownership of microwaves. More individual portion meals, both savoury and dessert.
- *Healthy eating trend*: placing more demands on producers for low fat, low cholesterol and vegetarian foods.
- *Broadening of tastes*: as more consumers are trying foreign and ethnic foods, including Indian, Italian, Asian and Caribbean dishes. There has been a corresponding increase in demand for these types of food in frozen and convenience formats.

FROZEN FOOD

The 1996 ICC report on the frozen food industry predicts that there is still great potential in the frozen food market, due largely to a 'culture lag' in consumers' perceptions of frozen foods. This potential will be exploited if shoppers can be persuaded to try out ranges of added value frozen meals. Specific areas for expansion might be frozen cooked rice and pasta as meal bases, frozen fruit and fruit desserts.

CHILLED FOOD

Overview

The UK market for chilled foods was worth approximately £4.52 billion in 1995, up 6.5 per cent from the 1994 (a poor year for the market). Chilled food accounts for 9 per cent of the total UK grocery food market in 1995. Ready meals and pizzas were the fastest growing sectors, both achieving around 60 per cent growth between 1991 and 1995. Yoghurts, desserts and prepared salads also performed well, with growth rates around 37 per cent for the same period. Sales are forecast to increase by 23 per cent between 1996 and 2000 to £5.81 billion.

Chilled meats

This is a diverse sector, including frankfurters, pre-packed and/or pre-cooked meats, sliced cooked meats and spreads. Due to the decline in meat consumption, growth of this sector has been relatively poor, 22 per cent over the period 1991–95, but acceptable in the circumstances. The introduction of more foreign meat types has been a major factor in slowing the decline.

Ham is still the biggest product in the sector, but others (including salamis, German wursts, pastrami, pepperoni and mortadella) now pose an increasing threat to the established meats. Continental types of ham are also doing well, such as Proscioutto and Parma. Cooked joints of poultry and other meats have a smaller but growing share of the sector; their advantage is convenience, mainly for single people and working mothers.

Around 75 per cent of chilled meat sales are dominated by own-label brands, due largely to supermarket chains' in-store delicatessens. Foreign products are fragmenting the market as they are becoming increasingly popular – numerous small Italian and German producers supply supermarket multiples and convenience stores direct. The largest Italian is Fiorucci Foods, with Giuseppe Citterio Salumificio Spa also gaining an increasing share.

Pizzas, pasta, salads and ready meals

The popularity of these food types has been growing rapidly due to the trends already mentioned above. Italian and American influences are dominant in this market area, helping sales of pizzas and changing the ingredients of many salads to include olives, foreign cheeses and pasta and rice as bases.

In 1995 the sector was worth around £692 million, growing faster than any other in the chilled foods market. Ready meals make up the largest part, worth around £415 million. Chilled meals are often seen as a cheaper alternative to eating out, and perform better than frozen meals largely due to perceived quality and versatility.

Ethnic and foreign dishes dominate the market with Italian, Indian and Chinese being the most popular. Bake type ready meals remain the market leaders (including lasagne and cannelloni), whilst British dishes continue to lose share. Meat-based dishes still dominate the sector, with chicken by far the most popular but fish and vegetable-based meals are gaining sales and share.

Chilled pizza sales rose by 13 per cent in 1995 and are worth £183 million, the fastest growing food type. Chilled pizzas command a higher price than frozen, although the quality difference is diminishing. Sales have been boosted by authentic Italian style pizzas, whilst vegetarian pizzas are becoming more popular in line with the decline in meat eating.

One important trend is that own label penetration stands at around 90 per cent, higher than for any other chilled food sector. Significantly, it is retailer led, with in-store preparation providing the advantage.

CONTRACTS, TENDERING AND SUPPLIERS

Definition

Compulsory Competitive Tendering (CCT) is a term and system applied to certain local and government authorities and bodies as the result of legislation. The main acts of law that affect this system are the:

- Local Government Act 1972, 1988 and 1992.
- Local Government Planning and Land Act 1980.
- Local Authorities Act (Goods and Services) 1970.

CCT requires Local Authorities to follow a set of procedural steps before undertaking work in certain defined areas. Generally, this means they have to invite tenders from companies for the work, and not to use exclusively in-house staff.

Application

CCT applies to:

- mainly Local Authorities in England, Wales and Scotland;
- urban and new town development authorities;
- police and fire services;

- metropolitan transport bodies;
- the Development Board for Rural Wales; and
- Northern Ireland (with amendments).

CCT covers:

- services which Local Authorities must provide to fulfil their statutory duties;
- services which Local Authorities provide to other public bodies;
- local Authorities entering works contracts with other public bodies; and
- activities defined in the Acts costing more than £100,000 in total or employing 15 or more people.

Specifically, CCT applies to catering supplied to schools; residential establishments and day centres; preparation of food for delivery to welfare clients; provision of ingredients, preparation, delivery and service; civic/municipal catering for social purposes or staff catering. However, it excludes 'meals on wheels' delivery, special schools maintained by Local Education Authorities (if food is prepared and consumed on the premises) and colleges of further or higher education.

Process

The Local Government Act 1988 has provisions to prevent anti-competitive behaviour in Local Authority contracting decisions. This covers the advertising process, invitations to tender and applicable time limits. Generally speaking, it is illegal for a Local Authority to include non-commercial considerations when evaluating tenders. Criteria often used include how long the company has operated for, their turnover and any previous experience of work with Local Authorities.

Contracts

Although Local Authorities and commercial bodies usually advertise contracts, lots of contract catering firms employ cold-calling to search for available contracts and business. In addition, consultancy firms compile lists of available contracts that can be acquired by contracting firms.

Profit margins for catering contracts can vary widely, but generally will be around 10 per cent, depending on the level of capital expenditure. Links with food manufacturers can enable contractors to get discounts on their supplies of up to 20 per cent.

SUPPLIER CHAIN

Outsourcing supplier activities is a common strategy of many contract caterers, including Sutcliffe and Marriott, as it allows them to source quality food materials from the best suppliers in the business whilst focusing on the core value-adding activities. In many cases, the large contract catering companies operate a 'one-stop-shop' concept that allows them to capitalise on lower costs and favourable credit term agreements with suppliers. The 'one-stop-shop' enables companies to purchase catering supplies varying from tomato ketchup to pre-packed lasagne.

Many of the catering companies source food suppliers from the large cash-and-carries such as Brakes Brother and Bookers, who are able to operate this 'one-stop-shop' concept and offer bulk purchasing for discount prices. Most large contract caterers will not consider individual suppliers unless the cash-and-carries have approved them on a supplier list, thus Gruppo Massone would have to consider gaining a 'nominated supplier' status to become part of the catering contract supplier chain.

Nominated suppliers

If it were to become a nominated supplier, Gruppo Massone must establish a 'hub store' or a central distribution operation to distribute their products to the cash-and-carries, who will consequently supply the products to customers around the country. By doing this, Gruppo Massone could reduce their distribution costs by undertaking only the transportation of products to a central distribution outlet.

Inferior distribution activities can occur when companies are required to deliver foods to remote locations as part of a contract. Consequently, many food suppliers to contract caterers do not undertake distribution activities that require them to supply products to diverse and somewhat remote locations, as the costs tend to outweigh the benefits.

GRANTS AND ASSISTANCE

UK sources

Government offices have been set up in the English regions to integrate the approach of the Departments of Trade and Industry, Education and Employment and Environment and Transport. This is meant to improve competitiveness and encourage partnership between regional organisations. A single regeneration budget has been established to combine 20 programmes into one budget directed towards partnership projects for local regeneration and economic development.

Within the offices, the Director (Trade and Industry) is responsible for the delivery of a wide range of services to business, including export advice, regional selective assistance and innovation. In Scotland and Wales the services delivered in England by the government offices are delivered by the Scottish and Welsh Offices. Within the UK there are various types of grants that are available to aid businesses looking to enter the UK market. These include:

- Local Assistance to Industry;
- Regional Assistance; and
- Finance from European Sources.

Local assistance

Local Authorities in England and Wales have a specific power to promote the economic development of their area. The power provides local authorities with considerable discretion in the way they choose to promote economic development, subject only to certain restrictions covering inappropriate activities. Local authority assistance under this power may include:

- providing grants, loans or guarantees of borrowing to persons;
- investing in a person's undertaking by acquiring share or loan capital in that body; and
- providing persons with property, services or other financial benefit.

In addition, local authorities in Britain have various general powers under which they may provide assistance to industry if this is in the interest of their area. These include the power to:

- advance money to acquire land;
- erect or carry out works on land; and
- dispose of land at below market value. (this requires the consent of the Secretary of State for the Environment, which is given only in exceptional circumstances).

Regional assistance

The UK Government offers a wide range of assistance to overseas as well as domestic companies locating in certain regions of the UK. The main aim of this policy is to encourage industrial investment. Assisted areas are locations of considerable development. They all have available workforce, competitive labour costs and high labour flexibility.

Need: does the grant make the difference?

A project will be considered for a grant if the company demonstrates convincingly that without grant the project would not go ahead at all in the assisted area, or would go ahead on a smaller scale or with fewer quality features.

Jobs

The project must create or safeguard jobs. The better the quality of jobs and the more the company is prepared to invest in its employees, the bigger the value placed on them when considering a grant.

Viability

The business should be viable and the project should have good prospects of being self-sustaining within a few years.

National and regional benefit

All projects should contribute positive benefits to both the regional and national economy. Consideration is given to how far the project will make a long-term contribution to the competitiveness of national and regional industry and the economy.

Private sector finance

Most of the finance for the project should come from the company's own or other private sector sources. The company will be expected to explore these sources before applying. Private sector finance can include loans from the European Investment Bank.

Figure C8.5   *Criteria for Grants Assessment*

Source: Department of Trade and Industry, September 1995

Grants are individually assessed against the criteria as outlined in Figure C8.5. The amount depends on the area, the needs of the project, the number of jobs created or safeguarded and the impact that the project will have on the economy. Grants can be significant, generally ranging between 5 per cent and 15 per cent of the fixed project costs. Over recent years in England, the average cost per job for projects assisted in development areas has been £4,600 and in intermediate areas £2,900.

Almost all businesses investing in manufacturing can apply for a grant, as can businesses in the service industries that serve a wide rather than a local market. The EC restricts assistance to some industries in which there is over-capacity, including iron and steel, coal and some fishery products.

If you are opening a new plant, expanding or modernising an existing plant or adding facilities such as a design and development division in an assisted area, eligible costs can include:

- plant and machinery;
- some associated one-off costs (such as patent rights, professional fees, re-installation and removal costs); and
- associated land, site preparation and buildings.

To qualify, a project must have a good core of spend on plant and machinery (except in some service sector cases). The working capital spend on a project does not qualify directly but can be taken into account in determining the level of the grant.

European sources

The European Investment Bank makes loans to aid development in the EU. These loans are available to overseas investors intending to invest in the UK. It provides loans for capital investment projects in industry or infrastructure. Typical sectors eligible for large loans include advanced technology, environmental protection, transport, telecommunications and energy. Loans may be for up to half the project capital costs in sterling or in other currencies and can be at either fixed or floating interest rates. Borrowers can draw loans in one or several instalments with flexibility on their timing.

Loan facilities to banks and finance houses (including leasing companies) help them provide finance to customers with eligible capital spending programmes or projects that may individually be up to £20 million. Under these schemes a small or medium-sized customer benefits through the financial terms applied by the clearing bank or finance house with access to European Investment Bank funds and not through increased credit availability, as the repayment risk is borne by the bank/finance house.

Incentives in Northern Ireland

The Industrial Development Board for Northern Ireland 'is responsible for assisting the growth of manufacturing and tradable sectors and promoting inward investment' (Mission Statement). The investment agency offers a flexible package of assistance tailored to a company's individual needs. The criteria on which they assess grants varies according to the precise location within Northern Ireland, however, it is possible to summarise the incentives:

- *Capital*: cash grants for building, machinery and equipment of up to 50 per cent to companies locating in areas of high unemployment.
- *Start-up cost grants*: employment grants related to the number of newly created jobs, designed to reduce initial start-up costs.

- *Factory rents*: grants to reduce rents up to 100 per cent of rental costs for up to 5 years.
- *Company development programme*: provide financial assistance of up to 50 per cent of total net training to develop personnel includes wage costs, fees and travel.
- *Depreciation allowances*: capital expenditure on machinery, equipment and construction costs of industrial buildings – may be written off at a rate of 25 per cent per year (reducing balance basis) for machinery and equipment and 4 per cent per year (straight line basis) for buildings.
- *Industrial de-rating*: 100 per cent for manufacturing.

The incentives operate most effectively within the first three years as companies need the most aid during these years. The most significant incentive for investing companies are the competitive tax rates that currently operate within Northern Ireland. The grants available are subject to assessment on an individual basis, thus it is impossible to state the financial assistance that Gruppo Massone may be entitled to receive.

Ireland

Southern Ireland is an ideal industrial manufacturing location for a food company, as it already has foreign investment of approximately 100 overseas companies. Other significant factors include one of the lowest labour and indirect labour costs in the EU and lowest prime interest rates within the EU.

Any company investing in Ireland is guaranteed a 10 per cent corporation tax until the year 2010 to improve the return on investment of projects. Development agencies such as Forbairt are able to inform foreign companies relating to the grant packages available. Gruppo Massone will be required to provide more specific information to enable the agencies to formulate a focused response to potential investment in Ireland. Below is a synopsis of the grant packages:

- capital investment up to 40 per cent capital grants; and
- staff training grants of £1200 to £1500 per employee.

Forbairt is the state agency with primary responsibility for funding the growth and development of the food and drinks processing industry in Ireland. As such it has responsibility for dividing an investment of some £525 million in the industry up to the end of the decade including substantial EU and state funding.

However, Forbairt's role goes far beyond mere funding. A key part of Forbairt's mission is to bring technology and innovation into the mainstream of industrial development – and this is particularly important in the case of the food and drinks industry.

Forbairt is supporting companies through assistance with new product development, management development, research and development and innovation. This is alongside assistance for new start-ups, expansion plans, and technology acquisitions and partnerships. Forbairt can provide a range of support to food and drinks companies. These include:

- the administration of EU and state funding;
- feasibility study grants;
- research and development grants;
- mentor support;
- technical assistance and advice;
- partnership identification;
- support for technology acquisition;
- joint ventures and world-class manufacturing initiatives;
- graduate placement supports;
- management development grants;
- equity investment and venture capital support; and
- business advisory support and strong links with banks and other institutions.

Inward

Inward is the only agency that promotes the whole of North West England to attract inward investment, and it is the opening to many opportunities the region has to offer. Funded by local and central government and the region's business community, Inward provide help and advice free of charge to those businesses seeking to expand, relocate, or set up a new operation.

Inward's area of operation covers Cheshire, Cumbria, Greater Manchester, Lancashire, Merseyside and the High Peak District of Derbyshire.

As with other agencies, its assistance to overseas companies does not cease once they are established within the region. Inward carry on offering a wide range of support and help on all aspects of setting up a new operation in North West England, *free of charge*. For example:

- availability and costs of sites and premises;
- suppliers of component parts;
- subcontract and other technical needs;
- access to research;
- transport and specialised services;
- labour and skill availability and costs;
- recruitment and training;
- government and other grants;
- european assistance; and
- finance.

GREENFIELD SITE

Overview

Gruppo Massone currently have a number of strategic investment opportunities available in the UK, including Northern Ireland. However, it is important to realise that Gruppo Massone will be subject to stringent criteria and assessed on an individual basis. No guarantee can be made at this stage, therefore, that assistance would be forthcoming.

Enterprise zones

There are various enterprise zones where the company may be able to locate their business operations. An enterprise zone is 'a designated industrial area which has been developed to re-invigorate depressed areas.' It may be beneficial to invest in such enterprise zones as they will be able to write down capital allowances for corporation tax purposes and qualify for full exemption on local property taxes on industrial buildings. In addition, the enterprise zones provide simplified planning procedures for development and expansion of the sites.

Site classification

The individual sites vary widely according to size and character. For example, some may be developed as business parks while others comprise of previous industrial areas with established infrastructure. All of the sites include opportunities to buy or rent land, some of which already have ready-built units of different sizes.

MERSEYSIDE

Knowsley Business Park South

This is described as a major development that comprises a cluster of greenfield sites located in an attractive business park. The site provides prospective companies with the opportunity to develop the area as sections or individual sites. There is a variety of tenure offered at the site either leasehold or freehold and is owned by the Knowsley Borough Council.

The site is deposited as a development plan for industrial and business development including light and general industrial, offices and storage/distribution. The location is ideal as it is easily accessible to the M57 motorway interchange and is within reach of major cities such as Liverpool and Manchester.

Guide price: £45,000 – £55,000 per acre subject to contract and specific areas.

Speke Development Company

The Speke Development Company is a joint venture initiative between English Partnerships and Liverpool City Council. Speke Development Company advises and provides information on property issues and sustains a network of business partnerships that can aid companies such as Gruppo Massone to access training and grants. The company provides a number of potential sites for development in the Liverpool Airport business park with established infrastructure and are able to facilitate fast-track planning arrangements.

The Northern Airport would provide Gruppo Massone with the opportunity to develop a greenfield site for a range of purposes. Infrastructure includes primary access to roads. The tenure will be long leasehold, but speke takes a flexible approach to meeting individual needs and can provide arrangements for owner occupation and joint ventures.

Guide price: £60,000 per acre subject to contract and specific areas.

Northern Ireland

Belfast and Londonderry were chosen as locations for enterprise zones to encourage private enterprise to start up or expand within these areas. This is achieved by offering a range of financial incentives through the Industrial Development Board, in conjunction with Government assistance. Sites include the North Foreshore near Belfast harbour and the Inner City.

SUMMARY

Pros

- Number of potential sites available for foreign investment in the UK.
- Many governmental agencies willing to provide free advice and assistance.
- Individual basis upon which grants and incentives are assessed enables a more tailored approach to each company.
- Gruppo Massone can pursue a number of options in relation to the building of a factory. This flexible approach includes occupancy of ready-built sites or building a new customised factory on a greenfield site.

Cons

- Gruppo Massone cannot make an informed decision until they have provided more detailed information.
- Qualification for grants is subject to stringent criteria, which is somewhat difficult to establish. For example, it is difficult to prove that a company is creating jobs.
- Cannot guarantee the enterprise zone status after the designated period (usually 10 years).

QUESTIONS FOR DISCUSSION

1   What do you see as the key reasons for Gruppo Massone's move into the UK market?
2   What changes have there been in consumer eating habits over the past 10 years and why ?
3   Do inward investment companies/organisations achieve results in stimulating business activity or do they lead to corporates moving from one good grant area to another?
4   'Once the aid runs out we move.' Discuss.
5   Is Gruppo Massone's marketing planning process likely to achieve success?
6   What major threats are there to this entry strategy?
7   Did the election of a Labour Government in 1997 have an impact on the business environment and Gruppo Masone's likelihood of success?

CS9   LEGO: THE TOY OF THE TWENTIETH CENTURY–THE CASE OF THE SIMPLE BUILDING BLOCKS

HANNE GARDNER

Internationalisation has become a central strategy for businesses the world over. What drives a business to become international? Is it the desire to expand a business in order to generate increased market share, turnover and profits? Or is it simply that the domestic market offers no further growth potential? These are some of the key questions to be addressed.

This case study considers the customers and consumers, the product, the market, the company itself as well as the company's strategies. It aims to give an historical account of some of the developments within the company, which have been crucial for the expansion of a small family-owned company, starting life in a very small Danish town – Billund – and staying there after achieving international success and recognition.

Recently LEGO has suffered a serious setback in terms of profit. The company made one of the classic mistakes so often made: that of becoming complacent and believing that the competitive environment would remain the same.

LEGO almost fell into the trap that Theodor Levitt referred to in his classic article 'Marketing Myopia', pointing out that the American Railroad Companies thought their market was railroads and not transportation. LEGO almost believed that the market was building bricks and not the toy, educational and entertainment markets!

THE CONSUMERS AND THE CUSTOMERS (NOT ALWAYS THE SAME)

Today, children in the Western world have more choice than ever of how they spend their free time. Most children have played with LEGO if not at home then either at school or at a friend's house. LEGO has been one of the most popular and enduring toys since the brightly coloured LEGO bricks were first launched in the mid 1950s. Why has this simple building system been so successful where so many other toys have failed? One explanation may be that the product transcends language and cultural barriers. Children the world over have been united in their enjoyment of building and creating anything from a simple tower to sophisticated 'high-tech' models. LEGO is a non-competitive toy that allows each individual child to push himself or herself to the limit of his or her own ability, using a child's unique imagination. The product has no boundaries. The LEGO brick facilitates the development of the imagination. The only limiting factors are the child's own ability and creativity and the availability of LEGO bricks. The combinations are endless.

LEGO bricks teach young children important spatial skills – one of the reasons why so many schools continue to buy the product. The bricks can be used over and over again. Children develop and change as they grow, and so do the models that they can make out of LEGO bricks. From the very large Duplo blocks aimed at the very young to the very sophisticated kits now available, LEGO allows children (and grown-ups for that matter) to have the opportunity to be design engineers working on any new prototype of their own choice. Many parents can remember the hours of enjoyment they themselves had from LEGO as children, thus becoming important 'sales agents' for the product. But perhaps one of the most important considerations is the very wide price points that the LEGO ranges offer. As a customer you can spend as little or as much as you wish; whether it is spending modest amounts of pocket money or buying a special gift for Christmas, each and every LEGO purchase adds to and enhances the LEGO collection.

THE PRODUCT

'The core product itself consists of one rectangular plastic brick, hollow on the inside except for one or more tubes, with rows of studs on the top emblazoned with the tiny LEGO logo' (Wiencek, 1987).

The LEGO brick has been described thus:

> The product is both simple and unique. Because of its simplicity it has been imitated by other manufacturers but none has been as successful as LEGO. This is in no small part due to the tenacity and focused strategy adopted by the company.

It has been LEGO's policy to maintain strong links with its machinery suppliers, making their own tools for plastic injection moulding. Tool-making could have been restricted to one location but, for reasons of competition and quality, six centres have been used (Denmark, Switzerland, the US, Germany, Brazil and South Korea) (Thompson, 1993). By spreading the manufacturing process across several continents, the company is not only spreading the risk but also inculcating an internal competitive market among the productive units helping to improve efficiency as well as quality. The product is tough and enduring, allowing children to play with the bricks for years without losing any through breakages.

To illustrate the high quality of LEGO and the continuous attention to quality control and standards, perhaps an example serves best. McDonald's in the US decided to use LEGO bricks in one of the company's sales promotions and as a result 37 million bricks were distributed in the course of 4 weeks (Langer, 1990). Only a dozen complaints were received.

To ensure that the product is as safe as possible each individual brick has a small hole which ensures that, should a child swallow a brick, air can still pass through and the child will not choke (*Jyllands-Posten*, 1988).

LEGO product development can best be described as variations upon a common theme. For example, the introduction of technical LEGO enabled older children to continue to develop their models using sophisticated gears and motors, thus extending the appeal of the product into a different, much older age group.

The LEGO company spends significant resources on developing new ideas and has a team of people 'playing' with LEGO to generate new ideas and models, extending the usage of the simple LEGO brick as well as researching and developing more advanced concepts which could extend the usage of LEGO.

Television, video and computer games have proved particularly important and this market has been growing fast. LEGO is aware of this threat and is working with projects which would allow the company to extend its operation into such new markets, but perhaps too late to be at the forefront of such activity (more about this later).

THE MARKET

LEGO's objective in doing anything is to enhance its image and to sell more LEGO. Market share is usually never quoted by the company itself, only by commentators or competitors. The LEGO philosophy is 'Why should we help the competition, let them find the information for themselves!' The market for LEGO bricks could be regarded as limited, particularly by many of LEGO's competitors and yet it is the infinite variety and the endless possibilities which the bricks offer that have appealed to the children the world over – just like the combination of different keys on a piano offer the composer and player.

However, one age group which LEGO recognises that it has been unable to capture is that of girls over four or five years old. Most girls play 'role model' games rather than games involving construction and model making. LEGO has now launched special ranges that seek to capture this particular market segment.

According to the Market Research Company Dodona, LEGO was number five in the world toy market with sales estimated to be in the region of US$1005 (Amsinck, 1992). At that time it was estimated to take one-third of all US toy sales. In 1991, the market for West Europe overtook the North American market.

The company has always sought to control growth – and did not attempt to achieve the maximum – which so many companies strive for. The figures quoted for market growth range from 5–10 per cent depending upon the country and the stage of development in that country. The marketing expenditure is dependent upon the development of the individual countries and an annual figure of between 6–7 per cent of turnover is quoted for well established countries, though there is no indication of the scale of expenditure for a new country (Roelsgaard, 1992).

The overall strategic objective for LEGO is a very ambitious one, namely that of every child in the world owning one cubic meter of LEGO!

> The LEGO story, which has lessons not just for toy manufacturers, but for businesses in other fast-changing industrial sectors, is centred on a long-term strategy of product development. (*Financial Times*, 1999)

But 'Like most things Lego ain't what it used to be. There was a time when Happiness was a bucket of coloured bricks' (*Daily Telegraph*, 1998). Children today expect fast action and interactive games, which many have come to take for granted to such an extent that that is the only activity in which they appear interested. For a long time LEGO sought to meet the creative needs and interests of a large proportion of the world's children. However, the march of innovation and technology has been relentless and although the company sought to develop computer-based activities, many other players occupy this fast growing and exceedingly competitive market.

'Mindstorm', a computer microchip that can be integrated into the Lego bricks and can have programmes downloaded for a PC and make possible different types of play, was launched in the autumn of 1998 and featured re-programmable bricks and sensors using Windows 95 softwear (*Daily Telegraph*, 1998). However, the price was well in excess of £100 in the UK and made many potential customers think twice before spending that amount of money.

THE COMPETITION

The LEGO principle 'Kids are kids and alike around the world' was the cornerstone of the global market strategy. 'However, in the US where competition has been at its fiercest, Tyco, a leading competitor, began to put its product in plastic buckets that could be used for storage after play. This utilitarian approach contrasted with LEGO's elegant see-through plastic cartons standardised worldwide. But American parents seemed to prefer the functional 'toys in buckets' idea over cartons. Seeing a potential for serious damage, LEGO's alarmed US management sought permission from Denmark to package LEGO toys in buckets. The head office flatly refused. The denial was based on seemingly sound arguments. The bucket idea could cheapen LEGO's reputation for high quality. Moreover, the LEGO bucket would be seen as a 'me too' defensive reaction, inappropriate for a renowned innovator. Finally, and perhaps most importantly, buckets would be a radical deviation from the company's policy of standardisation of marketing everywhere. Nevertheless, two years later LEGO's headquarter reversed its decision' (Kashani, 1989).

This example illustrates how LEGO initially adhered to its principles but recognised the need to change a policy decision based upon the facts presented over a two-year period. The important point is that the company was not rushed into a decision. This highlights that international conformity to global standards may have to be sacrificed to respond to shifting conditions in particular markets. As one LEGO executive put it ruefully, 'While kids will always be alike around the world, parents who buy toys may change their behaviour' (Kashani, 1989).

A battle concerning imitation or 'passing off' (a term used in intellectual property law implying imitation intended to mislead) was lost in court in the US. However, LEGO declared that although the company had lost the court battle it intended to win the real battle in the shops!

DIVERSIFICATION WITHIN THE MARKET

The decision to develop a theme park is one example of how the company has been able to capitalise and further enhance its image. The first theme park LEGOLAND in Billund celebrated its 25th anniversary in 1993 and is now the single biggest tourist attraction outside Copenhagen. In LEGOLAND everything is made out of LEGO bricks; all the different scenes ranging from the famous US Presidents' heads originally carved out of rock to the royal palaces of European countries.

The activities include trips in LEGO-copters, rides on board LEGO trains round the park, sailing in little LEGO boats to a gold-wash where youngsters can wash sand to collect sufficient gold nuggets, which are then turned into a LEGO key ring! Even the restaurants have LEGO bricks in the middle of the tables so the young customers need not be bored while they wait for food to arrive.

To ensure that there is something of interest to all generations, LEGO has also started a toy museum displaying Titania's Palace, a unique, exquisitely made very large doll's house, bought at Sotheby's for a small fortune in the 1970s. In addition there is also a unique collection of dolls and toys through the ages.

In 1993, LEGO bought Windsor Safari Park near London for the planned opening of the first theme park in the UK (Schwarck, 1992). The Windsor LEGOLAND opened in 1996 and now ranks as the seventh most popular tourist destination in the UK with over 1.5 million visitors (*Financial Times*, 1999). In the US there had been fierce competition between two states – California and Massachusetts – to get the third proposed LEGO theme park. However, LEGO was in no hurry and postponed the decision, which was due during the summer of 1993, while the two contenders continued to improve their offers of paying for improvements to the infrastructure and facilities to attract this universally popular theme park. In the end the choice was Carlsbad in California. The park eventually opened in March 1999.

THE RETAILERS

LEGO sells to 60,000 retailers in 130 countries around the world (LEGO website). Originally for countries outside Europe, North America and Japan the sales would take place through a distributor. However, 90 per cent of the entire sales took place through the company's own sales organisations. It has not been possible to identify exactly the stage at which LEGO sets up a sales company instead of using a distributor (Roelsgaard, 1992).

The sales organisation was radically changed in 1999 as in the recent downsizing or streamlining, known as 'LEGO's Fitness Programme', 30 different sales companies each with their own budgets have now been reduced to 7 (LEGO website).

BACKGROUND AND COMPANY HISTORY

The progress of the company has not been one of natural, easy success. On the contrary, it has been a long and arduous battle from the start. Success born out of adversity probably best describes the early years. The LEGO company was founded in 1932 by a carpenter in Billund, Ole Kirk Christiansen. During the recession, when there was little or no work for craftsmen in house building, Ole Kirk Christiansen started making toys. His toys were made of wood – hand-painted cars, animals and pull-toys. Even from its early days the company had one guiding principle, 'Only the best is good enough'!

Why choose the name LEGO? Simple! The Danish for 'play well' is 'leg godt' and Ole Kirk Christiansen simply took the first two letters of each word thus forming both the company name and the brand name 'LEGO'. It was only at a later date that it was discovered that the Latin meaning of LEGO was 'to put together'.

However, it was not until the late 1940s that an interest in building systems evolved and a factory and equipment capable of producing plastic bricks was purchased. In 1949 the first 'automatic binding bricks' were produced after inspiration from Kiddicraft in England (Thygesen Poulsen, 1993: 63).

The first LEGO system was launched in 1955 and the first patent taken out in 1958 (Olsen, 1975). Although other companies have sought to imitate the LEGO product, none has been as enduringly successful as LEGO. The decision to stop production of the original wooden toy was made in 1960 when a fire in the original wood store forced the company to make the decision to abandoned making wooden toys completely and thus became a single product company.

ANALYTICAL FRAMEWORK

Until the late 1990s the company had had three distinct phases:

- Formation and development.
- Transformation and internationalisation.
- Maintaining competitive advantage.

The three stages above can very clearly be linked to each of the generation, of the LEGO family. The first generation, Ole Kirk Christiansen, was the founder of the company and the one to get a toy making company established. He was also the man who identified the interest in a building system.

The second generation to become the leader was Godtfred Kirk Christiansen. He was self-educated, an entrepreneur with the unique ability to evolve long-term strategy. The only formal training he received was in the thatched Technical College in Haslev (Bach, 1989). Godtfred Kirk Christiansen was appointed as managing director designate in 1950, and he did, in fact, take over the management after his father's first stroke in 1951. However, the relationship between father and son was not without its trials and tribulations. Godtfred Kirk Christiansen handed in his resignation as a protest against his father's decision to expand again, at a time when the company could just see an end to its financial problems. Although he had resigned, he left with a box of samples and tried to establish sales in Sweden (but with little success until 1955). However, he was successful in Norway.

What had become clear was that the Danish market was too small and new markets had to be found. The German market was the next to be tackled, but the Germans were very critical of the product and complained about the quality. As a result, the construction of the basic LEGO brick was changed to the design we know today. This was the design that was patented in 47 countries.

Family disagreements led to Godtfred Kirk Christiansen buying out his three brothers. Tragedy almost led to the sale of the company when GKC's two children were involved in a serious traffic accident. However, a new top manager was head-hunted, Vagn Holck Andersen, and it was decided that Kjeld Kirk Kristiansen (grandson of the founder; note change in spelling of the surname at that time) should have further management training in Switzerland to equip him for leadership in the future.

Kjeld Kirk Kristiansen has been the only family member with modern business training from two business schools, one in Aarhus, Denmark (HA, a three-year full-time business course), the other in Switzerland, where he received his MBA (Bach, 1989).

THE CULTURE

'The LEGO culture is informal, more verbal than written, with consideration for the human being – sedate Jutlandish (*sindig jysk*) – without pressure and seeking prestige. They talk and have trust in each other and also in the leadership. It is a quality, which manifests itself in effectiveness and this contributes to making the LEGO Group so successful' (Thygesen Poulsen, 1993: 36).

The characteristics of the people living in and around Billund, the home of LEGO, include caution and the avoidance of taking rash decisions. Loyalty is considered one of the most important virtues mirrored in the style of management described earlier. In Billund, a job with LEGO was a job for life, particularly important in that part of Denmark where little alternative employment existed.

In the LEGO company, there is a reputed saying that no individual is important, it is the sum of the individuals. Just like the individual LEGO bricks. One brick on its own is not sufficient.

A Japanese-style of management is aspired to, in the sense of seeking consensus from the groups of managers rather than individuals making arbitrary decisions (Thygesen Poulsen, 1993: 5). The company prides itself on being both international and very professional. Its management style is one where there is no distinction in status between managers and workers in terms of canteen and car-parking facilities (Thygesen Poulsen, 1993: 14).

Words that have been used to characterise the management style (and this is also typical of the inhabitants around Billund) are: modest, frugal, sedate, obstinate, proud and loyal. As Thygesen Poulsen (1993: 15) points out:

> From the traditional management perspective LEGO's international success is itself a paradox.

A fundamental aspect of LEGO's long-term marketing strategy is to indoctrinate every employee at every level with this absolute and unshakeable faith in the single product of the company – the LEGO brick in all its adaptations.

Although the company, according to its website in 1999, had a worldwide operation and employs almost 10,000 people in 50 companies in 30 different countries around the world, LEGO's headquarters remains where the company was born and still bears the conservative stamp of a small-town farming culture. According to a detailed study of the LEGO company, it was described thus:

> The LEGO Group is a case study, an example from the real world of how a successful organisation grows and develops, not through a standard formula from management theory, but through organic growth using the organisation's own prosperity and based on its own belief and unique being, with very strong roots in the poor soil of Jutland. (Translated from Thygesen Poulsen, 1993: 20).

Lego had become accustomed to steady growth both in terms of market share and profits. However, 1997 saw a dramatic slump in the profit (before tax) from DKr 699 million in 1996 to DKr 171 million in 1997, to a loss of DKr 282 million in 1998 (*Jyllands-Posten*, 1999) as illustrated in Table C9.1.

However, the very first deficit in the company's history was recorded in 1998 and forced a dramatic departure from what had been existing company policy. LEGO made 1000 employees redundant, 486 in Denmark, which in a small community had a dramatic effect. Of the rationalisation the number of directors was reduced from 75 to 40 (*Jyllands Posten*, 1999).*

A number of different circumstances influenced this performance. The development of electronic toys by competitors forced Lego to change from the

---

*It should be noted here that because of differences in language, terminology and legislation, a director is not a member of the board as in the UK. In Denmark boards are two tier and by law require employee representation, one of the reasons LEGO decided to move part of the controls to Switzerland.

Table C9.1   LEGO's turnover and profit before tax (1995–98)

	1995	1996	1997	1998
Turnover	6,844	7,534	7,616	7,680
Profit before tax	676	699	171	–(282)

Source: Jyllands-Posten (1999)
Note: Million DKr (11DKr = £1)

traditional bricks to broader areas. An investment programme had been underway to introduce consumers to the electronic/computer-based toy as well as the development of softwear suitable for use with domestic PCs, which required significant investment in research and development before any pay-back could be anticipated. Agreements to collaborate with Walt Disney using a range of Disney characters as well as Star Wars films demonstrate how seriously the company viewed the situation.

The company is now managed by the third generation of the founder's family. However, a carefully selected management team, all steeped in the LEGO philosophy, supports the controlling family. LEGO is a very secretive company, which was one of the reasons for choosing Switzerland as home for part of the financial provisions safeguarding the family ownership of the organisation. Very little information is released from the company about its global operation unless it is seen to advance a particular element of the LEGO story. Financial informa-tion is limited to that which is required by law.

From time-to-time the company has recruited very senior managers from outside the company, when particular skills were deemed essential. For exam-ple, a lawyer (*landsretssagforer*) with particular expertise in setting up companies was recruited to reorganise the company into an organisation that could be controlled by the family, thus avoiding new legislation whcih required the company to have representatives on its main board. The solution adopted was a company structure with a number of different companies, 40 to be precise, some of which are registered in Switzerland, a country that offers the secrecy and protection which was deemed necessary to keep the company under family control.

More recently a new employee was head-hunted to give the company some new blood and ideas. In 1998 Paul Plougmann was recruited as 'crisis doctor' to help sort out the problems that manifested themselves in the first ever loss posted by the company (*Jyllands-Posten*, 1999).

THE STRATEGY

Quality is paramount for a toy company that has the simple but monumentally ambitious mission statement of 'Each and every child in the world to own to cubic meter of LEGO bricks'. It is a very clear and ambitious objective, one that does not depend upon comparisons with other companies and their activities. It is not subject to changing measurement criteria such as currency values, nor is it dependent on outside interests or economic growth.

In fact, what it does demonstrate is a simple and unshakeable faith in the product to such an extent that LEGO has put all its eggs in one basket. The company did not diversify into other toy products like so many other toy manufacturers until recently, when it was decided to enter into a range of collaborations with Walt Disney as well as launching LEGO clothes (*Jyllands-Posten*, 1999).

The company has, in the development of its culture, set up a protection against being diverted or forced into short-termism; through all this it begins to emerge that the key element of LEGO's successful strategy has been: CONSISTENCY.

So what has been the nature of the strategies that have underpinned the long-term consistency which so characterises LEGO? Like so many other businesses it started as a family business without reliance on the stock market and institutional support. Indeed, in the early years the bank refused to lend money and this event resulted in the firm belief in being self-sufficient. Most companies reach a certain size and then, to achieve more rapid growth, float themselves on the stock market. LEGO is one of the few companies to have eschewed this path, but nonetheless has achieved international ranking. In fact, LEGO has been listed among the top 25 brands in the world, with names like Levi and McDonald's (Irvin, 1999).

Three key factors have influenced and shaped the strategy adopted by LEGO. First, the small size of the Danish market forced the company to look towards the international market at an early stage in its development. Second, while other toy manufacturers diversified, LEGO single-mindedly maintained its focus on its original LEGO brick as the core product and have by and large stuck to that. Third, the company chose to remain a family-owned concern and has taken considerable trouble to safeguard and secure that status.

The company has adhered to two fundamental principles in achieving growth: organic expansion financed out of its own capital. Both are very cautious approaches, both of which have born rich rewards. Controlled growth has been the key, not rapid expansion.

The success of the company's marketing strategy has been the consistent and tenacious way in which the company has single-mindedly stuck to the one product and refused to stray into other areas in the toy market, which is littered with 'here today and gone tomorrow' products, thus maintaining a very clear focus on the core business. The reward has been the company's claim of 80 per cent of the global market for construction toys (*Marketing Business*, 1999).

The success of the company is perhaps best illustrated by the following claims:

- In 1993 the LEGO Group was among the world's 10 biggest toy manufacturers, the only one to be headquartered outside the US and Japan.
- In 1993, out of LEGO's sales only 2 per cent were in Denmark.
- The company is 100 per cent family owned and self-financing. (Thygesen Poulsen, 1993: 21)
- Most importantly, Lego was voted 'Toy of the Century' by *Fortune* magazine, an achievement that speaks for itself. (Anon: *Politiken*, 1999).

CONCLUSION

LEGO has mostly been successful, but there are also examples of how problems have developed and been solved.

All the decision-making has been underpinned by the very strong company culture, which reflects the nature of the inhabitants of Billund.

Whether LEGO will achieve its mission statement of every child in the world owning 1 cubic metre of LEGO bricks remains to be seen. What is certain, however, is that the evolution of the LEGO company demonstrates that consistent strategic management can shape and mould a company in a single-minded, consistent way to create an example of how success can be achieved on a global scale by a small company from a small country. More recently examples of developing joint ventures with Walt Disney demonstrate how difficult survival has become as new technology increases and forces the pace of change, for young consumers have also become far more demanding, expecting their toys to keep pace with the technical innovations in the marketplace.

QUESTIONS FOR DISCUSSION

1 How did LEGO start, and why has its success been so enduring in a market that is characterised by ever-changing trends and fads?
2 What are the enduring qualities that the products possess which have allowed such command of the toy market on a global basis?
3 Is LEGO's position based on genuine product superiority or is it superior management or a combination of both?
4 Or could it be the stability that a family-owned and managed company offers compared with the short-termism prevalent in public companies today – where profit, return on capital and earnings per share are paramount and where shareholders and City pressures are allowed to rule? These pressures are, to a large extent, absent in this family-owned company.
5 Did LEGO adopt a Japanese style strategy of long-term objectives to secure market share? And is this only possible within companies where employees feel secure and there is no practice of hiring and firing – which has characterised much of modern business in the West – thus maintaining the same, consistent company culture with its emphasis upon loyalty and continuity? What strategies did the family use to grow so successfully?
6 How did the company expand its business to become one of the world's best known and loved toy manufacturers, while still maintaining family ownership?

The following list of 11 paradoxes seeks to illustrate and explain the LEGO philosophy in terms of its management style. The list was put together following a period of rapid expansion in 1986 where a number of new employees had joined the company, but as yet had not been steeped in the company's philosophy. The list was produced at a management course to discuss a common leadership style for all.

LEGO's eleven paradoxes

1 To be able to establish a close relationship with one's co-workers
* to maintain a suitable distance.
2 To be able to go in front (to lead from the front)
* to keep in the background.
3 To show co-workers trust
* to keep an eye on what they do.
4 To be tolerant.
* to know how one wants things to work.
5 To think of one's own departments objectively
* and at the same time be loyal to the 'whole' (business).
6 To be able to organise one's time effectively
* to be flexible over time management.
7 To be able to express what one thinks
* to be diplomatic.
8 To have vision
* to keep one's feet on the ground.
9 To seek consensus
* to be able to cut through.
10 To be dynamic
* to be considerate (*eftertaenksom*).
11 To be self-assured
* to be humble.

(Thygesen Poulsen, 1993: 12–13).

Following the formulation of these 11 paradoxes it was decided that they should be sent out as the annual Christmas greeting headed by the Tao yang and yin symbol to illustrate the wholeness and complementary skills deemed necessary for the success of the company. How very different from some of the management thinking taught in some business schools.

REFERENCES

Many of the source are Danish and have been translated into English by Hanne Gardner, author of this case study.

Amsinck, H. (1992) 'LEGO's styrke ogsaa en svaghed', *Borsen*, 23 November.
Anon (1999) 'Lego Klodser Koaret', *Politiken Weekly*, 8 December.
Bach, C.(1989) 'Vi taenker Japansk', *Politiken*, 24 September.
Irvin, C. (1999) 'Construction site', *Marketing Business*, September: 36–39.
Kashani, K. (1989) 'Beware the Pitfalls of Global Marketing', *Harvard Business Review*, (Sept.–Oct.): 91–8.
Langer, M.W. (1990) 'Lego besejre USA', *Borens Nyhedsmagasin*, 19 October.
Levitt, T. (1960) 'Marketing Myopia', *Harvard Business Review*, (July–Aug.): 45–56.
Marsh, P. (1990) 'Family continuity holds the key to longevity in a one-product company', *Financial Times*, 20 June.

Olsen, K. (1975) 'LEGO og dens Godfather', *Berlinske Weekend*, 11 April.

Roelsgaard, J.M. (1992) 'LEGO leger ikke med markedsforing', *Borsen*, 23 November.

Schwarck, W. (1992) 'Lego indtager England', *Jyllands-Posten*, 3 December.

Thompson, J.L. (1993) *Strategic Management, Awareness and Change*, 2nd edn., London: Chapman & Hall.

Thygesen Poulsen, P. (1993) *LEGO – en virksonhed og dens sjael*. Albertslund: Schultz Information.

Wiencek, H. (1987) *The World of LEGO Toys*. New York: Harry N. Abrams.

Jyllauds–Posten (1988)

22 June

Daily Telegraph (1998) 'Connected', 17 September

Financial Times (1999) 3 May.

Jyllauds–Posten (1999) 12 May.

Jyllauds–Posten (1999) 12 August.

Jyllauds–Posten (1999) 22 October.

CS10 MANNESMANN MOBILFUNK: DISTRIBUTION CHANNEL DECISIONS IN THE GROWTH PHASE OF THE MOBILE PHONE MARKET IN GERMANY

H.J. SCHMENGLER AND MATTHIAS THIEME

THE DEREGULATION OF THE MOBILE PHONE MARKET IN GERMANY

There was no competition to the analogue mobile phone networks that were operating in Germany until the beginning of the 1990s. German Telekom was the operator of the analogue mobile phone networks and its high pricing and product policy only allowed around 240,000 mobile phone customers until 1990. This corresponded to a mobile phone penetration rate of approximately 0.2 per cent and meant that Germany's development was far behind that of other European countries. (European Mobile Communications Report, January 1998).

From 10 groups of applicants, the Mannesmann consortium was awarded the contract for the D2 license in 1989. Mannesmann Mobilfunk was able to operate the first private mobile phone network in Germany. This initiated competition for the first time in the sector of speech communication between the state utility German Telekom and a private provider of telecommunications. In the period that followed both built up a digital mobile phone network independently of each other in accordance with the GSM standard.

Since 1982 a working party of European Post and Telecommunications Administrations has been developing a cross-border digital mobile phone standard that is standardised throughout Europe. This is known as GSM (Global System For Mobile Communication).

The advantage of this uniform standard is not just that a mobile phone user can be reached abroad on thier own mobile phone, it has also meant that mobile phones were mass-produced right from the start, and so could be offered for sale at a more reasonable price. The lower telephone price reduced the customer's inhibitions against buying a mobile phone and the prices for use were set at a lower rate right from the beginning. Consequently the network operators could reckon with higher numbers of subscribers.

As a logical continuation of the analogue mobile phone networks called the A, B and C networks, the digital mobile phone networks of the new competitors were called D1 (German Telekom) and D2 (Mannesmann Mobilfunk).

MANNESMANN MOBILFUNK AND THE COMPETITION

The commercial operation of the D networks started in the middle of 1992. Until then German Telekom had a monopoly on the analogue C network. Reductions to the fee structure had increased the number of subscribers to around 600,000 by the time the D networks went into operation and a decision was made to continue to operate the C network parallel to the D networks. Therefore customers in Germany were able to choose between three networks, the D1, D2 and the C network. To further open the market and increase the competition, the German deregulation authorities first of all authorised 13 so-called service providers to market the D networks. Service providers are economically and legally independent telephone companies that use and operate the mobile phone networks of the network operators under their own name and make profits through their own tariff structures. Apart from this it must be emphasised that the service providers offer their own D1 and also D2 tariff structure. This means that a service provider is a partner as it markets the parent company's network, and is also a competitor as it also markets the competitor's network.

The aim of all competitors is to have as high a number of subscribers as possible, that is, to sign service contracts with customers and to keep the customers in their own network. The mobile telephones are simply an instrument for gaining customers and not for generating margins.

DISTRIBUTION CHANNELS

Mannesmann Mobilfunk GmbH built up a decentralised distribution structure for marketing the D2 network. Eight geographically defined branch offices are responsible for the operational business. Their aim is to guarantee proximity to the market and the fast implementation of distribution activities.

The regional branches set up the following distribution channels for handling the market: service providers, dealers, small and medium-sized business and key accounts. In addition, 14 D2-Centres were created as service support points.

The market opening function of the service providers and their special function as partners and competitors has already been described. The original marketing goal of the network operators is to support the partner firms with their distribution activities. As well as achieving the marketing goals set, the aim was also for Mannesmann to have subscriber numbers which exceed those of the competition and so result in the highest market share, that is, Mannesmann Mobilfunk is the market leader for a service provider if more of the service provider's customers use D2 than D1.

The following service providers were operating at the time the D networks were launched: Axicon Mobilfunkdienste, Bosch Telecom, Debitel, Dekratel, Hutchison, Martin Dawes, Mobilcom, Motorola, Proficom, Talkline, TMG and Unicom.

An important factor for high market penetration is the building up of a good partnership with dealers. A dealer becomes a D2 distribution outlet when a dealer contract is signed, which secures the dealer commission for selling a D2 card. In contrast to a service provider, a dealer does not market the D2 network under its own name. In order to guarantee blanket coverage, contracts were secured with dealers covering around 2000 sales outlets. These dealers are mainly classical communications retailers, entertainment electronics dealers, car dealers and car accessory dealers.

As well as the indirect distribution channels that have been described (service providers and dealers), direct distribution channels were also set up to ensure sales and to guarantee quality standards. The aim is for around 20 per cent of sales to be made through direct distribution channels.

The small and medium-sized company distribution channel deals with the target group that uses mobile phones for business purposes. In particular the small and medium-sized company distribution channel looks after customer groups from the self-employed and tradesmen, to industrial and service companies.

The distribution channel 'key accounts (corporations)' was created to fulfill the particular requirements of large companies. To distinguish them from the 'small and medium-sized companies' distribution channel, large customers are defined as companies with a turnover of more than DM 100 million and more than 500 employees.

The D2-Centres, which are spread throughout Germany, serves as service support points rather than as distribution channels and so support the direct distribution channels. These are one-stop shops, and their services include the installation of mobile phones, a telephone replacement service in the case of complaints, the sale of accessories, and securing of D2 contracts. With particular relevance to the installation of car phones, a high-quality standard has been established as an example to specialist dealers.

GROWTH PHASE: MARKET SEGMENTATION THROUGH PRODUCT AND PRICING POLICY

The main target group in the product introduction phase was users who use mobile phones for business purposes, typically occupational groups such as top and middle management employees of key accounts, sales representatives, service technicians, tradesmen, haulage contractors and security services. The mobile phone usually served as a productivity factor here, as the user is a procurer rather than a consumer by generating additional value through the service. The only private persons to be reached were image-conscious trendsetters or technical innovators with very low price sensitivity. For although the distribution channels marketed the D2 network with different types of telephones (car phones, mobile phones) and telephone manufacturers (Siemens, Nokia, Ericsson and so on), only one original telephone service product was available. This was the D2 Classic Tariff with a monthly basic fee of DM 78.20 and call charges of

DM 1.39 at peak time (workdays 7 a.m. – 8 p.m.) and DM 0.56 at off-peak time (the remaining time).

The time at which the tariff structure had to be expanded was decisive. New target groups had to be reached to prevent the market growth from slowing down. The moment for this was May 1995. The D2 Fun Tariff was introduced in addition to the D2 Classic Tariff. The basic price of DM 49.95 for the D2 Fun Tariff, which was further reduced to DM 24.95 in the autumn of 1996, and the minute price at off-peak time of DM 0.39, is geared to the target group of 'leisure time callers'.

- **Tariff**
  D2 Classic (until 5/95)
  D2 Fun (from 5/95)

- **Basic price (per month)**
  DM 78.20
  DM 49.95 (DM 24.95)

- **Price per minute – peak time**
  DM 1.39
  DM 1.89

- **Price per minute – off-peak**
  DM 0.56
  DM 0.39

At the same time the competitor, D1, also introduced a similar 'leisure' tariff. In addition to this, the German Post Ministry awarded a further mobile phone licence to a private consortium, which meant a further market participant. This new competitor, E-Plus, targets mainly private individuals.

The focus on further target groups considerably expanded the market potential. Figure C10.1 clearly shows the market growth expected from 1995.

ADAPTATION OF DISTRIBUTION CHANNELS TO THE CHANGED MARKET CONDITIONS

When it became clear that a differentiated pricing and product policy alone does not mean a clear positioning of the competition, competitive advantages had to be created, particularly in the distribution structure. The distribution channels of Mannesmann Mobilfunk had to adapt to the new target groups and the increased market growth, and to the growth phase that started with this. Figure C10.2 shows the result.

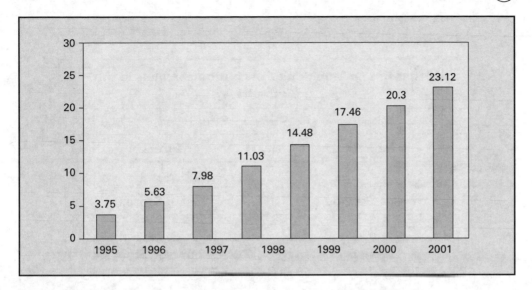

Figure C10.1   *Development of the mobile market in Germany (millions of subscribers)*
Source: Mobilcom Markt 6/97, Plica Market Research Analysis

KEY ACCOUNT MANAGEMENT FOR THE SERVICE PROVIDERS

The end of the product introduction phase and the beginning of the growth phase was characterised by concentration processes. In this market adjustment phase, where mergers meant that subscribers were also taken over, service providers developed with very large numbers of customers and so great market influence. As decisions about the fundamental organisation of market activities for the service providers are made centrally, Mannesmann Mobilfunk set up a central key account management to look after the service providers' head offices. Additional sales personnel were employed in the branches of Mannesmann Mobilfunk to implement decisions made centrally in the sales outlets of the partner firms.

SEGMENTATION OF DEALERS

As more than 2000 sales outlets of the D2 dealers had the highest market presence of all distribution channels and so the greatest access to the new target group, the organisation of the dealers was optimised through segmentation. There now followed a differentiated handling of the market divided into partner agencies, exclusive retailers, megastores and distributors.

Dealers were gained as partner agencies. A dealer that is a partner agency remains legally independent, although its external appearance is so similar to

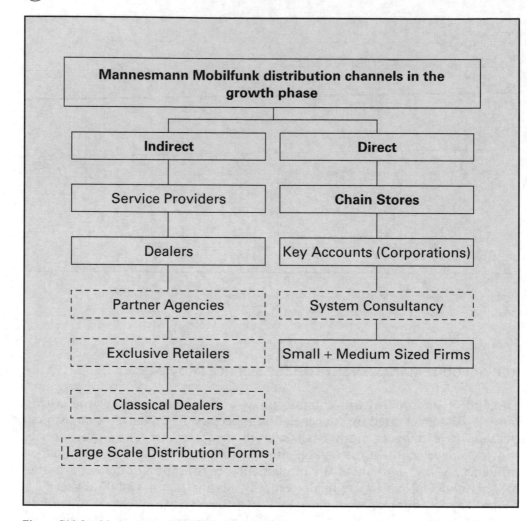

Figure C10.2 *Mannesmann Mobilfunk distribution channels*
Source: Mannesmann Mobilfunk

that of Mannesmann's own stores that the customer barely notices any difference. The locations are chosen so as to be a sensible supplement to Mannesmann's own D2 sales outlets. In places where the market potential means that a Mannesmann D2 store cannot work economically and there was already a dealer, this dealer was gained as a partner agency. Moreover, one or two of Mannesmann's own stores in cities are often not sufficient to absorb the market potential. Partner agencies can often be a sensible supplement. In addition to this, partner agencies are advertised as D2 sales outlets in the local press to ensure frequent customers.

The exclusive retailer was strengthened as a further segment, that is, dealers who only market the D2. Various measures were implemented that were particularly connected to the regional requirements of the branch offices. The same applied to forms of bulk distribution such as megastores and distributors whose market position means they have access to a considerable market potential.

INTRODUCTION OF THE 'CHAIN STORE' DISTRIBUTION CHANNEL

The D2 Classic Tariff was directly marketed through 'small and medium-sized companies' and 'key accounts' distribution channels. Mannesmann Mobilfunk decided that the D2 Fun Tariff should be marketed not only through indirect distribution channels, but also through a direct distribution channel. This is why they set up their own chain of retailers from the D2-Centre structure, the aim of which can be described as follows: in the private customer sector a defined market share must be generated through a separate distribution channel, so that the handling of this target group, which will have the most growth in future, remains independent of the indirect distribution channels.

In addition to this, an independent chain of stores must set quality standards for retailers and compete with these in an area. Last but not least, a separation from the retail structure of the competition must be achieved, that is, especially with regard to German Telekom.

ACHIEVEMENTS IN SETTING UP A CHAIN OF STORES

The setting up of a chain of stores achieved the following aims:

- blanket coverage;
- competition in Mannesmann's own distribution channels;
- high rate of turnover;
- sales promotion;
- quality standards;
- management of sales personnel; and
- chain stores as mobile phone specialists.

In contrast to the D2-Centre, the retail shops to be created did not need their own installation workshops. The product placement on the market, price reductions and continuous technical improvements to mobile phones provided a platform for shops in 1A situations in town centres without installation workshops. By the end of 1997 the chain of stores had been extended to 150 outlets, providing blanket coverage throughout Germany.

This blanket coverage means that the customer can take out a D2 service contract either in one of Mannesmann's own D2 shops or at a dealer. The proximity of these sales outlets, which are independent of each other, means that they must constantly implement improved procedures to compete with each other.

The mass market that begins in the growth phase demands immediate implementation of marketing and distribution decisions. This is why the retail distribution structure has been designed to enable fast reactions and a high turnover ratio.

The product range was limited to a fairly small variety of telephones. The same applies to the accessories available. Products which were not directly connected to the conclusion of a D2 service contract were not included in the product range. A goods management system was introduced to speed up the cash transactions. The format of the service contract was reduced to the basic essentials and only consists of one page in order to speed up the signing of a contract at the point of sale. The regular placement of advertisements in the regional press ensures many enquiries at the D2 branches.

Measures were implemented so that the customer experiences high service quality in the D2 chain stores in spite of a high turnover ratio. Quality standards were fixed for the exterior and interior of the stores. The D2 shops differ from classic retailers in that the relatively small product range means that there is no shelf space competition. This enables a generous interior design, which leads to improved customer satisfaction. The employees are regularly trained to improve the quality of advice they give. The planning and so the definition of marketing goals for every single sales person in the store is also part of the implementation of a distribution channel. The employees of the stores have variable earnings depending on goals achieved.

These measures promoted the exceptional status of the D2 stores. However, this was finally achieved through the D2 stores selling exclusively the core product of mobile phones, in contrast to the retail outlets of the main competitor, the German Telekom (T-Punkt shops). The German Telekom's T-Punkt shops sell fixed network and other German Telekom telecommunication products as well as mobile telephone products. The specialist dealers also market very different kinds of products, which meant that the D2 shops and D2 centres were the sales points specialising in mobile phones.

HIGHER MARKET PRESENCE IN SMALL AND MEDIUM-SIZED FIRMS AND KEY ACCOUNTS

In the sector of key accounts, the market growth could clearly be seen through increased areas of application for mobile phones. The customers, that is, the firms, remained the same. However, the target groups within the company structures expanded. Improved technology meant that fax and data applications via mobile phones became solutions for company requirements. Examples of this are applications for managing sales representatives, telemetry or for the company's internal phone system.

As the market growth in the business customer sector in particular took place through these applications and firms needed intensive expert customer care, the sales areas in the 'small and medium-sized companies' and 'key accounts' distribution channels were successively scaled down. A sales representative now has a smaller number of customers to look after and so is better able to meet the customer's requirements. In addition to this system, consultants were introduced to provide technical support. The tariff structure was expanded accordingly with the introduction of D2 data, a product used exclusively for data transmission and the transmission of short messages.

As decisions about contracts are made by the heads of large companies, Mannesmann Mobilfunk's 'key account' distribution channel also set up a key account management system to manage the penetration of the closed conditions in the subsidiaries and associated companies of the group. The key account manager negotiates the conditions here and is responsible for their implementation throughout the subsidiaries and associated companies of the groups by the regional sales representative.

CONTROL INSTRUMENTS OF SELECTIVE MARKETING POLICY

When controlling marketing activities it is particularly important to react quickly to market developments in the growth phase. The differentiated distribution control system was constantly optimised for this. This enables the sales management to analyse the sales activities from daily, weekly and monthly reports and to implement corrective action. In particular this means analysing which sales results are achieved by whom, where, and using which means. The sales are depicted daily according to tariffs in the separate distribution channels. This information can be provided right up to the individual sales outlets, be they specialist dealers, retailers or sales representatives, centrally and regionally. To supplement the distribution channel-orientated depiction of the results, market shares are also determined according to area in order to analyse better the penetration achieved. Decisions about distribution channels, for example, locations for retailers or partner agencies, are in turn derived from this.

The funds used, that is, the profitability of the distribution channels, must also be monitored. For this, comparisons of the individual distribution channels are available.

RESULTS AND OUTLOOK

Until the start of the growth phase, the market shares between D1 and D2 were about the same, although D1 tended to be the market leader. With the introduction of the Fun Tariff aimed at 'leisure time users', D2 achieved market leadership and continued to extend this until the end of 1997. At the end of 1997 around 3.5 million customers telephoned in the D2 network. A main reason for the market leadership was the consistent portrayal of product and pricing policy in the distribution channel policy.

The next fundamental change to the mobile phone market in Germany was the introduction of rechargeable mobile phone cards. The introduction of these cards again requires an adaptation of the distribution channel structure. Furthermore, on 1 January 1998 the go-ahead was given for the liberalisation of fixed network telecommunications in Germany, which also has an influence on the distribution channel structure of Mannesmann Mobilfunk through the involvement of Arcor, the fixed network subsidiary of the Mannesmann group. After all this it is becoming clear that, in future, decisions made by Mannesmann Mobilfunk concerning distribution channels will be constantly reviewed and steadily developed.

MANNESMANN MOBILFUNK'S D2 PRIVATE NETWORK

In December 1989 the go-ahead was given for D2 Privat when the Minister for Post and Telecommunications, Dr Christian Schwarz-Schilling, awarded Mannesmann Mobilfunk the licence to operate the first private digital mobile telecommunications network in Germany. For the first time, competition in the field of speech transmission was opened up between the German government-owned telephone company, Deutsche Bundespost Telekom, and a private operator.

Only two and a half years after obtaining the licence, Mannesmann Mobilfunk began the commercial operation of the D2 Privat network in June 1992. Six months later, Mannesmann Mobilfunk welcomed its 100,000th customer. At the end of 1993, almost 500,000 subscribers were registered with D2 Privat and at the end of 1997 3,500,000 customers made calls in the D2 network. This trend continues to be very positive. Mannesmann Mobilfunk has been operating in the black since 1994, one year earlier than expected. In 1997 Mannesmann Mobilfunk's revenues amounted to DM 5.6 billion

Mannesmann Mobilfunk's headquarters are located in Düsseldorf. D2 Privat has approximately 5500 employees throughout Germany. Eight branch offices (Berlin, Dortmund, Radebeul/Dresden, Ratingen/Düsseldorf, Frankfurt, Langenhagen/Hanover, Munich and Stuttgart) are responsible for sales and distribution, radio network planning and network operations in their respective regional markets. Today the D2 network covers more than 98 per cent of the total area of Germany.

EXTENSIVE RANGE OF SERVICES

Another decisive factor in the success of D2 Privat was its extensive range of services that enhance the ease of use of mobile phones. Mannesmann Mobilfunk constantly strives to improve and to expand its services. The range of services starts with D2 mailbox (the free-of-charge network-integrated voice mail service), call barring, call forwarding and caller number display, and also includes information services such as directory information and call completion, traffic information, D2 breakdown service and travel and hotel reservation services. Furthermore, facsimilie and data transmission services make it possible to exchange written information through the D2 network.

TELEPHONING ABROAD WITH THE D2 CARD

D2 customers can make calls across national borders. This service is part of the GSM standard on which the D2 network is based. This standard creates uniform guidelines for digital mobile radio communications and allows cross-border roaming throughout Europe without requiring any customs formalities for the purchase of mobile phones. As a result of this joint standard, it was possible to create a uniform infrastructure as the basis for a pan-European mobile communications market. Moreover, many overseas countries have also accepted the GSM standard.

MANNESMANN MOBILFUNK FACTS AND FIGURES

- *Licence awarded*: December 1989
- *Start of commercial operation*: June 1992
- *Ownership*: 65 per cent Mannesmann AG
  35 per cent Air Touch Communications
- *Turnover*:
31.12.1992	DM 138 million
31.12.1993	DM 902 million
31.12.1994	DM 1.745 billion
31.12.1995	DM 2.7 billion
31.12.1996	DM 4.2 billion
31.12.1997	DM 5.6 billion
- *Subscriber numbers*:
December 1992	100,000
December 1993	500,000
December 1994	850,000
December 1995	1,450,000
December 1996	2,300,000
December 1997	3,500,000

QUESTIONS FOR DISCUSSION

1 How would you assess the service delivery and product differentiation within the product life cycle of Mannesmann D2 mobile phones?
2 What are the prerequisites to start market segmentation?
3 How would you assess the conception of D2 chain stores in contrast to the chain stores of the prime competitor, German Telekom – D1?
4 What are the advantages of key account management when looking after large customers and service providers?
5 What alternative distribution structures could you imagine for Mannesmann Mobilfunk – D2? What advantages and disadvantages do you see in those chosen by D2?
6 From your own experience, what future developments do you think are possible for Mannesmann Mobilfunk – D2, particularly in relation to the structure of distribution channels?
7 What was the business environment like for this business from 1997 to 2002?
8 What was the impact of the takeover of Mannesmann by Vodaphone in 2000?

CS11 EUROPEAN BUTTER BATTLES THE NEW ZEALAND DAIRY BOARD AND SPREADABLE BUTTER

MAUREEN BENSON-REA AND
RICHARD HADLEY

The New Zealand Dairy Board (NZDB) was the statutory marketing body for the New Zealand dairy industry. As the country's largest multinational food marketing organization with a 1997–98 turnover of NZ$7.7 billion, the NZDB exported to over 115 markets, employed approximately 6500 people, and possessed an international network of 80 subsidiaries and allied companies. In July 1999 the New Zealand Dairy Board was contemplating rebuilding a European product market that it had originally opened and which was suddenly taken away from it in the space of a few short years. As the NZDB began its campaign to win back its market share in spreadable butter, the organization reflected on the events of the past couple of years and on current trading conditions for its products in Europe.

The NZDB had been created in 1961 as the marketing arm of a cooperative industry. The farmers owned the dairy manufacturing companies, which in turn were shareholders in the Board. The NZDB then purchased the dairy produce from the companies and subsequently sold it through a worldwide marketing infrastructure. Thus the Board played a valuable coordination role in the industry, capturing market information and ensuring that the dairy companies were satisfying demand. In summary, the NZDB's two functions were to administer and coordinate the sector, and to market and distribute the industry's produce, with the industry's structure invoking comparisons to a vertically integrated multinational business.

While the Board held an export monopoly in the New Zealand dairy industry, it operated in an extremely competitive and protected international environment. Although only around 5 per cent of global milk production was traded internationally in the form of dairy products, of this 5 per cent New Zealand accounted for approximately 25 per cent of world trade, second only to the European Union (EU) on 47 per cent. Hence, the Board could wield considerable influence in the international dairy trade arena, demonstrated by its domination (with the EU) of the International Dairy Arrangement, which set baseline prices. Since its inception, increasing competitive pressures had seen the NZDB progress from being a subsidised commodity exporter to a competitive international marketer of predominantly value-added products.

THE NZDB IN THE EU (1996–98)

The NZDB operations in the EU came under the umbrella of its subsidiary Milk Products Holdings (Europe) Ltd. This holding company and its subsidiaries provided the NZDB with revenues of NZ$1,487,170 for 1997–98, up approximately 19 per cent from the previous period. Dairy products accounted for 20 per cent of New Zealand's total merchandise trade earnings, covering milk powders, cheeses, proteins and milk fat.

The Uruguay round of GATT

New Zealand's access to the EU market had been restricted for some years. The negotiation of a special agreement, Protocol 18 (1971), allowed New Zealand, under certain criteria, to continue to export to the UK on that country's accession to the EU. However, the conclusion of the Uruguay Round of the General Agreement on Tariffs and Trade (GATT) in 1995 offered considerable promise for the NZDB and the dairy industry, with improved steps towards liberalising world trade and the dismantling of protectionist measures. As a result, the quota for butter access to the EU increased from 52,180 tonnes to 76,767 tonnes annually, while there was also an increase in cheese sales permitted. Furthermore, quotas were guaranteed until the year 2000, rather than the previous system of regular re-negotiation.

Butter had been an important New Zealand export to the EU, and competition with the subsidised local competitors was intense. As butter was a commodity product there was also a strong need to differentiate the Board's produce, thus increasing the opportunity to maximise returns for New Zealand dairy farmers. Introducing spreadable butter under the Anchor brand in the early 1980s was an attempt to do just that, and this product had since experienced considerable growth in demand. In 1996 it remained unchallenged in its market segment.

The GATT agreement allowed New Zealand to export 77,000 tones of butter a year to the EU. Of this, spreadable butter made up 5000 tonnes, with a retail value of about NZ$45 million a year. In comparison, the same quantity of ordinary butter would earn about NZ$34 million. While the added value was important to New Zealand, the flow on opportunities it created were also valuable. Spreadable butter was increasing New Zealand's customer base, attracting in particular the young and affluent.

Common Agricultural Policy reforms

In 1992, the EU began initialising reform of its Common Agricultural Policy (CAP). Along with a decrease in financial assistance, the completion of the GATT Uruguay Round increased the competitive pressure on the European agricultural sector. New Zealand's increased access to their market added to the discontent amongst EU agriculture officials. It also led to the suspicion in New Zealand that its exports could be hit by non-tariff trade barriers, a protectionist measure whereby a country's trade appears open but uses strict regulatory regimes to discriminate against imports. Indeed, the European Dairy Association acknowledged that 'Australia and New Zealand are the EU's main competition in the world market' and that recent EU reforms would ultimately expose the EU dairy sector to even more intense competition both at home and in world markets.

THE DISPUTE BEGINS

New Zealand butter already adhered to strict guidelines under a concession made upon the UK's membership of the EU. Apart from the UK, most butter manufactured and consumed in the rest of the EU was unsalted, with a fat content usually between 82 per cent and 85 per cent. Therefore, to be eligible under the export quota and retain access to the UK, yet still protect producers in the other member countries, New Zealand butter had to meet certain conditions. It had to be:

- of New Zealand origin;
- at least six weeks old;
- of a fat content by weight of not less than 80 per cent but less than 82 per cent; and
- manufactured directly from milk or cream.

In September 1995, Dutch Customs officers took samples of New Zealand butter for laboratory analysis of the fat content. The test results showed a fat content of more than 82 per cent, with the range of excess fat content between 0.1 per cent and 1.5 per cent. Consequently, the Dutch authorities imposed a penalty of NZ$1.8 million worth of extra duties. However, the Board claimed that the Dutch analytical instruments employed were inaccurate, as the figures generated were inconsistent with the NZDB's own measurements of the shipment before it left New Zealand. The Dutch denied this claim, and while the Board paid the outstanding duties, appeal proceedings with the European Commission were initiated.

The 'direct manufacture' criterion

In November 1996, the British Department of Customs and Excise notified the NZDB that its right to export spreadable butter under the preferential tariff of

Protocol 18 was to be challenged. This serious threat arose from a difference in interpretation over the definition of the butter manufacturing process. Customs contended that spreadable butter was manufactured from a butter concentrate, a process deemed as indirect, thus violating the EU regulations. A couple of days later several members of the NZDB Anchor Foods subsidiary were arrested by British customs officers: a technicality under British customs law enabled officials to question the Board's staff about the content and manufacturing method. However, the British officials refused to believe that the spreadable butter product, which was made from a fractionated process where the hard fats were separated and removed, was a continuous process resembling direct manufacture from milk or cream. The NZDB, along with the New Zealand Government, protested to the Commission regarding the definition criteria and the manner in which the investigation was being conducted.

Around the same time further allegations arose, asserting that on a couple of occasions in 1995 and 1996 the NZDB had exceeded its butter quota, and though noted by British Customs, the excess had been passed through under a lesser tariff. This sequence of events triggered a closer scrutiny of New Zealand's imports and the search for further potential regulatory improprieties.

In spite of these events, the NZDB Chairman, Sir Dryden Spring, commented that he was confident that the Board would beat the challenges, but did acknowledge that they were using up Board time, money and energy. This optimism was tested, however, when a couple of weeks later the Commission ruled in favour of the British Customs and Excise. As a result the Board now faced having to pay an extra NZ$3500 a tonne in extra duty on its spreadable butter exports. During a subsequent appeal the NZDB had been handicapped by commercial sensitivity, as fully disclosing the spreadable butter manufacturing process would have aided competitors, since no rival had yet managed to duplicate the process. The Board spokesperson, Neville Martin, responded to the judgement expressing the frustration felt by the Board:

> It is what butter always has been – butter made from cream with nothing else but salt and water. It is just that this butter is soft and ordinary butter is hard.

As a result of the ruling the Board was left with no option but to begin to assemble its appeal case for the Commission, and consider utilising World Trade Organisation (WTO) reconciliation avenues. The Board asserted that definitions needed to be clarified to include spreadable butter. At the same time, in order to maintain its UK market stake and avoid the increased tariffs, the NZDB moved its technology to a European company and a local milk supply. November 1996 eventually brought brighter news for the embattled NZDB. Since the ruling and the increase in duty on spreadable butter, sales had doubled thereby reconfirming the decision to change manufacturing locations. In addition, industry commentators suggested that British media coverage of the dispute had created the impression amongst British consumers that officials were trying to keep the product from them.

1997: more trouble for the board

Unfortunately 1997 started badly for the Board, with the Commission upholding the earlier ruling. As a result, the Board considered taking the case to the European Court of Justice. A further consequence was that even though it had to pay compensation to the New Zealand dairy companies that produced for export, the Board decided to continue with its European spreadable butter production to avoid paying the extra tariff.

The ruling also coincided with the visit to New Zealand by Dr Franz Fischler, the EU Commissioner for Agriculture. However, NZDB and government talks with the Commissioner failed to make progress towards resolving the dispute over spreadable butter exports. Dr Fischler told New Zealand officials that he supported the European Commission ruling and felt it was more of a technical nature than politically based. The suggestion that this dispute could lead to wider trade ramifications for exports of primary produce saw the New Zealand Government prepare to have the matter referred to the WTO.

At the same time as the Commissioner's visit to New Zealand, the NZDB was faced with yet another challenge to its European butter exports. It was revealed that the Commission was also questioning the Board's use of a more conventional butter production method that had been in use for a number of years. The Europeans claimed that this process, like that used for spreadable butter, did not meet the technical specifications for New Zealand's reduced tariff. Again the spectre of increased import duties loomed. Nevertheless, although only approximately 10 per cent of New Zealand's total butter production was made with this process, the NZDB halted exports of this butter too until the matter could be resolved. In the following month, March, it was the turn of NZDB's cheese exports to be challenged.

The 'End Use' criterion

This new objection had arisen out of a European Court of Auditors' report. From the audit findings, the Commission ruled that the Board would have to pay an extra NZ$2808 per tonne in duty if it wished to keep supplying one of its British customers. This ruling came despite the Board having supplied the customer for nearly four years under the low-tariff that applied to New Zealand's cheese quota. The cheese contract itself only represented approximately 2.5 per cent of New Zealand's 'cheese for processing' 4000-tonne quota. The EU had decided that the British customer's use of the cheese for sauces did not fall within the quota's definition of acceptable end uses of 'cheese for processing'. In addition, the Commission also ordered the NZDB to back-pay the extra duty, though subsequently dropping that particular request when contested by the Board. Although the NZDB could have managed without this one customer, it decided to appeal against the decision on principle. On 24 March the New Zealand Government formally asked the WTO to begin a dispute resolution process in order to resolve the dispute over the spreadable butter. This was the first time New Zealand had initiated a formal settlement process on its own under either the WTO or its predecessor, the GATT.

Criminal charges laid

In a surprise move on 18 April, British Custom officials arrested the entire London-based management team of the NZDB European operations. The six executive managers, Monny Verschuren, Alan Absolon, Fernando Guerra, Jens Haughstrup, Gualb Sharma and Colin Bell, were charged with a NZ$12.8 million fraud relating to butter exports in 1995 and 1996. Customs asserted that the Board had claimed lower tariffs on some butter consignments in 1996, knowing that its quota had already been exhausted. It turned out that two parcels of butter representing 1 per cent of New Zealand's annual butter imports to the UK were behind the charges, with two misdemeanours alleged:

- the butter contained more fat than allowed; and
- the NZDB paid a lower, old GATT agreement quota levy, when it should have paid the higher new GATT tax.

Customs had investigated five consignments in 1995 and 1996 and alleged that some had been declared at the preferential rate when the relevant quota was believed to have been exhausted, and that others had failed to meet all the qualifying conditions. On appearance in the City of London magistrates' court the executives pleaded not guilty, and were subsequently released on bail. An interesting point in the proceedings was that the Board had not been named as a defendant in the case. Instead the executives were charged with committing crimes for the Board's financial benefit rather than for personal gain. Verscheuren, the Board's highest ranking official in Europe, faced six charges laid under the 1979 Customs and Excise Act, while the others including Guerra, the Managing Director of Anchor in the UK, faced three. Along with unlimited fines, the charges carried jail terms of up to seven years. During this time the NZDB argued that this was a trade matter rather than a criminal matter, but Customs countered with the argument that duty evasion was in fact fraud and therefore a criminal offence.

Unsurprisingly, the news of the arrests was received in New Zealand with astonishment and anger, with the belief developing that they were part of a European campaign of harassment against New Zealand dairy exports. While the Board admitted to regulatory confusion, it had since paid the outstanding tax, an extra NZ$420,000, on the two parcels. However, it continued to strenuously deny that the butter fat composition was in breach of the regulations. British Customs representatives also arrived in New Zealand to gather evidence, though the New Zealand Government insisted that only relevant documents would be provided.

Around the same time there was more disturbing news for the NZDB. Reports began to surface that the supermarket chain Sainsbury's, in partnership with a newly privatised farm research and consultancy company, ADAS, had begun to produce the UK's first spreadable butter, achieved by feeding the cows a special oil-rich diet. However, better news for the Board was that the spreadable butter line was growing by 20 per cent a year in Britain. Anchor believed that demand existed for at least twice the 6000 tonnes of spreadable butter it was allowed to sell.

During this time the New Zealand Government received a fair share of media and public criticism for their lack of action in the dispute. However, in their defence, the court charges against the NZDB executives hindered government action, for it could not interfere in the British legal system. The arrests had coincided with the British election when, in effect, Britain was without a government for New Zealand to approach. Furthermore, because the Board was a private company, the government was only looking to deepen its involvement if there was evidence that the charges were trumped up and if the case raised any broad trade policy issues.

The case took a significant step forward in July 1997 when the Board's lawyers did not contest committal proceedings and the case was set down for the Old Bailey for mid-August. The Board wanted the case heard in the higher court rather than by magistrates, to speed up the legal process. Even so, it did not expect the case to come to trial until September 1998. The Board also revealed that it had set aside NZ$10 million to fight the case, with none of that a contingency fund in case it lost the case.

A positive development in the court proceedings occurred in early October 1997, when British Customs decided to drop five of its seven charges against the Board's executives. While the Board applauded the move, it also signalled its intentions to vigorously pursue its right under British law to recover costs. It also saw the move as justification of its belief that the charges were unjustified. As well as this move, the Board had also begun to prepare its test case for the British legal system, with the hearing set to be heard in early December.

The appeals

In late January 1998 the British Customs Duty and Value Added Tax Tribunal ruled in favour of the Board, thus beginning to clear the way for the normalisation of its European operations. The legally binding nature of the ruling meant that the WTO case was now suspended. However, a month later Customs decided to appeal the Tribunal ruling. Board Chairman, Sir Dryden Spring, commented that while the NZDB was disappointed and exasperated with the decision, it would vigorously contest the appeal and was confident that the decision would be upheld. Also as expected the Board approached the New Zealand Government to reactivate the WTO case. Again it was reported that the prolonging of the legal battle continued to cost the New Zealand dairy farmer in terms of legal costs and lost market opportunities.

The Court of Auditors' report

However, that was not to be the last setback for the Board. April was to prove a stormy month for the Board, with the European Court of Auditors revealing another damaging report regarding New Zealand's butter exports to the EU. Essentially, the report claimed that the NZDB owed the EU almost NZ$900 million in unpaid import duties from the period 1973 to 1995. However, due to the three-year restriction on seeking back duties the claim was limited to NZ$236 million. The basis for the claim revolved around the contention that butter imported during this period exceeded butterfat limits, and thus was ineligible for New Zealand's preferential tariff. It also made the assertion that the legitimacy of the exports during this period were questionable, because they were not subject to a system of import licensing. Regarding the latter point, the Board was quick to point out that the regulations of that time did not require it. The Court also recommended that the Board be stripped of its approval to issue import certificates. In addition, the report also criticised the slack monitoring practices of the EU and British Customs.

While it queried the Court's interpretations, the NZDB also expressed serious misgivings about the methodology employed to calculate the duties owed. However, because of the matter of excessive butterfat already before the British courts, the NZDB was unable to formally challenge those findings. While the Board was confident of determining the Auditor's findings as wrong in fact and law, to do so would probably have taken many years and dollars. The New Zealand Government also suggested that the assessment compliance with the quota requirements raised complex technical and statistical issues that the Luxembourg Court appeared to have completely ignored.

In Brussels, however, the Commission agreed that because the audit did not accurately reflect either a loss of anticipated revenue to the EU or any potential benefit that might have been accrued to the NZDB, then recovery of the full amount would be unlikely. But it was also considered unlikely that the Board would escape without being forced to pay some of the NZ$236 million. Regarding a possible political settlement, the big question mark as the political and trade commentators saw it was the attitude of the European Parliament, which included a large number of MEPs representing rural constituencies, therefore making them more likely to favour punitive action against New Zealand. Furthermore, even if a reduced claim passed Parliament it would then require a unanimous vote by the Commission, including its French and Irish members, countries traditionally hostile towards the NZDB's success.

On a more optimistic note, the NZDB did manage to win a couple of its ongoing battles against British Customs, as the remaining fraud charges were dropped and Custom's High Court appeal against the earlier Tribunal ruling dismissed. Unfortunately, the case had weakened Anchor's spreadable butter market leadership, with competitors now arriving in increasing numbers. Nonetheless, the Board contended that rival products included vegetable oils and that its Anchor brand was the only pure spreadable butter. But a few days after their appeal failed, British Customs lodged another appeal, this time with the Court of Appeal in London, leaving Sir Dryden Spring further exasperated by the whole process:

> We confront some extraordinary situations in marketing our butter around the world. This, however, is the most absurd of all. It is astounding that trade barriers are erected when even the courts of the country concerned dismiss them.

This appeal was finally dismissed and the Board awarded costs. However, the Board could not celebrate yet, as it still had a number of other legal battles continuing in the UK and EU courts.

Thus, at the peak of Anchor spreadable butter sales in the UK, the British Customs had quite unexpectedly begun to investigate the butter quota regulations. During the ensuing battle over spreadable butter, the EU-based competition had seized the opportunity built in this new product category and plugged the gap that Anchor had created in an innovative leadership position.

QUESTIONS FOR DISCUSSION

1 Would the NZDB and its Anchor brand be able to reclaim lost ground?
2 What is NZDB's future in the EU market?
3 Why did New Zealand have almost a veto right on the UK's entry into the EU in 1971?
4 How important is it for non-member countries to lobby within the EU?
5 Is organic status important for New Zealand?
6 How is New Zealand increasingly marketing its food products within Europe and the US?

CS12 PERKINS FOODS: THE PLACE OF PUBLIC RELATIONS IN THE PROFILE OF A EUROPEAN FOOD BUSINESS

DANNY MOSS AND DAVID DAVIES

This case examines the role that public relations has played in helping a growing European own-label food company, Perkins Foods, to strengthen its position in both the UK and European frozen and chilled foods markets. The case illustrates how a carefully crafted public relations strategy can help to build a strong corporate profile within key markets and within the City for a company that does not have the advantages of a prominent consumer brand image.

BACKGROUND

Perkins Foods PLC is unusual among stock market listed food industry groups in the UK. In contrast with those companies that began as manufacturers or suppliers in a particular product sector, growing and diversifying by acquisition, Perkins was created in 1987 as a listed, customer-led, flexible and varied European convenience foods group.

On the face of it, that would seem to present a company with a clear identity profile – the starting point for a cohesive, consistent and effective strategy. However, the first five years or so of Perkins Foods' existence had somewhat different implications for its public relations (PR) function.

Perkins existed initially as a City entity. Its profile as a group existed according to its share value and prospects – its attractiveness and performance for shareholders and potential shareholders. For some considerable time it did not have any widespread or consistent PR profile in its business sectors, which were the north European grocery retail, wholesale, food service and food manufacturing environments. The companies that had become members of the Perkins group continued to operate and trade in their own names and, in almost every case, with the same senior management. Perkins' companies were based in the UK, The Netherlands, Luxembourg, Germany and France, manufacturing and/or selling frozen and chilled meat products, pizzas, pasta and other ready meals, potato specialities, seafoods, processed mushrooms and fresh fruit and vegetables.

In each case, Perkins' companies had established reputations in their respective market sectors.

THE FROZEN AND CHILLED FOOD MARKET

The frozen and chilled food sector has been one of the fastest growing sectors of the food market throughout Europe over the past 30 years. The growth of frozen food sales has been driven by a number of factors. First, changes in consumer lifestyles have seen an increased emphasis on convenience food purchases. Improvements in refrigeration and packaging technology have allowed huge improvements in storage times, and the growth of major supermarket chains across Europe has enabled consumers to have access to a vastly increased range of reasonably-priced frozen foodstuffs. This desire for greater convenience and ease of storage of foodstuffs on the part of consumers, together with the falling real costs of refrigeration equipment, has encouraged consumers to embrace the convenience food culture that has been long established in the US.

Chilled foods emerged on the market during the 1980s, again targeted at the growing convenience sector of the food market, but with a higher quality reputation than frozen foods (because of their 'fresher', less 'processed' appearance). Consumers have tended to perceive chilled foods as better quality than their frozen alternatives and hence have been prepared to pay a premium for them. Ironically, many consumers having purchased chilled products put them in the freezer, unaware that a frozen-at-source version would undoubtedly be of better quality than a slowly home-frozen one.

Frozen and chilled foods have become popular even in countries such as France, where traditional cooking and preparation methods using only fresh ingredients have long been seen as a central part of their culture. However, consumption patterns for frozen and chilled foods do vary across Europe, with Denmark having the largest per capita consumption (41.4 kg) followed by the UK (38.5 kg) and Norway (32.9 kg), whereas in countries such as The Netherlands (19.8 kg), Spain (20.6 kg) and Italy (10.1 kg) consumption of frozen foods in particular is far lower.[1]

To some degree, these variations in consumption patterns reflect the differing climates and agricultural traditions across Europe, but also reflect differing consumer attitudes and traditions with respect to food preparation and consumption.

Estimates of the size of the frozen and chilled food market in Europe vary considerably because of the diverse and fast-changing range of products within this sector and because of the different measurement methods that have been

---

[1]Estimates taken from *European Frozen Food Economy 1997*, Quick Frozen Foods International.

employed. One set of estimates of frozen food consumption within Europe suggest that total consumption reached around 8.8 billion metric tons in 1997 (excluding frozen poultry – 9.96 billion metric tons including poultry[2]). Here the UK had by far the largest consumption of frozen food, with sales of over 2.6 million metric tons, followed by Germany (2.1 million) and France (1.9 million). In contrast, frozen food consumption in Italy amounted to only 596,000 metric tons and in Austria 184,000 metric tons. A recent *Key Notes* report suggests that frozen food sales in the UK will rise from £4 billion in 1994 to around £6 billion in 2003 (at retail values), a growth rate of 3–4 per cent per annum. However, within this overall figure, the *Key Notes* report suggests that more 'traditional' product sectors such as frozen vegetables, meat, poultry and fish have experienced more limited growth, with newer 'value-added' products such as ready meals experiencing far faster growth in sales. Here, for example, frozen pizza sales have grown by 48 per cent during 1994–98, while frozen vegetarian foods have grown by 35 per cent over the same period.

Figures for the consumption of chilled foods are more difficult to estimate, and vary wildly depending on what products are included in the estimates. Some estimates include such products as yoghurts and cheeses and prepared salads. If estimates are confined only to chilled versions of established frozen convenience foods (chilled ready-meals, pizza and pasta and so on), the figure for UK sales has been estimated to be currently in the region of £4 billion. However, despite the lack of accurate figures, there is little doubt that the chilled food sector has expanded remarkably both within the UK as well as within Europe in recent years.

Given the size and growth of the frozen and chilled food market in Europe, it is not hard to see why Perkins Foods have enjoyed considerable success in recent years. However, like all food sectors, the frozen and chilled foods market is an extremely competitive one, particularly for producers and suppliers. To be successful, firms need to ensure rigorous quality standards and constant product innovation, as well as needing to build strong relationships with the major retailers who increasingly dominate the consumer marketplace.

PERKINS' GROWTH STRATEGY

Many medium-sized and larger parent groups in the food industry have often acquired companies in order to obtain assets, facilities, brands and market positions, shaping or absorbing their acquisitions into their existing profile and culture. Perkins set itself up to be an acquisitor not as an end in itself, but in order to construct a group to grow and compete with the most powerful in Europe. It set out to this goal by identifying and acquiring companies providing it with:

---

[2]Estimates taken from *European Frozen Food Economy 1997*, Quick Frozen Foods International.

- a variety of product sector coverage of interest to European multiple retailers;
- expertise in the production/sale of satisfying products across those sectors;
- sound respective market knowledge and management skills towards the profitable; manufacture and sale of these products; and
- high-quality manufacturing and new product developement (NPD) facilities with potential for expansion and positive return on investment.

PERKINS WHO?

This initial strategy for the construction and success of the group had two very distinct consequences in PR and marketing communications terms:

1 Perkins Foods PLC very quickly acquired a strong reputation in the City – as a skilled acquisitive group with a lean and efficient management structure and good prospects for shareholders – *but* ... a low-level physical presence coupled with acknowledged City skills did not give it a clear reputation as a food business.

2 Perkins Foods companies retained their existing identities as good companies in their respective product sectors, *but* ... they were not clearly badged as Perkins Foods companies, and their positive reputations as food manufacturers and suppliers was not rubbing off on Perkins Foods PLC.

Perkins' determination to buy viable food businesses and to construct an expert, customer-led European food group had enabled it to become a genuinely skilled food business. However, doing the right thing is often not enough. Being *seen* to be doing the right thing can be an essential management tool in maintaining corporate success. For this reason, public relations needed to be treated as far more than window dressing or 'spin'.

A few years into the so far short yet successful history of Perkins Foods, it was recognised that PR had an important role to play.

PUBLIC RELATIONS STRATEGY

Having recognised that Perkins Foods had not established a reputation as a 'hands on' food business, the company recognised the need for a strategically-orientated PR campaign. In other words, Perkins consciously avoided the common mistake of pursuing the broad objective of 'raising awareness', despite the obvious conclusion that a straightforward *lack* of awareness in the wider trade environment presented a problem.

From the outset (in 1991), in considering a PR strategy it was accepted that all communications (PR and marketing communications) should be carefully aligned with, and integral to, the company's corporate and commercial strategy. Having carefully constructed a group of trusted, expert food businesses in tune with European retail markets, it was recognised that any campaign to raise Perkins' profile should be based on the core values that comprised Perkins' identity.

TACTICS: PREACHING TO THE CONVERTED

The initial PR campaign for Perkins Foods PLC had a ready-made audience in the grocery and food trade press that serve its markets, and in many cases they were aware of the existence, activities and reputation of Perkins member companies. The task for PR was to place a Perkins 'branding' on this awareness – that a success for a Perkins company was a success for, and because of, Perkins Foods and the way it does business.

This media audience was also largely concentrated in the business-to-business sector. Perkins was and is primarily interested in the retail own-label sector, so there is little need to raise a public or consumer profile. Not only is there no 'profit' in this, with very few Perkins branded products in the marketplace, but also most major multiple retail customers would prefer their suppliers to actively avoid a strong consumer profile. A retailer prefers its customers to perceive a product bearing its name to be 'all its own work' and to protect relationships with its suppliers with as much anonymity as possible.

As already pointed out, Perkins Foods had built up a portfolio of companies across a wide range of product categories, chosen in simple terms because they did things the 'right way'. Creating a stronger corporate profile for the group as a whole meant promoting the activities of these companies as essentially 'The Perkins Way'. This created a symbiotic relationship demonstrated through trade media, in which good products, practices and service by Perkins' member companies showed Perkins Foods PLC to be a skilled and professional *food* business. At the same time, those individual companies could greatly enhance their existing reputations in the trade by being seen to have the gravitas of a progressive, growing and increasingly successful PLC behind them – with all of the investment, development and positive collaborative potential that that implied.

In practical terms, the PR campaign for Perkins Foods did not involve remarkable activities. It comprised traditional media relations support in the form of: product launch press releases; personnel appointment press releases; factory, production line or quality assurance facility investment stories; inclusion in trade press previews and reviews of major trade exhibitions; regular articles within trade press scheduled features on relevant product sectors, such as meat products, ready meals, pizza and pasta and so on. These fairly traditional, trade PR mechanisms were used, however, to support corporate PR objectives, in terms of the consistent themes applied to them.

Trade media relations activity resulted in coverage relating to a range of Perkins companies, activities and product ranges. Although the coverage and range of publications targeted has been quite varied, all of the articles were negotiated and written (some fully prepared for the publications, and some written by the publication based on information supplied), with the conscious objective of reflecting key strategic messages about Perkins Foods, that is: the range of specialised convenience food manufacturers within the group; the emphasis on continuous development of customer-orientated quality frozen and chilled convenience foods; a clear strategic focus on the frozen and chilled convenience sectors; and Perkins' understanding of, and concerted service provision to, multiple retail and food service customers.

Whatever their specific content, press materials would stress the concept of 'The Perkins Way', the principal elements of which comprised: technical and product knowledge; investment in leading-edge technology; cross-fertilisation of skills and ideas across the major European markets; understanding of retail customer (and consumer) needs; and partnership working methods with customers. Here key personnel from both the parent group and member companies would be quoted at every opportunity in order to apply a human face to these principles and to demonstrate that the parent group and Perkins' member companies thought and acted as one.

Another consequence of Perkins' low 'point of sale' presence has been very limited advertising activity. Some trade advertising has appeared in key trade directories and media, but chiefly as a PR more than purely advertising mechanism – demonstrating support by an important player for its marketplace and media, more than seeking a commercial response.

Perkins' advertising, as well as exhibition presences and group and divisional brochure materials, have been devised, written and produced to be consistent with the PR programme. In a sense, PR has taken the lead in setting the tone and emphasis for other market-related communications activities. One example of promotional support material used was the creation of a set of full colour brochure inserts included in a presentation leather Filofax offered to key buyers and City analysts to mark the Millennium.

EVOLUTION – FOCUS ON CONVENIENCE

Perkins Foods is still a relatively young food group, but it has changed substantially over the past 12 years. Strategic change, most notably in terms of the disposal of some of its member companies and the acquisition of new ones, has taken place as the evolution of its original purpose and ethos – not as a reaction to error or as any kind of U-turn in its mission or philosophy.

Companies have been acquired regularly by Perkins over the last seven years, again on the original basis of strong existing people, products, facilities and practices. The pattern of acquisitions has not signalled any significant change of direction in the company's strategy. However, Perkins' more recent disposal of its fresh produce division and its move into markets apart from own-label retail products, most notably the food service sector in 1999, has raised some eyebrows in the retail and food industries and in the City.

In 1996 it was decided to dispose of the UK-based speciality seafood's business and of two companies processing mushrooms in various packaged forms. This was not as a result of their performance; the seafood business in particular was extremely successful, and still is, in supplying exotic fish and seafoods for supermarket fresh fish counters. Neither was compatible with the dynamics of the increasingly successful convenience foods businesses. More than a dozen of these businesses, operating in five countries, were working well together, sharing expertise and market knowledge and even combining products to meet specific new opportunities. The seafood and mushroom businesses did not effectively fit into this pattern.

The evolution of Perkins Foods as a modern frozen and chilled convenience foods business by the end of 1997 suggested the logic of disposing of its Dutch-based interests in fresh produce (sold for £33.6 million to Greenery International). The Fresh Produce Division was a major importer and supplier of high-quality fruit and vegetables to European supermarkets, but this is a very different business from convenience food manufacture and sales. Its disposal presented a sizeable PR challenge, as in the first half of 1998 it reduced the turnover of Perkins Foods PLC by almost 30 per cent, to £240.9 million. Thus, in handling the news of this disposal, great care had to be taken to communicate to the City that the move was entirely in line with the group's evolving business strategy.

This presented an excellent example of 'background' PR effects in one area of media supporting the impressions created in another. Coverage in food, retail and grocery trade press explaining the disposal in terms of a strategic business focus on the thriving and rapidly increasing sectors of frozen and chilled foods, are viewed in City circles as convincing evidence of clear business thinking on the part of the PLC. Analysts are perhaps more likely to take a cynical view of this focus being explained through direct briefings and coverage in the financial press (although this is also important) on a 'they would say that, wouldn't they' basis, than they are of positive coverage of this kind in core trade press. Analysts do follow relevant trade press closely for corroborative evidence of a listed company's strategic thinking and actions, and this route of information was covered by Perkins' City PR specialist, Square Mile Public Relations, quoting trade press coverage generated by trade PR consultant David Davies, in dealings with financial audiences.

Positively, the disposal of the fresh produce business enabled Perkins to post a £33.6 million pre-tax profit on the sale after writing off £46 million of goodwill, previously charged against its reserves. This windfall profit resulted in a trebling of Perkins' earnings per share (29.7p compared with 9.7p in 1997), although basic earnings per share, excluding the profits of the disposal, were slightly lower than the previous year. This was due mainly to currency movements and the effects of adverse weather and poor Christmas trading in the UK.

Following the sale of the fresh produce division, Perkins made a number of acquisitions to strengthen its core business including, among others, companies manufacturing international high-quality ready meals and premium chilled sandwich fillings, pickles and relishes.

A feature of Perkins' growth strategy has been its move into new market sectors, in particular into the food service sector. Here Perkins has utilised the expertise, skills and products from within its remaining convenience food activities to form a UK-based specialist division serving major food service customers with products (uniquely with frozen *and* chilled products) from throughout the Perkins group. At the same time, a French-based initiative combining the products of four Perkins companies in three countries has launched a specialised service for the international in-flight catering sector.

These developments have been part of a carefully thought-out evolutionary strategy, rather than simply opportunist tactics. Here PR has played a vital role in communicating Perkins' strategy to these new markets and the established retail sector, where loyalty must be preserved. The key task for PR activity has been to portray Perkins, accurately, as a major European, customer-led convenience foods group, and a recipe for continuing success.

The launch of Perkins Foodservice is a case in point. Having presented itself consistently as something of a specialist in the multiple retail sector, not least in own-label, this move could have been seen as a 'U-turn' or as evidence that perhaps modest success in the retail sector needed to be supplemented by a move into food service. The rationale explained through trade publicity and complementary brochure work and trade advertising was that the food service sector has evolved from a basic 'manufacturer – wholesaler – scaterer' chain to a professional customer-orientated product and service provision. The major food service customers therefore serve their markets in a very similar way to the leading retailers, based on consistency, efficiency, quality and value, in turn relying upon sophisticated management control. Perkins' pedigree was in fact ideal to command the kind of expertise and knowledge necessary to meet the needs of these modern food service customers, indeed as the only truly integrated European group providing a vast range of (uniquely) frozen *and* chilled products all manufactured within a single group. This was the tone of the PR activity launching Perkins Food service.

PERKINS EXPERTISE AND CUSTOMER PARTNERSHIPS – 'RECIPES FOR SUCCESS'

Retailer own-labels may have been born as cheaper alternatives to television-advertised proprietary brands, but over the last 10 years or so they have been developed more as brands in their own right – competing with the brands on quality, convenience, innovation and interest more than on price. The major multiples are now major spenders on television advertising designed to promote their brand name, with separate, self-proclaiming economy alternatives established, such as Tesco Value and Kwik Save's 'No Frills'. Perkins has from the outset been unashamed about its role as an own-label manufacturer, and this has been central to its PR profile throughout the 1990s.

The challenges presented by the modern own-brand environment in terms of developing products that can compete with established brands for quality and value for money, as well as satisfying the rigorous demands of dominant multiple retailers, have been addressed by Perkins Foods by strengthening its product development teams and continuously introducing new ranges of convenience products. Here for example, Perkins has strengthened its teams of food technologists and chefs in the UK, The Netherlands, Luxembourg, Germany and France. The French team includes a Michelin Star Chef. Recent own-label successes include the launch of a range of frozen English fruit crumbles into France and a variety of restaurant-quality chilled complete meal solutions, such as Beef Bourguignon and Chicken Chasseur, in UK supermarkets.

Another popular assumption about the own-label sector is that it conveniently avoids brand support costs, but Perkins argues that this enables investment to be channelled into the evolution of convenience food development and manufacturing. Perkins has continued to invest in manufacturing facilities and technologies, as well as supporting retail customers' promotional costs. Regular unannounced factory audits are an accepted part of the working life of the modern own-label manufacturer, and the highest possible standards have to be maintained at all times.

The own-label sector is not governed by a single set of considerations. Operating across a number of European markets, different consumer attitudes come into play. Product quality, convenience and innovation top consumer 'wish lists' in the UK and France, but in Germany people still seek out own-label products, with price primarily in mind. This is perpetuated and accentuated by the strength of the hard discounters in Germany.

The move from own-label towards own-brand has also brought the importance of packaging into focus. This was one area in which earlier 'cheaper alternative' own-label products could save on costs, but today the strength of design and quality of photography and materials used is as important in own-label as it is in proprietary brands. Focus group research is now as common in Perkins Foods own-label product development, including packaging, as it is in branded products.

Discussions about new products are invariably two-way, with both parties drawing on a wealth of expertise in sourcing, technology, quality assurance, logistics, marketing, merchandising and a vital understanding of consumer attitudes and trends.

The process described above, of own-label evolving into own retailer's brand, has provided Perkins Foods with tremendous business opportunities over more than a decade. Many food manufacturers claim to work 'in partnership' with their customers, but this is really the only way to succeed in the own-label environment of the late 1990s. For Perkins Foods, by the mid-1990s the single most important factor in its business strategy has been to apply the best possible technology and skills, via detailed understanding of customers and their markets, to partnership working methods alongside Europe's biggest retail and food service customers.

This emphasis in Perkins Foods' strategy is in effect its 'recipe for success', and it is clearly visible in every strand and element in the company's PR-dominated (marketing) communications strategy. It is a strategy that has been of vital support to the commercial performance of Perkins Foods and to the continued success of its City profile. Moreover, it is a strategy that is continuously evolving in order to provide such support as the company approached its 13th year, and a new millennium.

As all of Perkins' communications activities have been formulated and executed, from a single cohesive 'brand essence' and positioning, a strapline has emerged to sum up Perkins' strengths within the convenience foods environment. This line is used consistently through all marketing communications materials and activities to sum up what makes Perkins Foods 'tick'.

All Perkins' products are now chef-developed and recipe-based convenience foods. Hence recipes for success. The key elements characterising Perkins Foods' professional offer – expert personnel, the latest technology, NPD skills, quality assurance, customer and market understanding, integration across companies and countries – also represent a recipe for success. Finally, Perkins Foods' unrivalled commitment and ability to work in partnership with customers to develop and provide products their customers want to buy is its ultimate recipe for success.

Everything the company does and everything it says through its PR and marketing communications strategies observes and communicates the ingredients that combine to make … *Perkins Foods ~ Recipes for Success.*

QUESTIONS FOR DISCUSSION

1 How can public relations be used to promote a company ?
2 What is bad public relations?
3 Is 'spin' used by some companies to promote their position in the marketplace?
4 Give three examples of bad and good public relations practice used by companies.
5 How do you build a corporate reputation?

CS13   ROYAL PHILIPS ELECTRONICS

MATT DODD, IRENE HARRIS
AND PHIL HARRIS

In the nineteenth century, the industrial revolution ushered in technological changes that reshaped industry, commerce and trade. Now at the beginning of the twenty-first century, a digital revolution is poised to have an equally dramatic impact.

In this case we consider if Europe's leading electronics conglomerate, Koninklijke ('Royal') Philips Electronics, is ready to challenge Japan's finest and examine how it is reshaping its businesses to take a lead role in the new digital world.

KEY ISSUES

The key issues of this development are:

- restructuring the business for profit;
- rebuilding brand confidence; and
- exploiting the opportunities of the digital convergence.

Digital is set to challenge the very structures and disciplines that Philips has put into place over its 100-years existence. It poses many questions for the Dutch conglomerate – how far can digital integration go; how should it structure its businesses as technology converges from one platform to another; and how far should it collaborate with its rivals to reduce the inhibitive costs involved whilst still retaining a competitive edge?

BACKGROUND

Philips grew from a small, family-run Dutch lamp factory founded in 1891 to become one of the world's largest electronics corporations employing over 230,000 people and with annual sales of DF67 billion (£19 billion). It prospered as a result of Gerard Philips' technical expertise and his brother's, Anton, foreign sales efforts.

By 1900, it had become Europe's third largest lightbulb maker. It adopted the name Philips Gloeilampenfabrieken (lightbulb factory) in 1912. The Netherlands' neutrality during the First World War allowed Philips to expand and integrate into glass manufacturing (1915) and X-ray and radio tubes (1918). The company started building plants abroad in the 1930s to avoid trade barriers and tariffs. During the Second World War Philips created US and British trusts to hold majority interests in North American Philips (NAP) and in Philips' British operations. Following the War, the company established hundreds of subsidiaries worldwide. It repurchased its British businesses in 1955; NAP in 1987. The company started marketing televisions and appliances in the 1950s. It entered a joint venture in electronic components with Matsushita in 1952. Philips introduced audiocassette, video-cassette recorders (VCR) and laser disc technology in the 1960s but had limited success with computers and office equipment. Despite its development of new technologies, in the 1970s Philips was unable to maintain market share against the onslaught of inexpensive goods from Japan. Meanwhile, NAP acquired the US consumer electronics corporation Magnavox in 1974. NAP acquired GTE Television in 1981 and Westinghouse's lighting business in 1983. In 1972 Philips launched Polygram, the music recording label, adding Island Records and A&M to the stable in 1989 and 1990 respectively.

Thus by the early 1990s Philips was left with a myriad of businesses that were testing the company's resources and resolve. Moreover, Philips' slowness to bring its new products to market saw its superior inventions usurped by inferior products such as the V2000 video system and the digital compact cassette (DCC), the former being out-marketed by the video home system (VHS) recorder and the latter by Sony with its mini disc system. These failures contributed to huge losses in the early 1990s. Philips has cut some 60,000 jobs and sold many of its loss-making businesses, including its computer division, its Magnavox Electronics Systems unit, and its stakes in appliance maker Whirlpool. For the first time Philips recognised that it must collaborate because the technology jumps were now too big and risky (see Gugler, 1992, Appendix 1, p. 88 of the original text). However, these partnerships have often ended in disaster since Philips' multi-business unit structure was often at odds with its alliance strategy. This was most vividly demonstrated by the collapse of the mobile phone joint venture with Lucent Technologies at the end of 1998.

These problems have led to poor productivity and profitability and an overall lack of focus. Drastic action was required and the first step was to decide which businesses should stay and which ones should go. This rationalisation process was started in the late 1980s and is still not finished. In a break with tradition, Philips appointed its first non-technical Chairman in 1996, Cor Boonstra. The former Sara Lee marketeer's first act that year was to sell the company's cellular communications business to AT&T, take a DF1 billion (£297 million) restructuring charge and merge the company's system integration unit with BSO/Origin to form Origin BV. Boonstra quickly realised that unravelling over 100 year's of

Table C13.1   Sales/profits during the period 1994–98

Year	Sales DF billions	Gross profits DF billions	Profit margin %
1994	52.4	2.7	5.2
1995	55.7	3.0	5.3
1996	59.7	0.9	1.6
1997	65.4	3.8	5.8
1998	67.1	1.5	2.2

Source: Philips Annual Report 1998

history has and is taking longer than expected. However, now at the beginning of the twenty-first century, a digital revolution is poised to make as dramatic impact as the one that heralded the twentieth century. If Philips is to survive the next 100 years it must act quickly – unless, of course, it wants to revert back to being a lightbulb manufacturer.

PERFORMANCE INDICATORS

Despite a steady improvement in sales, profitability still remains weak (see Table C13.1) and the company still has some way to go to rival the margins enjoyed by its Japanese counterparts.

Despite disposing of Polygram and Philips Car Systems, 1998 revenues remained on a par with 1997. However, Boonstra has moved quickly to reinvest the DF12 billion (£3.4 billion) gained from the sale of these businesses. The company has spent nearly 70 per cent of these monies; DF5.6 billion (£1.6 billion) on acquiring VLSI Technology, the microchip manufacturer, and bought a 50 per cent stake in the flat panel display maker, LG LCD, with an additional DF2.6 billlion (£0.7 billion) being earmarked for a new semi-conductor plant in Singapore.

As can readily be seen from Table C13.2, the two commodity sectors of lighting and semi-conductors are the only areas that generated healthy profits for the company in 1998. These two have been 'cash cows' for Philips for many years and without their contribution Philips would have made a loss in 1998. Cor Boonstra's challenge is to improve the fortunes of the Consumer Products division, which continues to under perform, notably the failed mobile telephone partnership with Lucent Technologies, but it accounts for more than 40 per cent of revenues and is now seen as the key cluster for future prosperity of the company.

RESTRUCTURING FOR PROFIT

Philips initiated a major restructuring initiative, Operation Centurion, in 1987. The overriding objective was to improve organisational productivity and

Table C13.2 Sales by product sector (1998)

Product sector	Sales (DF billions)	% of total	% profits
Lighting	9.8	15.0	13.2
Consumer products	27.5	41.0	(2.2)
Components	8.4	12.5	0.8
Semi-conductors	7.1	11.0	19.3
Professional products	10.0	15.0	(1.2)
Origin	2.3	3.0	3.6
Miscellaneous	2.0	3.0	(4.1)
Total	67.1	100.0	2.2

Source: Philips Annual Report 1998

profitability, which was still one of the poorest in the sector. The process is far from over as the sale of Polygram in 1998 demonstrates.

To sharpen the corporation's focus further, on his arrival Boonstra divided the company into two distinct entities: consumer and business electronics.

Some observers feel that Boonstra has not gone far enough and that Philips must decide whether it is to become a consumer- or business-led electronics business. The new chairman, however, sees no conflict between the high-volume consumer business and the business-to-business division, with the latter acting as 'breeding ground' for the high-volume consumer electronics division.

As Boonstra explains, 'Business Electronics has technology clusters that are of great value. We let them grow, operate them, and at a certain moment we evaluate whether we can grow them further, move them into a consumer area or part with them' (Philips Press Office, 1997).

There is a question mark over the medical systems division. It is not emotionally attached to the company, nor is it one of the fundamental blocks of the organisation. However, the acquisition of ATL Ultrasound in 1998 for US$800 million put paid to the rumours that it was likely to be sold off. Medical is a 'cash cow', it is a sound performer, maintains a market leading position (third in the world) and generates healthy revenues and profits for Philips, so there is no hurry to dispose of it in the short term.

This is in marked contrast to Polygram, wherein falling sales and profits meant that an approach in mid-1998 from Seagram to acquire the division was too good to refuse. The acquisition of Polygram in the 1980s made strategic sense, since it allowed Philips to push its new formats by producing music and videos on their newly developed systems.

However, Philips' newly developed DCC system never really captured the public's imagination and failed to establish itself as a major format. This was in stark contrast to Sony's mini disc system, which after a slow gestation period paid dividends. This is in spite of the fact that the Philips system was a superior product offering, since the end user could play old analogue cassettes on the system whereas Sony's system did not offer this functionality. Yet again Philips had been outsmarted by Sony's superior marketing. This, coupled with flagging sales and increased marketing costs at Polygram, only seemed to rub salt into Philips' already deep wounds.

In the Consumer Products division the major disappointment was Philips Consumer Communications (PCC), the company's mobile telephone joint venture with Lucent Technologies. The major reason that PCC ran into trouble was due to a clash of cultures. Both Philips and Lucent (formerly part of the AT&T empire) had old and strong cultures, which just did not gel when the venture hit hard times. Nonetheless, consumer communications is a vital component for the company's push into the digital convergence market and cannot be dropped from the portfolio.

> …We intend to stay in this business because of its strategic importance for our Consumer Electronics business … The consumer communications business has a natural spin-off to our products in the home and away areas and it offers us the capabilities needed for future digital products and home networks. (Philips Press Office, 1998b)

The alliance was a disaster. Formed in October 1997, in its 12 months of trading it did not make any profit despite heavy investment from both partners. Philips has now regained control of its original assets. It cannot exit the market because as telecommunications, computer and multimedia technologies converge, Philips must maintain a presence as it will be an important part of the 'digital mix' in tomorrow's high-volume electronics industry.

The company still hopes to find another partner for its 'third generation' (3G) mobile phone and in the medium term is focusing its efforts on improving the quality and functionality of its GSM model. In the other areas of Consumer Products the company is entrusting its faith in a number of new products that embrace the new digital arena. These include its digital video disc (DVD) player, flat-screened television, set-top boxes, Ambi – which turns your television into a PC – web television, digital television and most controversially its Super Audio CD System, which was developed with Sony as a rival to DVD audio products. Only time will tell if Philips wins this particular battle. The comforting thing this time around is that Sony is also committed to the new platform.

REBUILDING BRAND CONFIDENCE

Until the 1980s Philips was renowned for its ability to innovate. Notable achievements include X-ray technologies, audio-recording systems, television sets and energy-efficient lighting systems. Its ill-fated video recorder system, the V2000, brought an end to the company's Midas touch. This has been followed by two further white elephants, the Digital Compact Cassette (DCC) and Compact Disk Interactive (CDI) in the early 1990s.

These failures were costly, hitting company profits and credibility. The new chairman, Cor Boonstra, recognised the importance of rebuilding confidence in the Philips brand.

For many years the Philips brand statement was 'Philips invents for you'. However, the results of the company's first global consumer survey revealed that Philips was not living up to its brand promise. Cor Boonstra soon discovered:

> ...that testing led us to develop a policy for the consumer where we stimulate certain products because we now know that there is an interest at the consumer level. That should lead, and has led, technology in the organisation. You cannot do it the other way round. (Philips Press Office, 1997).

However, changing an organisation's culture does not happen overnight, particularly one with over 100 years' history and with offices spread across the globe.

To reinforce the company's efforts to become a market-led corporation, Philips launched its largest ever consumer marketing campaign in September 1998. The £45.4 million campaign 'Let's Make Things Better' shifted the emphasis from the product itself to the lifestyle benefits afforded by using a Philips product. The ongoing campaign features selected 'star' products such as the new 42" × 4" deep flat television, DVD player and the Nino 300 (palm-sized PC). The aim is that these 'star' products will create a 'halo effect' across the entire Philips product range. As Gerard Dufor, Philips' Marketing Director, explains:

> ...by featuring products with unique and superior benefits we simultaneously pay off the brand promise of how we make things better while benefiting from the halo effect these products provide to the entire range of products. (Philips Press Office, 1998a)

Prior to the launch, Dufor was busy creating a new global marketing support structure including a new consumer intelligence unit in New York, supported by newly created regional brand champions across all six Philips geographic regions.

These brand champions report directly to Dufor who, in turn, reports directly to Boonstra. This streamlined support network contrasts with previous cumbersome hierarchies at Philips, which stifled the company's efforts. This was vividly demonstrated in the late 1970s when Philips' US sales and marketing team rejected the company's own VCR system, the V2000, in favour of Matsushita's rival platform! Those days are long gone. The challenge these marketing men now face is to woo customers to the Philips' family of products on what is, by contrast to Japanese standards, a paltry advertising budget.

Moreover, the company must not lose sight of its overriding goal, which is to develop and manufacture new and superior products. However, if it is truly to succeed, it must marry its inventiveness with its ability to bring these new products to the market whilst at the same time convincing those consumers who bought defunct systems that they should have renewed confidence in the Philips brand.

> We need to do more with it. To seal the quality and make consumers confident that this is a purchase they can make with complete trust. (Philips Press Office, 1997)

There is no short fix and the company will need to invest heavily in areas it has traditionally overlooked. Philips lead cycles are much longer than classic fast moving consumer goods (FMCG) brands; a Philips consumer will probably buy a new television set probably once every five years or a shaver once every three years. So whilst sharpening its marketing the company must develop new products that 'make things better' for the consumer, which is something that Philips has failed to do in recent times.

DIGITAL CONVERGENCE

Philips also sought to sharpen up its act both internally and externally, to ensure that it was well positioned to take advantage of the opportunities afforded by digital 'connectivity'. Convergence will allow once disparate technologies, such as phones, computers and television sets, to 'talk' to each other. Philips' strategy is simple:

> If you are going to be a main player, you must be big across the board in audio, video and also in terms of computing power. This is a game for people with deep pockets and a wide range of products. (*Marketing Week*, 1998a)

This is in stark contrast to Pioneer, which is concentrating its efforts on two core products, the DVD player and the plasma flat screen television.

Philips is gambling on the fact that there will be few companies that will have the capabilities to develop the software to make the different pieces of equipment talk to each other in a 'highly intuitive way'. Products from the same company will have the advantage of fitting together seamlessly, thus leaving niche players such as Pioneer on the sidelines.

Patrick Barwise, chairman of the future media research programme at the London Business School, disagrees with this synopsis, '... If the smaller companies are able to introduce technology that will lower costs, then they will be successful' (*Marketing Week*, 1998a).

However, he does feel that the strength of the larger company's brand will give them an edge. Hence the launch and continuation of the 'Let's Make Things Better' campaign, which is building confidence in the Philips 'star' brands.

But while convergence brings a number of opportunities, it also brings a number of threats. Philips will have to anticipate how far integration will go. The past is littered with examples where this has failed. Combined satellite televisions were discontinued by Toshiba, space-saving washer/dryers failed to catch on and integrated televisions and VCRs have been slow to take off.

Observers point to consumers' fear of dependence on one piece of equipment, which, if it breaks down, will need a major part or the whole system to be replaced. Philips' place in the convergent world will depend heavily on how successfully it anticipates trends. The new global consumer intelligence unit will clearly have to work hard in this area to make sure the company maximises its opportunities in future years.

Since the next technology jump is so great, and to minimise both the cost and risk, Philips has joined forces with leading electronics firms and film companies to ensure that DVD does succeed. Philips' DVD partners include Grundig, Hitachi, Matsushita (Panasonic), Sharp, Sony, Thomson and Toshiba as well as Warner Brother, Buena Vista, Columbia Tristar, MGM and Polygram.

DVD is the replacement for VHS technology. It is more versatile, with additional applications for music and home computers. Sound quality from DVD is better than CD quality and many new computers have integrated DVD drives.

The philosophy behind the collaboration was simple: 'There is a recognition that the costs of the launch of a new format are so high that it is no longer feasible to do it single handedly. The days of Betamax and VHS are long gone' (*Marketing Week*, 1998b).

When Toshiba and Sony each presented their own, different formats to the film studios several years ago, the studios insisted that they would only back a single industry format. The unanimous backing bodes well for the launch of the new product.

Already in the US some 3.42 million DVD players have been sold (*Audio Week*, 1999). However, one of the key disadvantages of the present system is that it does not record and this may prove to be a hard sell to consumers, especially if they expect a recorder. Pioneer's focus strategy seems to have worked, for the company launched the first recordable DVD player in Japan in December 1999, followed by Europe and the US in early 2000. This was hotly pursued by Samsung, who launched its system in Autumn 2000. Philips clearly has its work cut out if it is going to catch up with its Asian rivals.

The key threat to DVD is the 'near video on demand' service offered by digital television, wherein the same film is available at 15-minute intervals across a number of channels. Philips and its partners are pinning their hopes on the 'collector mentality' of the public, which industry figures reveal shows no signs of abating.

The next stage in the strategy is a joint promotion to achieve critical mass as quickly as possible. Whether this is achievable in the short term is debatable. Jumping technology hurdles such as non-recordable formats and the arrival of digital television will be no mean feat. However, a combined marketing offensive based on mutual cooperation will be a powerful proposition.

CONCLUSION

Is Philips still struggling to find its true identity in the global landscape?

Despite several restructures during the 1980s and 1990s, it still struggles to deliver double-digit profit margins. Consumer Products remains the 'problem child' and Philips has entered into a plethora of strategic alliances and made a number of acquisitions, all to no avail. Philips has stated that it wants to become a leading player in the new digital world, but is it stretching itself too thinly?

Do recent acquisitions – VLSI and ATL Ultrasound – reveal a sea-change in corporate direction? Semi-conductors and medical generate healthy profits and are not as risky as consumer electronics; however, with the division accounting for 41 per cent of revenues it is unlikely that the company would exit this market.

Perhaps Philips would best be advised to follow Pioneer's lead and focus on key consumer niches. This approach has already reaped dividends for Pioneer, which recently launched the first recordable DVD player.

Alternatively, Philips could hope to strike gold with its new Super Audio CD system. What is encouraging is that the Philips have forged an alliance with Sony, a company that has tended to have the Midas touch in product development in recent years.

QUESTIONS FOR DISCUSSION

1 Has Philips been successful in restructuring its business for profit?
2 Has the Philips brand been strengthened by these activities?
3 How would you apply a branding strategy to Philips?
4 What do you see as the core markets for Philips products?
5 Is Philips an innovator or an inventor?
6 What marketing strengths and weaknesses do you perceive Philips having at a strategic and brand level?

REFERENCES

Audio Week (1999), 4 October.

Gugler, P. (1992) 'Building transitional alliances to create competitive advantage', *Long Range Planning*, 25(1): 90–99.

Marketing Week (1998a) 'Can Pioneer profit from convergence?', 3 September.

Marketing Week (1998b) 'Will collaboration pay off for DVD?', 29 October.

Philips Annual Report, 1998

Philips Press Office (1997) *Clearing the Decks*. 23 December.

Philips Press Office (1998a) *Building The Brand*. 13 February.

Philips Press Office (1998b) *Lucent Technologies and Royal Philips Electronics end Joint Venture*. 22 October.

CS14   **SHELL: ENVIRONMENTAL STANCE IN EASTERN AND WESTERN EUROPE**

LIZ WALLEY AND JULIA CLARKE

This case study examines the environmental stance of Royal Dutch/Shell (hereafter referred to as Shell) across the national borders in which it operates. Specifically it compares the different business environments of Eastern and Western Europe and the impact these might have on Shell's local environmental performance. The question raised in this case study is the extent to which a multinational's environmental performance is reactive to drivers in the external environment rather than being motivated by the company's own ethical stance.

The rest of this case study is divided into four sections. The first section provides a brief background on Shell and the oil industry in general; the second provides company-produced materials and information about Shell's environmental and ethical policies and standards; the third section compares the general business environments of Central and Eastern Europe (and specifically Romania) with that of Western Europe (specifically the UK) and the extent to which these might impact on Shell's environmental performance in these regions. Finally, we introduce an analytical framework within which to model the interactions of external drivers and the company's own ethical stance. We suggest that this may be used to explain the extent of variation of environmental performance of a multinational, such as Shell, between Central and Eastern Europe (CEE) and Western Europe. The case study was written with publicly available information up to mid 1999.

BACKGROUND TO THE COMPANY AND INDUSTRY

Shell was formed in 1907 and is today one of the world's largest multinational businesses, consisting of more than 2000 companies worldwide. Ultimate control is vested in two parent companies: the Shell Transport and Trading Company, a UK registered company, and the Royal Dutch Petroleum Company, a Dutch company. The group's activities include oil and gas exploration, production, refining, transportation and marketing, chemicals and other operations in coal and metal mining, forestry and biotechnology. The oil industry is often described as having an oligopolistic market structure; that is, it is dominated by a small number of big players, which include Exxon, Mobil, Chevron, BP and Shell. A slump in oil prices in the late 1990s resulted in heavy cutbacks in staff and operating costs in 1998–99 and mergers between BP and Amoco and Exxon and Mobil.

Shell has operating companies throughout CEE, but Romania is the only CEE country that has both an oil products and an exploration/production company. Shell Romania was established in Bucharest in 1992. The company markets Shell lubricants and chemicals in Romania and supports the trading of other Shell products in the country. Shell Romania Exploration BV (100 per cent) is involved in oil and gas exploration and production in Northern Transylvania.

SHELL'S ENVIRONMENTAL STANCE

Shell provides an appropriate case study for examining the environmental stance of a multinational across national borders for two main reasons. First, it has extensive worldwide operations (and specifically has around 14 operating companies in CEE). Second, it has debated and written extensively about its business principles in general and environmental principles in particular.

One of the reasons why Shell has engaged in public debate on environmental issues in recent years is because of its Brent Spar (and Shell Nigeria) controversies. Brent Spar, a huge redundant North Sea storage and loading buoy, was the centre of controversy over Shell's plans for its deep sea disposal in 1995. The extensive consultation exercise that resulted helped Shell 'promote a different approach to decision-making in the Group, and has shown new ways in which Shell companies can be more open and accountable' (Royal Dutch/Shell Group, 1998a). Shell recognised that hitherto its decision making had been too internally focused and technically based. 'We have learned that we must change the ways we identify and address issues and interact with the societies we serve. Brent Spar has taught us the value of dialogue with our critics and other interested parties' (Royal Dutch/Shell Group, 1998b). In a 1996 speech by C.A.J. Herkstroter, the President of Royal Dutch on 'Dealing with contradictory expectations – the dilemmas facing multinationals', he said '... we have sometimes made mistakes and misjudgements. These are not, however, issues only for Shell. They affect all companies, particularly those working across borders or across cultures' (Herkstroter, 1996).

Shell has had a formal Statement of General Principles since 1976 and, as part of its stated commitment to being open and to engage in dialogue, this is now joined by a wide range of company literature on the subject. This includes not only stand-alone environmental reports (group and business), but also more open-ended, questioning, discussion documents and speeches on social responsibility and the dilemmas facing multinationals (see references below). This material provides us with the opportunity to examine the ethical and environmental principles behind Shell's environmental stance. The materials may help us address the question posed at the outset of this case – to what extent Shell's environmental performance is reactive to drivers in the external environment or motivated by the company's own ethical stance.

Shell's own main reference point is the relevant General Business Principle – No. 6 on Health, Safety and the Environment, namely:

'Consistent with their commitment to contribute to sustainable development, Shell companies have a systematic approach to health, safety and environmental management in order to achieve continuous performance improvement. To this end Shell companies manage these matters as any other critical business activity, set targets for improvement, and measure, appraise and report performance.' (Royal Dutch, Shell Group, 1998a).

In the context of globalisation and the role of multinationals, Shell is conscious of the accusation of operating double standards in areas such as wages, safety and the environment. The following extract comes from a Radio 4 interview with Mark Moody Stuart, Chief Executive of Royal Dutch/ Shell.

Interviewer: Do you in fact apply different environmental standards in different parts of the world?

Mark Moody-Stuart: For new facilities we would apply exactly the same *principles*, so we would look at environmental impact and study what you actually needed to do. We would certainly apply universal base minimum standards; there are quite clearly things below which you would shut an operation down. But to say that you apply identical standards everywhere is *plainly* untrue. Look at the US; we don't have the same standards in California as we do in the rest of US and people say we are not talking about Californian standards, we are talking about some other standards. You have to ask – what standards are you actually talking about? The answer is, it has to be related to the overall environment in which you work.

(Extract from Radio 4, *Analysis*, 23 November 1998)

More formally, in its 'Profits and Principles' document, in the context of outlining Shell's approach to globalisation, the company addresses the 'standards' issue explicitly:

Standards

Special standards governing private and public enterprise may be helpful to consumers, workers and the public at large. The appropriate authorities should decide on these standards and Shell companies will then conform to them. The Business Principles act as a safety net against abuse or inadequate exercise of such authority.

The principle of different standards is enshrined in a United Nations agreement (Principle 11 of the Rio Declaration of 1992), which makes it clear that national environmental standards have to be effective but 'standards applied by some countries may be inappropriate and of unwarranted economic and social cost to other countries, in particular developing countries'.

Shell companies do not pretend to operate in an identical manner around the world, although some standards are global by their very nature. The importance of human life is the same worldwide and Shell operates to the same standard in the areas of occupational health, and safety.

Other standards to which we adhere must depend on local circumstances, such as the condition of the region's environment, what the customer wants and is willing to pay for, and the law. In any event, each Shell company has adopted and will conform to the Group's Statement of General Business Principles and HSE Policy.

(Royal Dutch/Shell Group, 1998a: 37)

In the same section, Shell also acknowledges the view that multinationals with long-term investments, and which are also under public scrutiny, have sufficient incentives to observe relatively strict standards worldwide.

Shell also addresses the issue of double standards in the 'Dealing with contradictory expectations' speech, but this time set in the context of environmental standards versus economic development:

There are groups who call for one set of standards – whether it be wages, environment or any other issue – to be applied worldwide ... Representatives of many developing countries argue that to apply those standards would effectively lock them out of competition ... What is the ethical way to proceed? Should we apply the higher cost western standards, thus making the operation uncompetitive and depriving the local workforce of jobs and the chance of development? Or should we adopt the prevailing legal standards at that site, while having clear plans to improve towards 'best practice' within a reasonable time frame? That way, of course, we would risk condemnation in the West.

(Herkstroter, 1996)

THE GENERAL BUSINESS ENVIRONMENTS IN CEE AND WESTERN EUROPE

As a multinational operating across many borders, Shell faces differing external factors that may impact upon its activities and environmental stance. The first driver we identify is legislative. Shell has to work within different legislative frameworks in the different regions in which it operates. Second, companies will be subject to a market pull. The strength of this pull towards environmentally friendly strategies will depend upon, for example, the level of environmental awareness amongst consumers and suppliers and the resulting demand for green products and services. The final category concerns legitimation pressures. Legitimacy theory argues that organisations will only survive (and prosper) if they are operating in line with the value system of that society (Gray et al., 1996).

Legislation

Government acts as a driver to companies both through environmental legislation and market instruments, the former having by far the most direct influence at present. In fact, some would say that the development of environmental legislation has been *the* most important factor influencing the environmental behaviour of companies to date (Welford and Gouldson, 1993). Within the European Union (EU), the objectives of environmental legislation are determined by the various institutions of the EU, particularly the European Commission, although in many instances the mechanisms through which objectives are to be reached are determined nationally, particularly in relation to the implementation of EU policies. National legislation remains an important influence, however, although its influence, varies from country to country. For instance, in the UK the EU, through its Directives and Environmental Action Programmes, is a major (if not the main) driver for legislative action, whilst relatively it is a less significant influence in other member states that have more progressive domestic environmental policies.

The EU has also been a very significant driver of the Romanian government's recent environmental initiatives since it is an 'associated country' and has been going through the process of approximating EU environmental legislation, which is a prerequisite of EU membership. This resulted in new legislation – the Environmental Protection Act (EPA) – and the adoption by government of an environmental strategy and National Environmental Programme in 1995. One set-back has been the failure of Romania to be included in the 'first wave' of countries to begin accession negotiations to the EU. Yet it seems likely that the government will continue to pursue this objective of joining the EU in the next wave. Thus the EU approximation process will continue to be the most significant driver of environmental legislation and the associated institutions for implementation and enforcement in Romania.

With the adoption of the EPA, the environmental law approximation process will be well progressed and we can say that in terms of legislative drivers, the UK and Romania are converging quite quickly, at least formally. However, it is widely recognised that the main problems with environmental legislation in Romania concern the implementation of, and compliance with, laws and other regulations. The Regional Environmental Centre for Central and Eastern Europe (REC) (1996) identifies the main reasons as being related to enforcement alleviation, lack of incentives, insufficient technology, financial implications and obstacles to public participation. These result in big differences between the formalities of legislation and their actual influence on company behaviour and performance. Caddy (1997) comments on this implementation gap in the context of Central Europe as 'hollow harmonisation' and calls for greater attention to be paid to the strengthening of both informal and formal institutions.

Market forces

Within this category we include those stakeholders who make their influence felt directly through market forces (customers, suppliers and insurers), the market-based instruments used by government (such as carbon taxes, EMAS and eco-labelling schemes) and environmental efficiency drivers.

Both the supply chain driver and green consumerism have become significant factors driving corporate environmental strategy in certain UK sectors, for example, supermarkets and DIY stores. In Romania neither has yet developed as a driver of environmental performance. Whether or not trans-boundary supply chain pressure is an issue for Shell will depend on whether it is selling within Romania or overseas.

In relation to environmental efficiency, clearly it is in the interests of companies to minimise their costs, and in the environmental context this means the cost of raw materials and waste disposal. In the longer term it is anticipated that the reduced ability of the environment to continue to supply raw materials will result in much higher raw materials costs. In the UK, companies are experiencing tougher legislation and as a result higher costs of waste disposal, and so this is already becoming an important incentive towards waste minimisation. In Romania, until recently energy costs were kept artificially low, but since the abolition of the relevant price controls in early 1997, the price of oil has now moved closer to EU levels.

Legitimation

Under this heading we include those stakeholder categories that are most closely linked with ethical concerns: the community, employees, investors, media and pressure groups.

Looking at community and employees together, these groups in the UK are able in many instances to demand a high level of environmental performance from their industrial neighbour or employer. For communities, the freedom of access to environmental information is very important in this respect, since it is the means by which they gain power to question the activities of companies. The extent to which pressure is actually exerted is variable and relates to a range of factors, not least the state of the economy. In Romania, the new 1991 constitution does guarantee the right to information, but this is a very undeveloped area given the context and culture of the decades before the revolution. Furthermore, given the desperate economic plight of Romania over the last 10 to 15 years, economic prosperity is still a much higher priority for most people than environmental quality. So for a MNC, such as Shell, in Romania, legitimation is more likely at present to come from providing job opportunities, job security and improved wage levels than from operating to a high environmental standard. However, there have been some horrendous examples of environmental pollution in Romania (for example, Copsa Mica's carbon-black plant, Zlatna's copper smelter and Suceava's artificial fibre factory) and recently environmental problems have been receiving much more media attention. REC (1994) comments that one phenomenon noted by local observers is the increased coverage of environmental matters by the broadcast and print media, which is likely to have the effect of increasing environmental awareness.

It is interesting to note that after the Romanian revolution, two ecological parties were set up and gained 4 per cent of the vote in 1990. Initially the parties received strong support from highly industrialised areas, but this has since waned. Moreover, the general public tends to associate direct political involvement with the crude opportunism of pre-revolutionary public life. Yet, as Shell knows only too well in the wake of the intense media scrutiny of its activities in Nigeria and Brent Spar, it is often the Western media and pressure group activists, rather than the local media and pressure groups, who are likely to act as a more significant driver on the environmental stance of the MNC.

ANALYTICAL FRAMEWORK

From the above discussion it is clear that for each of the three categories external drivers are likely to be a more significant influence in the UK than in Romania. If we designate these drivers as 'high' in the UK, then for comparative purposes we would classify the three variables as combining to demand a 'lower' level of environmental performance in Romania.

If we hypothesise that environmental performance arises either from *reaction* to external drivers, or a *pro-active* ethical stance, or a combination of both, then comparing the performance of an MNC such as Shell in the two regions may help us to isolate the effect of the latter. Figure C14.1 presents a model that may be used to categorise the environmental performance of organisations operating across different regions where they face differing external drivers, such as Eastern and Western Europe.

MNCs that implement the same high environmental policies across all the regions they operate in, even where these exceed requirements in certain localities, may be designated as 'honourable players' in that they are taking a pro-active environmental stance by performing to the highest common factor. Indeed some organisations, the 'saints', may exceed expectations in all regions in which they operate (one example might be the Body Shop). Other MNCs may take a more pragmatic approach, hence 'pragmatist', and simply react to local legal, legitimacy and market requirements, implementing different environmental policies in different regions. Finally, the 'sinners' may take advantage of the lack of effective regional sanctions to break local environmental laws. For example, Dobson (1992) discusses the dumping of hazardous waste by US firms in Ireland where they faced 'trifling' fines for illegal disposal of toxic materials.

CONCLUSIONS

This case study has presented a framework that models corporate environmental performance as a combination of *reaction* to external drivers and a *pro-active* ethical stance. It has highlighted how the external drivers in CEE (specifically Romania) combine to demand a lower level of environmental performance than the external drivers in the EU (specifically the UK). Whilst it is recognised that the UK and Romania are not necessarily representative of Western and Central

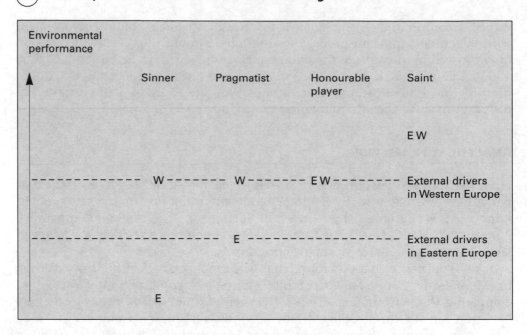

Figure C14.1   *Variations in the environmental stance of MNCs in Eastern and Western Europe*

E	Performance in Eastern Europe (region with lower drivers).
W	Performance in Western Europe (region with higher drivers).
Saint	Consistently adopts the same high-level policies in all regions where it operates; outperforms requirement in all localities in which it operates.
Honourable player	Consistently adopts the same high-level policies in all regions where it operates; meets highest common factor even where this surpasses regional minimum requirements.
Pragmatist	Meets only local requirements even though these may be lower than in other regions where it operates.
Sinner	Takes advantage of lack of effective sanctions to break local legal and legitimacy requirements.

Source: Key

and Eastern Europe, this analysis does provide an example of the general assertion that external drivers are higher in Western Europe than in Central and Eastern Europe. Information has been provided about Shell's environmental principles and standards, both in general terms and specifically about how this relates to operating across national frontiers. An analytical framework is presented to enable the reader to categorise Shell according to how they might vary their environmental strategies across the two regions.

It will be interesting to see how future developments close the gap between the external drivers identified in this paper. The approximation process is already moving the legislation of the CEE towards that of the EU, although the implementation and enforcement of that legislation is more problematic. If living standards in CEE improve and countries continue their transition towards market economies, market pull can be expected to be a stronger influence in the future. Finally, the globalisation of the media and its use by environmental pressure groups means that the environmental and ethical stances of companies such as Shell are being subjected to worldwide scrutiny. In terms of the analytical framework presented, this process may be forcing would-be 'pragmatists' to perform as 'honourable players'. As these companies could then exert a more significant influence on local companies, particularly through the supply chain, local expectations of corporate environmental performance could be increased in a way that increases the pressure derived through the need to secure legitimacy. Thus, it is possible (but far from certain) that the various pressures could become self-reinforcing. Clearly, policy makers may be able to encourage this virtuous circle in a number of ways, although it remains to be seen whether the harmonisation process will generate such effects.

QUESTIONS FOR DISCUSSION

1   How would you characterise Shell's likely environmental stance in Romania in terms of the 'Saints–Honourable Players–Pragmatists–Sinners' model? Justify.
2   In what ways does the objective of many CEE countries to join the EU provide an opportunity for European policy makers to influence the development of CEE market economies in the direction of more sustainable business operations?
3   Why are Western style environmental policies not necessarily appropriate to CEE economies?
4   Outline the likely environmental impact of foreign direct investment in Romania.
5   What differences are there, or might there be, between a multinational's stance in CEE compared to its environmental stance in other lesser-developed parts of the world?
6   Is it possible or desirable for a profit-making multinational such as Shell to adopt a stakeholder model of the corporation?
7   Shell has produced many publications outlining and discussing its ethical position with regard to its business activities. Does this mean that the company itself, as distinct from its shareholders or management, is a moral person?
8   If you were a shareholder in Shell, what would you consider to be the nature and extent of your ethical responsibilities with regard to its environmental performance in CEE countries such as Romania?

REFERENCES

Caddy, J. (1997) 'Hollow harmonisation? Closing the implementation gap in Central European environmental policy', *European Environment*, 7 73–9.
Dobson, J. (1992) 'Ethics in the transnational corporation: 'the "moral buck" stops where?', *Journal of Business Ethics*, 11(1): 21–7.

Gray, R., Owen D., and Adams, C. (1996) *Accounting and Accountability.* Hemel Hempstead: Prentice Hall.

Herkstroter, C.A.J. (1996) 'Dealing with contradictory expectations – the dilemmas facing multinationals'. Speech, October.

REC (1994) *Manual on Public Participation: Country Report: Romania.* Regional Environmental Centre for Central and Eastern Europe.

REC (1996) *Approximation of European Union Environmental Legislation: Case Studies of Bulgaria, Romania etc.* Regional Environmental Centre for Central and Eastern Europe.

Royal Dutch/Shell Group (1994) 'Shell in the CIS, Central and East Europe,' *Shell Briefing Note*, August.

Royal Dutch/Shell Group (1998a) *The Shell Report* 'Profits and principles – does there have to be a choice?', April.

Royal Dutch/Shell Group (1998b) *Health, Safety and Environment Report 1998*, June.

Welford, R. and Gouldson, A. (1993) *Environmental Management and Business Strategy.* London: Pitman.

AUDREY GILMORE AND DAVID CARSON

Sealink British Ferries were bought by the Scandinavian company Stena Line in late 1990. Prior to this acquisition Sealink British Ferries had been privately owned by the Sea Containers Group, for six years. Before this, the company was owned by British Rail throughout the 1970s and early 1980s.

The acquisition of Sealink British Ferries more than doubled the size of the Stena Line company, making them one of the largest car ferry operators in the world.

This case study focuses on price-led competition on one sea route that the new Stena Line company had to address immediately upon acquisition.

IRELAND–GB FERRY TRAVEL PRE-1992

In 1991, Stena had approximately 72 per cent market share on the Northern Irish sea route. The only other competitor, P&O, had 28 per cent. Stena had 3 ferries operating 18 sailings per day between the port of Larne in Northern Ireland and the port of Stranraer in the west of Scotland. The 3 Stena ferries were 10 years old and were purpose-built specifically for this route at the Harland and Wolffe shipyard in Belfast.

These ferries were refurbished on a yearly basis to ensure that the on board facilities were up to date and of a high quality. The facilities on board included: a modern open-plan cafeteria, a large bar area with entertainment, a television lounge, a confectionery/newspaper shop, a children's play area with children's entertainment and gaming machines in the corridor areas.

P&O had 2 ferries on the route and they operated 12 sailing's per day. These 2 ferries were 30 years old, and one of them was a freight ship rather than a passenger ferry but was used to carry small numbers of passengers during busy periods. However, P&O announced the replacement of these 2 ships by 'newer' 20-year-old ships that had previously been used on the English Channel routes. These ferries were due to arrive in February and May 1992 respectively.

The facilities on board these ferries included: a cafeteria, a bar, a television lounge, a confectionery/newspaper shop and gaming machines. A children's play area was planned for later in the year. Thus these were similar to the Stena ferries' on-board facilities.

The major peak season for this ferry route was from June to September, the local market regions' main holiday period. The ferry companies traditionally started their advertising campaigns in late January with reminder campaigns until June, plus an additional surge of activity before the Easter holiday.

The ferry companies' marketing activity had been established over many years with only minor changes to brochures, schedules and prices. The only variation in this activity occurred when the introduction of a new ferry, as with P&O at this time, was exploited. Otherwise comfortable complacency prevailed, especially with regard to pricing strategy.

NEW COMPETITOR – A THIRD COMPANY COMMENCES OPERATIONS

The North Irish sea route (the North Channel) was receiving much public and media attention at the beginning of 1992. The arrival of a new fast craft, the Seacat catamaran, was announced in January. Much of the local press heralded its arrival with excited anticipation of the change this would bring to the ferry-using public of Ireland and Scotland, since for many years this route had been shared by the two major ferry operators, P&O and Stena (formally Sealink).

In March, the Seacat (the name of the new company, a sub-division of Sea Containers, and the generic name of the new craft) public relations (PR) announcements began in the press, providing information about the new exciting catamaran, its speed and modern facilities. There was no announcement in relation to pricing. The constant press 'hype' about the new catamaran, together with the PR announcements by Seacat, reduced the traditional ferry companies' (P&O and Stena) annual advertising campaign messages to relative insignificance.

COMPETITOR'S REACTIONS

In late April, P&O announced that they would reduce the price of their core product, the 'standard return fare', from approximately £120 (sterling) to £49 for a car plus two passengers return ticket. This would effectively mean that they would be running at a loss or break-even point at best. Within a short time, Seacat announced the beginning of their service for 1 June with special holiday rates for new customers: £49 for a car plus two passengers return ticket. When this news was announced in the media, Stena management called an emergency meeting.

RESULTS/IMPACT OF COMPETITOR PRICE DECISION

In 1992 the average price for a car plus two passengers return ticket was £120. By 1996, four years later, the average comparable price was £49. This equates to less than one-third of price levels in real terms, allowing for inflation. Obviously the three competitors' revenue 'yields' were substantially reduced. Of course, some recompense was achieved through greater volumes of travellers as the market size almost doubled as a result of the price-led marketing activity.

However, the major impact of the market pricing strategies was in market/customer expectations. Prior to 1992 the relatively complacent dormant market *expected* to pay something over £100 to travel between Great Britain and Ireland. The main consumer concern was to secure a desired travel schedule and time; the price paid for the service was simply whatever was on offer and which conformed broadly with expectations. By 1996 market expectations had changed significantly. Consumers now expected to pay something around £50; anything greater than this would be perceived as poor value or too expensive. Further, because of almost continuous price-led 'special promotions', consumers had become accustomed to 'shopping around' for the best deals on offer. Even though one in three travellers were regular customers, there was little customer loyalty to any one ferry company.

To summarise this situation in broad marketing terms, what had happened was: the market price levels and expectations had spiralled downwards as a result of continuous price discounting; and competitors had 'entrapped' themselves in a high-volume, low-yield market circumstance.

Obviously, each competitor would have a desire to increase price levels whereby they would generate easier/acceptable revenues and profits. However, market competitiveness remained at such a level as to make it impossible for any one competitor to 'break ranks' and increase prices; having gained new market share percentages with substantially increased volumes, any company would find it difficult to relinquish these.

The best option open to the ferry companies was to attempt to achieve market differentiation by improving the product offering. This is what each company began to do:

- *P&O*: P&O introduced a new craft on the North Irish route. This was a mono-hull fastcraft, call a 'Jetliner'. This craft shortened the route from Larne–Scotland by half, effectively offering a one-hour crossing. This feature became the main selling point and promotional message for this service. Indeed, this was the first time a one-hour crossing was possible for the ferry-travelling market of Northern Ireland.
- *Seacat*: At this time, Seacat had their craft completely refurbished and promoted it as an even better service. However, their advertising campaign focussed heavily on the speed of the service, linking it with 'flying' across the sea.
- *Stena*: Stena (formally Sealink) decided to build on the strength of their service improvement activities of the past few years, where they had dramatically improved the 'intangible' aspects of the service delivery. They felt that investing in the 'tangible' quality of their product through operating a new fast catamaran would be the natural progression in their service delivery.

The Stena company ordered a new 'top of the range' craft for this ferry route. This craft was bigger and better operationally than the earlier designs of both P&O and Seacats' fast crafts. The high technical specification and quality of this craft would 'balance' the quality of service offering on this route by operating a 'top of the range' craft that could also deliver the best in 'intangible' service offerings because of experience and dedication of the service staff and management of this route. These local staff had practised, monitored and continually improved the on-board service over time. By providing the best in tangible and intangible service delivery, Stena planned to be the leaders in the ferry-travelling market for some time to come.

To increase differentiation further, Stena moved its entire operation from the port of Larne to the port of Belfast. The logic behind this decision was that this provided easier access to the city and its greater conurbations than the relatively isolated coastal port of Larne.

CONCLUSION

The circumstance of competitive pricing is problematic in an industry where differentiation is based upon the added value aspect of a product/service rather than on the core product itself. In this case the core product is transport from one port to another (A–B). The added value aspect of the product is manifested in dimensions of comfort and service. In order to overcome this problem of differentiation and to move prices upward, marketing efforts and messages must begin to emphasise other components related to the core product, for example, through emphasising variables such as speed, frequency, convenience and/or length of journey. Otherwise in this industry context competitive pricing leads to a downward price spiral. The only scope for price premiums is to differentiate travel products by convenience of time; peak rates; days; times' early/late booking differentiation. However, the scope remains limited unless the whole market moves broadly together.

QUESTIONS FOR DISCUSSION

1 Should Stena change their prices, and if so, to what levels?
2 In 1992, Seacat was launched at £49 for a car and two passangers. What are the marketing issues that this situation presents?
3 What implications should Stena consider before changing their prices?
4 What impact do you think each company's initiatives had on profit yield and market share?
5 How can competitors increase profit yields?

CS16 UNILEVER GROUP: MARKETING STRATEGIES FOR EASTERN EUROPE

JULIA DJAROVA AND CARLA MILLAR

The Unilever Group was established when Margarine Unie and Lever Brothers decided to merge, whilst retaining their separate legal identities. Unilever NV and Unilever PLC, as they are known now, are the parent companies of what today is one of the largest consumer goods businesses in the world, with its corporate centres located in London and Rotterdam.

Unilever's business in branded food and drinks has developed from its original base in edible fats, established in The Netherlands nearly 125 years ago by Simon van den Bergh and Anton Jurgens. More than 100 years ago, William Hesketh Lever opened his first factory in the UK and launched the famous Sunlight soap brand. From its origin in the early eighteenth century, when famous brand names like Atkinsons and Pears were first introduced in UK, Unilever's personal products business has developed to become a diverse and internationally successful world leader.

The greater part of Unilever's business is in branded and packaged goods, primarily foods, detergents and personal products. Over 1000 strong and successful brands are marketed by Unilever companies worldwide.[1] The total sales of the company defines its position amongst the top industrial producers in the world. Unilever ranked 15 by net profit in the Fortune List 1994.

Unilever has been developing its range of products and organisational structure along a broad vertical integration: 'from the palm tree to the soap-kettle'.[2] 'It is easy to forget how diverse our activities were only 10 years ago. We were in transport, distribution, market research, advertising, fishing, printing, plastics and packaging – you name it, Unilever had tried it.'[3] In the early 1980s, most of those businesses – accounting for nearly a quarter of group sales – were sold off, which resulted in more business focus and in the increase of operation margins.

UNILEVER'S PRODUCT MIX AND MARKETS

Unilever's core product mix consists of foods, home care and professional cleaning and personal care products, which now account for about 90 per cent of the total turnover and about 89 per cent of the operational profit (Table C16.1).

Table C16.1 Turnover and operational profit by operation, 1997

Core operation	Turnover*	Operational profit
Foods:	43,899	2,540
• Oil and dairy foods and bakery	16,614	940
• Ice-cream and beverages	13,134	1,006
• Culinary and frozen foods	14,151	594
Home care and professional cleaning	17,606	1,388
Personal care	19,756	2,313
Speciality chemicals **	3,700	474

Source: Unilever Annual Review 1997
* In Dfl million at constant rates.
** Special chemicals are not considered as a core operation, since most of it had been disposed by 1999.

Especially in the food business, where the three giants – Unilever, Nestlé and Danone – are dominating Europe, good profits depend mainly on boosting sales volume and expanding market share. In the last decade, two major trends in this industry limited growth options for the producers. These were strengthening of the position of the retailers and cost-conscious consumers with flat incomes. With raw material costs starting to rise in the latter years, there was severe pressure on margins and a need to maintain low selling prices. In these conditions competitors strove for cheap production with peak efficiency of their factories, and innovation and clever marketing. As a reaction, two types of actions were typical for the global players in the sector: closure of factories and portfolio restructuring. The latter limits the competition into massive scale production in fewer strong brands and products while freeing capital to invest in new markets.

As part of its restructuring programme, Unilever bought some 64 food businesses and disposed of 28 others in the years 1992–96.[4] Of the purchased businesses, 18 are ice-cream and 8 margarine producers. Unilever is reorganising its Western European and North American operations and it is investing in developing and emerging markets. In 1996 these new markets generated around US$ 7.1 billion, or twice the figure for 1992 and around 26 per cent of the total turnover.[5] 'The greater part of our future growth is likely to come from regions outside Europe and North America,' states the Annual Review 1994. The priority regions for Unilever are: Central and Eastern Europe, China, India, South East Asia and South Latin America. These regions represent more than 30 per cent of the turnover and 34 per cent of the operating profit of the company, with a tendency of steady growth (Table C16.2).

There are three priority foods for Unilever, which at this moment represent more than half of the foods division's turnover and profit: margarine being very much a commodity, ice-cream and tea belonging to the impulse products. In all three products, Unilever is the world's leading producer.

Although being on two different sides of the market (commodity market and impulse products market), Unilever approaches the three product groups with a common policy – new product development. Unilever's share on the North

Table C16.2   Turnover and operating profit by geographical area, 1997

Geographical area	Turnover*	Operational profit
Europe	39,869	3,351
North America	15,558	790
Africa and the Middle East	5,604	434
Asia and Pacific	12,993	1,102
Latin America	9,169	775

Source: Unilever Annual Review 1997
* In Dfl million at constant rates.

American market has grown from 10 per cent in the 1980s to 45 per cent today, mainly because of new products based on a new formula – low-fat and cholesterol-reducing spreads.[6] Unilever spends almost 2 per cent of its turnover each year on research and development. As much as 9000 people are involved in research and development (R&D) in 6 major laboratories and in 68 innovation centres that feed market research and ideas into the research laboratories. Albeit its traditional mastery in oils and fats technology, use of biotechnology and other leading science fields, Unilever still has to master the bridging of the scientists, marketeers and business managers. 'Unilever has stronger basic science than Nestlé, but is less good in exploiting it,'[7] is the opinion of Andrew Smith, ABN AMRO Hoare Govett.

While innovations in the product portfolio are of great importance for the developed markets, expansion in well-established worldwide brands is the company's approach in Central and Eastern Europe. Rama margarine is now the number one brand in Russia and several other Central European countries.

Fabrics cleaning and conditioning products (Omo, Skip, Wisk and Comfort) is the largest product group in the home care and professional cleaning business. The year 1997 was the first full year of operation of Diversey Lever, which resulted from a merger in 1996 and is now one of the leading professional cleaning companies in the world.

The Western market is difficult for the detergents of Unilever. In Europe the volume of sales of fabrics cleaning and conditioning products declined by 13 per cent in 1994 and the profits went down. This weakened the overall market position of Unilever in fabrics cleaning. Cost saving and market support measures or helped the operating profits to grow by 1997. Developing and emerging markets shown a steady progress in volume and operating profit in the last years.

In the home care sector, Unilever's brands continue to grow. The product Cif/Jif is a market leader in many counties.

Similar to the food products, markets outside Western Europe and North America offer growth opportunities for the company. Sales in developing and emerging markets represent almost half of Unilever's worldwide sales of detergents.[8]

Personal wash products show stable market performance with continued growth of the major brands. Dove and Lux took leading market positions almost everywhere. Lifebuoy maintains its position as a key brand in the health segment. In personal care products, growth can mainly be observed outside Europe. To be successful in personal products requires sustained and effective innovation in the marketplace, presenting to the consumer a continuing and relevant range of choices to meet his or her changing personal grooming needs.

THE MULTI-LOCAL MULTINATIONAL

The product–market policy of Unilever is based on the 'getting it right' concept: the right product for the right market. In the business of foods, detergents and personal products, a producer should know individual consumer trends of different markets and adapt its product concept accordingly. A producer should have 'the sensitivity to know when a global brand makes sense or when local requirements should take precedence … when to transfer innovation and expertise from one market to another and, equally, when a local idea has global potential … when to bring international teams together fast to focus on key opportunities'[9].

While stagnated markets are approached by Unilever with innovations and new formulae products, emerging markets host its worldwide brands and existing local brands with improved quality. The right choice of product–market combinations should provide high performance in developing markets, compensating declines in saturated markets. For instance, the decline of volumes in Unilever's West European markets in 1995 was partly compensated by the continued growth in Central and Eastern Europe (CEE).

ORGANISATIONAL AND DECISION-MAKING STRUCTURE

Since the 1960s till recently, Unilever has been operating under a matrix organisational structure distinguished by product groups and geographical area. As any other multinational company, Unilever has been changing the balance between decentralisation and centralisation in its organisational and decision-making structure over the years as a response to global trends in the industry and the markets. In the matrix structure the company combined high operational and restricted strategic decentralisation. In search of more simple and effective organisational structure, Unilever introduced a series of top-level changes in March 1996. The changes aimed at clearer allocation of responsibility for corporate strategic leadership and operational execution, strong regional focus within a framework of agreed category strategies, and operational decision-making close to the market.[10]

Unilever has two levels of management: Executive Committee, which is responsible for the corporate strategic leadership, and Business Groups

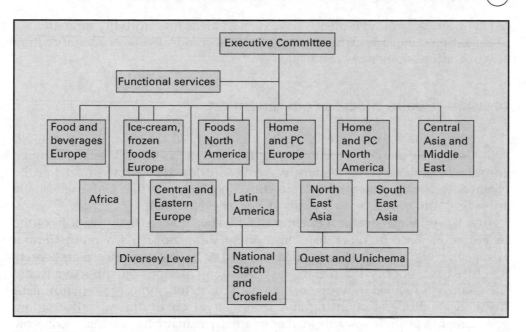

Figure C16.1 *Organisational structure of Unilever*

Presidents, which are responsible for operational management. All operating units are organised into 14 business groups (see Figure C16.1). The two levels of management together form the Unilever Executive Council (UEC), which is the principal discussion forum on policy matters.

The Executive committee is responsible for:

- agreeing priorities and corporate resource allocation, setting overall corporate targets, and defining the role of each category and business group;
- agreeing and monitoring business group strategies and annual plans;
- identifying and exploiting those areas of opportunity where Unilever's scale and scope can add significant value;
- managing relations with the external world at corporate level; and
- identifying and overseeing the careers of the future leaders of Unilever.

The Business Groups Presidents are responsible for:

- the profit in their groups;
- development of regional strategies and plans to execute corporate strategy;
- the understanding of the local market needs, providing input to the development of corporate strategy and for the allocation of corporate resources;
- the representation of Unilever in their region; and
- specific corporate issues.

The Business Group Presidents have management responsibility for a number of operating companies which belong to their groups. Unilever has more than 120 operating companies worldwide.

DECISION-MAKING PROCESS CONCERNING CEE

'To expand where the market is' is the philosophy of Unilever. In this respect, CEE offers a big market (close to 500 million people, as big as Western Europe), consumer habits close to Western patterns, and low disposable income at the moment but with potentials of growth. Global players like Unilever usually enter this kind of market in its early stage of development.

After the principal decision to enter CEE had been taken, investigations of the region took place in order to define prime sub-regions. As a result Central European countries – Czechoslovakia (before 1992), Hungary and Poland – were identified as a priority sub-region. As a selection criterion, the attractiveness of the country is defined in terms such as: political stability, business environment (banking, auditing, accounting and so on), legal environment, privatisation, government's attitude towards market reforms, the maturity of macro-economic policy. In addition to the attractiveness of the country, an important criterion for investment is the market potential.

There are no CEE countries which are not considered by Unilever as potential markets, although such countries as Chechnia might not be in its present list of actions. Countries are prioritised in sub-regions. Russia, one of the priority countries, is considered special for its huge market potential and at the same time high risk. If a new option comes up in a country which does not belong to the priority areas, it is taken into consideration, but with limited resources and limited time spent on analysis. If, for instance, export people say there is an option for an acquisition, then after a follow-up discussion the checklist procedure starts. A team of technical, marketing and other experts will visit the place for about two weeks. As a result of the desk and ground research, a decision is taken how to proceed further.

Local company's advantages and disadvantages

Overall, three characteristics can be distinguished of local companies in the CEE, acquired by Unilever:

- they are traditional producers of products within Unilever's portfolio (the consumer buys brands, not assets);
- they hold strong positions on their national markets; and
- they have potential to grow in volume and range of products.

These three characteristics match with Unilever's prime objectives: to take up leading positions in the local market and to establish operational bases in the countries as soon as possible.

Local and international brands

Unilever relies on strong brands. Strongly-built brand names assure their sustainability in recession-hit markets and their role as an instrument of growth elsewhere.[11] This philosophy of the company is applied to CEE, but taking into account some important specifics in the brand names tradition and in the consumer behaviour:

- The markets in the region don't have strong traditions in brands and thus the consumers do not become attached to a certain brand name. The low variety of local products, which did not provide much choice, built up a passive consumer attitude towards goods in general. Now, not only foreign but also local companies are facing the problem of building consumer loyalty towards brands.
- Building up a brand loyalty is difficult in these countries where good brand counts less than a good price and where a constant flood of products keeps consumers curious. While in developed markets mostly young people tend to change brands frequently, in Hungary for instance 40 per cent of brand switchers are older than 35. In addition, consumers are still experimenting moving from one brand to another.[12]
- After a stage of explosion of CEE consumer interest towards Western products, a stage of 'nostalgia' for local brands can be observed. This is caused by several reasons: there is a substantial price gap between foreign and local products in favour of the latter; the quality of some Western products appeared to be lower than expected; and emotional attachment. 'Calling it a renaissance of local brands puts a wrong touch on it,' says Mr J. Berner, former Unilever Director for CEE. He calls shoppers' affinity for home-grown goods 'an economic necessity'.[13] The local competition is especially influencing the food sector where consumers spend most of their income.

As a rule, Unilever combines its mature international brands with local brands with substantial market share in one product portfolio in the CEE companies that Unilever has acquired. For instance, Lever Polska is now marketing detergents and cleaners and personal care products under international brand names. At the same time it is selling local brands such as Pollena 2000 washing powder, which leads on the market and earns high popularity with its advertisement based on a Polish caption.

The production range at SZPT, Poland is progressively expanding to include international Unilever brands in margarine and edible fats where products should show constantly high quality. Similar is the case with the Czech PTZ where Unilever moves towards a manufacturing of its international brands after investing in production technology and methods. The local margarine brands of

PTZ are maintained and improved because of the market position of the local company. To ensure a constant quality is one basis on which to estabilise one's international brand name to a new producer. The quality is influenced not only by the production technologies and methods adapted in the company, but also very much by the supply in terms of constant quality and regularity. This is one of the reasons, for instance, why Unilever decided not to buy two margarine companies in Kazakhstan. 'With laundry detergent, it's not crucial, but margarine, a perishable food product, has to be available every day,' says J. Berner.[14]

One of the advantages of Unilever in building up consumer loyalty in CEE is the popularity of some of its international brands much before the changes in these countries have started. Brands such as Lux toilet soap, Axe, Denim and Impulse deodorants and after-shaves, Rama margarine and Omo detergent are not new to East Europeans. The challenge is to replace the import with home-made Unilever brands with the same quality, at the same time maintaining the local brands wherever possible. For instance, in Hungary the sales of Panda, the local brand of ice-cream produced by VNTV, melted away after Unilever began importing products from Western Europe.[15] Successful local brands can answer consumer's requirement for high quality for low price and satisfy their patriotism for so long as it exists.

For a complete list of Unilever's acquisitions in CEE, see Appendix 1.

Unilever action plans

For every acquisition in the CEE there are three main components in Unilever's action plan:

- building up the product portfolio;
- improving or very often setting up the distribution and the supply chain; and
- training local staff.

All this is backed up with a follow-up investment.

Many CEE companies used to have a diversified, but not optimal product portfolio. To consolidate the product range within the core business, which is also coinciding with Unilever's core business, was one of the first steps into companies' restructuring. The establishment of a market-sensitive combination between local and international brands was the next step, which led to measures to improve the production technologies and methods or to the introduction of new ones, and to defining optimal size of production. In order to succeed, any restructuring in CEE companies needs to be accompanied by training of the local staff. The main policy of Unilever everywhere in the world is to build up a strong local management team. Therefore, programmes for recruitment and training take an important part in the action plans. Training programmes are also introduced at the levels of manufacturing, marketing and distribution of branded products and so on.

In some places of CEE the distribution can be the main ingredient for success. To get the product to the customer and to do it efficiently has been, and still is, one of the problems there because of the lack of structured national distribution channels. The same applies for the supply. In practice, a producer should consider building-up its own supply chain in order to ensure quality and regularity.

In all three elements Unilever has invested substantially. For instance, since the establishment of Unilever Magyarorszag in August 1991, Unilever has invested more than US$ 100 million in Hungary on acquisitions, investment programmes, training of personnel and the development of distribution systems and marketing and sales organisations.[16]

A good summary of an action plan of Unilever in CEE can be seen in the address given by Mr Floris Maljers, former Chairman of Unilever, at the signing ceremony of the acquisition of its company Polena in Warsaw:

> However more important than money are people. We will set up a major programme to train people in the latest technology in processing. In addition, we will have to consider the best way to distribute and sell our products. We intend to strengthen the existing marketing by appointing two expatriates and one Polish director in addition to the already functioning board. The introduction of more efficient production methods will reduce the number of labour places in the existing departments. On the other hand the increase of the production capacity of powders and the new liquid department will provide new opportunities for employment.[17]

DEALING WITH CONSTRAINTS IN CEE

The first type of external constraint comes from governmental policy concerning inflation, commercially sound taxation system, accounting system and so on. International financial institutions insist on keeping the inflation low, but the inflation is a also a sign of creating the market in these countries. A typical reaction is that the governments increase taxation and introduce all kinds of new taxes. Costs like advertising are not always tax deductible. As a result, a distortion between profit and investment occurs.

Red tape also causes problems. Procedures sometimes are not clear and often contradictory. Some things, which are common in the West, do not exist in CEE. This can be an advantage for those who are first because they can 'create' procedures or they can be 'precedent cases'. The first companies to enter CEE build up their own learning experience.

The short-term thinking of many people in CEE is disturbing: the wish to have the cash today. Therefore, partnerships with local companies are difficult and often tricky. The same applies to the expectations of the employees whose understanding of working for a foreign company is very often identified with higher salaries.

In order to diminish the internal constraints, Unilever applies management control structure. Cash and assets management is one of the first to be introduced. Market research takes place in order to tune the product to the customer.

Refurbishing of the factories takes place as the backlogs are identified. People are trained on the spot and in training sessions.

Move of the suppliers to CEE

Unilever doesn't have a specific approach in influencing its traditional suppliers to establish activities in CEE. Nevertheless, it encourages them through informal talks to follow its lead. Some of the packaging companies moved, so did advertisement agencies, market research institutes, accounting companies, consultants and so on. The pioneers in CEE don't have many of the necessary elements of the business infrastructure, including the supply. This can serve not only as a disadvantage, but also very often as an advantage because these companies have the chance to build a large part of the infrastructure themselves in a way which suits them the best. Unilever have established relationships with local suppliers in CEE. Local suppliers are capable of setting up supply activities provided there is a little help from outside. In cases where strategies for Unilever products are produced, foreign suppliers are used.

QUESTIONS FOR DISCUSSION

1 Evaluate Unilever's policy on marketing in Central and Eastern Europe.
2 From a CEE consumer point of view, what are the attractive and unattractive points of Unilever's marketing policy?
3 Compare and contrast Unilever's internationalisation strategy (mode of entry) with alternatives.
4 Is Unilever's entry strategy geared to long-term or short-term profit?
5 Who will be Unilever's major competitors in these markets?

NOTES

1 Unilever Annual Review 1994.
2 Words of the founder William Lever quoted in 'Days of making hay are over', *Financial Times*, 26 July 1993.
3 Words of Unilever's Chairman Michael Perry (see 2).
4 'Munching on change', *Economist*, 6 January 1996.
5 Unilever Annual Report 1996.
6 The brand 'Promise Ultra', introduced in 1993 in the US, has the lowest fat content of any product in this category on the market. Following the acquisition of Bertolli in 1994, Unilever holds a strong position in all major olive oil markets in Southern Europe.
7 'Munching on change', *Economist*, 6 January 1996.
8 Unilever Annual Review 1995.
9 Unilever Annual Review 1995.
10 'Unilever's Organisation: Shaping for Outstanding Performance', 1996.

11 Opinion of Mr Floris Maljers, former Unilever Chairman, in 'Unilever relies on strong brands', *Netherlander*, 28 August 1993.

12 'Maturing consumers' in *Central European Economic Review*, Summer 1994.

13 'Maturing consumers' in *Central European Economic Review*, Summer 1994.

14 C. Rohwedder, 'Western consumer goods giants set sights on burgeoning Russian market', *NewsEDGE/LAN*, 20 March 1995.

15 'Cleaning up after communism', *Financial Times*, 3 July 1992.

16 'Unilever to acquire quick frozen vegetables producer in Hungary', *Unilever-News*, 14 December 1993, Budapest.

17 'Unilever acquires first privatised Polish detergents company', *Unilever-News*, 17 June 1991, Warsaw.

Appendix 1: Unilever acquisitions in Central and Eastern Europe

Country	Year	Local company (description)	Transaction data (share, price, acquired business)	Local company's advantage	Unilever's actions (in the coming years)
1	2	3	4	5	6
Poland	1991	Pollena Bydgoszcz (new name Lever Polska); 430 people	80% (now 100%) US$ 20 milllion detergents	Leading laundry detergents producer in Poland; popular local brands (Pollena, 2000)	Total investment of US$ 24 milllion; increase capacity; add international brands; train employees
Poland	1992	Slaskie Zakladey Przemyslu Tluszczowego (SZPT 'Olmex'); annual turnover US$ 30 milllion; 800 people; 45,000 tonnes margarine; two production locations	70% (now 100%) US$ 25 milllion margarine, edible oils and fats	Leading position in man-ufacturing and marketing of margarine and edible fats in the country; local brands	US$ 14 milllion investments; new production lines for international brands; education and training of locals; establishment of marketing and sales organisation
Poland	1993	Roma International; private	ice-cream		US$ 17.5 million investments; establishment of nation-wide sales and distribution network for ice-cream in Poland; introducing inter-national brands
Hungary	1992	NMV; 3000 people; 6 pro-duction locat; turnover US$ 290 milllion	80% (now 100%) margarine, soaps and detergents	market leader in margarine in Hungary; one of the most important companies in	international brands for margarine will be added; NMV detergents product ranges

(Continued)

Appendix 1 (*Continued*)

				oilseed sector in Eastern Europe; strong market position in detergents and soaps	will be upgraded as quickly as possible; to compete with businesses outside Hungary; training of locals
Hungary	1993	Bajai Hutoipary; 500 people	96.3% US$ 3.7 milllion quick frozen vegetables	significant producer for local market and for export; links with farmers	US$ 5 milllion investments; improving facilities; expanding capacities; transfer of new technologies; improvement of the supply chain
The Czech Republic	1992	Povltavske Tukove Zavody (PTZ); turnover US$ 20 milllion; 400 people	100% more than US$ 10 milllion edible oils and fats, toilet soap and skin cream	significant share of the market; traditional exporter of soap to other Eastern countries	US$ 15 milllion investments; new line for Rama; expanding production of soap; training
Russia	1994	Severnoye Siyaniye, St. Petersburg; 1000 people	90% (now over 95%) fragrances, after shave and colour cosmetics	leading producer in the region	US$ 10 milllion investments; broaden company's portfolio; training
Romania	1995	DERO; 1000 people	70% (now 100%) about US$ 20 milllion detergents	leading detergents manufacturing; leading market position in fabric powder with popular local brands; successful export	investments in modernisation; environmental standards; training

(*Continued*)

Appendix 1   (*Continued*)

| Russia | 1998 | MMZ; 350 people | Controlling interest | leading Moscow producer of margarine, cooking fats and mayonnaise; understanding of Russian yellow fats market | initial investment of US$ 20 million to up-grade the production facilities to the standards of Unilever; training of staff |

INDEX